About the Author

Professor David Weisburd is a leading researcher and scholar in the field of criminal justice. He received his Ph.D. from Yale University, and has held positions as research associate at Yale Law School, senior research associate at the Vera Institute of Justice, as associate professor at the School of Criminal Justice at Rutgers University, and as director of the Center for Crime Prevention Studies at Rutgers University. Professor Weisburd is currently director of the Institute of Criminology of the Hebrew University Law School in Jerusalem, and senior research scientist at the Police Foundation in Washington, D.C.

Professor Weisburd has broad experience in research and statistics in criminal justice. He has served as a principal investigator for a number of federally supported research studies, including the Minneapolis Hot Spots Experiment and the Jersey City Drug Market Analysis Project. He has also served as a scientific and statistical advisor to local, national, and international organizations, including the National Institute of Justice, the Institute of Law and Justice, the Office of National Drug Control Policy, the New Jersey Administrative Office of the Courts, the British Home Office Research Unit, and the Israeli Ministry of Police.

Professor Weisburd serves as associate editor of the *Journal of Quantitative Criminology,* and is on the editorial boards of the *Journal of Research in Crime and Delinquency, Advances in Criminology Theory, The Israel Law Review,* and *Policing: An International Journal of Police Studies.* He is author or editor of six other books, including *Crimes of the Middle Classes* (Yale University Press, 1991), *Police Innovation and Control of the Police* (Springer Verlag, 1993), and *Crime and Place* (Criminal Justice Press, 1996). His articles have appeared in numerous scholarly journals including the *American Sociological Review, Criminology, Crime and Delinquency, Crime and Justice, The Journal of Quantitative Criminology, Justice Quarterly, Law and Social Inquiry,* and *The American Criminal Law Review.*

statistics

in Criminal Justice

David Weisburd

West/Wadsworth Publishing Company

I⊤P® **An International Thomson Publishing Company**

Belmont, CA • Albany, NY • Bonn • Boston • Cincinnati • Detroit • Johannesburg •
London • Madrid • Melbourne • Mexico City • New York • Paris • San Francisco •
Singapore • Tokyo • Toronto • Washington

Criminal Justice Editor: Sabra Horne
Assistant Editor: Claire Masson
Editorial Assistant: Kate Barrett
Project Editor: Cathy Linberg
Permissions Editor: Robert Kauser
Marketing Manager: Mike Dew
Print Buyer: Karen Hunt

Production: Professional Book Center
Designer: Andrew Ogus ■ Book Design
Copy Editor: Professional Book Center
Cover: Cuttriss & Hambleton
Compositor: Professional Book Center
Printer: Courier Westford, Inc.

Printed in the United States of America
1 2 3 4 5 6 7 8 9 10

For more information, contact:
Wadsworth Publishing Company, 10 Davis Drive, Belmont, CA 94002, or electronically
at http://www.thomson.com/wadsworth.html

International Thomson Publishing Europe
Berkshire House 168-173
High Holborn
London, WC1V 7AA, England

Thomas Nelson Australia
102 Dodds Street
South Melbourne 3205
Victoria, Australia

Nelson Canada
1120 Birchmount Road
Scarborough, Ontario
Canada M1K 5G4

International Thomson Publishing GmbH
Königswinterer Strasse 418
53227 Bonn, Germany

International Thomson Editores
Campos Eliseos 385, Piso 7
Col. Polanco
11560 México D.F. México

International Thomson Publishing Asia
221 Henderson Road
#05-10 Henderson Building
Singapore 0315

International Thomson Publishing Japan
Hirakawacho Kyowa Building, 3F
2-2-1 Hirakawacho
Chiyoda-ku, Tokyo 102, Japan

International Thomson Publishing Southern Africa
Building 18, Constantia Park
240 Old Pretoria Road
Halfway House, 1685 South Africa

Library of Congress Cataloging-in-Publication Data
Weisburd, David.
    Statistics in criminal justice / David Weisburd.
        p.   cm.
    Includes index.
    ISBN 0-534-51840-0. (Windows) — ISBN 0-534-51841-9 (Macintosh)
    1. Criminal statistics.   2. Criminal statistics—Mathematical
models.   3. Criminology—Statistical methods.   4. Criminal justice.
Administration of—Statistics.   I. Title.
HV7415.W43   1997
364'.01'5195—dc21   97-36514

 This book is printed on acid-free recycled paper.

For Shelly
With all my love and admiration

Contents

chapter four

How Typical Is the Typical Case?
Measuring Dispersion 56

chapter five

Representing an Array of Data: Frequency Distributions 78

chapter six

The Logic of Statistical Inference: Making Statements about Populations on the Basis of Sample Statistics 102

chapter eight

Steps in a Statistical Test: Using the Binomial Distribution to Make Decisions about Hypotheses 138

chapter nine

Chi Square: A Commonly Used Test for Nominal-Level Measures 158

chapter eleven

Parametric Tests Comparing Means and Proportions in Two Samples 210

chapter twelve

Comparing Means among Multiple Samples: Analysis of Variance 240

chapter thirteen

Statistical Power: Avoiding Studies That Are Designed for Failure 274

chapter fourteen

Introduction to Correlation and Regression   296

chapter fifteen

An Introduction to Bivariate and Multivariate Regression Modeling 336

Oliver Wendell Holmes, the distinguished associate justice of the Supreme Court, was noted for his forgetfulness. In one story told about him, he is said to have been approached by a conductor who requested his ticket on a train leaving Washington, D.C. Holmes, searching through his case and his pockets, could not locate his pass. After a few awkward moments, the conductor recognized the distinctive looking and well-known jurist, and suggested that he might just send the rail company the ticket when he finds it. Justice Holmes, however, is said to have looked sternly at the conductor and responded, "Young man, the problem is not where is my ticket, the problem is where am I going."

For the student of statistics, a textbook is like a train ticket. It not only provides a pass the student can use for entering a new and useful area of study, it also defines the route that will be taken and the goals that are important to achieve. Different textbooks often take different approaches, and often emphasize different types of material. *Statistics in Criminal Justice* takes an approach that emphasizes the uses of statistics in research in crime and justice. This text is meant for students and professionals who want to gain a basic understanding of statistics in this field. In the first chapter, the main themes of the text are outlined and discussed. In this preface, it is important to describe the way the text is organized.

The text takes a building-block approach. This means that each chapter helps prepare you for the chapters that follow. It also means that the level of sophistication of the text increases as the text progresses. Basic concepts that are discussed in early chapters form an introduction to more complex statistical issues raised later. One advantage to this approach is that it is easy to see, as time goes on, how much you have learned about statistics. Concepts that would have seemed impossible to understand had they been introduced at the outset, are surprisingly simple when you encounter them later on. If you turn to the final chapters of the book now, you will see equations that are quite forbidding. However, when you come to these equations after covering the material in earlier chapters, you will be surprised at how easy they are to understand.

Throughout the text there is an emphasis on *comprehension* and not *computation*. The approach is meant to provide the reader with an accessible but sophisticated understanding of statistics that can be used to examine real-life criminal justice problems. In the opening chapters of the book, basic themes and materials are presented. Chapter 1 provides an introduction to how we use statistics in criminal justice and the problems that we face in applying statistics to real-life research problems. Chapters 2 through 5 introduce basic concepts of measurement and basic methods for using statistics to describe data. Many of the statistics provided here will be familiar to you; however, remember that more advanced statistics presented in later chapters build on the themes provided in these early chapters.

One of the fundamental problems that researchers face is that they seek to make statements about large populations (such as all U.S. citizens), but they are generally able to collect information or data on only a sample, or smaller group drawn from such populations. In chapters 6 through 12 our focus is on how researchers use statistics to overcome this problem. What is the logic that underlies the statistics we use for making statements about populations based on samples? What are the different types of statistical procedures or tests that can be used? What special problems are encountered in criminal justice research, and how should the researcher approach them? Some texts skip over the basics, moving students from test to test before the logic behind such tests is understood. The approach here is to focus in greater detail on relatively simple statistical decisions before moving on to more complex ones.[1]

Because our emphasis is on research in criminal justice, chapter 13 examines methods for improving the design of a research project. The statistical concept that is central to this chapter, statistical power, follows directly from the concepts developed in the prior chapters. Sta-

---

[1] This is why, for example, the binomial sampling distribution is introduced before the more commonly used normal distribution significance tests. In this way, the student can examine the logic behind statistical tests in the context of a distribution that is relatively simple to construct.

tistical power is often ignored in introductory statistics texts. However, it has become a central concern in criminal justice research, and is accordingly given strong emphasis in this text.

The final chapters of the book examine correlation and regression. These are likely to be new topics for you though they are statistics commonly used in criminal justice. The text ends with a discussion of multivariate regression modeling. While it is always difficult in statistics to decide where an introductory text should stop, with the introduction of these techniques you will have the basic tools to understand and conduct criminal justice research. Of course, these tools provide a building block for more advanced methods. The goal of the text is not only to bring you to this point in learning statistics, but also to leave you with the confidence and tools for tackling more complex problems on your own.

In each chapter there is a statement of the basic concepts and problems addressed at the outset, and a full chapter summary at the end. There is also a list of equations, when relevant, at the end of each chapter. These materials should help you to review what you have learned, and help identify the basic knowledge you need to move on to subsequent chapters. For all of the chapters, with the exception of the introduction, there is also a list of key terms with short definitions. The key terms are identified with boldface type the first time they are mentioned in the chapter. Sometimes a term may be briefly explained in an earlier chapter, but not placed in bold and defined until a later chapter when that concept is more central. A general glossary of key terms is placed at the end of the book.

There are also a set of questions at the end of each chapter, from chapters 2 through 15. The questions are designed to make you think about the subjects covered in the chapter. Sometimes they are straightforward, following directly from the text. Sometimes the questions ask you to develop ideas in slightly different ways from those that have been presented in the text. In constructing the questions, we sought to make working on statistical issues as much fun as possible. In statistics it is crucial to go over the materials covered more than once. The questions are meant to reinforce the knowledge you have gained.

A working knowledge of computers is not required to understand the statistical concepts or procedures presented in the text. However, computers have become a very important part of research in statistics, and thus we provide in the text computer exercises for relevant chapters and attach a data disk for those exercises. You are encouraged to use the data disk. It will help you to see the connection between the topics discussed in the chapters and statistical computing.

Statistics in Criminal Justice will allow you to approach statistics within a context that is familiar. It emphasizes the statistics and the problems that are commonly encountered in criminal justice research. It emphasizes understanding rather than computation. However, it takes a serious approach to statistics, which is relevant to the real world of research in crime and justice. The text is meant not only as an introduction for students but as a reference for researchers. The approach taken will help not only students gaining an introduction to statistics, but professionals who seek a straightforward explanation for statistics that have become a routine tool in contemporary criminal justice systems.

Acknowledgments

In developing this text, I have been helped by colleagues and students. I owe a particular debt to Daniel Salem, who not only crafted questions included at the end of the chapters, but also helped in framing the tone and content of the text. His perspective as a student of statistics continually reminded me of the importance of clarity and simplicity in presentation of statistical concepts. A debt is owed as well to Mary Ann Zager who prepared the computer disk and associated questions for the text. I am particularly grateful for her interest in the text, her thoughts for improving it, and her success in developing computer exercises that fit the perspective and tone of the work. Support for the work was provided by the former director of the Institute of Criminology, Professor Simcha Landau, and the dean of the Hebrew University Law School, Professor Uriel Procaccia. Their recognition of the importance of scholarly efforts made it possible for me to devote significant time to this project.

The text would not have been completed without the continual encouragement and persistence of Sabra Horne, the Criminal Justice editor of Wadsworth Publishing. Her faith in the importance of the text and her energy in pursuing it to its completion are much appreciated. I want to thank others as well, that have helped in the production of the work, including Claire Masson, Cathy Linberg, Kate Barrett, Elaine Jones, and Jennifer Ballentine and Professional Book Center. I owe special appreciation to my administrative assistant at the Police Foundation, Allison Dalseg, who played a very important role in keeping my communications organized even as I traveled from continent to continent. Finally, as with all of my academic successes, I want to thank my wife, Shelly, for her support and advice, and of course her patience.

Though anonymous reviewers cannot be thanked at the outset, they always play a major role in improving the quality of scholarly work. I was fortunate to have a large number of reviewers who read and commented on my work. The final product reflects their keen insights and thoughtful suggestions.

Thomas L. Austin, Shippensburg University

Steven G. Brandl, University of Wisconsin–Milwaukee

Chester L. Britt, Pennsylvania State University

Jerald C. Burns, Alabama State University

Michael H. Hazlett, Western Illinois University

Frank Horvath, Michigan State University

Edward Latessa, University of Cincinnati

Janet Lauritsen, University of Missouri–St. Louis

Michael D. Maltz, University of Illinois–Chicago

Greg Manco, Rutgers University

Kimberly McCabe, University of South Carolina

Terance D. Miethe, University of Nevada–Las Vegas

Larry S. Miller, East Tennessee State University

Joseph I. Naus, Rutgers University

Albert J. Reiss, Yale University

Richard Sluder, Central Missouri State University

Thomas Tomlinson, Western Illinois University

Elin Waring, Lehman College

Alexander Weiss, Indiana University

Mary Ann Zagar, Northeastern University

Statistics

in Criminal Justice

initial hurdles

Do Statisticians Have to Be Experts in Mathematics?

Are Computers Making Statisticians Redundant?

key principles

What Is Our Aim in Choosing a Statistic?

What Basic Principles Apply to Different Types of Statistics?

What Are the Different Uses of Statistics in Research?

T HE PURPOSE OF STATISTICAL ANALYSIS is to clarify and not confuse. It is a tool to answer questions. It allows us to take large bodies of information and summarize them using a few simple statements. It makes it possible to come to solid conclusions even when the realities of the research world make it difficult to isolate the problems we seek to study. Without statistics it would be virtually impossible to conduct research about crime and justice. Yet, there is perhaps no other subject that criminal justice students find so difficult to approach in their university studies.

A good part of the difficulty lies in the links that students make between statistics and math. A course in statistics is often thought to mean long hours solving formulas and managing equations. In developing our understanding of statistics in criminal justice research, we will develop a better understanding of the formulas that underlie statistical methods, but our focus will be on concepts and not on computations. There is just no way to develop a good understanding of statistics without doing some work by hand. But in the age of computers, the main purpose of doing computations is to provide a deeper understanding for how statistics work.

Researchers no longer spend long hours calculating statistics. In the 1950s, social scientists would work for months developing results that can now be generated on a computer in a few minutes. Today, it does not take a whiz kid in math to carry out a complex statistical analysis. Such analyses can be done routinely with user-friendly computer programs. Why then do we need a course in statistics? Why not just leave it to the computer to provide us with answers. Why do we need to learn the basics in the computer age?

The computer is a powerful tool and has made statistics accessible to a much larger group of criminal justice researchers. However, the best researchers still spend many hours on statistical analysis. The computer age has freed us from long and tedious calculations. What is left is the most challenging and important part of statistical analysis: identifying the statistical tools that will best serve the researcher in interpreting his or her research to others.

The goal of this text is to provide you with the basic skills you will need to choose statistics for research and interpret them. It is meant for students of criminology and criminal justice. As in other fields, there are specific techniques that are commonly used and specific approaches that have developed over time among researchers who specialize in this area of study. These statistics are the focus of this text. Not only do we draw our examples from crime and justice issues, we also pay particular attention to the choices that criminal justice researchers make when approaching statistical problems.

Before we begin our study of statistics in criminal justice, it is useful to state some basic principles that underlie the approach we take in this text. They revolve around four basic questions. First, what should our purpose be in choosing a statistic? Second, why do we use statistics to answer research questions? Third, what basic principles apply across very different types of statistics? And finally, what are the different uses for statistics in research?

The Purpose of Statistics Is to Clarify and Not Confuse

It sometimes seems that researchers use statistics as a kind of secret language. In this sense, it is a way for the initiated to share ideas and concepts without including the rest of us. Of course, it is necessary to develop a common language to report research results. This is part of the reason why it is important for you to take a course in statistics. But the reason we use statistics is to make research results easier, not more difficult, to understand.

For example, if you want to provide someone with a description of three offenders, that you had studied, you would not need to search for statistics to summarize your results. The simplest way to describe your sample would be to just tell us about your subjects. You could describe each offender and their criminal histories without creating any real confusion. But what if you want to tell us about twenty offenders. It would take quite a long time to tell us about each in some detail, and it is likely that those listening would find it difficult to remember who was who. It would be even more difficult to describe 100 offenders. With thousands of offenders it would be just about impossible to take this approach.

This is one example of how statistics can help to simplify and clarify the research process. Statistics allow you to use a few summary statements to provide a comprehensive portrait of a large group of offenders. For example, instead of providing the name of each offender and telling us how many crimes he or she committed, you could present a single statistic that describes the average number of crimes committed by the persons you studied. You might say, that on average the people you studied committed two to three crimes in the last year. Accordingly, although it might be impossible to describe each person you studied, you could, by using a statistic, give your audience an overall picture of them. Statistics thus make it possible to summarize information about a large number of subjects with a few simple statements.

Having said that statistics should simplify research results, it follows that the researcher should utilize the simplest statistics that are appropriate in answering the research questions that he or she raises. Nonetheless, it sometimes seems as if researchers go out of their way to identify statistics that few people recognize and even fewer understand. This approach does not help the researcher or his or her audience. There is no benefit in using statistics that are not understood by those who are interested in your research findings. Using a more complex statistic when a simpler one is also appropriate serves no purpose beyond that of reducing the number of people that will be influenced by your work.

The best presentation of research findings is one in which the investigator communicates results in a clear and understandable way. When using more complex statistics, the researcher should present them in as straightforward a manner as possible. The mark of good statisticians is not that they can mystify their audiences, but rather that they can communicate even complex results in a way that most people can understand.

Statistics Are Used to Solve Problems

Statistics develop because of a need to deal with a specific type of question or problem. In the example above, we were faced with the dilemma that we could not describe each person in a very large study without creating a good deal of confusion. Instead, we suggested that an average might provide a way of summarizing a characteristic of all of the people we studied with one simple statistic. The average is a statistical solution. It provides the researcher with a tool for solving the problem of how to describe many subjects with a short and simple statement.

As we will see in later chapters, statistics have been developed to deal with many different types of problems that researchers face. Some of these may seem at the outset difficult to understand, and indeed it is natural to be put off by the complexities of some statistics. However, the solutions that statisticians develop are usually based on simple common sense. Contrary to what is often thought about statistics, they follow a logic that you will find quite easy to follow. Once you learn to trust your common sense, learning statistics will turn out to be surprisingly simple. Indeed, my own experience is that students that have good common sense, even those with very little formal background in this area, tend to become the best criminal justice statisticians.

But in order to be able to use common sense it is important to approach statistics with as little fear as possible. Fear of statistics is a greater barrier to learning statistics than the computations or formulas that we will use. It is just very difficult to learn anything well when you approach it with great foreboding. Statistics is a lot easier than you think. The job of this text is to take you step-by-step through the principles and ideas that underlie basic statistics for criminal justice researchers. At the beginning, we will spend a good deal of time examining the logic behind statistics and illustrating how and why statisticians choose a particular solution to a particular statistical problem. What you must do at the outset is take a deep breath and give statistics a chance. Once you do, you will find that the solutions that statisticians use make very good sense.

Basic Principles Apply across Statistical Techniques

There are a few basic principles that underlie much of the statistical reasoning you will encounter in this text. Stating them at the outset will help you to see how statistical procedures in later chapters are linked one to another. To understand these principles you do not need to develop any computations or formulas, but rather to think generally about what we are trying to achieve when we develop statistics. You should not worry if you do not understand each principle thoroughly.

The first is simply that *in developing statistics we seek to reduce the level of error as much as possible.* The purpose of research is to provide answers to research questions. In developing those answers we want to be as accurate as possible. Clearly, we want to make as few mistakes as we can. The best statistic is one that provides the most accurate statement about your study. Accordingly, a major criterion in choosing which statistic to use, or indeed in defining how a statistic is developed, is the amount of error that a statistic presents. In statistics we try to minimize error whenever possible.

Unfortunately, it is virtually impossible to develop any description without some degree of error. This fact is part of everyday reality. For example, we do not expect that our watches will tell perfect time, or that our thermostats will be exactly correct. At the same time, we all know that there are better watches or thermostats, and that what makes them "better" is that they provide information with less error. Similarly, although we do not expect our stockbroker to be correct all of the time, we do choose a broker who we believe will make the fewest mistakes.

In choosing a statistic, we will also use a second principle to which we return again and again in this text. *Statistics based on more information are generally preferred over those based on less information.* This principle is common to all forms of intelligence gathering and not just those that we use in research. Good decision making is based on information. The more information that is available to the decision maker, the better he or she can weigh the different options that are presented. So also in statistics. A statistic that is based on more information, all else being equal, will be preferred over one that utilizes less information. There are exceptions to this rule, often resulting from the quality or form of the information or data that you collect. We discuss these in detail in the text. But as a rule, the best statistic utilizes the maximum amount of information.

Our third principle relates to a danger that confronts our use of statistics as a tool for describing information. In many studies there are cases that are very different from all of the others. Indeed, they are so different that they might be termed deviant cases or, as statisticians sometimes call them, "outliers." For example, in a study of criminal careers there may be one or two offenders who have committed thousands of crimes, whereas the next most active criminal in the sample has committed only a few hundred crimes. Although such cases form a natural part of the research process, they often have very significant implications for your choice of statistics and your presentation of results.

In almost every statistic we will study, we will find that outliers present a distinct and troublesome problem. A deviant case can make it look like your offenders are younger or older than they really are. It can make it look like they are less or more criminally active. Importantly, deviant cases often have the most dramatic effects for more complex statistical procedures. And it is precisely here, where the researcher is often preoccupied with other relevant statistical issues, that deviant cases go unnoticed. But whatever statistic is used, the principle remains the same: *Outliers present a significant problem in choosing and interpreting statistics.*

The final principle is one that is often unstated in statistics, because it is assumed at the outset: *Whatever the method of research, the researcher must strive to systematize the procedures used in data collection and analysis.* As Albert J. Reiss, Jr., a pioneer in criminal justice methodologies, has noted, "systematic" means in part "that observation and recording are done according to explicit procedures which permit replication and that rules are followed which permit the use of scientific inference."[1] While Reiss's comment will become clearer as statistical concepts are defined in coming chapters, his point is simply that you must follow clearly stated procedures and rules in developing and presenting statistical findings.

It is important to approach statistics in a systematic way. One cannot be sloppy or haphazard, at least if the statistic is to provide a good answer to the research question you raise. The choice of a statistic should follow a consistent logic from start to finish. One should not jump from statistic to statistic merely because the outcomes are favorable to the thesis that you raise. In learning about statistics, it is also important to go step-by-step—it is important to be well organized and prepared. You cannot learn statistics by cramming in the last week of classes. It is a systematic process that must be followed each week. This is the key to learning statistics.

Statistical procedures are built on all of the steps of research that precede them. If those steps are faulty, then the statistics themselves are faulty. In later chapters we often talk about this process in terms of the assumptions of the statistics that we use. We assume that all of the rules of good research have been followed up to the point where we decide on a statistic and calculate it. Statistics cannot be disentangled from the larger research process that comes before it. The numbers that we use are only as good as the data collection techniques

---

[1] A. J. Reiss, Jr. (1971), "Systematic Social Observation of Social Phenomenon," in Herbert Costner (ed.), *Sociological Methodology* (San Francisco: Jossey Bass), 3–33.

that we have employed. Very complex statistics cannot hide bad research methods. A systematic approach is crucial not only to the statistical procedures that we learn about in this text but to the whole research process.

The Uses of Statistics

In the chapters that follow we examine three types of statistics, or three distinct ways in which we use statistics in criminal justice. The first is called descriptive statistics, because it helps in the summary and description of research findings. The second, inferential or inductive statistics, allows us to make inferences or statements about large groups of people from studies of smaller groups, or samples, drawn from them. Finally, we introduce the problem of multivariate statistics toward the end of the text. Multivariate statistics, as its name implies, allows us to examine a series of variables at one time.

Descriptive Statistics

We are all familiar with descriptive statistics in some way. We use them often in our daily lives, and they appear routinely in newspapers and on television. Indeed, we use them so often that we sometimes don't think of them as statistics at all. During an election year, everyone is concerned about the percentage support that each candidate gains in the primaries. Students at the beginning of the semester want to know what proportion of their grades will be based on weekly exercises. In deciding if our salaries are fair, we want to know what the average salary is for other people in similar positions. These are all descriptive statistics. They summarize for us in one simple statement the characteristics of many people. As we discussed above using the example of criminal histories, descriptive statistics make it possible for us to summarize or describe large amounts of information.

In the chapters that follow we are concerned with two types of descriptive statistics: measures of central tendency and measures of dispersion. Measures of central tendency are measures of typicality. They tell us in one statement what the average case is like. If we could take only one person as the best example for all of the subjects we studied, who would it be? If we could choose only one level of crime activity to typify the frequency of offending of all subjects, what level is the best snapshot we could provide? If we wanted to give our audience a general sense of how much on average a group of offenders stole in a year, what amount would provide the best portrait? Percentages, proportions, and means are all examples of measures of central tendency that we commonly use. In the coming chapters we learn more about these statistics as well as more complex measures with which you may not as yet be familiar, such as correlation or regression coefficients.

Having a statistic that describes the average case is very helpful in describing research results. However, we might also ask how typical this average case is of the subjects in our study as a whole. The answer to this question is provided by measures of dispersion. They tell us to what extent the other subjects we study are similar to the case or statistic we have chosen to represent them. Although we don't commonly use measures of dispersion in our daily lives, we do often ask similar questions without the use of such statistics.

For example, in deciding whether our income is fair, we might want to know not only the average income of others in similar positions, but the range of incomes that such people have. If the range is very small, we would probably decide that the average provides a fairly good portrait of what we should be making. If the range is very large, we might want to investigate more carefully why some people make so much more or less than the average. The range is a measure of dispersion. It tells us about the spread of scores around our statistic. In the chapters that follow we speak about many other measures of dispersion, for example, the standard deviation or variance, which may be less familiar to you. Without these measures, our presentation of research findings would be incomplete. It is not enough simply to describe the typical case, we must also describe to what degree other cases in our study are different or similar to it.

Inferential Statistics

Inferential statistics allow us to make statements about a population, or the larger group of people we seek to study, on the basis of a sample drawn from that population. This is a very important and powerful tool, without which it would be very difficult to conduct research in criminal justice. The reason is simple. When we conduct research, we do so to answer questions about populations. But in reality we seldom are able to collect information on the whole population, so we draw a sample from it. Statistical inference makes it possible for us to infer characteristics from that sample to the population.

Why is it that we draw samples if we are really interested in making statements about populations? In good part it is because it is usually impractical or too expensive, or both, to gain information on most populations. For example, if we seek to examine the attitudes of

U.S. citizens toward criminal justice processing, we are interested in how all citizens feel. However, to study all citizens would be a task of gigantic proportion and would cost millions of dollars. Such surveys are done every few years and are called censuses. The last census in the United States took many years to prepare and implement and cost hundreds of millions of dollars. If every research effort about attitudes demanded a census, then we would have very few research projects indeed. It would make criminal justice research about such attitudes virtually impossible to complete.

Even when we look at much smaller populations in the criminal justice system, examination of the entire population is often beyond the resources of the criminal justice researcher. For example, if we merely wanted to study all U.S. prisoners, we would have to study about 1,000,000 people. Even if we want to look at only the 50,000 or so women prisoners, it would still likely cost millions of dollars to complete a simple study of their attitudes. This is because even the most inexpensive data collection can still cost tens of dollars for each subject studied. When you consider that the National Institute of Justice, the primary funder of criminal justice research in the United States, provides a total of about $100,000,000 a year for all research, it is clear that criminal justice research cannot rely on studies of whole populations.

It is easy to understand, then, why we want to draw a sample or subset of the larger population to study, but it is not obvious why we should believe that what we learn from that sample applies to the population from which it is drawn. How do we know, for example, that the attitudes toward criminal justice expressed in a sample of U.S. citizens are similar to the attitudes of all citizens. The sample is a group of people drawn from the population, it is not the population itself. How much can we rely on such estimates? And to what extent can we trust such statistics?

I think you have probably raised such issues already either in regard to the surveys that form so much a part of public life in recent years, or from the studies that you read about in your college classes. When a news organization conducts a survey of 1,000 people to tell us how all voters will vote in the next election, they are using a sample to make statements about a population. This is very similar to the criminal justice studies you read about, which also base their conclusions about populations—whether of offenders, criminal justice agents, or criminal justice events—on samples. Statistical inference provides a method for deciding to what extent you can have faith in such results. It allows you to decide when the differences you discover in your sample can be generalized to the population from which it is drawn. Statistical inference is a very important part of statistics and one we spend a good deal of time discussing in this text.

Taking into Account Competing Explanations: Multivariate Statistics

Multivariate statistics allow us to solve a different type of problem in research. It is often the case that the issue on which we want to focus is confounded by other factors in our study. Multivariate statistics allow us to isolate one factor while taking into account a host of others. For example, there are many criminal justice studies that examine the impact of imprisonment on the future criminal behavior of offenders. In general, they compare offenders who are found guilty in court and sentenced to prison with those who are found guilty but do not receive a prison sanction. Such studies are interested in whether the criminal behavior of prisoners is different from that of nonprisoners once they are released into the community. Most of these studies are faced with a very difficult research problem. Prisoners and nonprisoners are often very different types of people, and some of these differences are likely to impact upon their criminal behavior in the community.

For example, prisoners are more likely than nonprisoners to have been arrested before, since a prior arrest is often an important factor in the judge's decision to incarcerate a defendant in the first place. But we know from research about criminal careers that people with a prior history of arrest are also much more likely than people without such a history to commit a crime in the future. Accordingly, prisoners are more likely to commit crime in the future irrespective of the fact that they have served a prison sentence. This makes it very difficult to assess the impact of·imprisonment on future offending. If we discover that the prisoners are more likely than nonprisoners to commit a crime once released into the community, how can we tell whether this was a result of the experience of imprisonment? It might be due to the simple fact that prisoners are more likely than nonprisoners to commit crimes in the first place. Their more serious arrest histories would predict this result.

It is easy to see how complex it is for the criminal justice researcher to isolate the specific impact of imprisonment itself from all of the other possible explanations for differences in reoffending between prisoners and nonprisoners. Multivariate analysis provides a statistical solution for this problem. It allows the criminal justice researcher to isolate the impact of one factor, in this case imprisonment, from other factors that might confound the researcher's conclusions.

Chapter Summary

Statistics seem intimidating because they are associated with complex mathematical formulas and computations. Although some knowledge of math is required, an understanding of the concepts is much more important than an in-depth understanding of the computations. Today's computers, which perform complex calculations in a matter of seconds, or fractions of seconds, have drastically cut the workload of the researcher. They cannot, however, replace the key role a researcher plays in choosing the most appropriate statistical tool for each case.

The researcher's aim in using statistics is to communicate results in a clear and simple form. As such, the researcher should always choose the simplest statistic appropriate in answering the research question. Statistics offer common sense solutions to research problems.

The following principles apply to all types of statistics: The statistician should strive (a) to keep the levels of error down to an absolute minimum, (b) to base the statistic on the maximum amount of information possible, (c) to find solutions to the nagging problem of outlying cases, and (d) to take a systematic approach to both the collection and the analysis of data.

There are three principal types of statistics. Descriptive statistics allow the researcher to summarize large amounts of information in an efficient manner. Two types of such statistics, which go hand in hand, are measures of central tendency, which describe the characteristics of the average case, and measures of dispersion, which tell us just how typical this average case is. Inferential statistics allow us to make statements about a population on the basis of a sample drawn from that population. Multivariate statistics allow us to isolate the impact of one factor from others that may distort our results.

of Research

MEASUREMENT LIES AT THE HEART of statistics. Indeed, no statistic would be possible without the concept of measurement itself. Measurement is also an integral part of our everyday lives. We routinely classify and assign value to people and objects without giving much thought to the processes that underlie our decisions and evaluations. In statistics, such classification and ordering of value must be done in a systematic way. There are clear rules for developing different types of measures, and defined criteria for deciding which are most appropriate for answering a specific research question.

Although it is natural to focus on the end products of research, it is important for the researcher to remember that measurement forms the first building block of every statistic. Even the most complex statistics, with numbers that are defined to many decimal places, are only as accurate as the measures upon which they are built. Accordingly, the relatively simple rules we discuss in this chapter are crucial for developing solid research findings. The researcher can build a very complex structure of analysis. But if the measures that form the foundation of research are not appropriate for the analyses that are conducted, the findings cannot be relied upon.

We begin chapter 2 by examining the basic idea of measurement in science. We then turn to a description of the main types of measures in statistics, and the criteria we use to distinguish among them. We are particularly concerned with how statisticians have ranked measurement based on the amount of information that a measure includes. This concept, defined as levels of measurement, is very important in choosing which statistical procedures are appropriate in research. Finally, we discuss some basic criteria for defining a good measure.

Science and Measurement:
Classification as a First Step in Research

Criminal justice research is a scientific enterprise. By that we mean that it seeks to develop knowledge about the nature of crimes, criminals, and the criminal justice system. The development of knowledge can, of course, be carried out in a number of different ways. Criminal justice researchers may, for example, observe the actions of criminal justice agents or speak to offenders. They may examine the routine information collected by government or criminal justice agencies, or develop new information through analyses of the content of records in the criminal justice system. Knowledge can be developed by historical review, and even through examining archaeological records of legal systems or sanctions of ancient civilizations.

The methods that criminal justice researchers use vary. Nonetheless, they have in common an underlying philosophy about how knowledge may be gained and what scientific research can tell us. This philosophy, which is predominant in scientific study in the modern world, is usually called positivism.[1] At its core is the idea that science is based on facts and not values. Science, in this sense, cannot make decisions about the way the world should be (although scientific observation may inform such decisions). Rather, it allows us to examine and investigate the realities of the world as we know it. The major tool for defining this reality in science is **measurement.**

Measurement in science begins with the activity of distinguishing groups or phenomena one from another. This process, which is generally termed **classification,** implies that we can place objects or people in clearly defined categories. What differentiates measurement in science from measurement in our everyday lives is that there must be systematic criteria for determining both what each category represents and the boundaries between categories. We now turn to a discussion of those criteria as they relate to different **levels of measurement.**

---

[1] See D. Black (1973), "The Boundaries of Legal Sociology," in D. Black and M. Mileski (eds.), *The Social Organization of Law* (New York: Seminar Press), 41–47.

Levels of Measurement

Classification forms the first step in measurement. However, there are a number of different ways that we can classify the people, or places, or phenomena we wish to study. We may simply distinguish one category from another. But we might also be interested in how those categories relate to one another. Do some represent more serious crime or less serious crime? Can we rank how serious one crime is to another in a clear and defined order? Is it possible to define exactly how serious one crime is relative to another?

These types of questions suggest that measurement can be a lot more complex than simply distinguishing one group from another. Recognizing this complexity, statisticians have defined four basic groups of measures, or **scales of measurement,** based on the amount of information that each takes advantage of. The four are generally seen as occupying different positions or levels on a ladder of measurement (see figure 2.1). Following a principle we stated in chapter 1—that statistics that take advantage of more information are generally preferred—measures that include more information rank higher in the ladder of measurement.

Nominal Scales

At the bottom of the ladder of measurement are **nominal scales.** Nominal scale measures simply distinguish one phenomenon from another. Suppose, for example, that you wanted to measure crime types. In your study, you are most interested in distinguishing be-

Figure 2.1   *Ladder of Measurement*

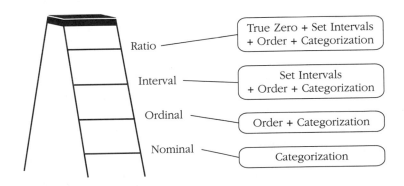

tween violent crime and other types of crime. To fulfill the requirements of a nominal scale, and thus the minimum requirements of measurement, you would need to be able to take all of the crime events in your study and place them in the category of either violent crime or other crime. There can be no overlap.

In practice you might come across many individual events that seem difficult to classify. For example, what would you decide to do with a crime event in which the offender first stole from his victim and then assaulted him? This event includes elements of both violent and property crime. What of the case where the offender does not assault the victim, but merely threatens her? Would you decide to include this in the category of violent crime or other crime?

In measurement, you must make systematic choices that can be applied across events. You cannot decide one way for one event and another way for another. In this case, you might conclude that the major issue in your study is the presence of violence. Thus all cases with any violent events would be placed in the violent category. Similarly, you might conclude that violence must include physical victimization. Whatever your choice, to meet the requirements of measurement you must define clearly where all events in your study would be placed.

Nominal scales can include any number of different categories. For example, in classifying crime, the Uniform Crime Reporting system, which keeps track of arrests in the United States, includes some 29 categories of crime. These range from violent crimes such as murder or robbery, to vagrancy and vandalism. Although there is no statistical difficulty with defining many categories, the more categories that are included, the more confusing that description of the results can be. If you are trying to provide a sense for the distribution of crime in your study, it is very difficult to practically describe 20 or 30 different crime categories. Keeping in mind that the purpose of statistics is to clarify and simplify, you should try to use the smallest number of categories that can best describe the research problem you are examining.

At the same time, do not confuse collection of **data** with presentation of your findings. You do not lose anything by collecting information in the most detailed way that you can. If you collect information with a large number of categories, you can always collapse a group of categories into one. For example, if you collect information on arrest events utilizing the very detailed categories of the criminal law, you can always combine them later into more general categories. But if you collect information in more general categories (for example, by violent crime or property crime), you cannot identify specific crimes such as robbery or car theft without returning to the original source of your information.

Nominal scale measures are common in criminal justice. We often seek simply to distinguish whether people are offenders or nonoffenders, whether they have served time in prison or not, whether they are female or male, or whether they have received one type of treatment versus another. Nominal measures, although they are commonly used, provide us with very limited knowledge about the phenomenon we are studying. As we will see in later chapters, they also limit the types of statistical analyses that we may use. In the hierarchy of measurement, nominal scales form the lowest step in the ladder. One step above are what we define as **ordinal scales.**

Ordinal Scales

What distinguishes an ordinal from a nominal scale is the fact that we assign a clear order to the categories included. Now we not only can distinguish between one category and another, we also can place those categories on a continuum. This is a very important new piece information; it allows us to rank events and not just categorize them. Taking the example of type of crime, we might decide to rank them in order of seriousness. In measuring crime in this way we would not only distinguish between categories, such as violent, property, and victimless crimes, we might also argue that violent crimes are more serious than property crimes and that victimless crimes are less serious than both violent or property crimes. We need not make such decisions arbitrarily. We might rank crimes by the amount of damage done, or the ways in which the general population rates or evaluates different types of crime.

Ordinal scales are also commonly used in criminal justice and criminology. Indeed, many important criminal justice concepts are measured in this way. For example, in a well-known London survey of victimization, fear of crime was measured using a simple four-level ordinal scale. Researchers asked respondents: "Are you personally concerned about crime in London as a whole? Would you say you are: (1) very concerned, (2) quite concerned, (3) a little concerned, or (4) not concerned at all?"[2]

---

2 See R. Sparks, H. Genn, and D. Dodd (1977), *Surveying Victims: A Study of the Measurement of Criminal Victimization* (New York: Wiley).

Ranking the seriousness of crime and people's fear of crime are only two examples of the use of ordinal scales in criminal justice research. We could also draw examples regarding severity of court sentences, damage to victims, complexity of crime, or seriousness of prior records of offenders. What all of these measures have in common is that they classify events and order them. What is missing is a precise statement about how various categories differ one from another.

Interval Scales

Interval scales utilize this missing piece of information. They not only classify and order people or events, they also define the exact differences between them. Thus an interval scale would not simply rank prior record by seriousness, it would allow us to say how much more serious one offender's record is than another's. Indeed prior record is often measured as an interval scale, usually by the number of events that are on an offender's criminal history record. For example, one offender may have 20 prior arrests and another offender only 5. This scale of number of arrests allows us not only to say that the offender with 20 arrests has a more serious arrest history, but also that his history is 15 arrests more serious.

Criminal justice researchers use interval scales to present findings about resources, criminal sentences, and a whole host of other issues that relate to crimes and criminals. There is the amount spent by criminal justice agencies and the amount stolen by offenders. We can measure the number of years of prison served or sentenced, or the age at which offenders were first arrested. These measures all have in common a precise statement of the relationship among categories described. They not only distinguish one category from another, and order the categories, they also allow us to define the exact differences between them. By using interval measures, we can describe how much more one offender stole than another, how many more years he served in prison, and how much older he was at first arrest. This additional information provides a whole range of new possibilities both for describing our research findings and, as we will see in later chapters, for analyzing them.

Statisticians define one additional step up the ladder of measurement. Interval measures that have what is described as a nonarbitrary or true zero point can also be defined as **ratio scales.** Thus, for example, age and number of arrests meet the requirements not only for an interval scale, but also for a ratio scale. This because zero age and zero arrests means simply that the individual has no arrests and no age. While ratio scales represent the highest level of measurement, it is very seldom that a statistic will require more than an interval-level scale. Nonetheless, whenever a statistic is appropriate for an interval scale, you should assume that it is also appropriate for a ratio scale.

Relating Interval, Ordinal, and Nominal Scales: The Importance of Collecting Data at the Highest Level Possible

As you move up the ladder of measurement, the amount of information that is gained grows. At the lowest level, you have only categorization. At the next level, you add knowledge about the order of the categories included. With interval scales you not only classify and order your measure, but you also define how much categories differ one from another. The fact that each higher level of measurement includes additional information means that you cannot transform a lower-level measure to a higher one.

Take for example, measurement of victimization. If you decide to simply compare the types of victimization involved in a crime event, you would measure victimization using a nominal scale. You might choose the following categories: events involving loss of money or property, events including physical harm, a combination of such events, and all other events. But let us assume, for a moment, that at some time after you collected your data, a colleague suggested that it is important to distinguish not only the type of event but the seriousness of crimes within each type. In this case, you would want to distinguish not only whether a crime included monetary loss or violence, but the seriousness of loss in each. However, because your measure is a nominal scale it does not include information on the seriousness of loss. Accordingly, from the information available to you, you could not create an ordinal-level measure of how much money was stolen or how serious was the physical harm.

Similarly, if you had begun with information only on the order of crime seriousness, you could not transform that measure into one that defined the exact differences between the categories you examine. Let us say, for example, that you received data from the police that ranked monetary victimization for each crime into four ordinally scaled categories: no monetary harm, minor monetary harm (less than $500), moderate monetary harm ($501–10,000), and serious monetary harm ($10,001 and above). If you decide it is important not just to know the general order of monetary harm, but also the exact differences in harm between crimes, these data are insufficient. Such information would be available only if you had received information about harm at an interval level of measurement. In this case the police would provide information not on which of the four categories of harm a crime belonged to, but rather on the exact amount of harm in dollars caused by each crime.

While you cannot move up the ladder of measurement, you can move down it. Thus, for example, if you have information collected at an interval scale you can easily transform that information into an ordinal-scale measure. Taking the example of victimization, if you have information on the exact amount of harm caused by a crime in dollars, you could at any point decide to group crimes into levels of seriousness. You would simply define the levels, and then place each crime in the level appropriate for it. For example, if you define crimes involving harm between $501 and $10,000 as being of moderate victimization, you would take all of the crimes that include this degree of victimization and redefine them as falling in this moderate category. Similarly, you could transform this measure into a nominal scale, by just distinguishing between those that include monetary harm and those that do not.

Beyond illustrating the connections between different levels of measurement, our discussion here emphasizes a very important rule of thumb for research. You should always collect information at the highest level of measurement possible. You can always decide later to collapse such measures into lower-level scales. However, if you begin by collecting information lower on the ladder of measurement, you will not be able to decide later to use scales at a higher level.

What Is a Good Measure?

In analysis and reporting of research results, measures that are of a higher scale are usually preferred over measures that are of a lower scale. Higher-level measures are better measures, based on the principle that they take into account more information. Nonetheless, this is not the only criterion we use in deciding what is a good measure in research. The researcher must raise two additional concerns. First, does the measure reflect the phenomenon to be described? Second, is it a measure that will yield results that can be trusted?

The first question is one that involves what those who study research methods call **validity.** Validity asks whether the measure used actually reflects the concept or theory you seek to examine. Thus, for example, collecting information on age in a sample does not provide a valid measurement of criminal history. Age, although related to criminal history, is not a measure of criminal history. Similarly, work history may be related to criminality, but it does not make a valid measure of criminality. But even if we draw measures that directly reflect criminal history, there are often problems of validity to address.

Let us say that you wanted to describe the number of crimes that offenders have committed over a one-year period. One option you might have is to examine their criminal history information as it is recorded on the Federal Bureau of Investigation's (FBI) criminal history record, or rap sheet. The rap sheet includes information on arrests, convictions, and incarcerations. Although each of these measures tells us something about a person's criminal history, they are not all equally valid in terms of answering the research question we have proposed.

The most valid measure of frequency of offending is the one that most directly assesses how many crimes an individual has committed. Each of the three measures in the rap sheet includes some degree of threat to validity. This means that we can criticize each because it does not quite reflect the concept we wish to study. Incarceration, for example, is more a measure of seriousness of crime than frequency of offending. This because judges may impose a number of different types of sanctions, but they are are more likely to impose a prison sentence for more serious crimes. Many crimes that result in a conviction do not lead to incarceration but rather to probation, fines, or community service. Thus, if we used incarceration to measure frequency of offending we would be likely to miss many crime events in an offender's criminal record. Incarceration accordingly provides a biased picture of the number of offenses committed by an offender. It is not a highly valid measure of this concept.

Using this logic, criminologists have generally assumed that arrest is the most valid measure of frequency of offending that can be gained from official data sources, such as the FBI rap sheet. Arrests are much closer in occurrence to the actual behavior we seek to study and do not include the filtering of negotiations found at later stages of the legal process. Criminologists have assumed that arrests reflect criminal behavior more accurately than convictions or incarceration. Nonetheless, some legal scholars would contend that arrests are a less valid measure of criminality precisely because they come before prosecutors and defense attorneys can argue out the innocence or guilt of offenders. They contend that someone has not committed a crime until the legal system defines it as such.

Although arrests are generally assumed to provide the most valid official measure of an offender's criminal history, the validity of arrests as a measure of frequency of offending can also be challenged. Many crimes go unreported to police, and many crimes that are reported are never solved. This means that an arrest reflects only part of an offender's criminal history, because he or she is not likely to be arrested for every crime that is committed. This threat to validity has been a major issue in criminology in recent years and has led to the development of estimates of the relationship between actual offending and arrests. In general, criminologists have used self-report surveys to examine such biases. In a self-report survey we can ask the offender directly how many crimes he or she has committed over the last year. Thus self-reports provide for a more valid measure of offending than official data. But such studies are sensitive to another issue in measurement, which also provides insight into whether a measure is a good measure.

Reliability questions whether a measure gains information in a consistent manner. Will you get the same result if you repeat measurement of the same case or person? If different people have similar characteristics, will your measure reflect that similarity? Taking the above example of criminal history, we would ask in this case not whether the measure reflects the concept of frequency of offending, but whether its measurement of the concept is reliable across different subjects.

Self-reports, which allow us to ask valid questions about the number of crimes that a person commits, have been challenged on the basis of their reliability. One problem is that people may lie about their criminal histories. This is a sensitive question, and no matter what efforts the researcher takes to assure subjects of confidentiality, people may be hesitant to talk about crimes in their past. Accordingly, depending on the degree of hesitancy of subjects, a researcher might gain different answers irrespective of a person's actual criminal history. But even if a person is willing to provide accurate responses to such questions, he or she may not be able to. Some people have better memories than others. Accordingly, the reliability of this measure depends in part on a person's ability to recall events generally.

Such issues of reliability have begun to be addressed directly by criminologists, who are trying to increase the reliability of self-report methods by improving interview techniques and protocols.

Returning to the FBI rap sheets, we can also assess problems of reliability. In general, arrest not only is assumed to be the most valid of official measures, it is also the measure most reliably recorded on the FBI rap sheets. This is the case in good part because the rap sheets are built around fingerprint records, and police agencies have come to routinely send such records to the FBI. This helps the police agencies as well, because they often use this information to check the identities of arrestees and to assess their criminal histories. Other types of agencies are less consistent in their transfer of information to the FBI, and as a result convictions and incarcerations are less reliably recorded.

Validity and reliability in criminal history information are good examples of the kinds of problems you will encounter in assessing measures in criminal justice. You should keep in mind that no measure is perfect. Some threat to validity is likely to be encountered no matter how careful you are. Some degree of unreliability is almost always present in measurement. Your task is to develop or choose the best measure you can. The best measure is one that most closely reflects the concept you wish to study and assesses it in a consistent and reliable way across subjects or events.

Chapter Summary

In science we use **measurement** to make accurate observations. All measurement must begin with a **classification** process—a process which in science is carried out according to systematic criteria.

There are four **scales of measurement:** nominal, ordinal, interval, and ratio. Information in a **nominal scale** is organized by simple classification. The aim is merely to distinguish between different phenomena. There can be no overlap between categories nor can there be cases that do not fit any one category. There is no theoretical limit to the number of nominal categories possible. With an **ordinal scale,** the information is not only categorized, but these categories are then placed in order of magnitude. An **interval scale** is one that, in addition to the processes of categorization and ordering, also defines the exact difference between objects, characteristics, or events. A **ratio scale** is an interval scale for which a value of true zero can be identified.

Data collected at a higher level of measurement may be subsequently reduced to a lower level, but data collected at a lower level may not be transformed to a higher one. For this reason it is always advisable to collect data at the highest level of measurement possible.

There are three separate factors that affect the quality of a measure. The researcher should strive for a measure that has: (a) a high scale of measurement (i.e., one that uses more information); (b) a high level of **validity** (i.e., one that provides an accurate reflection of the concept being studied); (c) a high level of **reliability** (i.e., one that provides the most consistent results).

Key Terms

Classification The process whereby data are organized into categories or groups.

Data Information used to answer a research question.

Interval Scale A scale of measurement that uses a common and standard unit and, in addition to categorizing and ordering data, enables the researcher to calculate exact differences between scores.

Levels of Measurement Types of measurement that make use of progressively increasing amounts of information.

Measurement The assignment of numerical values to objects, characteristics, or events in a systematic manner.

Nominal Scale A scale of measurement that assigns each piece of information to an appropriate category without suggesting any order for the categories created.

Ordinal Scale A scale of measurement that categorizes information and places it in an order of magnitude without using a standard scale of equal intervals.

Ratio Scale A scale of measurement identical to an interval scale in every respect except that, in addition, a value of zero on the scale represents the absence of the phenomenon.

Reliability The extent to which the measure chosen will consistently assign the same value to whatever is being measured.

Scale of Measurement Type of categorization used to arrange or assign values to data.

Validity The extent to which the measure chosen accurately reflects the concept being measured.

Exercises

2.1   For each of the following examples of criminal justice studies, state whether the scale of measurement used is: nominal, ordinal, or at least interval (i.e., interval or ratio). Explain your choice.

a In a door-to-door survey, residents of a neighborhood are asked how many times over the past year they (or anyone in their household) have been the victims of any type of crime.

b Parole-board members rate inmate behavior on a scale of 1 to 10, where a score of 1 represents exemplary behavior.

c One hundred college students are asked whether they have ever been arrested.

d A researcher checks prison records to determine the racial background of prisoners assigned to a particular cell block.

e In a telephone survey, members of the public are asked which of the following statements best matches how they feel about the performance of their local police force: totally dissatisfied, dissatisfied, indifferent, satisfied, or very satisfied.

f A criminologist measures the diameters of the skulls of inmates who have died in prison in an attempt to develop a biological theory of the causes of criminality.

g Secretaries at a top legal firm are asked the following question: "Over the past year, have you been the victim of sexual harassment—and if so, how many times?" Answers are categorized as follows: never, once, two or three times, more than three times, or refused to answer.

2.2 You have been given access to a group of 12 jurors with a mandate from your senior researcher to "go and find out about their prior jury experience." Devise a question to ask the jurors under each of the following three sets of restrictions:

a The information may be recorded *only* on a nominal scale of measurement.

b The information may be recorded on an ordinal scale but not on any higher scale of measurement.

c The information may be recorded on an interval scale.

Your senior researcher subsequently informs you that she wishes to know the answers to the following five questions:

■ How many of the jurors have served on a jury before?

■ Who was the juror with the most prior experience?

■ What was the sum total of previous jury experience?

■ Was there anyone on the jury who had served more than three times?

■ What was the average amount of prior jury experience per juror?

d If you had collected data at the nominal level, which (if any) of the above questions would you be in a position to answer?

e If you had collected data at the interval level, which (if any) of the above questions would you be in a position to answer?

2.3 Because the Ministry of Transport (MOT) is concerned about the number of road accidents caused by motorists driving too close together, it has, on an experimental 2 km stretch of road, painted "chevrons" (lane markings) every few meters in each lane, . By the roadside it has erected a sign that reads: "KEEP YOUR DISTANCE: STAY AT LEAST 3 CHEVRONS FROM THE CAR IN FRONT!" The MOT has asked you to measure the extent to which this instruction is being followed. There are a number of possible measures at your disposal. For each measure suggested below, assess its reliability and validity. Which is the best measure?

a To stand on a bridge over the experimental stretch of road and count how many of the cars that pass below are not keeping the required distance.

b To compare police figures for how many accidents were recorded on that stretch of road for the period before it was painted with those for the period after painting.

c To study the film from a police camera situated 5 km farther down the same stretch of road (after the end of the experimental stretch) and count how many cars are not keeping to a safe distance.

2.4 The police are planning to introduce a pilot "community relations strategy" in a particular neighborhood and wish you to evaluate whether it has an effect on the willingness of citizens to report crimes to the police. There are a number of possible measures at your disposal. For each measure suggested below, assess its reliability and validity. Which is the best measure?

a Telephone every household and ask them to measure, on a scale of 1 to 10, how willing they are to report particular types of crime to the police. Repeat the experiment six months after the scheme has been in operation.

b A list of offenses reported by members of the neighborhood in the six months before the introduction of the scheme is compared with a similar list for the six months after the introduction of the scheme. (It is standard procedure for the police to record the details of the complainant every time a crime is reported to them.)

2.5 You are comparing the psychological condition of three inmates serving out long terms in different high-security prisons, and you are interested in the amount of contact each one has with the outside world.

You wish to determine how many letters each one has sent over the past 12 months. No official records of this exist. There are a number of possible measures at your disposal. For each measure suggested below, assess its reliability and validity. Which is the best measure?

a Ask each prisoner how many letters he or she sent over the past year.

b Check the rules in each of the prisons to see how many letters high-security prisoners are allowed to send each year.

c Check the records of the prison postal offices to see how many times the prisoners bought a stamp over the past year.

Computer Exercises

The questions in this section, as well as the computer exercise sections in subsequent chapters, are written for use with the data diskette included with the text. These questions provide examples of data analysis with a large sample, and allow the student to develop a fuller understanding of the statistical concepts discussed in the text. The data are provided as an SPSS data file (1994UCR.sav) and as an ASCII file (1994UCR.txt). Questions are written referring to SPSS commands but may be answered using any statistical analysis package.

The data are drawn from the Uniform Crime Reports (UCR) provided by the Federal Bureau of Investigation. These data are transferred voluntarily to the FBI by local law enforcement agencies on a monthly basis, and are designed to give a general description of crime in the United States. The UCR reports only crimes known to the police. The data on the diskette includes a portion of the 18,482 cases in the 1994 "Offenses Known and Clearances by Arrest" file. The diskette includes a random sample of 500 cases, with total data for the year rather than monthly data, and a small subset of the variables that are included in the original file. The full file, as well as many other criminal justice data files, is available from the Interuniversity Consortium for Political and Social Research.

Before you start your work, it is a good idea to make a copy of the original data set just in case you accidentally erase something you will need later.

1. To view a list of the variables that are included in the data on the diskette, open the data set and choose File Info from the Utilities menu. Remember that each case is a criminal justice agency. Referring to the output produced from the File Info command, identify the variable that would classify the type of agency as "U.S. Park Police and State Police" or "Other Agency." This is a nominal scale with two categories. Using the Numeric State Code variable, create a new nominal variable that identifies the agency location as within your home state or from another state. Remember to use the Transform menu and the

Recode into Different Variable command so you can use the state information later.

2. Variables measured on an ordinal scale reflect a range of values from high to low. Recode the Group Code variable as an ordinal scale with three levels. The first level is a city, the second level is a county, and the third level is the state police. This new variable will reflect the type of agency that is reporting. Again, use the Recode into Different Variables command found in the Transform menu.

3. Look through the file information produced in question 1 (you may want to print a copy for easy reference) and familiarize yourself with the variables that are provided. Identify all of the variables that are measured on an interval or ratio scale.

4. Using the file information, identify all of the measures of crime that are available in the UCR data. Which measure do you think is the most valid measure of the number of crimes against persons (e.g., assault attempted)? Which is the most valid measure of the number of crimes against persons that resulted in an arrest? Could you use the information provided in the UCR to create a new measure that is better than those that are provided?

5. Which crimes do you think are likely to be most reliably reported in the UCR? Which reports are likely to be most valid? Explain why in each case.

chapter three

Describing the Typical Case:
Measures of Central Tendency

THE NATURAL FIRST STEP in research is to provide a basic portrait of the characteristics of a sample or population. What is the typical case? If the researcher could choose one case to represent all others, which would be the best? When a sample is very small, it is possible merely to show the array of cases and let the reader decide. However, as the number of cases grows, it becomes difficult to make a decision about typicality from the distribution as a whole. This is the function of measures of central tendency in statistics. They provide us with a simple snapshot of our data that can be used to gain a picture of the average case.

In this chapter, three basic measures of central tendency that are commonly used are discussed and compared. The first, the mode, is used primarily with nominal-level data. It is the simplest measure of central tendency, drawing information only about the frequency of events in each category. The median, the second measure, takes into account not only frequency but the order or ranking of study subjects. Finally, the mean adds the additional factor of the exact scores associated with each subject you study. As with the discussion of levels of measurement, we emphasize in this chapter the benefits gained from statistics that use more information. But, we also illustrate the importance of looking carefully at the distribution of cases in your study before deciding which measure of central tendency is most appropriate.

The Mode: Central Tendency in Nominal Scales

Faced with a nominal-scale measure, how would you define a typical case? Take the example of table 3.1. Here you have a nominal scale of legal representation in a sample of offenders convicted of white-collar crimes in U.S. federal courts. Offenders were placed into one of five

Table 3.1   White-Collar Crime Legal Representation

CATEGORY	FREQUENCY (N)
No Attorney	20
Legal Aid	26
Court Appointed	92
Public Defender	153
Private Attorney	380
Total (Σ)	**671**

categories indicating the type of attorney that represented them: no lawyer present; legal-aid attorney, court-appointed attorney, public defender, and privately retained legal counsel. The number of individuals, or in statistical language the "N" of cases, that fall in each category is reported.

Clearly, you have very limited information upon which to make a choice about typicality from this example. Here, as in other nominal-scale measures, you simply know how many cases fall into one category or another. You would probably choose the category "private attorney" as the most representative type for this sample because it contains by far the most cases (380). And indeed, this is precisely how statisticians define typicality for nominal-level scores. We call the category with the largest N, or number of cases, the **mode.** In this sample of white-collar offenders, the modal category for type of representation is "private attorney."

By defining one category as the modal category, we are able to provide a summary view of the type of case that is typical of our sample or population. Such statements are common in criminal justice research. We often are interested in the racial category that appears most in our data, or the type of offense that is most common. The modal category can also provide a basis for making comparisons among samples. For example, let us say that a sample of offenders convicted of nonviolent property crimes that would not ordinarily be defined as white collar was compared to this larger white-collar crime sample. In this case, as is apparent from table 3.2, the modal category is not "private attorney" but rather "court appointed attorney." Although this comparison of the two samples is not a complex one, it illustrates the different backgrounds of the two groups. White-collar offenders are much more likely than common criminals to have the resources to pay for private legal representation.

Table 3.2   Common Crime Legal Representation

CATEGORY	FREQUENCY (N)
No Attorney	40
Legal Aid	7
Court Appointed	91
Public Defender	22
Private Attorney	70
Total (Σ)	**230**

In general, we do not use the mode to describe central tendency in ordinal or interval scales. The reason, in good part, is that the mode does not take advantage of the additional information that such scales provide. The average case should not be chosen simply on the basis of the frequency of events in a particular category, because higher-level scales also provide information on the order or nature of the differences between categories.

Nonetheless, there are cases when researchers choose to use the mode to describe ordinal or interval-level measures. This occurs generally when there is a very large grouping of cases in one particular category. Table 3.3, for example, provides an ordinal-level measure of the financial harm caused in a sample of convicted offenders. Because almost two-thirds of the individuals studied fall in the category "$101–$2,500," you might want to describe typicality in this case by saying that this category is the modal category. Similarly, if you were examining prior arrests and two-thirds of the offenders in your sample had no prior arrests, you might want to report no arrests as the modal category. Even though this measure is an interval measure, the mode provides a fairly good summary of the typical case in your sample.

Table 3.3   Financial Harm in a Sample of Convicted Offenders

CATEGORY	FREQUENCY (N)
Less than $100	15
$101–$2,500	92
$2,501–$10,000	20
More than $10,000	19
Total (Σ)	**146**

The Median: Taking into Account Position

In constructing the **median** we utilize information not only on the number of cases found in a particular category, but also the position of the categories. The median may be defined simply as the middle score in a distribution. For ordinal scales it is the category in which the middle score lies. For example, in table 3.4 we present results from a survey of students regarding the seriousness of public drunkenness. The students were presented with an ordinal-scale measure that allowed them to rate the seriousness of a series of crimes. The ratings ranged from "not serious at all" to "most serious." The median for this distribution is "somewhat serious," because the middle score (or the 141st score in this distribution) falls in the "somewhat serious" category.

The advantage of the median over the mode for use in describing ordinal scales is well illustrated from this example. If we used the mode to describe typicality in student assessments of the seriousness of public drunkenness, we would conclude that the typical student does not see drunkenness as serious at all. But even though the "not serious at all" category includes the largest number of cases, almost three-quarters of the students rate this behavior more seriously. The median takes this fact into consideration by placing the typical case in the middle of a distribution. It is concerned not only with the number of cases in the categories, but also their position.

The median is sometimes used for defining typicality in interval scales. For example, in table 3.5, the average number of minutes of public disorder (per 70-minute period) observed in a sample of 31 city blocks with high levels of crime, or "hot spots of crime," is presented. The hot spots are arranged in ascending order on the basis of

Table 3.4   Student Views on Public Drunkenness

CATEGORY	FREQUENCY (N)
Not Serious at All	73
A Bit Serious	47
Somewhat Serious	47
Serious	27
Very Serious	26
Extremely Serious	39
Most Serious	22
Total (Σ)	**281**

the number of minutes of disorder observed. In this case the median score is the middle, or 16th, score, 2.12. Accordingly, by using the median we would describe the average hot spot as having a little more than two minutes of disorder in each 70-minute period.

One problem with using the median for defining central tendency in interval scales is that it is ambiguously defined when there is an even number of cases. Let us, for example, delete the hot spot with a score of 6.57 from table 3.5. In this case there is no single middle

Table 3.5   Hot Spots: Minutes of Public Disorder (A)

HOT SPOT SCORE	FREQUENCY (*N*)	CUMULATIVE *N*
0.35	1	01
0.42	1	02
0.46	1	03
0.47	1	04
0.52	1	05
0.67	1	06
1.00	1	07
1.06	1	08
1.15	1	09
1.19	2	11
1.48	1	12
1.60	1	13
1.63	1	14
2.02	1	15
2.12	1	16
2.21	1	17
2.34	1	18
2.45	1	19
2.66	1	20
3.04	1	21
3.19	1	22
3.23	1	23
3.46	1	24
3.51	1	25
3.72	1	26
4.09	1	27
4.47	1	28
4.64	1	29
4.65	1	30
6.57	1	31
Total (Σ)	**31**	**31**

value for the array of cases in the table. Should we choose the 15th case, representing 2.02 minutes of disorder, or the 16th case, with 2.12 minutes of disorder, as our measure of typicality? Both could be considered as middle values. By convention, we take a compromise position. When there is an even number of cases in a study, we take the score exactly between the two middle scores. In this example, the median would be defined as 2.07, a value exactly between 2.02 and 2.12.[1]

Working It Out

15th case = 2.02

16th case = 2.12

$$median = \frac{2.02 + 2.12}{2} = 2.07$$

The median is generally more appropriate than the mode for assessing central tendency for both ordinal and interval-level measures. However, the median does not take advantage of all of the information that is included in interval-level scales. Although it recognizes the position of the values of a measure, it does not take into account the exact differences among those values. In many cases this can provide for a misleading estimate of typicality for interval-level measures.

For example, let us say that the distribution of disorder in hot spots was that represented in table 3.6. In this case the median would be 1.83. But is 1.83 a good estimate of central tendency in this distribution? The 17th score is 3.34, not very close to 1.83 at all. The score of 1.83 provides an estimate of typicality that is much below half the scores in this distribution. The median is not sensitive to this gap in the values of the 16th and 17th cases in our measure. This is because it looks only at position and not at the size of the differences between the cases. The median does not take advantage of all of the information provided by interval-level measures.

Another way to describe the median in interval-level measures is to say that it is the 50th percentile score. A percentile score describes the

---

[1] In some introductory textbooks in statistics, there is a section on developing the mean and median from tables that had grouped interval level data into ordinal categories. At one time, criminologists were commonly faced with such grouped data, and thus it was quite useful to develop procedures for gaining estimates of the mean or the median from such tables. Today, however, it is usually possible to obtain the raw data from which such tables are constructed. Accordingly, estimates of the mean and median can be developed directly.

point or score below which a specific proportion of the cases is found. The 50th percentile score is the score below which 50 percent of the cases in a study lie. In table 3.6 you can see that if we define the median in this way, we also would choose 1.83 as the median minutes of disorder observed in the hot spots. In this case if we add the percent of cases for all of the scores up until the middle, or 16th, score, we come to a total (or cumulative percent) of 51.6. At the

Table 3.6   Hot Spots: Minutes of Public Disorder (B)

HOT SPOT SCORE	FREQUENCY (N)	CUMULATIVE N	CUMULATIVE %
0.35	1	01	3.2
0.42	1	02	6.5
0.46	1	03	9.7
0.47	1	04	12.9
0.52	1	05	16 1
0.67	1	06	19.4
1.00	l	07	22.6
1.06	1	08	25.8
1.15	1	09	29.0
1.19	2	11	35.5
1.48	1	12	38.7
1.60	1	13	41.9
1.63	1	14	45.2
1.73	1	15	48.4
1.83	1	16	51.6
3.34	1	17	54.9
3.44	1	18	58.1
3.45	1	19	61.3
3.66	1	20	64.5
4.04	1	21	67.7
4.19	1	22	71.0
4.23	1	23	74.2
4.46	1	24	77.4
4.51	1	25	80.6
4.72	1	26	83.9
5.09	1	27	87.1
5.47	1	28	90.3
5.64	1	29	93.5
5.65	1	30	96.8
5.57	1	31	100.0
Total (Σ)	**31**	**31**	**100.0**

15th score, or 1.73, the cumulative percent is only 48.4, less than 50 percent.

The Mean: Adding Value to Position

The **mean** takes into account not only the frequency of cases in a category and the position of the scores in a measure, but also the value of those scores. To calculate the mean, we add up the scores for all of the subjects in our study and then divide the total by the total number of subjects. In mathematical language, this can be written as a short equation:

Equation 3.1

$$\overline{X} = \frac{\displaystyle\sum_{i=1}^{N} X_i}{N}$$

Even though equations sometimes put students off, they are an important part of statistics. Indeed, equations are the language of statistics. They represent how a statistic is constructed and the way in which we can calculate it. Equations provide a short way of writing out what would often take a number of sentences to describe in English. One of our tasks in this text is to help you to translate such equations and to become more comfortable with them.

In the case of the mean, we introduce what are for most students of criminal justice some new symbols and concepts. First, when expressing the mean, statisticians provide us with a shorthand symbol, $\overline{X}$ or, in English, "X bar." The equation also includes the summation symbol, Σ. Under the symbol is an $i = 1$ and above it is an N. What this means is that you should start summing your cases at the first subject in your sample and end at the last one (represented by N because, as we have already discussed, N is the number of cases in your sample). But what should you sum? X_i represents the measure of interest—in the case of our example, minutes of disorder. So the equation above, says that you should sum up the scores for minutes of disorder from the first to the last case in your study. Then you should divide this number by the total number of cases.

Let us take the example of minutes of disorder in crime hot spots from table 3.5. According to equation 3.1, the first step is to sum up all of the scores:

Working It Out

$$\sum_{i=1}^{N} X_i =$$

0.35 + 0.42 + 0.46 + 0.47 + 0.52 + 0.67 + 1.00 +

1.06 + 1.15 + 1.19 + 1.19 + 1.48 + 1.60 + 1.63 +

2.02 + 2.12 + 2.21 + 2.34 + 2.45 + 2.66 + 3.04 +

3.19 + 3.23 + 3.46 + 3.51 + 3.72 + 4.09 + 4.47 +

4.64 + 4.65 + 6.57

= 71.56

We then take this number, 71.56, and divide it by N, or 31, the number of cases in our sample.

Working It Out

$$\overline{X} = \frac{\sum_{i=1}^{N} X_i}{N}$$

$$= \frac{71.56}{31}$$

$$= 2.308387097$$

The result, 2.308387097 (rounded to the ninth decimal point), illustrates an issue that often arises in reporting statistics. Do you really need to provide your audience with the level of precision that is given by your statistic? In our case, for example, at what level of precision should minutes of disorder be presented?

A basic rule of thumb is to use your common sense in answering such questions. Don't provide statistics developed out to a large number of decimal points just to impress others. In making this decision you should ask, what is the simplest presentation of my results that provides the reader or listener with enough information to understand and evaluate my work? Overall, criminal justice researchers seldom report the mean to more precision than two decimal points. This is also a good choice in our example. Rounding to the second decimal point provides a mean of 2.31. Providing a more precise representation of the mean here would not add important information for the reader.

In some cases it is useful to develop estimates with much greater precision. In particular, if the values for the cases you are examining are very small in the first place, you will want to present a more precise mean. For example, Lawrence Sherman and his colleagues looked at the mean daily rate of reported domestic violence in a study that compared the impacts of arrests versus warnings as a strategy of controlling spouse abusers.[2] Had they reported their findings only to the second decimal point, as recommended above, they would have ended up with a mean daily rate over the longest follow up period (361–540 days) of 0.00 for short arrest and 0.00 for warning. The difficulty here is that it is unlikely for individuals to report cases of domestic violence on a very frequent basis. Sherman et al. needed a much higher degree of precision to show the differences between the two groups they studied. Accordingly they reported their results to the fourth decimal point. For arrests the rate is 0.0019 and for warnings it is 0.0009.

Comparing Results Gained Using the Mean and Median

Returning to our example, the mean for minutes of disorder from table 3.5, 2.31, is very similar to the median, 2.12. In this case adding knowledge about value does not change our portrait of the typical hot spot very much. However, we get a very different sense of the average case if we use the data from table 3.6. Here, the median provided a less than satisfying representation of the average case. It was not sensitive to the fact that there was a large gap in the scores between the 16th and 17th cases. Accordingly, the median, 1.83, was very close in value to the first half of the cases in the sample, but very far from those hot spots with higher values. The mean should provide a better estimate of typicality here, because it recognizes the actual values of the categories and not just their position. Let us see what happens when we calculate the mean for table 3.6.

---

[2] L. Sherman, J. D. Schmidt, D. Rogan, P. Gartin, E. G. Cohn, D. J. Collins, and A. R. Bacich (1991), From Initial Deterrence to Long-Term Escalation: Short-Custody Arrest for Poverty Ghetto Domestic Violence, *Criminology* 29:821–850.

Following our equation, we first sum the individual cases:

$$\sum_{i=1}^{N} X_i =$$

0.35 + 0.42 + 0.46 + 0.47 + 0.52 + 0.67 + 1.00 +

1.06 + 1.15 + 1.19 + 1.19 + 1.48 + 1.60 +1.63 +

1.73 + 1.83 + 3.34 + 3.44 + 3.45 + 3.66 + 4.04 +

4.19 + 4.23 + 4.46 + 4.51+ 4.72 + 5.09 + 5.47 +

5.64 + 5.65 + 5.77

= 84.41

We then divide this number by the total number of cases:

$$\overline{X} = \frac{\sum_{i=1}^{N} X_i}{N}$$

$$= \frac{84.41}{31}$$

$$= 2.7229$$

In this case we gain an estimate of typicality of 2.72 (rounding to the second decimal point). As you can see, this score is much better centered in our distribution than is the median. The reason is simple. The median does not take into account the values of the categories. The mean does take value into account and thus is able to adjust for the gap in the distribution presented.

There are cases in which the sensitivity of the mean to the values of the categories in a measure can give misleading results. For example, let us say that you have one case in your study that is very different from the others. As noted in chapter 1, researchers call such a case an **outlier,** because it is very much outside the range of the other cases you study. Taking the example of minutes of disorder from table 3.5, let us say that the last case did not have 6.57 minutes, but rather 70 minutes of disorder (the maximum amount possible). If we calculate the mean now, the sum of the cases is very much larger than before:

Working It Out

$$\sum_{i=1}^{N} X_i =$$

$0.35 + 0.42 + 0.46 + 0.47 + 0.52 + 0.67 + 1.00 +$

$1.06 + 1.15 + 1.19 + 1.19 + 1.48 + 1.60 + 1.63 +$

$2.02 + 2.12 + 2.21 + 2.34 + 2.45 + 2.66 + 3.04 +$

$3.19 + 3.23 + 3.46 + 3.51 + 3.72 + 4.09 + 4.47 +$

$4.64 + 4.65 + 70.0$

$= 134.99$

Dividing this by the total number of cases:

Working It Out

$$\overline{X} = \frac{\sum_{i=1}^{N} X_i}{N}$$

$$= \frac{134.99}{31}$$

$$= 4.3545$$

provides us with a mean of 4.35 (rounded to the second decimal point). The mean we gained without the score of 70 was 2.31. Accordingly, merely by changing one score to an outlier, we have almost doubled our estimate of typicality. In this case the sensitivity of the mean to an extreme value in the distribution has led it to overestimate the average case. Another way of saying this is to note that the mean is sensitive to outliers. Because the mean is used to develop many other more complex statistics, this principle is relevant not only to the mean itself but to a number of other important statistical techniques used by researchers.

So what should you do if you have one, or just a few outliers in your study? One solution is simply to exclude the outliers from specific analyses and to let your reader or audience know that some cases have been excluded and to explain why. If the number of extreme cases is large enough, you may want to analyze those cases separately. Another solution is to transform the outliers. That is, you may want to replace them with a value closer to that of the rest of the distribution (e.g., the highest value that is not an outlier). In this way you can include the cases, but minimize the extent to which they impact upon your estimate of typicality. However, you should be cautious in developing such transformations of your scores, keeping in mind that you are changing the character of cases in your study.

Other Characteristics of the Mean

Two other traits of the mean are important because they play a role in how we develop other statistics. The first relates to what happens when we look at **deviations** (or differences) **from the mean.** This issue will become a consideration in the next chapter, when we discuss measures of dispersion. The second, often termed the **least squares property** of the mean, will become important to us later, when we discuss regression in chapter 15.

If we take each score in our distribution, subtract it from the mean, and sum these differences, we will always get a result of 0. Written in equation form, this principle is represented as follows:

Equation 3.2
$$\sum_{i=1}^{N} (X_i - \overline{X}) = 0$$

In English, this equation says that if we sum each of the deviations from the mean, from the first to the last case, we will always get a result of 0. This principle is illustrated in table 3.7 using the example of minutes of public disorder from table 3.5. Here we have taken the 31 scores and subtracted each of them from the mean. We then added these differences. Because the positive scores balance out the negative ones, the result is 0. This will always happen when you use the mean.

The second trait, the least squares property, is very important for understanding a commonly used technique for describing relationships among **variables** in criminal justice called regression. For the moment, it is enough to note this fact, and to remember that the issues that we address early on in statistics are often the bases for much more complex types of analysis. "Don't forget the basics" is a good rule. Many mistakes that researchers make in developing more complex statistics come from a failure to think about the basic issues that we are raising in the first few chapters of this text.

Table 3.7   Hot Spots: Minutes of Public Disorder (A), Deviations from the Mean

SCORE (X)	DEVIATION FROM THE MEAN $(X_i - \overline{X})$	DEVIATION FROM THE MEAN
0.35	0.35 – 2.31	–1.96
0.42	0.42 – 2.31	–1.89
0.46	0.46 – 2.31	–1.85
0.47	0.47 – 2.31	–1.84
0.52	0.52 – 2.31	–1.79
0.67	0.67 – 2.31	–1.64
1.00	1.00 – 2.31	–1.31
1.06	1.06 – 2.31	–1.25
1.15	1.15 – 2.31	–1.16
1.19	1.19 – 2.31	–1.12
1.19	1.19 – 2.31	–1.12
1.48	1.48 – 2.31	–0.83
1.60	1.60 – 2.31	–0.71
1.63	1.63 – 2.31	–0.68
2.02	2.02 – 2.31	–0.29
2.12	2.12 – 2.31	–0.19
2.21	2.21 – 2.31	–0.10
2.34	2.34 – 2.31	0.03
2.45	2.45 – 2.31	0.15
2.66	2.66 – 2.31	0.35
3.04	3.04 – 2.31	0.73
3.19	3.19 – 2.31	0.88
3.23	3.23 – 2.31	0.92
3.46	3.46 –2.31	1.15
3.51	3.51 – 2.31	1.20
3.72	3.72 – 2.31	1.41
4.09	4.09 – 2.31	1.78
4.47	4.47 – 2.31	2.16
4.64	4.64 – 2.31	2.33
4.65	4.65 – 2.31	2.34
6.57	6.57 – 2.31	4.26
Total (Σ)		**0***

*Due to rounding error, the actual column total is slightly less than zero.

The least squares property is written in equation form as follows:

Equation 3.3

$$\sum_{i=1}^{N} (X_i - \overline{X})^2 = MIN$$

What this says in English is that if we sum the squared deviations from the mean for all of our cases we will get a minimum possible score. That is, if we take each individual's score on a measure and subtract that score from the mean and then square the difference, and then sum all of those scores, we will get an amount that is smaller than we could get using any other number besides the mean. You might try this by calculating the result for minutes of disorder using the mean. Then try other scores and see if you can find some other number of minutes that will give you a smaller score. The least squares property says you won't.

Using the Mean for Noninterval Scales

The mean is ordinarily used for measuring central tendency only for interval scales. However, in practice, researchers sometimes use the mean to represent ordinal scales as well. Is this wrong? In a pure statistical sense it is. However, some ordinal scales have a large number of categories and thus begin to mimic some of the characteristics of interval-level measures

This is particularly the case if you believe that the movement from one category to another in an ordinal scale can be looked at as equivalent no matter which category you move from. Taking our example of student attitudes toward public drunkenness from table 3.4, a researcher might argue that the difference between "somewhat serious" and "a bit serious" is about equivalent to that of "very serious" to "extremely serious," and so forth. Thus, the difference between these categories is not just a difference of position, it is also a movement of equal units up the scale. Taking this approach, this measure takes into account both position and value, although the values here are not as straightforward as those gained in looking at true interval scales such as number of crimes or dollar amount stolen.

A researcher might argue here that the mean is appropriate for presenting these findings because this ordinal-scale measure of attitudes is like an interval-scale measure. Although it is easy to see the logic behind this decision, it is important to note that it takes a good deal of justification. In general, you should be very cautious in using the mean for ordinal-level scales, even when such criteria are met.

Statistics in Practice:
Comparing the Median and the Mean

When measuring central tendency for an interval scale, the general rule is that the mean provides the best measure. This follows a principle we stated in chapter 1. In statistics, as in other decision-making areas, more information is better than less information. When we use the mean, we not only take into account the frequency of events in each category and their position, but the values or scores of those categories. We can say that the mean is a more stable measure of central tendency than the median. Because more information is used, the mean is less likely to be affected by changes in the nature of the sample that a researcher examines. It is useful to note as well that the mean has some algebraic characteristics that make it more easily used in developing other types of statistics.

The mean is generally to be preferred, but when a measure is strongly **skewed,** the median provides a better estimate of central tendency than the mean. What is meant by "skew" is that the scores of a variable are very much weighted to one side. A good example of this in criminal justice is criminal history as measured by self-reports of prisoners. Horney and Marshall, for example, report results on the frequency of offending in a sample of prisoners.[3] As is apparent from figure 3.1, most of the offenders in their sample have a relatively low offending rate—between 1 and 20 offenses in the previous year. But there are a number of offenders who have rates of more than 100, and a fairly large group with more than 200. The mean that is gained from this distribution is 175.

Clearly, 175 offenses provides a misleading view of typicality for rates of offending of their sample. Because the mean is sensitive to value, it is being inflated by the very high frequency scores for a relatively small proportion of the sample. One solution we suggested earlier to the problem of outliers was to exclude such cases. But here, this would mean excluding almost 30 percent of the sample. These are not outliers in the traditional sense. Another option mentioned earlier is to analyze the "outliers" separately. But again, there is quite a spread of scores even if we were to look at those above 50 or 100 separately, and the analyses of the outliers might in itself provide a misleading view of central tendency. A common solution to this type

[3] J. Horney and I. H. Marshall (1992), An Experimental Comparison of Two Self-Report Methods for Measuring Lambda, *Journal of Research in Crime and Delinquency* 29:102–121.

Figure 3.1   *Individual Offender Frequency for a Sample of Offenders: Showing How the*
Mean Can Be a Misleading Measure of Central Tendency

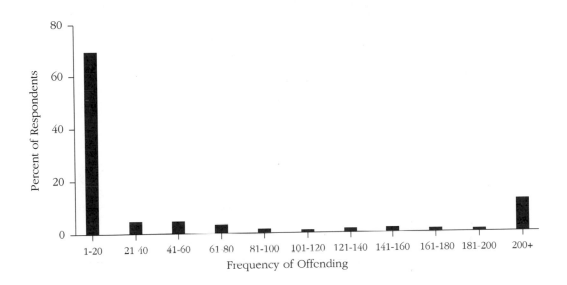

of skewed distribution is to use the median rather than the mean to
describe central tendency. The median for this distribution is 4, which
is certainly more representative of the average case than is the mean.
But even if you choose this solution, it is very important to note to
your audience that the distribution is skewed and to tell them a bit
about the nature of the distribution.

How should you decide when a distribution is skewed to a large
enough degree that it is preferable to use the median as opposed to
the mean? You should begin by comparing the mean and the median.
When there is a very large difference between them, it may be the result of skewness. In such cases, you should look at the distribution of
the scores to see what is causing the mean and median to differ
widely. But there is no solid boundary line from which to choose.

In extreme cases such as that of prior record in our example, or if
the mean and median provide relatively close estimates, your choice
will be clear. In the former case you would choose the median, and in
the latter the mean. However, when your results fall somewhere in
between you will have to use common sense and the experiences of
other researchers working with similar data as guidelines. What seems

to make sense? What have other researchers chosen to do? One way of being fair to your audience is to provide results for both the mean and the median, irrespective of which you choose as the best measure of typicality.

Chapter Summary

The **mode** is calculated by identifying the category that contains the greatest number of cases. It may be applied to any scale of measurement. Because the mode uses very little information, it is rarely used with scales of measurement higher than the nominal scale. It can occasionally serve as a useful summary tool for higher-level scales, however, when a large number of cases are concentrated in one particular category.

The **median** is calculated by locating the middle score in a distribution and identifying in which category it falls. It is also known as the 50th percentile score, or the score below which 50 percent of the cases lie. The information used includes both the number of cases in a particular category and the position of the categories. The median uses more information than does the mode and requires a scale of measurement that is at least ordinal in magnitude. It may be used with interval scales, but with caution. When there is an even number of cases and a single middle case value cannot be identified, we assign a value that is exactly between the two middle scores.

The **mean** is calculated by dividing the sum of the scores by the number of cases. The information used includes not only the number of cases in a category and the relative position of the categories, but also the actual value of each category. Such information normally requires at least an interval scale of measurement. Only in exceptional circumstances do researchers use the mean to describe an ordinal scale. The mean uses more information than the mode and the median. It is, however, sensitive to extreme cases—**outliers.** When faced with the distorting effect of outliers, the researcher may choose to keep them, to transform them to other values, or to delete them altogether. If a distribution of scores is substantially **skewed,** then it may be more appropriate to use the median than to use the mean. The sum of each score's **deviation from the mean** always adds up to 0. If the deviation of each score from the mean is squared, then the total of these squares will be less than if any number other than the mean were used. This is called the **least squares property.**

Key Terms

Deviation from the Mean The extent to which each individual score differs from the mean of all the scores.

Least Squares Property A characteristic of the mean whereby the sum of all the squared deviations from the mean is a minimum—it is lower than the sum of the squared deviations from any other fixed point.

Mean A measurement of central tendency calculated by dividing the sum of the scores by the number of cases.

Median A measurement of central tendency calculated by identifying the value or category of the score that occupies the middle position in the spread of scores.

Mode A measurement of central tendency calculated by identifying the score or category that occurs most frequently.

Outlier(s) A single or small number of exceptional cases that substantially deviate from the general pattern of scores.

Skewed A description of a spread of scores that is clearly weighted to one side.

Variable A trait, characteristic, or attribute of a person/object/event that can be measured at least at the nominal-scale level.

Symbols and Formulas

X Individual score.

$\overline{X}$ Mean.

N Number of cases.

Σ Sum.

To calculate the mean of a sample:

$$\overline{X} = \frac{\sum_{i=1}^{N} X_i}{N}$$

To show how the sum of the deviations from the mean equals 0:

$$\sum_{i=1}^{N} (X_i - \overline{X}) = 0$$

To express the least squares property:

$$\sum_{i=1}^{N} (X_i - \overline{X})^2 = MIN$$

Exercises

3.1   Calculate the mode, median, and mean for the following data:

a   Number of previous employments held by 25 convicts:

3, 3, 1, 1, 0, 1, 0, 2, 1, 0, 8, 4, 3,
1, 2, 1, 9, 0, 1, 7, 0, 7, 2, 0, 1

b   Weeks of training undergone by 20 prison guards:

10, 16, 12, 16, 16, 16, 10, 08, 10, 12
16, 18, 12, 16, 16, 08, 00, 12, 10, 16

c   Heights of 100 convicts:

1.72, 1.78, 1.73, 1.70, 1.81, 1.64, 1.76, 1.72, 1.75, 1.74,
1.88, 1.79, 2.01, 1.80, 1.77, 1.79, 1.69, 1.74, 1.75, 1.66,
1.77, 1.73, 1.72, 1.91, 1.80, 1.74, 1.72, 1.82, 1.86, 1.79,
1.80, 1.79, 1.63, 1.80, 1.99, 1.77, 1.72, 1.71, 1.73, 1.69,
1.77, 1.79, 1.81, 1.74, 1.81, 1.82, 1.77, 1.70, 1.73, 1.75,
1.74, 1.76, 1.83, 1.80, 1.77, 1.70, 1.80, 1.77, 1.66, 1.71,
1.72, 1.72, 1.73, 1.73, 1.74, 1.69, 1.88, 1.78, 1.80, 1.94,
1.76, 1.73, 1.78, 1.71, 1.75, 1.74, 1.70, 1.72, 1.77, 1.77,
1.68, 1.80, 1.77, 1.76, 1.84, 1.76, 1.93, 1.80, 1.73, 1.89,
1.70, 1.80, 1.75, 1.77, 1.72, 1.73, 1.88, 1.74, 1.77, 1.75.

3.2   A researcher checked the response times of police to 10 emergency
telephone calls. The data listed below record the number of minutes
that elapsed from when the telephone call ended to when the police
arrived:

24, 26, 14, 27, 198, 22, 27, 17, 19, 29

a Calculate the mode, the median, and the mean.

b Which of these measures is the most suitable for this particular case? Explain your choice.

3.3   Airport officials wished to check the alertness of their security officers in the two busiest weeks of the summer. During this period, they sent 50 undercover staff onto flights carrying suspicious items of hand luggage. Five of them were stopped at the entrance to the airport. Six made it into the airport, but were stopped at check-in. Thirteen more got into the airport and through check-in, only to be stopped at the hand luggage inspection point. Two passed the airport entrance, check-in and hand-luggage inspection, but were stopped when presenting their boarding cards at the gate. Four people made it past every one of these stages only to be stopped when boarding the plane. Twenty of the undercover staff were not detected at all.

a Categorize the data and calculate the median category.

b Is the median a good measure of central tendency in this case? Explain your answer; if you think not, suggest an alternative.

3.4   Of five prisoners in the high security wing in a prison—Albert, Bert, Charlie, Dave, and Eddie—only Eddie's biographical details have been lost. The information available is as follows.

	AGE	PREVIOUS CONVICTIONS
Albert	23	1
Bert	28	4
Charlie	18	1
Dave	41	1
Eddie	??	??

a Can we compute any of the following: (i) the mode, (ii) the median, or (iii) the mean for previous convictions of the five prisoners? If any or all of these three measures may be calculated, what are their values?

b If we know that the median age for the five prisoners is 28, does this tell us anything about Eddie's age? If so, what?

c The mean age for the five prisoners is 28.2. How old is Eddie?

3.5   A researcher sits on a bench on the main shopping street of a city center on 10 successive Saturdays from 11:00 A.M. to 2:00 P.M.—the three busiest shopping hours of the day—and records the number of times a police officer passes by. The results for the 10 weeks are as follows:

Week No.:	1	2	3	4	5	6	7	8	9	10
Observations:	4	3	6	4	4	5	4	35	3	5

On week 8, local unionists held a demonstration in the city center, and the high number of observations for that week can be explained by the extra officers called in to police the rally.

a Calculate the mode, median, and mean of these data.

b Discuss the issues involved in choosing the most appropriate means of describing the data. What would you recommend?

Imagine that the unionists had decided to hold a regular demonstration in the city center on alternating weeks. The results recorded for the same study were as follows:

Week No.:	1	2	3	4	5	6	7	8	9	10
Observations:	4	30	6	31	6	52	4	35	4	34

c Would your recommendation to the researcher as to how to represent the results now be any different? If so, explain why.

3.6 Using the first set of data from question 3.5, show how:

a The sum of the deviations from the mean equals 0.

b The sum of the squared deviations from the mean is less than the sum of the squared deviations from the median.

Computer Exercises

1. The variable you created that identifies each agency as from your home state or from another state is measured on a nominal scale. The Agency Count variable, which separates "U.S. Park Police and State Police" from "Other Agencies" is also a nominal variable. For each variable, use the Graph menu to create a bar graph and identify the modal value.

2. Next, let's examine a variable that is measured on an ordinal scale. Using the variable you created in chapter 2 that identifies each agency as a city-, county-, or state-level agency, obtain the 50th percentile score. The easiest way to obtain a percentile score is using the Statistics subcommand in the Frequencies command. Since you do not need the frequency table (frequency distributions are discussed in chapter 5), click on the Display Frequency Tables box so there is no check in it. The Frequencies command is found in the Statistics (Summarize) menu.

3.   Many measures used in criminal justice research are counts of the number of events that occur (such as the counts of the number of crimes included in the UCR data). Looking over the crime measures in your data, choose two types of crime (e.g., Total Robberies and Auto Theft). Using the Frequencies command, compute the median number of those crimes that were reported to the police, and the median number that were cleared by an arrest. Are these differences large or small?

4.   Using the two measures that you chose for question 3, compute the mean number of crimes reported, and the mean number that were cleared by arrest. Are the mean and the median the same? If not, what does this tell you about the measures you have chosen?

measures of dispersion

What Do They Tell Us about Our Data?

measuring dispersion in nominal and ordinal scales: proportions, percentages and the variation ratio

How Are They Calculated?

What Are Their Characteristics?

Are There Any Alternative Measures?

measuring dispersion in interval scales: range, variance and standard deviation

How Are They Calculated?

What Are Their Characteristics?

Are There Any Alternative Measures?

$\mathbf{M}$EASURES OF CENTRAL TENDENCY provide a snapshot for describing the typical case; however, the same statistic could be obtained from samples or populations that are in fact quite dissimilar. For example, a class of police recruits with a mean or median age of 23 is not likely to include people younger than 18 or older than 30, because most police departments have age requirements for incoming officers. A sample of offenders with a mean or median age of 23, however, will include offenders much younger than 18 and much older than 30. In both these samples the average person studied is 23 years old. But the sample of offenders will include more younger and older people than that of police recruits. The ages of the offenders are dispersed more widely around the average age.

Measures of dispersion allow us to fill this gap in our description of the samples or populations we study. They ask the question: How typical is the typical case? They tell us to what extent the subjects we study are similar to the case we have chosen to represent them. Are most cases clustered closely around the average case? Or, as with the sample of offenders above, is there a good deal of dispersion of cases both above and below the average?

Measures of Dispersion for Nominal- and Ordinal-Level Data

In nominal scales we define the typical case as the category with the largest number of subjects. Accordingly, in chapter 3 we chose "private attorney" as the modal category for legal representation in a sample of white-collar offenders. But how would we describe to what extent the use of a private attorney is typical of the sample as a whole? Put another way, to what degree are the cases concentrated in the modal category?

The Proportion

The most straightforward way to answer this question is to describe the **proportion** of cases that fall in the modal category. In statistical language, a proportion is represented by the following equation:

Equation 4.1

$$Proportion = \frac{N_{cat}}{N_{tot}}$$

That is, we take the number of cases in the category and divide it by the total number of cases in the sample. Taking the example of legal representation, we would divide the N of cases in the modal category (private attorney) by the total N of cases in the sample (see table 4.1):

Working It Out

$$Proportion = \frac{N_{cat}}{N_{tot}}$$

$$= \frac{380}{671}$$

$$= 0.5663$$

In this example (following our earlier suggestions regarding rounding to the second decimal place), about 0.57 of the white-collar offenders in the sample were found in the modal category.

The Percentage

Sometimes, researchers like to transform a proportion to a **percentage** because most people find percentages easy to understand. For a percentage, we merely take a proportion and multiply it by 100:

Equation 4.2

$$Percentage = \left(\frac{N_{cat}}{N_{tot}} \right) 100$$

Table 4.1   White-Collar Crime Legal Representation

CATEGORY	FREQUENCY (*N*)
No Attorney	20
Legal Aid	26
Court Appointed	92
Public Defender	153
Private Attorney	380
Total (Σ)	**671**

For our example:

Working It Out

$$Percentage = \left(\frac{N_{cat}}{N_{tot}}\right) 100$$

$$= \left(\frac{380}{671}\right) 100$$

$$= 56.6319$$

That is, about 57 percent of the cases in the sample fall in the modal category.

The Variation Ratio

Another way to describe the degree to which the modal category represents the cases in a sample is to use a statistic called the **variation ratio** (VR). The variation ratio is based on the same logic as a proportion, but it examines the extent to which the cases are spread outside the modal category, rather than concentrated within it. It subtracts the proportion of cases in the modal category from one.

Equation 4.3

$$VR = 1 - \left(\frac{N_{cat}}{N_{tot}}\right)$$

For our example:

Working It Out

$$VR = 1 - \left(\frac{N_{cat}}{N_{tot}}\right)$$

$$= 1 - \left(\frac{380}{671}\right)$$

$$= 0.4337$$

The variation ratio for legal representation in this sample of white-collar offenders is about 0.43. But what does this say about the extent to which cases in the sample are clustered around the typical case? Is a variation ratio of 0.43 large or small? What type of rule can we use for deciding more generally whether the distribution we are examining is strongly clustered?

One way to do this is to define at the outset the upper and lower limits for the variation ratio or proportion for a particular measure. Obviously the largest proportion, regardless of your study, is 1.0, which would mean that all of the cases are in the modal category. In regard to the variation ratio, all of the cases in the modal category would lead to a statistic of 0, indicating no dispersion.

The smallest proportion (or largest VR) depends, however, on the number of categories in your measure. The mode is defined as the category in your measure with the most cases, so it must have at least one more case than any other category. If you have only two categories, than the modal category must include one more case than half of the cases in your study. So in the instance of two categories, the least concentration that can be gained is just over 0.50 of the cases. The least amount of dispersion, as measured by the variation ratio would be one minus this proportion, or just under 0.50. If you have four categories, the modal category must have more than one-quarter of the cases. Accordingly, the smallest variation ratio would be a bit smaller than 0.75.

What of our example of legal representation? We have five categories and 671 cases. The smallest modal category that could be gained with these numbers is 135. In this instance, each of the other four categories would have 134 cases. This is the maximum amount of dispersion of the cases that you can gain in this sample. This amounts to about 20.12 percent of the total number of cases in the sample, or a variation ratio of 0.7988. As noted earlier, the greatest degree of concentration in the modal category would yield a proportion of 1 and a variation ratio of 0. The estimates we gained for legal representation (proportion = 0.57; *VR* = 0.43) lie somewhere between these two extremes.

Is this dispersion large or small? The answer here, as in many of the statistics that we will examine, is that it depends on the context in which you are working. Large or small is a value, not a statistical concept. Statistically, you know that your estimate falls somewhere between the largest degree of concentration and the largest degree of dispersion that can be gained. But whether this is important or meaningful depends on the problem you are examining and the results that others have gained in prior research.

For example, if in a study of legal representation in white-collar crime in England it was found that 90 percent of the cases were concentrated in the private attorney category, then we might conclude that our results reflect a relatively high degree of dispersion of legal representation in the United States. If in England only 25 percent of the cases were found in the modal category, we might conclude that there was a relatively low degree of dispersion of legal representation in the United States.

The proportion and the variation ratio are primarily useful for describing dispersion in nominal-level measures. They can in some circumstances, however, be useful in describing ordinal-level variables as well. This is primarily true when there are just a few categories in our measure, or when there is a very high degree of concentration of cases in one category. The problem in using a simple proportion or variation ratio for ordinal-level measures is that the mode, upon which these statistics are based, is often a misleading measure for ordinal scales. As discussed in chapter 3, the mode does not take into account the position of scores in a measure, and thus it may provide a misleading view of the average case.

Index of Qualitative Variation

One measure of dispersion that is not based on the mode, and can be used for both nominal and ordinal scales, is the **index of qualitative variation** (IQV). The IQV compares the amount of variation in a sample to the total amount of variation that is possible given the number of cases and categories in a study. It is a standardized measure. This means that whatever the number of cases or categories, the IQV can vary only between 0 and 100. An IQV of 0 means that there is no variation in the measure, or all of the cases lie in one category. An IQV of 100 means that the cases are evenly dispersed across the categories.

Equation 4.4

$$IQV = \left(\frac{\sum\limits_{(i,j)} Nobs_i \, Nobs_j}{\sum\limits_{(i,j)} Nexp_i \, Nexp_j} \right) \times 100$$

Equation 4.4 provides a guide for how to compute the IQV. We are already familiar with the summation symbols within the parentheses. Here we are summing not across cases, but across products of distinct categories. *Nobs* represents the number of cases we observe within a category in our study. *Nexp* represents the number of cases we would expect in a category if the measure were distributed equally across the categories. That is, it is the N we would expect if there was the maximum amount of dispersion of our cases. We use the subscripts i and j here as a shorthand way to say that we should multiply all of the potential pairs of categories.

Taking a concrete example will make it much easier to develop this statistic in practice. Let us say that we wanted to describe dispersion in an ordinal-scale measure of fear of crime in a college class of 20 students. The students were asked whether they were personally concerned about crime on campus. The potential responses were: "very concerned," "quite concerned," "a little concerned," and "not concerned at all." The responses of the students are reported under the *N observed* column in table 4.2. As you can see, the cases are fairly spread out, although there are more students who are in the "very concerned" and "quite concerned" categories than in the "a little concerned" or "not concerned at all" responses. The expected number of cases in each category under the assumption of maximum dispersion is 5. That is, if the cases were equally spread across the categories, we would expect the same number in each. Following equation 4.4, we first multiply and then sum the number of cases in each observed category by every other observed category. We then divide this by the sum of each expected category multiplied by every other expected category. This amount is then multiplied by 100:

Working It Out

$$IQV = \left(\frac{\sum\limits_{(i,j)} Nobs_i\, Nobs_j}{\sum\limits_{(i,j)} Nexp_i\, Nexp_j} \right) \times 100$$

$$= \left(\frac{(3 \times 4) + (3 \times 6) + (3 \times 7) + (4 \times 6) + (4 \times 7) + (6 \times 7)}{(5 \times 5) + (5 \times 5) + (5 \times 5) + (5 \times 5) + (5 \times 5) + (5 \times 5)} \right) \times 100$$

$$= \left(\frac{145}{150} \right) \times 100$$

$$= 96.6667$$

Table 4.2   Fear of Crime among Students

CATEGORY	N OBSERVED	N EXPECTED
Not Concerned at All	3	5
A Little Concerned	4	5
Quite Concerned	6	5
Very Concerned	7	5
Total (Σ)	**20**	**20**

The observed variation for the *IQV* is 145. The expected variation is 150, representing the maximum amount of dispersion possible in the measure. The *IQV* for this measure is 96.67, meaning that the cases studied are very dispersed among the categories of the measure.

Measuring Dispersion in Interval Scales: The Range, Variance, and Standard Deviation

A common method for describing the spread of scores in interval or higher scales is to examine the **range** between the highest and lowest scores. Take, for example, the distribution of cases in table 4.3. Let us say that this was a distribution of crime calls at specific places in a one-year period. In describing typicality in this distribution, we would report the mean number of calls for the 12 places, which is 21.50. In describing how dispersed the scores are, we would report that the scores range between 2 and 52, or that the range of scores is 50.

The range is very simple and easy to present. Its attraction lies precisely in the fact that everyone understands what a range represents. However, the range is a very unstable statistic because it uses very little of the information available in interval-level scales. It bases its estimate of dispersion simply on two observations, the highest and lowest scores. This means that a change in just one case in your distribution can completely alter your description of dispersion. For example, if we change the case with the most calls in table 4.3 from 52 to 502, the range would change from 50 to 500.

Table 4.3   Crime Calls at Specific Places in a Year

HOT SPOT NUMBER	NUMBER OF CALLS
1	2
2	9
3	11
4	13
5	20
6	20
7	20
8	24
9	27
10	29
11	31
12	52

One method for reducing the instability of the range is to examine cases that are not at the extremes of your distribution. In this case, you are likely to avoid the problem of the range being magnified by a few very large or small numbers. For example, you might choose to look at the range between the 5th and 95th percentile scores, rather than that between the lowest and highest scores. It is also common to look at the range between the 25th and 75th percentile scores, or the 20th and 80th percentile scores. But however you change the points at which the range is calculated, it still relies on just two scores in determining the spread of cases in your distribution. The range provides little insight into whether the scores below or above those cases are clustered together tightly or dispersed widely. Its portrait of dispersion in interval scales is thus very limited.

How can we gain a fuller view of dispersion in interval scales? Remember that we became interested in the problem of dispersion because we wanted to provide an estimate of how well the average case represented the distribution of cases as a whole. Are scores tightly clustered around the average case or dispersed widely from it? Given that we have already described the mean as the most appropriate measure of central tendency in such scales, this is the natural place to begin our assessment. Why not simply examine how much the average scores differ from the mean?

In fact, this is the logic that statisticians have used to develop the main measures of dispersion in interval scales. However, they are faced with a basic problem in taking this approach. As we discussed in chapter 3, if we add up all of the deviations from the mean we will always gain a value of 0. You can see this illustrated again using our example of crime calls at hot spots (see table 4.4). Taking the sum of the differences of each score minus the mean, written in equation form as:

$$\sum_{i=1}^{N} (X_i - \overline{X})$$

we gain, as expected, the result of 0.

As discussed in chapter 3, when we add up the deviations above and below the mean, the positive and negative scores cancel each other out. In order to use deviations from the mean as a basis for a measure of dispersion, we must develop a method for taking the sign or direction out of our statistic. One solution to our problem is to square each deviation from the mean. Squaring will always yield a positive result because multiplying a positive number or a negative

Table 4.4   Crime Calls at Hot Spots in a Year: Deviations from the Mean

HOT SPOT NUMBER	SCORE (X)	DEVIATIONS FROM THE MEAN $(X_i - \overline{X})$
1	2	$2 - 21.5 = -19.5$
2	9	$9 - 21.5 = -12.5$
3	11	$11 - 21.5 = -10.5$
4	13	$13 - 21.5 = -08.5$
5	20	$20 - 21.5 = -01.5$
6	20	$20 - 21.5 = -01.5$
7	20	$20 - 21.5 = -01.5$
8	24	$24 - 21.5 = 02.5$
9	27	$27 - 21.5 = 05.5$
10	29	$29 - 21.5 = 07.5$
11	31	$31 - 21.5 = 09.5$
12	52	$52 - 21.5 = 30.5$
		Total (Σ) = 00.0

number by itself will result in a positive outcome. This is the method that statisticians have used in developing the most commonly used measures of dispersion in interval scales.

The Variance

The **variance** takes the average deviation from the mean using this approach. It is the sum of the squared deviations from the mean divided by the number of cases. Written in equation form, it is:

Equation 4.5

$$Variance = \frac{\sum_{i=1}^{N} (X_i - \overline{X})^2}{N}$$

In practice, this means you must take the following steps in computing the variance (as we do for our example in table 4.5):

1. First you take each case and subtract its score from the mean (deviation from the mean). For our example of crime calls at hot spots, this means that you would first take the case with 2 calls and subtract it from the mean of 21.5, giving a score of −19.5.

2. You then take that score and square it. For the first case our result would be 380.25.

3. You then repeat these steps for each of your cases, and sum them. In our example this yields a result of 1839.

4. Finally you divide this result by the number of cases in your study. This leads to a variance for our 12 cases of 153.25.

Table 4.5　Crime Calls at Hot Spots in a Year: Calculating Variance

HOT SPOT NUMBER	SCORE	$(X_i - \overline{X})$	$(X_i - \overline{X})^2$
1	2	−19.5	380.25
2	9	−12.5	156.25
3	11	−10.5	110.25
4	13	−8.5	72.25
5	20	−1.5	2.25
6	20	−1.5	2.25
7	20	−1.5	2.25
8	24	2.5	6.25
9	27	5.5	30.25
10	29	7.5	56.25
11	31	9.5	90.25
12	52	30.5	930.25
		Total (Σ) 0.0	Total (Σ) 1839.00

Working It Out

$$Variance = \frac{\sum_{i=1}^{N} (X_i - \overline{X})^2}{N}$$

$$= \frac{1839}{12}$$

$$= 153.25$$

We now have a statistic for computing dispersion that is based on deviations from the mean. However, how can we interpret whether 153.25 is large or small? If you are having trouble making sense of this, you are not alone. While squaring solves one problem (that the raw deviations from the mean equal 0), it creates another. By squaring, we generally obtain numbers that are much larger than the actual units in the distributions that we examine.[1]

---

[1] In the special case of a fraction, the result will be smaller numbers.

The Standard Deviation

In part because of this, another measure of dispersion, based on the variance, has been developed. This measure, the **standard deviation,** is calculated by taking the square root of the variance. Accordingly, it reduces our estimate of dispersion using a method similar to that we employed to solve the problem of positive and negative differences from the mean adding to 0. The standard deviation (*s*), provides an estimate of dispersion in units similar to our original scores. It is described in equation form as:

Equation 4. 6

$$s = \sqrt{\frac{\sum_{i=1}^{N} (X_i - \overline{X})^2}{N}}$$

In calculating the standard deviation, we add one step to our calculation of variance: we take the square root of our result. In the example of crime calls at 12 hot spots (where the variance equaled 153.25), we obtain a standard deviation of $\sqrt{153.25} = 12.38$. If you were to define on average how much the scores differed from the mean just by looking at these 12 cases, you would probably come to a conclusion close to that provided by the standard deviation.

The standard deviation has some basic characteristics which apply generally to its use:

1. When the standard deviation of a measure is 0, it means it has no variability. For this to happen, all of the scores in a measure have to be the same. For example, if you examine a group of first-time offenders, there would be no variation in the number of offenses in their criminal records. By definition, because they are all first-time offenders, it would be zero for all. The standard deviation here (and the variance) would be zero.

2. The size of the standard deviation (and the variance) is dependent on both the amount of dispersion in your measure and the units of analysis that are used. When cases are spread widely from the mean, there is more dispersion and the standard deviation will be larger. When the cases are more tightly clustered around the mean, the standard deviation will be smaller.

   Similarly, when the units of analysis in your measure are larger, the standard deviation will reflect the larger units. That is, if you report the standard deviation of police salaries in a particular city in dollars, your standard deviation will be larger than if you report those salaries in units of thousands of dollars. For example, if

Table 4.6   Duncan SEI for Bribery and Antitrust Offenders

CATEGORY	N	$\bar{X}$	s
Bribery	83	59.27	19.45
Antitrust	112	61.05	11.13
Total (Σ)	195		

the standard deviation is 3,350 in dollars, the standard deviation will be 3.35 using the unit of thousands of dollars.

3. Extreme deviations from the mean have the greatest weight in constructing the standard deviation. What this means is that you should be concerned here, as with the mean, with the problem of outliers. In this case, the effect of outliers is compounded because they impact not only upon the mean itself, which is used in computing the standard deviation, but also upon the individual scores that are obtained by subtracting cases from the mean.

The standard deviation is a useful statistic for comparing the extent to which characteristics are clustered or dispersed around the mean in different samples. For example, in table 4.6 a sample of offenders convicted of antitrust violations is compared to a sample of offenders convicted for bribery. The characteristic examined is social status, as measured by the interval scale Duncan socioeconomic index (SEI).[2] The index is based on the average income, education, and prestige associated with different occupations. The mean Duncan scores for these two samples is very similar (61.05 for antitrust violators; 59.27 for bribery offenders), but the standard deviation for those convicted of bribery is about twice that of those convicted of antitrust violations.

Figure 4.1 illustrates why these two samples yield similar means but very different standard deviations. The scores for most antitrust offenders are clustered closely within the range of 55 to 75. For bribery offenders, in contrast, the scores are much more widely spread across the distribution, including many more cases between 75 and 90, and below 50. What this tells us is that antitrust includes a fairly homogeneous group of offenders, ranking on average relatively highly on the Duncan socioeconomic index. Bribery is a much more diverse category. Although the average cases are similar, the bribery category includes many more lower- and higher-status individuals than does the antitrust category.

---

[2] See Albert J. Reiss (1961), *Occupations and Social Status* (New York: Free Press).

Figure 4.1a   *SEI for Antitrust Offenders*

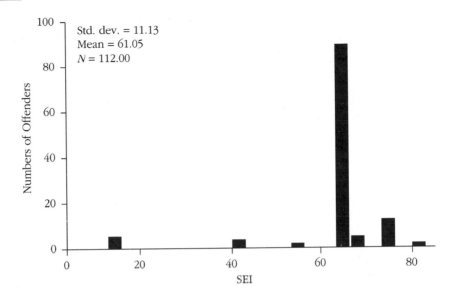

Figure 4.1b   *SEI for Bribery Offenders*

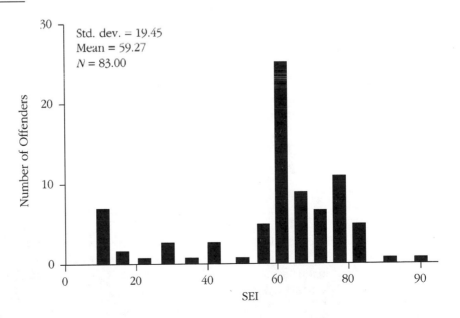

The Coefficient of Relative Variation

In this example, in which the means of the two groups are fairly similar, a direct comparison of their standard deviations provides a good view of the differences in dispersion between them. When the means of two groups are very different, however, this comparison may not be a fair one. If the mean Duncan score for one group was 10 and for the other it was 50, we might expect a larger standard deviation in the latter group simply because the mean is larger and provides for a greater potential for dispersion. Similarly, if two measures use different units of analysis, for example, dollars and number of offenses, a direct comparison of standard deviations does not make sense.

One solution to this problem is to use the **coefficient of relative variation** (CRV). The coefficient of relative variation looks at the size of the standard deviation in a measure relative to the size of its mean:

Equation 4.7

$$CRV = \frac{s}{\overline{X}}$$

In the example of the SEI for antitrust offenders, we divide the standard deviation (11.13) by the mean (61.05) to obtain a CRV of 0.18, meaning that the standard deviation is about one-fifth the size of the mean. Because the CRV expresses dispersion in a measure in a standardized form relative to the mean, we can compare the CRV across measures that have widely different means and standard deviations. A measure that has a CRV of one, for example, may be considered to include much greater relative variation than that found in our sample of antitrust offenders.

Working It Out

$$CRV = \frac{s}{\overline{X}}$$

$$= \frac{11.13}{61.05}$$

$$= 0.1823$$

A Note on the Mean Deviation

The standard deviation allows us to measure dispersion in interval scales taking into account the deviation from the mean of each case in our sample or population. But it is not the only measure that allows us to do this. The **mean deviation** takes a similar approach, but relies on the concept of absolute values, rather than squaring, to overcome the fact that the sum of the deviations from the mean equals 0. When you take the absolute value of a number, you ignore its sign. Accordingly, –8 and 8 both have an absolute value of 8, or in mathematical notation, $|-8| = |8| = 8$.

The equation for the mean deviation is similar to that for the variance. The only difference is that we take the absolute value of the difference between each score and the mean, rather than that value squared:

Equation 4.8

$$\text{Mean Deviation} = \frac{\sum_{i=1}^{N} |X_i - \overline{X}|}{N}$$

Using the example of crime calls in hot spots from table 4.3, we take the following steps to obtain the mean deviation. We first take the absolute value of the difference between each score and the mean (see table 4.7). We then sum up the 12 scores. Notice that we obtain a positive number now (111), and not zero, because we are taking the absolute values of the differences. Dividing this by the number of cases, N, we get a mean deviation of 9.25.

Table 4.7 Crime Calls at Hot Spots in a Year: Mean Deviation

HOT SPOT NUMBER	SCORE (X)	ABSOLUTE DEVIATION FROM THE MEAN $|X_i - \overline{X}|$
1	2	2 – 21.5 = 19.5
2	9	9 – 21.5 = 12.5
3	11	11 – 21.5 = 10.5
4	13	13 – 21.5 = 8.5
5	20	20 – 21.5 = 1.5
6	20	20 – 21.5 = 1.5
7	20	20 – 21.5 = 1.5
8	24	24 – 21.5 = 2.5
9	27	27 – 21.5 = 5.5
10	29	29 – 21.5 = 7.5
11	31	31 – 21.5 = 9.5
12	52	52 – 21.5 = 30.5
		Total (Σ) = 111.0

Working It Out

$$Mean\ Deviation = \frac{\displaystyle\sum_{i=1}^{N} |X_i - \overline{X}|}{N}$$

$$= \frac{111}{12}$$

$$= 9.25$$

The mean deviation and standard deviation provide similar estimates of dispersion, but the mean deviation here is a bit smaller than the standard deviation of 12.38 that we calculated earlier. Which is the better estimate of dispersion? In some sense the mean deviation is more straightforward. It simply looks at the average deviation from the mean. In obtaining the standard deviation we first must square the deviations, and later, to return our result to units similar to those of the original distribution, we must take the square root of the variance.

Given our rule that we should use the least complex presentation that is appropriate to answering our research question, you may wonder why it is that the standard deviation is almost always preferred over the mean deviation in criminal justice research. The answer, as we will see in the next few chapters, is that the standard deviation is relevant to a number of other statistics that we use in analyzing and describing our data.

Chapter Summary

Measures of dispersion describe to what extent cases are distributed around the measure of central tendency. They tell us just how typical the typical case is.

There are several measures of dispersion for nominal and ordinal scales. **Proportions** and **percentages** describe the extent to which cases are concentrated in the modal category. The **variation ratio** (VR) describes the extent to which cases are spread outside the modal category. A proportion of 1 (VR of 0) means that all the cases are in the modal category. This represents the least amount of dispersion. The value for the greatest dispersion can be determined by calculating the minimum possible value of the modal category and then translating that into a proportion or VR value. These measures can, in principle, be used with ordinal-level data, but the results may be misleading as they take into account only the value of the mode. As an alternative, The **index of qualitative variation** (IQV) is a standardized measure that does not use the mode. An IQV of 0 means that there is no variation; an IQV of 1 means that there is maximum variation across the categories.

A different set of measures is used to measure dispersion for interval and ratio scales. The **range** measures the difference between the highest and lowest scores. It has the advantage of simplicity, but it uses very little information (only two scores), and the scores used are taken from the two extremes. It is also very sensitive to outliers. A researcher may instead choose to measure the range between, say, the 95th and the 5th percentiles. Such measures, however, are still based on minimal information. The **variance** is the sum of the squared deviations of each score from the mean divided by the number of cases. The **standard deviation** (s) is the square root of the variance. If all the scores in a sample are the same, s will be 0. The more widely the scores are spread around the mean, the greater will be the value of s. Outliers have a considerable impact on the standard deviation. Comparing the standard deviations of means is problematic when the means compared are very different or when their units of measurement are different. An alternative measure, the **coefficient of relative variation** (CRV), enables comparisons among samples with different means. A further alternative, the **mean deviation,** differs from the variance by using absolute values rather than squared deviations from the mean. It is rarely used in statistical analysis, however.

Key Terms

Coefficient of Relative Variation A measure of dispersion calculated by dividing the standard deviation by the mean.

Index of Qualitative Variation A measure of dispersion calculated by dividing the sum of the possible pairs of observed scores by the sum of the possible pairs of scores expected (when cases are equally distributed across categories).

Mean Deviation A measure of dispersion calculated by adding the absolute deviations of each score from the mean and then dividing the sum by the number of cases.

Percentage The relation between two numbers for which the whole is accorded a value of 100, and the other is given a numerical value corresponding to its share of the whole. Calculating what percentage of the cases are found in the modal category serves as a simple measure of dispersion.

Proportion The relation between two numbers for which the whole is accorded a value of 1 and the other is given a numerical value corresponding to its share of the whole. Calculating what proportion of the cases are found in the modal category serves as a simple measure of dispersion.

Range A measure of dispersion calculated by subtracting the smallest score from the largest score.

Standard Deviation A measure of dispersion calculated by taking the square root of the variance.

Variance A measure of dispersion calculated by adding together the squared deviations of each score from the mean and then dividing the sum by the number of cases.

Variation Ratio A measure of dispersion calculated by subtracting the proportion of cases in the modal category from 1.

Symbols and Formulas

N_{cat} Number of cases in the modal category.

N_{tot} Total number of cases.

N_{obs} Number of cases observed in each category.

N_{exp} Number of cases expected in each category.

s Standard deviation.

To calculate the proportion of cases falling in the modal category:

$$Proportion = \frac{N_{cat}}{N_{tot}}$$

To calculate the percentage of cases falling in the modal category:

$$Percentage = \frac{N_{cat}}{N_{tot}} \times 100$$

To calculate the variation ratio:

$$VR = 1 - \left(\frac{N_{cat}}{N_{tot}}\right)$$

To calculate the index of qualitative variation:

$$IQV = \left(\dfrac{\displaystyle\sum_{(i,\,j)} Nobs_i\, Nobs_j}{\displaystyle\sum_{(i,\,j)} Nexp_i\, Nexp_j} \right) \times 100$$

To calculate the variance:

$$Variance = \dfrac{\displaystyle\sum_{i=1}^{N} (X_i - \overline{X})^2}{N}$$

To calculate the standard deviation:

$$s = \sqrt{\dfrac{\displaystyle\sum_{i=1}^{N} (X_i - \overline{X})^2}{N}}$$

To calculate the coefficient of relative variation:

$$CRV = \dfrac{s}{\overline{X}}$$

To calculate the mean deviation:

$$Mean\ Deviation = \dfrac{\displaystyle\sum_{i=1}^{N} |X_i - \overline{X}|}{N}$$

Exercises

4.1   Police records for 105 rape victims were analyzed to determine whether any prior relationship existed between the victim and the offender. The results were as follows:

Spouse	41
Family Member Other than Spouse	14
Acquaintance	22
No Prior Relationship	28

    a Calculate the modal proportion and the variation ratio.

    b What are the minimum and the maximum possible values for the variation ratio?

4.2   The persons convicted of minor traffic offenses who appear in the magistrate's court of a given locality on a given day are sentenced as follows: conditional discharge (14), fine (35), and license disqualification (11).

    a Calculate the variation ratio.

    b Calculate the index of qualitative variation.

    c Why do these two results differ?

4.3   A sample of women was drawn from town A and from town B. All the women were asked how safe or unsafe they felt walking alone at night in their neighborhoods. The results were recorded on a scale as follows: totally unsafe (town A: 40; town B: 25), quite unsafe (town A: 29; town B: 23), quite safe (town A: 10; town B: 15), and totally safe (town A: 21; Town B: 17).

    a For each town, describe the typical case using a measure of central tendency. Justify your choice.

    b For each town, describe how typical the typical case is using a measure of dispersion. Justify your choice.

    c In comparing the results for the two towns, what conclusions may be drawn about the attitudes of the women?

4.4   A group of 20 prisoners in a particular cell block were tested on their knowledge of the rules of the institution. The marks (out of a possible 70) were as follows:

31, 28, 27, 19, 18, 18,

41, 0, 30, 27, 27, 36,

41, 64, 27, 39, 20, 28,

35, 30

    a Calculate the range.

    b Calculate the range between the 5th and the 95th percentile.

    c How do you account for the difference between the results of the above two measures of dispersion?

4.5   Police crack a drug ring of 18 suppliers and discover that of the 18, only 4 have no previous convictions for drug- or theft-related offenses. Eight of those arrested have 1 previous conviction and the others have 2, 3, 4, 5, 6, and 8, respectively.

a Calculate the mean and the standard deviation of the 18 cases.

b If each of the drug suppliers is convicted this time around, does the extra conviction on each of their criminal records affect the mean or the standard deviation in any way? Explain your answer.

4.6   Refer to the data collected from tests of prisoners' knowledge of institution rules in exercise 4.4.

a Calculate the mean and the standard deviation for the data.

b If you remove the two most extreme scores, 00 and 64, what effect does this have on the mean and the standard deviation?

c How do you account for this effect?

4.7   A researcher takes a sample of shop owners in Tranquiltown and a sample of shopowners in Violenceville and asks them to estimate the value of goods stolen from their shops in the past 12 months. The mean figure for Tranquiltown is $11.50 ($s$ = $2.50), and for Violenceville it is $4,754.50 ($s$ = $1,026.00). When the study is published, the mayor of Violenceville protests, claiming that the mean sum for his town is a misleading figure. Because the standard deviation for Violenceville is much bigger than that for Tranquiltown, he argues, it is clear that the mean from Violenceville is a much less typical description of the sample than the mean from Tranquiltown.

What statistic might help the researcher to refute this criticism? Why?

Computer Exercise

1.   The range, variance, and standard deviation are all useful measures of dispersion discussed in the text. You can compute all of these simultaneously using the Options subcommand in the Descriptives command in the Statistics (Summarize) menu. Do this for the two crime measures you have chosen to analyze (for both the number of crimes reported and the number cleared by arrest). What differences do you notice in the dispersion of reports and arrests?

the frequency distribution

What Is It?

How Are Data Represented Visually?

sample distributions and population distributions

How Are They Defined?

What Symbols Are Used?

How Are the Two Interrelated?

the normal frequency distribution

What Are the Characteristics of the Normal Curve?

What Is the z-Score?

When Can We Use the Normal Distribution?

$\mathbf{M}$EASURES OF CENTRAL TENDENCY and dispersion are used to describe the basic character of a variable. In the language of statistics, they summarize the array of values in a distribution of scores of that variable. Although we have used the term "distribution" in earlier chapters, we have not looked specifically at what constitutes a distribution and the different types of distributions that we encounter in criminal justice.

In this chapter we begin with an introduction to the basic idea of a statistical distribution and a discussion of two types of distributions that the researcher ordinarily considers: the sample and the population. Examination of these distributions also provides an opportunity to introduce the limitations of the sample and the statistical problem of extrapolating from a sample to a population. In the last section of this chapter, we consider ways in which a researcher can compare sample scores to those of a population in the context of a very commonly used distribution in statistics: the normal distribution.

What Is a Frequency Distribution?

When we array scores according to their value and frequency we construct what is called a **frequency distribution.** Taking the data on a number of prior arrests in table 5.1 as an example, we would first group all of the cases with the same value together. Accordingly, we would group together the cases with no prior arrests, one prior arrest, two prior arrests, and so forth until we had covered all of the potential scores in the distribution. Then we would arrange those scores in order of magnitude, as is done in table 5.2. Looking at the data in this way allows us to get a sense for the nature of the distribution of scores.

Table 5.1   Previous Arrests of 100 Known Offenders

14	0	34	8	7	22	12	12	2	8
6	1	8	1	18	8	1	10	10	2
12	26	8	7	9	9	3	2	7	16
8	65	8	2	4	2	4	0	7	2
1	2	11	2	1	1	5	7	4	10
11	3	41	15	1	23	10	5	2	10
20	0	7	6	9	0	3	1	15	5
27	8	26	8	1	1	11	2	4	4
8	41	29	18	8	5	2	10	1	0
5	36	3	4	9	5	10	8	0	7

Table 5.2   Frequency Distribution of Prior Arrests for 100 Known Offenders

VALUE	FREQUENCY
0	6
1	11
2	11
3	4
4	6
5	6
6	2
7	7
8	12
9	4
10	7
11	3
12	3
14	1
15	2
16	1
18	2
20	1
22	1
23	1
26	2
27	1
29	1
34	1
36	1
41	2
65	1
Total (Σ)	**100**

In practice, this is usually the first step that a researcher takes in analyzing results in a study. Looking at the distribution of scores not only provides a first glance of the results of a study, it also allows the researcher to check to see whether there are scores that do not make sense. For example, there may be coding errors in the data set that result in impossible scores. In our case, a result of thousands of arrests would be very unlikely and would thus lead the researcher to take another look at that particular case.

Researchers in the 1990s almost never construct frequency distributions by hand. This task is done simply and easily by computer. If you decide it is important to present a frequency distribution of results of a study, however, you must choose what particular format to use. For example, the distribution of prior arrests could simply be presented as in table 5.2. The same information could be presented in the context of what is called a **histogram.** In a histogram we take the scores and values from a frequency distribution and represent them in pictorial form. In this case we use bars to represent each value. The height of the bars indicates the number of scores found in the category. A histogram of the data from table 5.1 is provided in figure 5.1. This presentation of the information in the table is somewhat easier to comprehend than a simple frequency distribution.

Figure 5.1   *Histogram of Frequency Distribution*

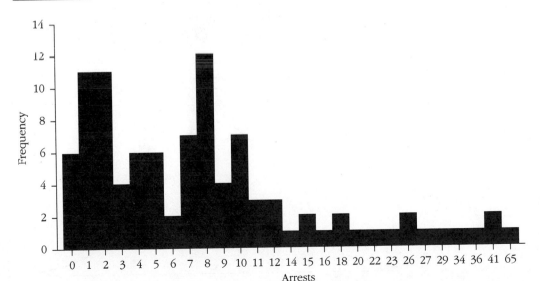

Because frequency distributions of interval-level variables are often dispersed across a large number of values, it is often necessary to group scores together into larger categories when presenting a frequency distribution or histogram. For example, if we were looking at the incomes of a random sample of thousands of people, we would likely not want to present the simple distribution of income scores. In such a case we might end up with thousands of scores, of which most include only one or two cases. It would take pages and pages to illustrate these data in the form of either a frequency distribution or histogram. The solution to this problem is to "group" data together into larger categories, for example by thousands, or tens of thousands, of dollars in the case of incomes. Although there is no hard-and-fast rule about how to create such larger groupings, it should be done in a way that fairly represents the raw distribution of scores. Do not create such a small group of categories that important variation in your data is hidden.

A common confusion for students of statistics develops from the fact that statisticians often represent distributions as "curves" rather than histograms or frequency distributions. For example, we speak in detail at the end of this chapter about a very important and commonly used distribution in statistics called the normal distribution. The normal distribution is ordinarily not represented in the form we have discussed so far, but rather as a smooth curve as illustrated in figure 5.2. What is the relationship between a frequency distribution or histogram and distributions represented by curves, such as the normal distribution?

It is important to begin with the difference between theory and practice in statistics. In practice our samples are generally relatively

Figure 5.2

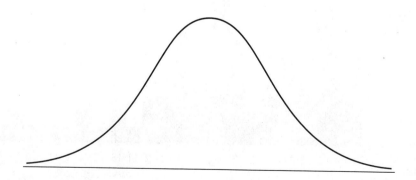

small. Even the largest samples collected by criminologists often include only a few thousand cases. But in theory we could define a distribution with a virtually unlimited number of cases. Such distributions are often the basis upon which statisticians develop statements and theories about statistics. When we represent a distribution as a curve, we are usually referring to a theoretical distribution with a very large number of cases. Such curves are the result of the fact that in a true interval-scale measure, as the number of cases becomes very large it is possible to construct a histogram in such a way that it begins to look like a curve. We do this by making the intervals of the scores smaller and smaller.

This process is illustrated in figure 5.3. We begin with a histogram of almost 10,000 cases, in which all of the scores are placed within 10 broad categories (see figure 5.3a). Here each category is represented as one large bar. When we increase the number of intervals or categories in the histogram to 30 (figure 5.3b), we can still see the individual bars but the shape of the distribution is not as jagged. When the number of categories is increased to 650 (see figure 5.3c) the histogram looks more like a smooth curve than a histogram, although if you look closely you will be able to identify the bars that make up the curve. If our distribution had included an even larger number of scores and categories, the curve would have become even smoother.

Figure 5.3a   *Distribution with 10 Intervals*

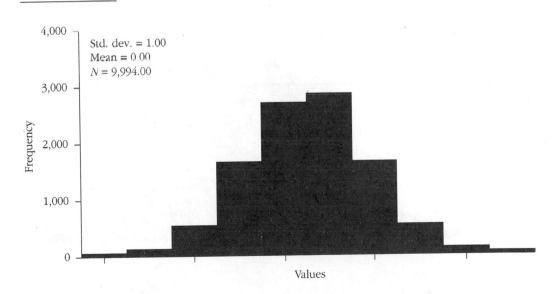

Figure 5.3b   *Distribution with 30 Intervals*

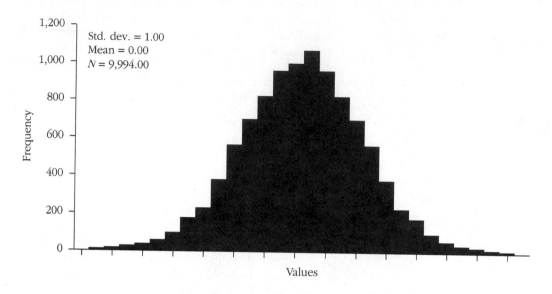

Figure 5.3c   *Distribution with 650 Intervals*

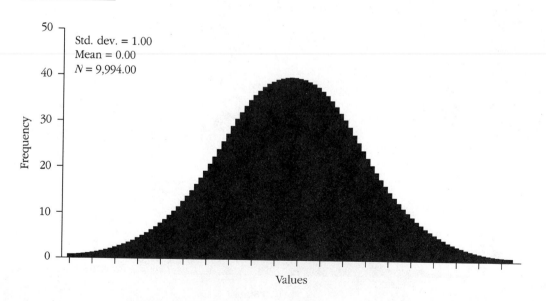

Types of Distributions in Statistics

In descriptive statistics there are two basic types of distributions. One is the distribution of scores in your **sample,** or the **sample distribution.** The second, is the distribution of scores in the **population** from which your sample is drawn. This is referred to as the **population distribution.** One of the fundamental problems in research in criminal justice, as in other fields, is that we want to make statements about the characteristics of the population distribution, but we generally have information only about the distribution of sample scores. For example, when we draw a sample of 2,000 voters in an election survey, we are not interested per se in knowing about how those people will vote. Rather, we examine their voting preference to learn something about how all people will vote in the election. In statistical terms, we want to use information on characteristics of the distribution of sample scores to make statements about characteristics of the distribution of population scores.

It is important to note at the outset that we can define populations in a number of different ways. There is, for example, the population of the entire United States, or the population of a particular state. There is a population of all prisoners in the United States, or a population of prisoners only in a specific state. Although the population of cases is fixed at any particular time, actual populations are constantly changing across time. For example, on any particular day we can speak of the population of prisoners. But every day new people enter the prison and some prisoners are freed. In this sense the population of prisoners changes every day, and data on the population of prisoners at any one time is only a sample of the population of prisoners across a longer period of time, for example, a year or two.

Statisticians use different symbols to denote statistics in a population as opposed to a sample (see table 5.3). Population statistics, or **parameters,** are defined using Greek letters. Of the statistics we have studied so far, the parameter for the mean in a distribution of population scores is represented by μ and the standard deviation by σ. For **sample statistics,** we use roman letters to represent statistics. We denote the mean in a distribution of sample scores as $\overline{X}$ and the standard deviation as s.

Why do we study sample statistics if we really want to say something about population parameters? It certainly makes more sense to collect information on the population if that is what is of interest in the long run. In practice, however, it is usually very difficult to gain information on the **universe,** or total group of cases in the popula-

Table 5.3   Representing Population Parametrics and Sample Statistics

	MEAN	VARIANCE	STANDARD DEVIATION
Sample Distribution	$\bar{X}$	s^2	s
Population Distribution	μ	σ^2	σ

tion. One reason is simply financial. As was pointed out in chapter 1, to carry out just one survey of the U.S. population regarding their attitudes toward crime would exhaust the budget of the National Institute of Justice (the major funder of research in criminal justice in the United States) for many years. But beyond the costs of such studies, there is the problem of their management. A study of entire populations will often demand contact with hundreds of thousands or even millions of people. Such an effort is likely to be not just expensive, but difficult to manage and take a long period of time to complete.

Because of the difficulty of gaining information on the characteristics of an entire population, it is generally the case that such parameters are unknown. However, when a parameter is available, there is no point in drawing statistics from a sample. In recent years, advances in computer technology and recognition by public officials of the importance of data in making policy decisions about the criminal justice system have led to the development of a number of data bases that include information on the population of cases involved. For example, we now have population parameters on characteristics of sentencing in the federal courts, and basic demographic characteristics of offenders held in jails and prisons. Information on the population of arrests and emergency calls to the police are routinely collected and computerized in most cities. One scholar suggests that this trend means that criminologists in the future will have to pay less and less attention to samples and the problems that they create for researchers.[1] However, whatever the future will bring, at present criminal justice researchers must rely primarily on sample statistics in trying to say something about the characteristics of a population.

Given our reliance on sample statistics, it is important at the outset to define how they might differ from population parameters. One obvious difference is that sample statistics are generally known, or put differently, they can be defined by the researcher in the context of a

---

[1] M. Maltz (1994), Deviating from the Mean: The Declining Significance of Significance, *Journal of Research in Crime and Delinquency* 31:434–463.

research study. In contrast, parameters are generally unknown, although, as we noted above, there is a trend toward development of parameters about major issues in criminal justice.

Even though parameters are often unknown, they are assumed to be fixed. By that, we mean that there is one true parameter for any measure. For example, there is a true mean age at first arrest for the population of all criminals in the United States at a specific time. In contrast, sample statistics vary from sample to sample. For example, if you were to draw 10 samples from a population, using exactly the same methods each time, each sample would likely provide different sample statistics.

This is what is done in table 5.4. Ten random samples of 100 offenders were drawn from a population of 1,940 offenders. Sample statistics are presented for mean age and number of prior arrests. Although the sample statistics gained are generally similar to the population parameters, each sample provides a somewhat different group of estimates, and in some cases the differences are relatively large. In the case of sample 10, for example, the average number of arrests for the sample is more than a third lower than the population score. In sample 4, the average age is more than two years older than the population parameters. This occurs despite the fact that we drew each of the samples using the same technique and the same population of scores. You might want to try this yourself by drawing a series of samples from your class or dormitory. Using the same methods, you will almost always obtain different sample statistics.

Table 5.4 Ten Random Samples of 100 Offenders Drawn from a Population of 1,940 Offenders

	MEAN AGE	MEAN ARRESTS
Population	39.7	2.72
Sample 1	41.4	2.55
Sample 2	41.2	2.19
Sample 3	38.8	2.09
Sample 4	42.1	3.45
Sample 5	37.9	2.58
Sample 6	41.1	2.62
Sample 7	39.2	2.79
Sample 8	39.2	2.48
Sample 9	37.8	2.55
Sample 10	37.7	1.72

This fact is one of the fundamental problems we face in statistics. We want to make statements about populations, but we generally must rely on sample statistics to do so. If sample statistics vary from sample to sample, how can we use them to make reliable statements about the parameters associated with a population? Put differently, what is the use of most studies in criminal justice, if they are based on samples rather than populations? Fortunately, there is an area of statistics that provides us with a systematic method to make decisions about population parameters based on sample statistics. This area is called statistical inference, and will form the major focus of our discussions in the next few chapters. However, before turning to inferential statistics, it is important to examine a specific distribution commonly used in developing an understanding of the relationship between samples and populations.

The Normal Frequency Distribution, or Normal Curve

Distributions may take many different forms. Sometimes there is no pattern to a distribution of scores. This is the case for the example in figure 5.4, in which the frequency of scores goes up and down without consistency. But often a distribution begins to take a specific shape. For example, Floyd Allport suggested more than half a century ago that the distribution of deviant behavior is shaped like a J.[2] His J curve, represented in figure 5.5, fits many types of rule-breaking behavior and suggests a theory of deviance in which social control leads to most people conforming more or less to societal rules. Allport fit a J curve to behaviors as diverse as parking violations, conformity to religious rituals in church, and stopping at a stop sign.

Although there is in theory an unlimited number of forms that frequency distributions can take, as the example of the J curve suggests, it is often possible to use one general shape to describe different types of behavior. The most widely utilized distributional form in statistics is what is defined as the **normal frequency distribution,** or **normal curve.** The normal distribution is the basis for a number of statistical tests that allow us to make inferences from a sample to a population. This is the case in good part because of a set of special characteristics that are associated with the normal curve.

---

[2] Allport, F. H. (1934), The J-Curve Hypothesis of Conforming Behavior, *Journal of Social Psychology* 5:141–183.

Figure 5.4   *Random Frequency Distribution*

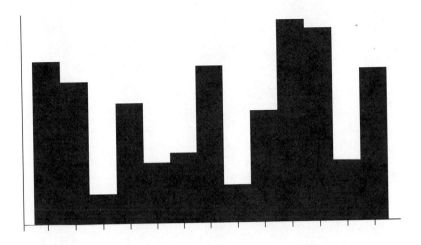

Characteristics of the
Normal Frequency Distribution

A normal distribution is always symmetrical and bell shaped. By that we mean that it is shaped exactly the same on both sides of its mean. If you were to represent a normal distribution as a curve, you should be able to fold it over at its mean and gain two half-curves that are exactly alike. Of course, there are many different potential bell-shaped curves that are symmetrical, as illustrated in figure 5.6. Curve 5.6a for example, is fairly flat. What this means is that the scores are

Figure 5.5   *The J Curve*

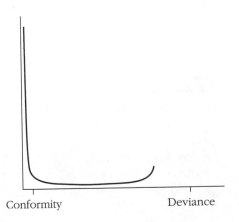

Conformity   Deviance

Figure 5.6   *Two Examples of Normal Curves: (a) Normal Curve with a Large Standard Deviation, and (b) Normal Curve with a Small Standard Deviation*

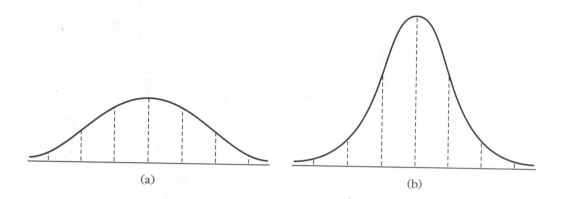

(a)   (b)

fairly widely spread around the mean. Curve 5.6b in contrast, is very peaked. Here, the scores are tightly clustered around the mean. In the statistical language we developed in earlier chapters, we can say that the standard deviation of the first distribution is much larger than that of the second.

In a true normal distribution, the mean, mode, and median are always the same. This can be seen in the normal curves represented in figure 5.6. If the distribution is completely symmetrical, then the 50th percentile score, or median, must be right in the middle of the distribution. In turn, since the middle of the distribution represents its highest peak, and thus the largest frequency of scores, this is also the location of the mode for the normal distribution. Finally, given the fact that there is an exactly equal distribution of scores below and above that peak, the same value must also be the mean for a normal distribution.

All of these traits help to define a normal distribution. However, the most useful characteristic of a normal curve develops from the fact that there is always a set number of cases between its mean and points a measured distance from the mean. The measure in this case is the **standard deviation unit.** A standard deviation unit is simply the standard deviation for the particular distribution being examined. For example, let us say you were examining the results of a standardized test for assessing adjustment of prisoners. You obtain a mean score of 90 and a standard deviation of 10 in your sample. The standard deviation unit of this distribution would be 10. That is, if you

Figure 5.7   *Percentage of Cases under Portions of the Normal Curve*

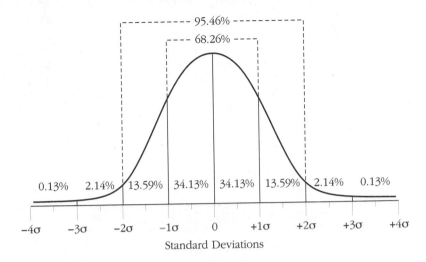

measured one standard deviation unit from the mean in either direction, you would move 10 points from the mean, to 100 and 80. If you measured two standard deviation units from the mean, you would move 20 points, to 110 and 70.

In a normal distribution, 68.26 percent of the cases in the distribution are found within one standard deviation unit above and below the mean (see figure 5.7). Because the normal distribution is symmetrical, this means that 34.13 percent of the cases lie within either one standard deviation unit to the right (positive side) or left (negative side) of the mean. Fully 95.46 percent of the cases are found within two standard deviation units above and below the mean. Virtually all of the cases in a distribution with a normal form are within three standard deviation units of the mean, although in theory the tails (or extremes) of this distribution go on forever. In the sample of inmates we discussed above, we thus know that slightly less than two-thirds have adjustment scores of between 80 and 100 (one standard deviation unit above and below the mean). Very few members of the sample have adjustment scores above 120, which represents a score that is three standard deviation units from the mean.

z-Scores

It is not necessary to limit our examination of the location of scores in a distribution with a normal shape. Using a simple equation, we can convert all normal distributions, irrespective of what their particular mean or standard deviation is, to a single **standard normal distribution.** This distribution can then be used to identify the exact location of any score. We do this by converting the actual scores in our sample or population to z-scores, which represent standard deviation units for the standard normal distribution. This distribution has a mean of 0 and a standard deviation unit of 1. The equation for converting a score in a sample to a z-score is represented by equation 5.1.

Equation 5.1

$$z = \frac{X_i - \overline{X}}{s}$$

The equation for converting a score in a population to a z-score is similar, except we now replace $\overline{X}$ with μ and s with σ.

Equation 5.2

$$z = \frac{X_i - \mu}{\sigma}$$

To identify the z-score for a specific sample in a population distribution we use equation 5.3.

Equation 5.3

$$z = \frac{\overline{X} - \mu}{\sigma}$$

In each equation we take the score of interest and subtract it from the mean score for the distribution (represented by $\overline{X}$ in a sample and by μ in a population distribution). We then divide that score by the standard deviation of the distribution we are examining (represented by s in the sample and by σ in the population). In practice what these formulas do is allow us to convert any specific score in any normal distribution to a z-score in a standard normal distribution. We can then use a standardized table to identify the location of that score. A concrete example may make this conversion easier to understand.

Intelligence quotient (IQ) scores are normally distributed in the U.S. population with a mean of 100 and a standard deviation of about 15. On average, studies have found the mean IQ score of offenders to be about 10 points lower, or about 90.[3] We might ask, where does the mean IQ score for U.S. criminals fit within the U.S. general population

---

[3] Whether these differences mean that offenders are on average less intelligent than nonoffenders is an issue of some controversy in criminology, in part because of the relationship of IQ to other factors, such as education and social status. This figure is drawn from R. J. Hernstein (1983), Some Criminogenic Traits of Offenders, in J. Q. Wilson (ed.), *Crime and Public Policy* (San Francisco: Insitute for Contemporary Studies), 31–49.

distribution of IQ scores? We can answer this question by transforming the mean IQ of offenders (about 90) to a z-score and then identifying where this z-score fits in the standard normal distribution.

We use equation 5.3 in defining the z-score for prisoners because we are locating that score in the population distribution of IQ scores. Following the numerator of the equation, we subtract the score of 90 from the population mean (μ) of 100. By doing this we have shifted the position of our score. We now have its location as if the mean of our distribution were 0—the mean of a standard normal distribution. If the mean were 0, then the score for offenders would be −10 (and not 90). As a second step, we divide this result by 15, the standard deviation (σ) of IQ scores in the U.S. population. This is equivalent to converting our sample standard deviation unit to 1, the standard deviation of the standard normal distribution, since each score of 15 is equivalent to one z standard deviation unit. Our result can be rounded to −0.67.

Working It Out

$$z = \frac{\overline{X} - \mu}{\sigma}$$

$$= \frac{90 - 100}{15}$$

$$= -0.6667$$

Our final step is to compare this z-score to an already prepared table of the standard normal distribution. This is provided in appendix 1. You will notice that the Z table goes up to only about 0.50 within its main part. This is because it provides us with only half of the normal curve. On this half of the normal curve, our z-score is equivalent to 0.2486, meaning that 24.86 percent of the scores lie between 0 and −0.67 standard deviations of 0. In figure 5.8 our result is illustrated in the context of the normal curve. Because our result is a negative score, we place the value on the left-hand side of the normal distribution. As you can see the score is about halfway between the mean and the tail of the normal curve. To identify the number of people in the general population with scores lower than the average prisoner, we subtract our result of 0.2486 from 0.50 (the proportion of cases in this half of the curve). Our result of 0.2514 means that a bit more than a quarter of the general population have IQ scores lower than the average prisoner. This also means, however, that a bit under three-quarters of the general population have IQ scores higher than the average prisoner.

In some fields in the social sciences, the normal distribution has provided a useful method for comparing individuals or samples to

Figure 5.8   *IQ Scores of Prisoners Compared to IQ Scores of the General Population*

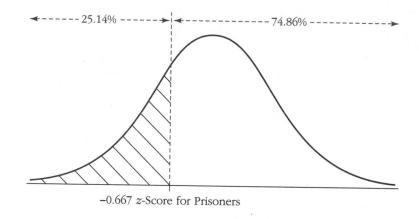

−0.667 *z*-Score for Prisoners

populations. This is particularly the case in the field of psychology, in which measures such as IQ have been assumed to be normally distributed in the population, and have been constructed in such ways that they are normally distributed in practice.[4] But in criminology, there has been much less use of distributions that are standardized in normal form, in part because the distributions of the behaviors and populations that we confront do not often conform to the shape of a normal curve. Even measures that do begin to approximate the shape of the normal distribution seldom meet all the requirements of a true normal distribution.

What this means in practice for criminologists is that the normal frequency distribution has limited use in understanding the distribution of scores in a sample or population. In cases in which standardized scores, such as IQ or certain personality tests, are used to compare offenders to the general population, the normal distribution has the most relevance. Then *z*-scores have a very direct and relevant meaning. In other cases, in which the shape of the distribution of scores begins to approximate a normal shape, the researcher can also refer to characteristics of the normal distribution. In this case, if an individual score is, for example, three standard deviation units above or below the mean, the researcher can conclude that the score is very

---

[4] In principle any distribution may be arranged in such a way so that it conforms to a normal shape. This can be done simply by ranking scores and then placing the appropriate number within standard deviation units appropriate for constructing a standard normal distribution.

different from the others. Importantly, however, even though the normal distribution is used as a general yardstick for understanding where a score is located within a wider distribution, only in a true normal distribution can a researcher make precise statements about the location of a specific score or group of scores.

Given the limitations of the use of the normal distribution in defining distributions in criminal justice, you might ask why we have given it so much attention in this chapter. The answer lies in our next topic, though we will not return to the normal distribution itself until chapter 10. Beginning in chapter 6 we explore the logic that researchers use in making statements about population parameters from knowledge about sample statistics. An important part of this logic will be to decide whether it makes sense to assume that the outcome we obtain in our sample was drawn from a specific type of population. That is, we will compare our sample statistics to a population distribution of scores. As we will discuss in chapter 10, it is often possible to use the standard normal distribution for this purpose even when the distribution of scores we examine does not conform to the standard normal form.

Chapter Summary

A **frequency distribution** is an arrangement of data according to the frequency with which each value occurs. The data may be represented in a table, or in graphic form through a **histogram** or curve.

There are two types of distributions in descriptive statistics. The **sample distribution** is the distribution of scores in your sample. The **population distribution** is the distribution of scores in the population from which the sample is drawn. Population statistics are known as **parameters,** and they have symbols different from those which we have encountered so far. The mean in a population distribution is μ and the standard deviation is σ. Parameters are assumed to be fixed and are generally unknown. Although we are usually interested in making statements about population parameters, we generally study sample statistics.

The **normal frequency distribution,** or **normal curve,** is widely used in statistics. It is symmetrical and bell shaped. Its mean, mode, and median are always the same. There will always be a set number of cases between the mean and points a measured distance from the mean. The measure of this distance is the **standard deviation unit.** All normal distributions, irrespective of their mean or standard deviations, can be converted to a single standard normal distribution by converting the actual scores in the sample or population to **z-scores.** In practice, there are few variables in criminology that are distributed normally.

Key Terms

Frequency Distribution An arrangement of scores in order from the lowest to the highest that shows the number of times each score occurs.

Histogram A bar graph used to represent a frequency distribution.

Normal Curve A normal frequency distribution represented on a graph by a continuous line.

Normal Frequency Distribution A frequency distribution, bell shaped and symmetrical in form. Its mean, mode, and median are always the same.

Parameter A characteristic of the population, for example, the mean number of previous convictions for all U.S. prisoners.

Population The universe of cases that the researcher seeks to study. The population of cases is fixed at a particular time (e.g., the population of the United States). However, populations usually change across time.

Population Distribution The frequency distribution of a particular variable within a population.

Sample A set of actual observations or cases drawn from a population.

Sample Distribution The frequency distribution of a particular variable within a sample drawn from a population.

Sample Statistic A characteristic of a sample, for example, the mean number of previous convictions in a random sample of 1,000 prisoners drawn from the entire prison population.

Standard Deviation Unit A unit of measurement used to describe the deviation of a specific score or value from the mean in a z-distribution.

Standard Normal Distribution A normal frequency distribution with a mean of 0 and a standard deviation of 1. Any normal frequency distribution can be transformed into the standard normal distribution by using the z formula.

Universe The total population of cases.

Symbols and Formulas

z The standardized score for a value in a normal distribution.

μ The mean of the population.

σ The standard deviation of the population.

To calculate the *z*-score for an individual in a sample:

$$z = \frac{X_i - \overline{X}}{s}$$

To calculate the *z*-score for a sample in a population:

$$z = \frac{\overline{X} - \mu}{\sigma}$$

Exercises

5.1   A team of researchers observed the behavior of 20 children during breaktime on a school playground. The observers recorded how many times each child performed a "violent act"—be it a push, a kick, or a punch—against another. The scores of the 20 children were as follows:

2, 0, 1, 0, 0, 4, 0, 10, 2, 1, 3, 3, 0, 1, 4, 11, 0, 0, 2, 0.

a   Construct a frequency distribution table for the above results.

b   Construct a histogram of the frequency distribution.

c   How might you interpret the results?

5.2   Workers at an inner city rape crisis center asked all the callers on a given night for their ages. Out of a total of 50 callers, the results were as follows:

28, 39, 17, 18, 22, 31, 26, 27, 16, 20
34, 35, 29, 26, 17, 23, 22, 23, 37, 28
24, 19, 14, 25, 27, 19, 24, 26, 41, 27
21, 24, 17, 16, 35, 25, 19, 23, 29, 18
23, 26, 24, 43, 28, 21, 21, 36, 26, 27

a   Construct a frequency distribution table for the above results.

b   Based on the frequency distribution, construct three different histograms whereby:

i.   The data are grouped in 10-year intervals.

ii.   The data are grouped in 3-year intervals.

iii.   The data are grouped in 1-year intervals.

c Which of these histograms would you say provides the most helpful visual representation of the results? Explain why.

5.3 A foundation has sponsored a review of all studies carried out over the past 15 years into the link between smoking and juvenile delinquency. Eric, a criminologist commissioned by the foundation, has unearthed five studies that seek to determine at what age delinquents who smoke began their habit. The five studies conducted at the same time use identical sampling techniques and sample sizes and draw their samples from a fixed data base of delinquents. The mean age, however, is different for each of the samples:

Study sample no. 1: mean age = 12.2

Study sample no. 2: mean age = 11.6

Study sample no. 3: mean age = 14.0

Study sample no. 4: mean age = 11.3

Study sample no. 5: mean age = 12.8

Overall computed mean = 12.38

a During Eric's presentation, one member of the foundation asks him to explain how it can be that each of the study samples produced a different result—does this mean that there was something wrong with the sampling techniques used? How should Eric respond?

b Another foundation member also seems confused. He asks if the overall computed mean is the mean age of the population. How should Eric respond?

5.4 A team of psychologists has created an index they claim measures an individual's "ability to control anger." The index is calculated from the answers to a detailed questionnaire and is normally distributed among U.S. adult males with a mean of 100 and a standard deviation of 30. Researchers assess a group of 10 prisoners, all of whom have been convicted for violent rapes. They discover that the mean score for the group is 50.8.

a What percentage of U.S. adult males would be expected to obtain a score equal to or less than that of the rapists?

b The psychologists who constructed the index consider the bottom 10 percent of U.S. adult males on their distribution to be "strongly inclined to use violence to solve social problems." Albert is a respectable businessman who scores 60.6 on the scale. Is Albert included in this category? Explain your answer.

c What percentage of U.S. adult males would be expected to score between 110 and 120 on the "anger index"?

5.5 A teacher gives the following assignment to 200 students: Each one is to check the local newspaper every morning for a week and is to count how many times the word "gun" is mentioned on the "local news" pages. At the end of the week the students report their totals. The mean result is 85 with a standard deviation of 8. The distribution of scores is normal.

a How many students would be expected to count fewer than 70 cases?

b How many students would be expected to count between 80 and 90 cases?

c Karen is a notoriously lazy student. She reports a total of 110 cases at the end of the week. The professor tells her that he is convinced she has not done the assignment but has simply made up the number. Are his suspicions reasonable? Why?

5.6 A noted criminologist, Leslie Wilkins, has suggested that the distribution of deviance in the population follows a normal bell-shaped curve, with "sinners" at one extreme, "saints" at the other, and most of us falling somewhere in between the two. Working on the basis of this theory, a researcher constructs a detailed self-report survey whereby individuals are given a score according to the amount of offenses they have committed in the past year, with the score weighted according to the relative triviality or seriousness of the offense. The lower the score, the nearer the individual approximates to "sinner" status, and the higher the score, the closer he is to being a "saint." From his initial sample of 100 adults in a specific state, he computes a mean score of 30 with a standard deviation of 5.

a If the researcher's model is correct, then below which score should he expect to find the 5 percent of U.S. society with the greatest propensity to deviance?

b From his sample of 100, the researcher is surprised to discover that 50 subjects score greater than 35 on the deviance test. How many cases would be expected under the assumption of a normal distribution of saints and sinners? What does this suggest about the original theory?

Computer Exercises

1. To get a better picture of the information you have been analyzing on the two types of crime you chose, use the Frequencies command, check the Display Frequency Tables box, and create frequency tables of crimes reported to the police and crimes cleared by arrest for the two types of crime you chose.

2. Now, let us finish our description of those crimes you are interested in. Using the graphs menu and the Histogram command, create a his-

togram (with the normal curve displayed) for each variable. Looking at these histograms, the frequency distributions, the mean values, and the median values, can you tell whether these measures are normally distributed?

3. To illustrate the principles of sample statistics discussed in this chapter, let's take a few samples of our own. Using the data menu and the Select Cases command, select a random sample of 5 percent of the cases in our UCR data. When you save this, be sure to give it a unique name, such as SAMPLE1.sav. Compute the mean value for the Grand Total of All Actual Offenses. Now, going back to the original data set, repeat this procedure (but name this data set SAMPLE2.sav). Repeat this until you have 10 samples, and 10 sample means. Compare the sample means, and explain what you find.

The Logic of Statistical Inference:

Making Statements about Populations

on the Basis of Sample Statistics

asking the research question

What Are the Research and Null Hypotheses?

How Are They Set Up?

answering the research question

How Can a Sample Teach Us about a Population?

What Types of Error Are Possible?

What Is an "Acceptable" Risk of Error?

When Might It Be Necessary to Accept a Different Level of Risk?

In THE PREVIOUS CHAPTER we introduced an important dilemma that we face in conducting criminal justice research. We seek to make statements about populations, but generally we collect data on samples drawn from such populations. Statistical inference provides a solution to this dilemma. It allows the researcher to make statements, or inferences, about the characteristics of a population from data collected from a sample drawn from the population. In this chapter we examine the logic of statistical inference and the statistical risks that are faced in using this logic. You will be introduced to how we set up null and research hypotheses, how we assess risks of error, and the ways in which levels of statistical significance are used to limit this error.

The Research Hypothesis

The first step in a research project is to define the questions that the researcher seeks to answer. Sometimes **research questions** in criminal justice are focused on specific agencies in the criminal justice system. For example, we may want to learn more about the police, or the courts, or probation services. Other times research questions revolve around broad theoretical concerns that can be applied across criminal justice agencies. We may, for example, seek to define common features of criminal justice programs that lead to a reduction in recidivism (reoffending). Sometimes our questions relate to offenders, other times to victims of crimes or criminal justice agents.

To answer a research question, we have to set up one or sometimes a number of **research hypotheses** related to it. A hypothesis is a proposed answer to our research question that we can then test in the context of a study. Stating a research hypothesis does not mean that we assume that the hypothesis is true. Rather, it focuses our research question in such a way that it can be directly examined in the context of a study.

For example, suppose we are interested in comparing drug-involved offenders with offenders who do not use drugs. Our research hypothesis might be simply that drug-involved offenders are different from offenders who do not use drugs. However, to test a research hypothesis in the real world, it is often necessary to state it in much more specific terms. It is not enough to state that drug offenders are different; we must define what is meant by "different." Do we mean that they commit different types of crimes, or that they are different in terms of their family or social backgrounds? If we are concerned only with their criminal records, are we concerned primarily with the seriousness of the crimes they commit or the number of crimes? In practice, we may want to examine each of these possibilities, and thus our study may include a series of related research hypotheses.

Common-Sense Reasoning and the Research Hypothesis

Having defined a research hypothesis, we will want to examine whether it is true for the population in which we are interested. In our example, if we are able to collect information about all offenders, we can simply look at the parameters drawn from our study and see whether they support the research hypotheses and, if so, to what degree. But ordinarily we will not be able to collect information on the population parameters and must rely upon the statistics that are drawn from our sample in making our decision. Our problem is that we cannot come to an absolute conclusion regarding the research hypothesis because we know that statistics vary from sample to sample.

On the basis of a sample, we can never be sure of the true value of a population parameter. Accordingly, we can never be absolutely certain as to whether the research hypothesis is true. But does the fact that we cannot be sure mean that we cannot come to a reasonable conclusion regarding our hypotheses?

In fact, we often make decisions about hypotheses on the basis of samples in our daily lives. For example, let us say that you are deciding whether to sign up for a course taught by an instructor named Professor Justice in the coming semester. One issue that you are particularly concerned about is the impact the course will have on your grade point average. To make an informed decision about the course, you might decide to ask friends of yours who took the course last year how Professor Justice grades in comparison to others at your college. Although you might not think of it quite in this way, your friends represent your sample. In turn, the conclusion that the professor grades differently from other faculty members in your college is similar to a research hypothesis.

If your friends give a mixed view, or generally are unable to say whether Professor Justice grades more harshly or more easily than other professors, you would likely conclude that the course would not have much impact on your grade point average. Put differently, you would decide that the research hypothesis is probably false. If most of your friends say that the professor is an easy grader, or conversely that she is a hard grader, you would take this as evidence that the research hypothesis is most likely correct—that the professor grades differently and that the course is likely to impact upon your grade point average.

Once you have made the decision that Professor Justice is different from others, you are likely to assess how she is different. If your friends define the professor as a hard grader, you might decide to avoid the course because you fear you would get a lower grade than is usual with other professors. If they define the professor as an easy grader, you might be encouraged to take the course, with the expectation that your grade will be higher than usual.

In effect, you make a decision about the research hypothesis based on information that you draw from your "sample" of friends. Your confidence in making a decision will depend greatly on how reliable you believe your friends' observations to be, and to what degree they represent other students in the class. This is very similar to the logic we use in making statistical inferences from samples to populations. However, in statistical inference we test hypotheses not in reference to the research hypothesis but to a type of hypothesis that statisticians define as the **null hypothesis.**

The Null Hypothesis

The null hypothesis—or H_0—gains its name because it usually states that there is no relationship, or no difference. It is generally the flip side of the research hypothesis (H_1) which usually posits that there is a relationship. In the example of the professor's grading, the null hypothesis would simply be that "there is no difference between the grading of Professor Justice and others in the university."

In practice in statistics, we make decisions about hypotheses in relation to the null hypothesis and not the research hypothesis. This is because the null hypothesis states that the parameter in which we are interested is a particular value. For example, returning to the comparison of drug-involved and other offenders, your null hypothesis (H_0) might be that there is no difference between the two groups in the average number of crimes committed, or, put differently, that the difference is equal to zero. In the case of Professor Justice's grading, the null hypothesis states that there is no difference, or again that the difference between the average grade given by Professor Justice and the average grade given by her colleagues is equal to zero.

In contrast, the research hypothesis is ordinarily not stated in exact terms. A number of potential outcomes can satisfy the research hypothesis. In the example of the professor's grading, any average grade that is different from that of other professors in the college is consistent with the research hypothesis. But only one result, that the professor's grading is the same as others, is consistent with the null hypothesis. The null hypothesis, accordingly, has the advantage of defining a specific value for the population parameter.[1]

The Null Hypothesis and Statistical Inference

By stating the null and research hypotheses, we have taken a first very important step in making statistical inferences. However, we still have the problem of how to make decisions about these hypotheses on the basis of sample statistics.

In fact, we generally do not come to concrete conclusions regarding our hypotheses. Whenever we rely on sample statistics to make statements about population parameters, we must always accept that our conclusions are tentative. The only way to come to a definitive conclusion regarding the population parameter is to actually examine the entire population. As we noted in chapter 1, this happens more

---

[1] Some statisticians prefer to call the research hypothesis the "alternative" hypothesis, because we can, in theory, choose any value as the null hypothesis, and not just the value zero or no difference. The alternative hypothesis, in this case, can be defined as all other possible outcomes or values. For example, you could state in your null hypothesis that the professor's grades are on average five points higher than those of other professors in the college. This five-point difference can then be defined as the null hypothesis. The alternative hypothesis would be that the professor's grades are not on average five points higher than those of other professors.

and more with criminal justice data today. However, in most research, we are still able to collect information only about sample statistics.

This means that when we test hypotheses in research, we generally do not ask whether the null hypothesis is true or false. To make such a statement would require knowledge about the population parameters. Rather we ask whether we can make an inference, or draw a conclusion, about our hypotheses based on what we know from a sample. In statistical inference, we use sample statistics to infer to, or draw conclusions about, population parameters.

In order to understand the logic of making inferences, it will help to return to our example of drug-involved offenders. Let us say that we are interested in the number of crimes that offenders commit in a given year. We decide to use arrests as our measure of criminal behavior. We might state our null hypothesis as follows: "Drug-involved offenders and offenders who do not use drugs have on average the same number of arrests in a given year." To test our hypothesis, we take a sample of drug-involved offenders and another sample of offenders who do not use drugs. We find that drug-involved offenders have a mean of five arrests per year, whereas offenders who do not use drugs have a mean of three arrests per year. Should we reject the null hypothesis? Should we conclude that there is a difference in the number of arrests in the population based on results from our sample?

As illustrated earlier in regard to Professor Justice's grading, in everyday life we make such decisions through a combination of intuition, prior experience, and guess work. In statistical inference we take a systematic approach to this decision making, which begins with the recognition that whatever decision we make has a risk of error.

Risks of Error in Hypothesis Testing

What types of error do we risk when making a decision about a population parameter from a sample? A simple way to examine this question is to compare the potential decisions that can be made about a null hypothesis with the value of the population parameter. Taking the example of our null hypothesis concerning arrests among drug-involved and non–drug-involved offenders, there are only two possible scenarios for the population. In the first case the null hypothesis is true, meaning that there is no difference in the average number of arrests of offenders who use drugs and those who do not. Alternatively, the null hypothesis may be false, meaning that there is a difference between drug-involved and other offenders. In this case, drug-involved offenders have on average either fewer or more arrests in a year than do offenders who do not use drugs.

Based on our sample statistic we can, as well, come to only two possible conclusions regarding the null hypothesis. We can reject the null hypothesis and infer that there is a difference in the average number of arrests of drug-involved and other offenders. Alternatively, we can fail to reject the null hypothesis and infer accordingly that drug-involved offenders and offenders who do not use drugs are similar.

If we cross these two sets of possibilities, we define four possible situations as represented in figure 6.1. Two of these are desirable, because they suggest that our decision about the null hypothesis is consistent with the population parameter. In one case (box 1), we fail to reject the null hypothesis, and in fact it is true. In the second (box 4), we reject the null hypothesis on the basis of our sample results, and the null hypothesis is false.

In the remaining situations, however, our decisions are not consistent with the population parameter. In one (box 2), we fail to reject the null hypothesis on the basis of our sample statistic, but in fact it is false. In this case we have made what statisticians call a **Type II (or Beta) error.** A Type II error in our example of arrests among offend-

Figure 6.1   *Types of Error in a Statistical Test*

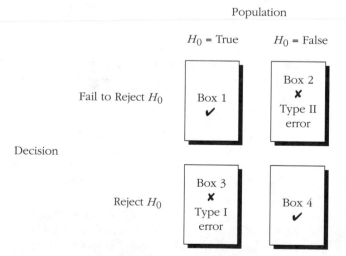

Population

	H_0 = True	H_0 = False
Fail to Reject H_0	Box 1 ✔	Box 2 ✘ Type II error
Reject H_0	Box 3 ✘ Type I error	Box 4 ✔

Decision

ers would occur if we did not reject the null hypothesis on the basis of our sample results, when in fact the average number of arrests for drug-involved and other offenders was different in the population to which we want to infer. We make a **Type I (or Alpha) error** (see box 3) when we reject the null hypothesis on the basis of sample statistics, but the H_0 is true. In this case, we would infer from our sample that drug offenders are different from offenders who do not use drugs, when in fact they are similar in the population.

Whenever we make a decision about a population parameter from a sample statistic we risk one of these two types of statistical error. If we fail to reject the null hypothesis, there is always the possibility that we have failed to reject it when it is false (Type II error). If we reject the null hypothesis, there is always the possibility that we have rejected it when it is true (Type I error). Although we cannot avoid the possibility of error when we study samples, we can define the amount of risk we are willing to take in making decisions about hypotheses.

Risks of Error and Statistical Levels of Significance

In statistical inference we assess the risk of making a wrong decision about the population parameter in reference to a Type I error. We define the amount of Type I error we are willing to risk as a **significance level.** If we are willing to take a good deal of risk of Type I error, we will set a very lenient significance level. This means that we are willing on the basis of our sample statistic to reject the null hypothesis, even though we are taking a fairly high risk that it is true for the population. If we set a very strict significance level, it means that we are unwilling to reject the null hypothesis except if we are fairly certain that our decision is correct.

If we use the example of Professor Justice's grading, the importance of Type I error in making statistical inferences will become clearer. Let us say that every one of the friends you ask reports that the professor is a much easier grader than other professors at your college. In this case you would probably assume that the risk of a Type I error would be very small. It is unlikely that all of your friends would say that the professor is an easy grader if she is in reality very similar to others in the college. Of course, your friends could provide a mistaken view of the professor's grading habits. But you would probably assume that this is not very likely.

But what if your friends provide you with a mixed view of Professor Justice's grading. What if 40 percent of your friends say that Professor Justice grades similarly to other professors and 60 percent say that she is easier. Would you be so confident in rejecting the null hypothesis with these results? Overall, the majority of your friends still say the professor is a relatively easy grader. But in this case there is a substantial group that reports that she grades similarly to other professors. If you set a strict significance level, you might not be willing to reject the null hypothesis, and you might simply conclude that there is not enough evidence on the basis of your sample of friends to say that Professor Justice grades differently.

It might seem at first that we would want to be fairly lenient in setting our significance level. Often, in defining the research hypothesis we are expressing what we believe to be true. Why, then, would we want to make it difficult to reject the null hypothesis? By rejecting the null hypothesis that there is no difference, we are led to infer that the research hypothesis is correct. This would seem in our best interest. In fact, by convention we set a fairly strict significance level. In order to establish a relationship, we are expected to provide convincing evidence that our conclusions reflect the true population parameters.

What is "convincing evidence"? How much risk of a Type I error should we be willing to take in a research project? In criminal justice, and in most of the social sciences, a five percent level of significance is generally considered rigorous enough for tests of hypotheses. This means that the risk of rejecting the null hypothesis (on the basis of a sample statistic) when it is in fact true for the population must be less than or equal to 5 percent. In the chapters that follow, we examine how statisticians calculate risks of error in statistical tests of hypotheses. For now, it is important to consider when we might choose to take either greater or less risk of a Type I error in a study.

Departing from Conventional Significance Criteria

In statistics, as in everyday life, it is simplest to follow the accepted conventions. Accordingly, most criminal justice researchers apply the 5 percent significance level fairly automatically to the research questions they consider. The problem with this approach is that the purposes of the research may be better served by departing from established norms. Sometimes this is the case because our criteria are not cautious enough for the issue we are examining.

For example, a criminal justice agency making a decision about its policies may want you to use a stricter standard than you would ordinarily apply to your research. This may be the case if your conclusions could lead to expensive or time-consuming changes in the structure or activities of the agency. The agency will likely not want to make such changes unless you are very certain that your conclusions are correct. In this situation you might decide to set your significance level at 0.01 or 0.001, meaning that you are willing to take only a 1 percent or a 0.1 percent risk of a Type I error in coming to a conclusion. Whenever you use a significance level more stringent than 5 percent, it is important to explain clearly why you have chosen to make it harder to reject the null hypothesis in your study.

Sometimes a researcher may decide to use a more lenient significance level than 5 percent. This ordinarily occurs when the researcher is particularly concerned with a Type II error rather than a Type I error. In the Minneapolis hot spots experiment, for example, which evaluated the impact of police patrol on street blocks with high crime activity, the principal investigators discussed the dangers of a Type II error at the outset of their study.[2] They argued that conventional significance criteria may be too strict for assessing the effectiveness of new police initiatives. Acceptance of the null hypothesis of no program impact in this case, if it were false, would lead the police not to pursue a potentially effective new method of police patrol. The principal investigators, accordingly, decided to use a 0.10, rather than 0.05, significance level.

Why would a concern with a Type II error lead us to change the significance level of our test of hypotheses? As we noted earlier, the significance level is based on a Type I error, not a Type II error. However, the two types of statistical error are related. When we increase the risk of a Type I error we reduce the risk of a Type II error. When we decrease the risk of a Type I error we increase the risk of a Type II error. This relationship is an obvious one, because setting a stricter significance level (by decreasing the risk of a Type I error) naturally makes it less likely that you will reject the null hypothesis. Similarly, when we make it easier to reject the null hypothesis by increasing the risk of a Type I error, it is that much harder in practice to support it. The relationship between Type I and Type II error is easy to understand, but it is not directly proportional. As we discuss in chapter 13, when we examine the concept of "statistical power," a series of other factors besides the significance level of a study impacts upon the risk of a Type II error that the researcher encounters.

---

2 See Lawrence Sherman and David Weisburd (1995), General Deterrent Effects of Police Patrol in Crime 'Hot Spots': A Randomized Study, *Justice Quarterly* 12(4):625–648.

You should always consider carefully the implications of risks of error in your research before setting your significance level. Even though you are likely in the end to rely on the conventional norm of 5 percent, there are, as discussed above, some cases for which you might want to consider stricter or more lenient levels of significance. If you do choose a level other than 0.05, you must explain to your audience the factors that have led you to depart from common practice in criminal justice.

The level of significance in a study should, as well, be defined at the outset, and not after your results are in. If you wait until you have your sample data, there will always be the temptation to adjust your significance level to fit your sample statistics. This is particularly important if you decide to use more stringent or more lenient criteria. If you use a more lenient criterion, others might argue that you have made that decision in order to allow rejection of the null hypothesis (and thus support for the research hypothesis). If you use a more strict criterion, others might argue that you are trying to avoid rejecting the null hypothesis. In many funded research studies, researchers specify in their original proposals the significance levels that they intend to apply to tests of hypotheses in order to prevent such criticism later on.

In this chapter we discussed the logic underlying statistical inference. In the coming chapters we examine how statisticians define risks of error in statistical tests, and we detail how such tests are applied to different types of statistics. You should not expect to have a full understanding of statistical inference at this point. We have only begun to develop these ideas, and will return to them again and again.

Chapter Summary

The **research hypothesis** and the **null hypothesis** are set up by the researcher to answer the broader **research question.** The research hypothesis is the proposed answer to a specific research question. It usually suggests that there is a meaningful relationship or a difference between the variables studied. The null hypothesis suggests that there is no such relationship or no difference. The null hypothesis is stated in exact terms. The research hypothesis encompasses a range of possible alternatives. It is thus easier to focus decisions on whether to reject the null hypothesis.

Given the difficulties involved in collecting information on an entire population, we are forced to work with samples. We have seen, though, how sample results vary from sample to sample. The tools of statistical inference enable us to infer from a sample to a population by identifying the risk of making a mistaken decision and determining the risk we are prepared to take. Two possible errors can be made when making decisions about a population from a sample. A researcher who rejects the null hypothesis when in fact it is true has made a **Type I error.** A researcher who fails to reject the null hypothesis when in fact it is false has made a **Type II error.**

The **significance level** defines the risk of Type I error that a researcher is willing to take. A commonly accepted standard significance level is 5 percent, but the researcher may choose to set a lower level if he wants it to be more difficult to reject the null hypothesis, or a higher level to make it easier. A researcher who wishes to depart from the accepted standard should explain the reasons for such a decision at the outset. Decreasing the risk of a Type I error increases the risk of a Type II error, and vice versa.

Key Terms

Null Hypothesis A statement that reduces the research question to a simple assertion to be tested by the researcher. The null hypothesis normally suggests that there is no relationship or no difference.

Research Hypothesis The antithesis of the null hypothesis. The statement normally answers the initial research question by suggesting that there is a relationship or a difference.

Research Question The question the researcher hopes to be able to answer by means of a study.

Significance Level The objective risk that the researcher may make a Type I error. In a test of hypotheses, the researcher sets a significance level. This level is the risk that the researcher is prepared to take of making a Type I error.

Type I Error Also known as "Alpha" error. The mistake made when a researcher rejects the null hypothesis on the basis of the sample (i.e., claiming that there is a relationship) when, in fact, the null hypothesis is true (i.e., there is actually *no* such relationship in the population).

Type II Error Also known as a "Beta" error. The mistake made when a researcher fails to reject the null hypothesis on the basis of the sample (i.e., claiming that there is no relationship) when, in fact, the null hypothesis is false (i.e., there actually *is* a relationship).

Symbols and Formulas

H_0 Null hypothesis.

H_1 Research hypothesis.

Exercises

6.1   A researcher collects data on the families of 20 delinquent and 20 nondelinquent children from the records of a school, and checks how many children from each group come from broken homes.

a   What might the null hypothesis be?

b   What might the research hypothesis be?

6.2   A study published in a distinguished journal reported the results of a series of tests carried out on 50 convicted burglars. One of the assumptions of the investigators was that the average IQ of convicted burglars is 120.

a   From the following list of options, choose an appropriate null hypothesis and research hypothesis for testing this assumption.

$IQ = 120$ $IQ \neq 120$ $IQ > 120$ $IQ < 120$

b   Explain your choices.

6.3   A gang of criminals is planning to rob a supermarket. Eddy, the gang leader, reports that he "staked the store out" the day before and saw the store detective going for a 15-minute coffee break at 9.15 A.M. He suggests that this would be the best time to strike. Clive, a gang member, thinks that this plan is too risky—how do they know that the detective takes his break at the same time each day? Eddy, who is desperate for the money, thinks that the plan is safe enough and he wants to carry out the robbery the next day. After an argument, they agree to compromise and watch the supermarket for three more days. On each of the three days, the store detective indeed takes his 15-minute break at 9:15 A.M. The gang decides to go ahead with the robbery on the fourth day.

   The robbers can be seen as having set themselves a research question, and having made a statistical decision based on a simple study.

a   How would you frame the robbers' null hypothesis and research hypothesis?

b   Based on these hypotheses, what is their decision?

    c What type of statistical error ought the robbers to be most concerned with making? Explain.

    d How does the argument between Eddy and Clive relate to the concept of statistical significance?

6.4   The government wishes to launch a pre-Christmas advertising campaign warning against the dangers of drunk driving. It suspects that drivers aged 18 to 21 are most likely to drive while under the influence of alcohol, and is considering targeting the campaign specifically at this age group. A preliminary study gathers data on the ages of drunk drivers apprehended in a particular district over a six-month period.

    a What are the null and research hypotheses?

    b How might the government make a Type I error?

    c How might the government make a Type II error?

    The government accepts that targeting this specific age group in the advertising campaign will not cost any extra money. There is a feeling that the new campaign will be "worth a try," even if the study doesn't find enormous differences between the offending rate of 18- to 21-year-olds and that of other ages.

    d How should these considerations affect the researchers' decision on what level of significance to set?

6.5   The head of the police force in the city of Cheadle suspects that increasing the pay of his officers might increase their efficiency. A police researcher is assigned to test whether there is a difference between the crime-solving rates of a group of detectives who have been randomly awarded pay rises and a control group. In writing up his report, the researcher concludes as follows:

> The results show that rejecting the null hypothesis would run a 14% risk of a Type I error. Although a 5% significance level is considered standard, in the light of the potential benefits of salary increases for crime control rates, a higher 15% threshold is justified here, and H_0 may therefore be rejected.

    a What is the null hypothesis to which the researcher refers?

    b How might you criticize the researcher's statistical reasoning?

6.6   A study explored whether there is a link between male aggression and climate. The researcher recorded her results as follows:

> 5% significance level set, H_0 could not be rejected.

    a Explain these results in plain English.

    b Why is it important for the researcher to set the significance level at the beginning of the research and not at the end?

Defining Risks of Error:
From Probabilities to a Sampling Distribution

probabilities
and probability distributions

How Does One Calculate the Probability of a Given Outcome?

What Are Probability Distributions?

How Are They Used?

the binomial distribution

What Is It?

How Is It Calculated?

What Are Its Characteristics?

sampling distributions

What Are They?

What Role Do They Play in Inferential Statistics?

W HEN WE MAKE INFERENCES to a population, we rely upon a statistic in our sample to make a decision about a population parameter. At the heart of our decision is a concern with Type I error. We want to be fairly certain if we reject our null hypothesis that it is in fact false for the population we are studying. For this reason we want the risk of a Type I error to be as small as possible. But how do statisticians calculate that risk? If we do not know the value of the population parameter, then how can we estimate our risk of rejecting our hypothesis concerning it?

The methods that statisticians use for calculating Type I error vary depending on the statistics examined. Sometimes those methods are very complex. Nonetheless, the overall logic that underlies these calculations is similar irrespective of the statistic used. This means that we can take a relatively simple example and use it as a model for understanding how Type I error is defined more generally in statistics. This is fortunate for us as researchers, because it means that we do not have to spend all of our time developing complex calculations for defining risks of error. Once we understand how risks of error are defined for one problem, we can let statisticians calculate the risks for other more complex problems. Our concern is not with the calculations themselves, but with understanding the general logic that underlies them.

We begin this chapter by discussing a very simple decision. When should we begin to suspect that a coin used in a coin toss is unfair or biased? Ordinarily, we might come to a conclusion based on common sense or intuition. In statistics we take a more systematic approach, relying upon the logic of hypothesis testing and a type of distribution called a sampling distribution. Using this example of the coin toss, we illustrate how statisticians use probability theory to define risks of Type I error.

The Fair Coin Toss

Imagine that you and your friends play a volleyball game each week against a group of criminal justice students from another school. You always begin the game with a coin toss to decide who will receive the ball first. Your opponents bring an old silver dollar, which you have agreed to use for the toss. They choose heads and continue to choose heads each time you play. At first, this does not seem like a problem. However, each week you play, the coin comes up heads and they receive the ball.

Suppose that this happens four straight weeks. Would you begin to become suspicious? What if it went on for six weeks? How many times would they have to win the coin toss in a row for you and your team to accuse them of cheating? Would they have to win for ten or twenty weeks? Perhaps you would hesitate in accusing them too quickly, because you know that even if the coin is fair it sometimes happens that someone is lucky and they just keep on winning. You would want to be fairly certain that the coin was biased before concluding that something was wrong and taking some action.

In everyday life, you are likely to make this decision based on intuition or prior experience. If you ask your classmates, each one is likely to come up with a slightly different number of coin tosses before they become suspicious. Some students may be willing to tolerate only four or five heads in a row before concluding that they have enough evidence to accuse their opponents of cheating. Others may be unwilling to reach this conclusion even after 10 or 15 tosses that come up heads. In part, the disagreement comes from personality differences. But more important, by using guess work or common sense you do not have a common yardstick for deciding how much risk you take in coming to one conclusion or another.

The Multiplication Rule

Statistics provides a more systematic method from which to make this decision. The coin toss can be thought of as a simple test of hypotheses. The research hypothesis, in this sense, is that the coin is biased in favor of your opponents. The null hypothesis is that the coin is fair. Each toss of the coin is an event or a trial that is part of a sample. If you toss the coin 10 times, you have a sample of 10 tosses. The population of cases is infinite since in principle you can flip the coin an unlimited number of times. Type I error is the error of falsely rejecting the null hypothesis that the coin is fair. If you follow the common norm in criminal justice, you would be willing to tolerate no more than a 5 percent risk of this type of error.

In order to calculate that risk you can use a simple rule about probabilities called the **multiplication rule.** The multiplication rule tells you how likely it is to gain a series of events one after another, in this case a series of outcomes in a toss of a coin. The multiplication rule generally used to establish probabilities in statistics is based on the assumption that each event in a sample is **independent.** In the case of the coin toss, this means that the outcome of one toss of a coin is unaffected by what happened in the prior tosses. Each time you toss the coin, it is as if you started with a clean slate. That would seem a fairly reasonable assumption for our problem. What worries us is that the coin is unfair overall, not that it is becoming less or more unfair as time goes on.

An example of a series of events that are not independent is draws from a deck of cards. Each time you draw a card you reduce the number of cards in the deck, thus changing the likelihood of drawing any card in the future. For example, let us say that in your first draw from a deck of 52 cards you drew an ace of spades. In your second draw you cannot draw an ace of spades because you have already removed it from the deck. The likelihood of drawing an ace of spades in the second draw has thus gone from 1 in 52 to 0 in 51. You have also influenced the likelihood of drawing any other card because there are now 51, not 52, cards left in the deck. If you want a series of draws from a deck to be independent one from another, you have to return each card to the deck after you draw it. For example, if you returned the ace of spades to the deck, the chance of choosing it (assuming the deck was mixed again) would be the same as it was in the first draw. The chances of choosing any other card would also be the same because you once again have all 52 cards from which to draw.

The multiplication rule for four independent events is stated in equation 7.1. It says that the likelihood of any series of events, represented as A, B, C, and D, happening one after another is equal to the probability of event A times the probability of event B times the probability of event C times the probability of event D. The rule can be extended to as many events as you like. We have chosen four here, because this was the number of volleyball games we began with. If you wanted to extend the rule, you would simply include the number of additional events to the left side of the equation, for example E and F, and include the probability of each on the right side of the equation [e.g., $P(E) \cdot P(F)$].

Equation 7.1 $P(A\&B\&C\&D) = P(A) \cdot P(B) \cdot P(C) \cdot P(D)$

Extending this to our example of the coin toss is straightforward. The probability of *A* and *B* and *C* and *D* can represent the probability of four tosses in a row coming up heads. Our main problem is to establish what the probability is of a head coming up on any particular toss of the coin. In this, we are helped by our null hypothesis, which states that the coin is fair. If the coin is fair, then there should be an even chance of a head or a tail coming up on any particular toss of the coin. Put differently, the likelihood of a head coming up under the assumption of the null hypothesis that the coin is fair is 0.50.

What, then, does the multiplication rule tell us about the chances of getting four heads in a row if the coin is a fair one? In table 7.1 (1), we calculate that probability by multiplying 0.50 (the likelihood of gaining a head on any toss of the coin) by itself four times, representing four tosses of an unbiased coin. The result is 0.0625. If you had decided at the outset to reject the null hypothesis that the coin is fair after gaining four heads in a row, then you have conducted a type of test. For this test the probability of a Type I error is about 6.25 percent.

This is not enough, however, for you to reject the null hypothesis if you use the norms of criminal justice research. Criminal justice researchers generally want the risk of falsely rejecting the null hypothesis to be less than 5 percent. A bit over 6 percent is still more than the 5 percent significance criterion that is used by convention. So after four tosses you would probably not want to reject the null hypothesis that the coin is fair and confront your opponents. Under this criterion the likelihood of falsely rejecting the null hypothesis would have to be below 0.05.

| Table 7.1 | Probabilities Associated with Tosses of a Fair Coin |

7.1(1)	$P(A \& B \& C \& D)$ $= P(A) \cdot P(B) \cdot P(C) \cdot P(D)$ $= (0.5)(0.5)(0.5)(0.5)$ $= \mathbf{0.0625}$
7.1(2)	$P(A \& B \& C \& D \& E)$ $= P(A) \cdot P(B) \cdot P(C) \cdot P(D) \cdot P(E)$ $= (0.5)(0.5)(0.5)(0.5)(0.5)$ $= \mathbf{0.0313}$
7.1(3)	$P(A \& B \& C \& D \& E \& F \& G \& H \& I \& J)$ $= P(A) \cdot P(B) \cdot P(C) \cdot P(D) \cdot P(E) \cdot P(F) \cdot P(G) \cdot P(H) \cdot P(I) \cdot P(J)$ $= (0.5)(0.5)(0.5)(0.5)(0.5)(0.5)(0.5)(0.5)(0.5)(0.5)$ $= \mathbf{0.0010}$

What about five heads in a row? As illustrated in table 7.1 (2), the multiplication rule tells you that the likelihood of getting five heads in a row if the coin is fair is 0.0313. This is smaller than our threshold of 0.05, and thus would lead you to reject the null hypothesis. Is this consistent with your earlier common-sense conclusions? Students are usually surprised at how quickly they reach the 0.05 significance threshold in this example.

If you had decided at the outset that you would need 10 or 15 heads in a row, you may want to reconsider, given what we have learned from the multiplication rule. The likelihood of getting 10 heads in a row if the coin is fair is only 1 in 1,000 (see table 7.1 (3)). The likelihood of getting 15 heads in a row is even lower, about 3 in 100,000. Of course, if you waited until getting 10 or 15 heads in a row before accusing your opponents, you would be on much stronger ground in challenging them. In this case, you take a very small risk of a Type I error. Nonetheless, the multiplication rule tells us that, even if the coin is fair, it is possible to get 10 or even 15 heads in a row. It just does not happen very often.

The multiplication rule and the logic of hypothesis testing have helped us to make a more systematic decision about when to challenge your opponents about the fairness of the coin. However, the problem as examined so far assumes that the coin will come up heads every time. What if the coin generally comes up heads, but not all the time? For example, what if you play ten games and the coin comes up heads nine times? The situation here is not as one-sided. Nonetheless, it would still seem unlikely for your opponents to win most of the time if the coin were fair. The multiplication rule alone, however, does not allow us to define how likely it is to get such a result.

Different Ways of Getting Similar Results

The multiplication rule allows us to calculate the probability of getting a specific ordering of events. This is fine so far in our coin toss because in each example we have chosen there is only one way to get our outcome. For example, there is only one way to get five heads in five coin tosses, or ten heads in ten coin tosses. In each case, your opponents must toss a head before each game. This would be the situation as well if your opponents tossed tails ten times in ten coin tosses. However, for any outcome in between, there is going to be more than one potential way to achieve the same result.

For example, if your opponents tossed nine heads in ten coin tosses, they could win the coin toss nine times (with a head) and then lose the toss (with a tail) in the tenth game. Or they could lose the first toss (with a tail) and then win the remaining nine. Similarly, they could lose the second, third, fourth, fifth, sixth, seventh, eighth, or ninth coin toss, and win all the others. We can call each of these possible ordering of events, an **arrangement.** As is illustrated in table 7.2, there are ten possible arrangements, or different ways that you could get nine heads in ten coin tosses. In the case of ten heads in ten coin tosses, there is only one possible arrangement.

It is relatively simple to list all of the arrangements for our example of nine heads in ten coin tosses, but this list becomes very cumbersome in practice as the split of events becomes more even. For example, if we were interested in how many ways there are of getting eight heads in ten coin tosses we would have to take into account a much larger number of arrangements. As table 7.3 illustrates, it takes a good deal of effort to list every possible arrangement even for eight heads. In the case of a more even split of events, for example five heads in ten tosses, it becomes extremely cumbersome to list each arrangement one by one. Because of this, we generally use the formula in equation 7.2 to define the number of arrangements in any series of events.

Equation 7.2

$$\binom{N}{r} = \frac{N!}{r!\,(N-r)!}$$

On the left side of this equation we have N "choose" r, where N is the number of events in your sample and r is the number of successes in the total number of events. In our case, N is the number of coin

Table 7.2 Arrangements for Nine Successes in Ten Tosses of a Coin

Arrangement #1	●	○	○	○	○	○	○	○	○	○
Arrangement #2	○	●	○	○	○	○	○	○	○	○
Arrangement #3	○	○	●	○	○	○	○	○	○	○
Arrangement #4	○	○	○	●	○	○	○	○	○	○
Arrangement #5	○	○	○	○	●	○	○	○	○	○
Arrangement #6	○	○	○	○	○	●	○	○	○	○
Arrangement #7	○	○	○	○	○	○	●	○	○	○
Arrangement #8	○	○	○	○	○	○	○	●	○	○
Arrangement #9	○	○	○	○	○	○	○	○	●	○
Arrangement #10	○	○	○	○	○	○	○	○	○	●

○ = Head; ● = Tail

Table 7.3   Arrangements for Eight Successes in Ten Tosses of a Coin

1 : ●●○○○○○○○○   16: ○●○○○○○○●○   31: ○○○○●●○○○○
2 : ●○●○○○○○○○   17: ○●○○○○○○○●   32: ○○○○●○●○○○
3 : ●○○●○○○○○○   18: ○○●●○○○○○○   33: ○○○○●○○●○○
4 : ●○○○●○○○○○   19: ○○●○●○○○○○   34: ○○○○●○○○●○
5 : ●○○○○●○○○○   20: ○○●○○●○○○○   35: ○○○○●○○○○●
6 : ●○○○○○●○○○   21: ○○●○○○●○○○   36: ○○○○○●●○○○
7 : ●○○○○○○●○○   22: ○○●○○○○●○○   37: ○○○○○●○●○○
8 : ●○○○○○○○●○   23: ○○●○○○○○●○   38: ○○○○○●○○●○
9 : ●○○○○○○○○●   24: ○○●○○○○○○●   39: ○○○○○●○○○●
10: ○●●○○○○○○○   25: ○○○●●○○○○○   40: ○○○○○○●●○○
11: ○●○●○○○○○○   26: ○○○●○●○○○○   41: ○○○○○○●○●○
12: ○●○○●○○○○○   27: ○○○●○○●○○○   42: ○○○○○○●○○●
13: ○●○○○●○○○○   28: ○○○●○○○●○○   43: ○○○○○○○●●○
14: ○●○○○○●○○○   29: ○○○●○○○○●○   44: ○○○○○○○●○●
15: ○●○○○○○●○○   30: ○○○●○○○○○●   45: ○○○○○○○○●●

○ = Head; ● = Tail

tosses and r is the number of times that the coin comes up heads. Put together, this statement establishes our question: How many ways are there of gaining r heads in N tosses of a coin? To answer our question we need to solve the right side of the equation. Each of the terms in the equation is defined as a **factorial,** indicated by the symbol !. When we take a factorial of a number, we merely multiply it by all of the whole numbers smaller than it. For example, 3! is equal to (3)(2)(1), or 6. Because factorials get very large very quickly, a table of factorials is presented in appendix 2. Note that 0! = 1.

Applied to our problem of nine heads in ten coin tosses, equation 7.2 is worked out below:

Working It Out

$$\binom{N}{r} = \frac{N!}{r!\,(N-r)!}$$

$$\binom{10}{9} = \frac{10!}{9!\,(10-9)!}$$

$$= \frac{10!}{9!\,1!}$$

$$= \frac{3,628,800}{362,880\,(1)}$$

$$= 10$$

Using this method, we get the same result as before. There are ten possible arrangements to get nine heads in ten tosses of a coin.

Applied to the problem of five heads in ten coin tosses, the usefulness of equation 7.2 becomes even more apparent. There are fully 252 different ways of getting five heads in ten tosses. Listing each would have taken us considerably longer than the calculation below.

Working It Out

$$\binom{N}{r} = \frac{N!}{r!\,(N-r)!}$$

$$\binom{10}{5} = \frac{10!}{5!\,(10-5)!}$$

$$= \frac{10!}{5!\,5!}$$

$$= \frac{3,628,800}{(120)\,(120)}$$

$$= 252$$

Solving More Complex Problems

Now that we have a method for calculating arrangements, we can return to our original problem, which was to define the probability of your opponents tossing the coin in ten games and getting heads nine times. Because there are ten different ways of getting nine heads in ten coin tosses, you need to add up the probabilities associated with each of these ten sequences. This is what is done in table 7.4. The multiplication rule is used to calculate the probabilities for each sequence, or arrangement, under the assumption of the null hypothesis that the coin is fair. Because we assume that the chances of gaining a head or a tail are even, the probability of any event, whether a head or a tail, is 0.50, and the probability of a sequence of ten events is always the same. This makes our task easier. But it is important to note that if the null hypothesis specified an uneven split (for example, 0.75 for a head and 0.25 for a tail), then each of the sequences would have a different probability associated with it. In any case the likelihood of getting any one of these sequences is about 0.001, rounded to the nearest one thousandth. When we add together the ten sequences, we get a probability of 0.010.

Table 7.4   The Sum of Probabilities for All Arrangements of Nine Heads in Ten Tosses of a Fair Coin

											PROBABILITY
Arrangement #1	●	○	○	○	○	○	○	○	○	○	0.001
Arrangement #2	○	●	○	○	○	○	○	○	○	○	0.001
Arrangement #3	○	○	●	○	○	○	○	○	○	○	0.001
Arrangement #4	○	○	○	●	○	○	○	○	○	○	0.001
Arrangement #5	○	○	○	○	●	○	○	○	○	○	0.001
Arrangement #6	○	○	○	○	○	●	○	○	○	○	0.001
Arrangement #7	○	○	○	○	○	○	●	○	○	○	0.001
Arrangement #8	○	○	○	○	○	○	○	●	○	○	0.001
Arrangement #9	○	○	○	○	○	○	○	○	●	○	0.001
Arrangement #10	○	○	○	○	○	○	○	○	○	●	0.001
									Total Probability:		**0.01**

Probability of throwing each arrangement of 10 throws:
$$= P(A) \cdot P(B) \cdot P(C) \cdot P(D) \cdot P(E) \cdot P(F) \cdot P(G) \cdot P(H) \cdot P(I) \cdot P(J)$$
$$= (0.5)(0.5)(0.5)(0.5)(0.5)(0.5)(0.5)(0.5)(0.5)$$
$$= 0.001$$

This means that we would expect to get nine heads in ten coin tosses only about 1 in 100 times in the long run if the coin was fair. But is this the total amount of risk we face in rejecting the null hypothesis? The answer to this question is no, although it may be difficult at first to understand why. If we are willing to reject the null hypothesis based on an outcome of nine heads in ten trials, then we are, by implication, also willing to reject the null hypothesis if our outcome is ten heads in ten trials. In calculating our risk of error, we must add together the risk of all potential outcomes that would lead us to reject the null hypothesis. This is why when testing hypotheses we generally do not begin with an estimate of the specific probability associated with a single outcome, but rather with the distribution of probabilities of all possible outcomes. Such a distribution is called a **probability distribution.**

The Binomial Distribution

To construct a probability distribution for all of the possible outcomes of ten coin tosses, we could continue to compute the number of permutations and the likelihood of any particular arrangement. However, equation 7.3 provides us with a more direct method for calculating the probabilities associated with each of the potential outcomes in our sample. Equation 7.3 is generally defined as the **binomial formula,** and the distribution created from it is called the **binomial distribution.** As the name suggests, the binomial distribution is concerned with events in which there are only two possible outcomes—in our example, heads and tails.

Equation 7.3

$$P\binom{N}{r} = \frac{N!}{r!\,(N-r)!}\,p^r(1-p)^{N-r}$$

The binomial formula may look confusing, but most of it is familiar from material we have already covered in the chapter. The left-hand side of the equation represents the quantity in which we are interested—the probability of getting r successes (in our case r heads) in a sample of N events (for us, ten tosses of a coin). The first part of the equation provides us with the number of arrangements for that number of heads. This quantity is then multiplied by $p^r(1-p)^{N-r}$, where p is the probability of a successful outcome (a head) under the null hypothesis and r is the number of successes. This formula gives us the probability associated with each arrangement. Although this part of the equation looks somewhat different from the multiplication rule we used earlier, as the example below illustrates, it provides a shortcut for getting the same result.

We have already calculated the likelihood of getting nine or ten heads in ten coin tosses. To complete the probability distribution, we need to compute probabilities associated with zero through eight heads as well. Let us begin with eight heads in ten coin tosses of an unbiased coin:

$$P\binom{10}{8} = \frac{10!}{8!\,(10-8)!}\,(0.5)^8\,(1-0.5)^{10-8}$$

Step 1: Calculating the number of arrangements

Working It Out

$$\binom{10}{8} = \frac{10!}{8!\,(10-8)!}$$

$$= \frac{10!}{8!\,2!}$$

$$= \frac{3,628,800}{(40,320)\,(2)}$$

$$= 45$$

In step 1 we simply follow the same method as earlier in establishing the number of ways there are of getting eight heads in ten tosses of a coin. Our conclusion is that there are 45 different arrangements.

Step 2: Calculating the probability of any specific arrangement

Working It Out $p^r(1-p)^{N-r}$

$$= (0.5)^8(1-0.5)^{10-8}$$

$$= (0.5)^8(0.5)^2$$

$$= (0.5)^{10}$$

$$= 0.00098$$

Step 2 provides us with the likelihood of getting any particular arrangement under the assumption of the null hypothesis that the coin is fair. As should be apparent, the outcome of this part of the equation is the same as would be obtained using the multiplication rule. This is because the expression $(0.50)^{10}$ means that we multiply the quantity 0.50 by itself 10 times. Using the multiplication rule we would have done just that.

Step 3: Combining the two outcomes

Working It Out $P\left(\dfrac{N}{r}\right) = \dfrac{N!}{r!\,(N-r)!}\,p^r(1-p)^{N-r}$

$$P\left(\frac{10}{8}\right) = (45)\,(0.00098)$$

$$= 0.0441$$

Combining the two outcomes, we find that the likelihood of tossing eight heads in ten tosses of a fair coin is about 0.044. In table 7.5 we calculate the probabilities associated with all the other potential outcomes in this binomial distribution: 0, 1, 2, 3, 4, 5, 6, and 7 heads in ten tosses. The resulting probability distribution is displayed in table 7.6 (page 129).

Table 7.5   Computation of Probability Distribution for Ten Tosses of a Fair Coin

	$\binom{N}{r} = \dfrac{N!}{r!\,(N-r)!}$	$\binom{N}{r} p^r (1-p)^{N-r}$
0 Heads	$\dfrac{3{,}628{,}800}{1(10-0)!} = \dfrac{3{,}628{,}800}{3{,}628{,}800} = 1$	$1(0.00098) = 0.0010$
1 Head	$\dfrac{3{,}628{,}800}{1(10-1)!} = \dfrac{3{,}628{,}800}{362{,}880} = 10$	$10(0.00098) = 0.0098$
2 Heads	$\dfrac{3{,}628{,}800}{2(10-2)!} = \dfrac{3{,}628{,}800}{80{,}640} = 45$	$45(0.00098) = 0.0441$
3 Heads	$\dfrac{3{,}628{,}800}{6(10-3)!} = \dfrac{3{,}628{,}800}{30{,}240} = 120$	$120(0.00098) = 0.1176$
4 Heads	$\dfrac{3{,}628{,}800}{24(10-4)!} = \dfrac{3{,}628{,}800}{17{,}280} = 210$	$210(0.00098) = 0.2058$
5 Heads	$\dfrac{3{,}628{,}800}{120(10-5)!} = \dfrac{3{,}628{,}800}{14{,}400} = 252$	$252(0.00098) = 0.2470$
6 Heads	$\dfrac{3{,}628{,}800}{720(10-6)!} = \dfrac{3{,}628{,}800}{17{,}280} = 210$	$210(0.00098) = 0.2058$
7 Heads	$\dfrac{3{,}628{,}800}{5{,}040(10-7)!} = \dfrac{3{,}628{,}800}{30{,}240} = 120$	$120(0.00098) = 0.1176$
8 Heads	$\dfrac{3{,}628{,}800}{40{,}320(10-8)!} = \dfrac{3{,}628{,}800}{80{,}640} = 45$	$45(0.00098) = 0.0441$
9 Heads	$\dfrac{3{,}628{,}800}{3{,}628{,}80(10-9)!} = \dfrac{3{,}628{,}800}{362{,}880} = 10$	$10(0.00098) = 0.0098$
10 Heads	$\dfrac{3{,}628{,}800}{3{,}628{,}800(10-10)!} = \dfrac{3{,}628{,}800}{3{,}628{,}800} = 1$	$1(0.00098) = 0.0010$

$$\Sigma = 1.0*$$

*The total in the last column is in fact slightly greater than 100%. This is due to rounding the numbers to the nearest decimal place in order to make the calculation more manageable.

Table 7.6   Probability Distribution for Ten Tosses of a Fair Coin

0 Heads	0.001
1 Heads	0.010
2 Heads	0.044
3 Heads	0.118
4 Heads	0.206
5 Heads	0.247
6 Heads	0.206
7 Heads	0.118
8 Heads	0.044
9 Heads	0.010
10 Heads	0.001

The probability distribution for ten tosses of a fair coin illustrates how likely it is to get any particular outcome. All of the outcomes together add up to a probability of 1.[1] Put differently, there is a 100 percent chance that in ten tosses of a coin you will get one of these 11 potential outcomes. This is obvious, but the probability distribution allows you to illustrate this fact. Following what our common sense tells us, it also shows that an outcome somewhere in the middle of the distribution is most likely. If the coin is fair, then we should more often than not get about an even split of heads and tails.

The largest proportion (0.247) in the sampling distribution is found at five heads in ten tosses of a coin. As you move farther away from the center of the distribution, the likelihood of any particular result declines. The smallest probabilities are associated with gaining either all heads or no heads. Like many of the distributions that we use in statistics, this distribution is symmetrical. This means that there are the same probabilities associated with outcomes on both its sides.

Using the Binomial Distribution to Estimate Type I Error

Using this probability distribution, we can now return to our problem of identifying the risks of error associated with rejecting the null hypothesis. Earlier we suggested that you might want to use a 5 percent

---

[1] Due to rounding error, the total for our example is actually slightly larger than 1 (see table 7.5).

level of Type 1 error in rejecting the null hypothesis, in part because this is the standard or conventional significance level used by most criminal justice researchers. Using this level, when would you be willing to reject the null hypothesis that the coin is fair and confront your opponents?

At first glance, you might decide to do this for outcomes 0, 1, 2, 8, 9, and 10. Each of these is below the threshold of 0.05 that we have suggested. However, at the outset we stated in our research hypothesis that we were concerned not that the coin was biased per se, but that it was biased against your team. This means that we set up our hypotheses in such a way that we would reject the null hypothesis only if the outcomes were mostly heads. Although it just as unlikely to toss zero, one, or two heads as eight, nine, or ten heads, your research hypothesis states your intention not to consider the former outcomes.

What of eight, nine, or ten heads? As we noted earlier, in calculating the risk of a Type I error you must add up the probabilities associated with all the outcomes for which you would reject the null hypothesis. So for example, if we want to know the risk of falsely rejecting the null hypothesis on the basis of eight heads in ten coin tosses, we have to add together the risk associated with eight, nine, and ten heads in ten tosses. The question we ask is, what is the risk of falsely rejecting the null hypothesis if we gain eight or more heads in a coin toss? The total risk here would be about 0.055, which is greater than our threshold of 0.05 for rejecting the null hypothesis. It is too large an outcome for you to confront your opponents and accuse them of cheating.

In the case of nine heads, the outcome is well below the threshold of Type 1 error we have chosen. By adding together the probabilities associated with gaining nine or ten heads in ten coin tosses, we arrive at a risk of falsely rejecting the null hypothesis of 0.011. For ten heads, as we noted earlier, the risk of a Type 1 error is even lower (0.001). Because there are no outcomes more extreme than ten heads in our distribution, we do not have to add any probabilities to it to arrive at an estimate of the Type 1 error.

You would take a very large risk of Type I error if you had decided in advance to reject the null hypothesis that the coin is fair based on six heads in ten tosses of a coin. Here, you would have to add the probabilities associated with six (0.206), seven (0.118), eight (0.044), nine (0.010), and ten heads (0.001).

Probability Distributions and Sampling Distributions

As the coin toss example illustrates, probability distributions play a very important role in inferential statistics. They allow us to define the risk of a Type I error that we take in rejecting the null hypothesis. Although most probability distributions we use in statistics are considerably more difficult to develop and involve much more complex mathematical reasoning than the binomial distribution, they follow a similar logic to what we have used here. For each distribution, statisticians use probabilities to define the likelihood of gaining particular outcomes. What we have learned here provides a basic understanding for how probability distributions are developed. In later chapters, we will rely on already calculated distributions. However, you should keep in mind that steps similar to those we have taken here have been used to construct these distributions.

Ordinarily in statistics we call the probability distribution that is used to make inferences from a sample to a population, a **sampling distribution.** A sampling distribution may be defined as a distribution of outcomes of a very large number of samples of a given size. In principle, one could create a sampling distribution by drawing thousands and thousands of samples from a population. For example, in the case of our coin toss, we could create a sampling distribution by taking a fair coin and flipping it ten times over and over again for thousands of trials. If we recorded the outcome for each trial and placed our results in a frequency distribution we would have a sampling distribution for a sample of ten tosses of a fair coin.

A probability distribution gives us the same result, and it saves us a good deal of effort. It relies on probability theory, rather than a burdensome effort to collect samples in the real world, to identify the likelihood of different outcomes in a sample. In the case of the binomial distribution, we rely on the multiplication rule and our understanding of arrangements of outcomes to identify the probabilities associated with specific outcomes. When we find that the likelihood of getting ten heads in ten tosses of a fair coin is 0.001, we are also saying that we expect one in every thousand samples of ten tosses of a fair coin to have an outcome of ten heads. Our probability distribution is in some sense a better estimate than that we are likely to gain from real samples, because it gives us the outcomes one would expect in a perfect world. In the real world, we might flip the coin slightly differently as we get tired, or the coin might become worn on one side or another, thus affecting the outcomes we gain. In probability theory, each toss is exactly the same as the one that came before.

You might ask why we assign the special term sampling distribution to probability distributions that are associated with statistical inference. The reason in good part is to remind us of the function of a sampling distribution and the problem that it solves. As we emphasized in the preceding chapters, samples vary one from another. This is what makes it so difficult to make inferences from a sample to a population. We can never be sure what the actual value of the parameter is based on a sample statistic.

However, as illustrated in the binomial distribution, samples drawn from the same population vary in a systematic way in the long run. It is very unlikely to get a sample in which there are ten heads in ten coin tosses from a fair coin. On the other hand, it is very likely to draw a sample in which at least five heads are tossed in ten tosses. Sampling distributions provide us with a precise method for defining risks of error in statistical tests of significance.

Chapter Summary

By using the **multiplication rule,** we can calculate the probability of obtaining a series of results in a specific order. The number of **arrangements** is the number of different ways of obtaining the same result. The total probability of obtaining any result is the individual probability multiplied by the number of different possible arrangements. The **probability distribution** is the distribution of the probabilities of all the possible outcomes. Whereas our intuition tends to produce inconsistent results, the probability distribution enables us to define in a systematic way the risk we take of making a Type I error.

The **binomial distribution** is the probability distribution for events with only two possible outcomes—success or failure, heads or tails, etc. It is calculated using the **binomial formula.** When deciding whether the result achieved passes the desired threshold for rejecting the null hypothesis, it is important to remember to take a cumulative total of risk.

Whereas a sample distribution is the distribution of the results of one sample, a **sampling distribution** is the distribution of outcomes of a very large number of samples, each of the same size. A probability distribution uses the laws of probability to calculate a sampling distribution without the need to take countless samples. The principal problem of inferential statistics is how we can make decisions about a population from a sample, when samples vary each time they are taken. But because repeated samples drawn from the same population vary in a systematic way, calculating a probability distribution can help to solve this problem.

Key Terms

Arrangements The different ways, or specific ordering of events, that result in a single outcome. For example, there is only one arrangement for gaining the outcome of ten heads in ten tosses of a coin. There are, however, ten ways, or ten different arrangements, for gaining the outcome nine heads in ten tosses of a coin.

Binomial Distribution The probability distribution for an event that has only two possible outcomes.

Binomial Formula The means of determining the probability that a given set of binomial events will occur in all its possible arrangements.

Factorial The product of a number and all the positive whole numbers lower than it.

Independent Two events are statistically independent when the occurrence of one does not impact upon the occurrence of the other.

Multiplication Rule The means for determining the probability that a series of events will jointly occur.

Probability Distribution A theoretical distribution, consisting of the probabilities expected in the long run for each possible outcome of an event.

Sampling Distribution A probability distribution of all the results of a very large number of samples, each one of the same size and drawn from the same population under the same conditions.

Symbols and Formulas

!	Factorial
r	Number of successes
N	Number of trials
p	The probability of a success

To determine the probability of events A, B, C, and D occurring jointly under the assumption of independence (the multiplication rule):

$$P(A\&B\&C\&D) = P(A) \cdot P(B) \cdot P(C) \cdot P(D)$$

To determine the number of arrangements of any combination of events:

$$\binom{N}{r} = \frac{N!}{r!\,(N-r)!}$$

To determine the probability of any binomial outcome occurring in all its possible arrangements (the binomial formula):

$$P\binom{N}{r} = \frac{N!}{r!\,(N-r)!}\,p^r(1-p)^{N-r}$$

Exercises

7.1   All of Kate's children are boys.

a Intuitively, how many boys would Kate have to have in succession before you would be willing to say with some certainty that for some biological reason, she is more likely to give birth to boys than girls?

b Now calculate the number of successive births required before you could make such a decision statistically with a 5 percent risk of error.

c How many successive boys would have to be born before you would be prepared to come to this conclusion with only a 1 percent risk of error?

7.2   The Federal Bureau of Investigation trains sniffer dogs to find explosive material. At the end of the training, Lucy, the FBI's prize dog is let loose in a field with four unmarked parcels, of which one contains Semtex explosives. The exercise is repeated three times, and on each occasion, Lucy successfully identifies the suspicious parcel.

a What is the chance of an untrained dog performing such a feat? (Assume that the untrained dog would always approach one of the parcels at random.)

b If, in the initial exercise, there were five parcels instead of four and the exercise was carried out only twice instead of three times, would the chances of the untrained dog finding the single suspicious parcel be greater or less?

7.3 Alex, an attorney, wishes to call eight witnesses to court for an important case. In his mind, he has categorized them into three "strong" witnesses and five "weaker" witnesses. He now wishes to make a tactical decision on the order in which to call the strong and the weaker witnesses.

For Example:

Strong Weak Weak Strong Weak Weak Weak Strong

a In how many different sequences can he call his strong and weaker witnesses?

b If Alex decides that one of his three "strong" witnesses is in fact more suited to the "weaker" category, how many options does he now have?

7.4 In a soccer match held at a low-security prison, the inmates beat the guards 4 to 2.

a How many different arrangements are there for the order in which the goals were scored?

b What would your answer be if the final score was 5 to 1?

7.5 At the end of each year, the police force chooses its "Police Officer of the Year." In spite of the fact that there is an equal number of men and women on the force, in the last 15 years, 11 of the winners have been men, and 4 have been women. Paul has been investigating whether women and men are treated differently in the police force.

a Do these figures provide Paul with a reasonable basis to suspect that the sex of the officer is an active factor? Explain your answer.

b Looking back further into the records, Paul discovers that for the three years before the 15-year span initially examined, a woman was chosen each time. Does this affect his conclusion? Explain your answer.

7.6 Tracy, a teacher, gives her class a ten-question test based on the homework she assigned the night before. She strongly suspects that Mandy, a lazy student, did not do the homework. Tracy is surprised to see that of the ten questions, Mandy scores seven correct answers. What is the probability that Mandy could have successfully guessed seven of the ten answers to the questions if:

a The questions all required an answer of "true" or "false"?

b The questions were all in the "multiple choice" format, with students having to circle one correct answer from a list of five choices?

7.7   After a recent supermarket robbery, four eye witnesses each reported seeing a "man with glasses" fleeing from the scene. The police suspect Eddy, and make up an identity parade of five men with glasses. Eddy takes his place in the parade alongside four randomly chosen stooges. Of the four eye witnesses who are brought in, three identify Eddy and the fourth points to one of the stooges. The detective in charge decides that there is enough evidence to bring Eddy to trial.

a The detective's superior wishes to know the probability that Eddy could have been chosen by three out of the four eye witnesses if each witness had chosen a member of the identity parade entirely at random. What is the probability?

b What is the probability of Eddy being chosen at random by only two of the four witnesses?

7.8   A gang of five child thieves draws straws each time before they go shoplifting. Whoever draws the short straw is the one who does the stealing. By tradition, Anton, the leader, always draws first. In the four occasions that the gang has performed this ritual, Anton has drawn the short straw three times. Should he accuse his fellow gang members of rigging the draw:

a If he is willing to take a 5 percent risk of falsely accusing his friends?

b If he is willing to take only a 1 percent risk of falsely accusing his friends?

7.9   Baron, a gambler, plays 11 rounds at a casino roulette wheel, each time placing a $100 note on either black or red.

a Construct a table to illustrate the binomial distribution of Baron's possible successes and failures for each of the 11 rounds.

b The casino croupiers have been told to "inform the management" if a client's winning streak arouses suspicion that he might be cheating. The threshold of suspicion is set at 0.005. How many successes does Baron need to score from the 11 trials to arouse the management's suspicion?

7.10   Nicola is playing roulette on an adjacent table. In 12 successive spins of the wheel, she places a $100 note on either the first third (numbers 1–12), the second third (numbers 13–24) or the final third (numbers 25–36).

a Construct a table to illustrate the binomial distribution of Nicola's possible successes and failures for each of the 12 spins.

b How many times out of the 12 would Nicola need to win, to arouse the suspicion of the casino manager that she was cheating, if the management policy is to limit the risk of falsely accusing a customer to 0.001?

Steps in a Statistical Test:
Using the Binomial Distribution
to Make Decisions about Hypotheses

statistical assumptions

What Type of Measurement Is Being Used?

Are Assumptions Made about the Population Distribution?

What Is the Sampling Method Being Used?

What Are the Hypotheses?

sampling distribution

Which Sampling Distribution Is Appropriate?

significance level

What Is the Rejection Region?

Where Is It Placed?

Should a One-Tailed or a Two-Tailed Test Be Used?

test statistic and decision

What Is the Test Statistic?

How Is a Final Decision Made?

IN THE PREVIOUS CHAPTER we saw how probability theory was used to identify the risk of type I error in testing hypotheses. But you cannot simply rely upon mathematical calculations to determine whether to reject the null hypothesis. You must make sure at the outset that the methods used are appropriate to the problem examined. You must state clearly the assumptions made. You must define the specific hypotheses that are tested and the specific significance criteria that are to be used. It is best to take a careful step by step approach to tests of statistical significance. Using this approach you will be much less likely to make serious mistakes in developing such tests.

In this chapter we introduce the basic elements of this step-by-step approach. To place this approach in context, we illustrate each step using a specific research problem that can be addressed using the binomial distribution. Although we use the binomial distribution as an example, you should not lose sight of the fact that our purpose here is to establish a general model for presenting tests of statistical inference that can be used whichever sampling distribution is chosen.

The Problem: The Impacts of Problem-oriented Policing on Disorderly Activity at Violent-Crime Hot Spots

In Jersey City, New Jersey, researchers developed a problem-oriented policing program that was directed at violent-crime hot spots.[1] Places in the city, for example, certain public areas such as a train station or

---

[1] See Anthony Braga (1996), "Solving Violent Crime Problems: An Evaluation of the Jersey City Police Department's Pilot Program to Control Violent Crime Places," unpublished dissertation, Rutgers University, Newark, N.J..

street where there was a very high level of violent-crime arrests or emergency calls to the police, were selected. Jersey City police officers, in cooperation with staff of the Rutgers University Center for Crime Prevention Studies, developed strategies to solve violent-crime problems at 11 places. The strategies followed a problem-oriented policing {POP} approach,[2] in which police first collect a wide variety of information about each hot spot, analyze that information to identify the source of the problem, develop tailor-made responses to do something about the problem, and finally assess whether their approach actually had an impact.

The evaluation involved a number of different components. One part of the research sought to identify whether "disorderly" activity at the violent-crime places had declined during the period of the study. For example, the researchers wanted to see whether the number of loiterers or homeless people had been reduced as a result of the efforts of the police. The treatment areas were compared to a matched group, or control group, of similar but untreated violent-crime places. Table 8.1 presents the overall results of pre- and posttest comparisons of outcomes for the 11 matched pairs of locations. In 10 of the 11 pairs, the experimental hot spots (receiving POP intervention) improved as compared with the control locations.

The research question asked by the evaluator is whether the POP approach impacts upon disorderly activity at violent-crime places. The statistical problem faced is that the 11 comparisons are only a sample of such comparisons. What conclusions can the researcher make regarding the larger population of violent-crime hot spots?

Assumptions: Laying the Foundations for Statistical Inference

When we rely upon statistics to make a decision about hypotheses, we call the process used a **statistical test of significance.** The first step in a statistical test of significance is to establish the **assumptions** upon which the test is based. These assumptions form the foundation of a test. No matter how elegant the statistics used or the approach

---

[2] Problem-oriented policing is an important new approach to police work formulated by Herman Goldstein of the University of Wisconsin Law School [see H. Goldstein (1990), *Problem-Oriented Policing* (New York: McGraw-Hill)].

Table 8.1   Results at Treatment and Control Locations Derived from Observations of Disorderly Behavior before and after Intervention

TRIAL	PLACE	OUTCOME
1	**Journal Square East** Newport Mall	−
2	**Stegman & Ocean** Clerk & Carteret	−
3	**Glenwood & JFK** Journal Square West	+
4	**Bergen & Academy** Westside & Duncan	−
5	**Westside & Clendenny** Franklin & Palisade	−
6	**Belmont & Monticello** MLK & Wade	−
7	**MLK & Atlantic** Neptune & Ocean	−
8	**MLK & Armstrong** Ocean & Eastern	−
9	**Westside & Virginia** JFK & Communipaw	−
10	**Park & Prescott** Dwight & Bergen	−
11	**Old Bergen & Danforth** Bramhall & Arlington	−

Note: Experimental locations are listed in bold face type.
+ = Relative increase in levels of postintervention incivilities
− = Relative decrease in levels of postintervention incivilities

taken, if the assumptions upon which they are built are not solid, then the whole structure of the test is brought into question.

Level of Measurement

Our first assumption is related to the type of measurement used. Different types of statistical tests demand different levels of measurement. Accordingly, it is important to state at the outset the type of measurement required by a test. For the binomial test, which is based on the binomial distribution, a nominal binary measure is required. A binary measure has only two possible outcomes, as was the case with the coin toss example in the last chapter. The type of outcome measure used for evaluating the impacts of problem-oriented policing on disorderly activity—whether the treatment hot spot improved (or got worse) as compared with the control location—fits this assumption. In stating our assumptions (as is done at the end of this section), we include a specific definition of the level of measurement required: *Level of Measurement: Nominal binary scale.*

Shape of the Population Distribution

The second assumption refers to the shape of the population distribution. In general, in statistical inference we are concerned with two types of tests. In the first type—termed **parametric tests**—we make an assumption about the shape of the population distribution. For example, in a number of tests we will examine in later chapters, there is a requirement that the scores of the variable for the population to which you infer, be normally distributed.

The second type of test does not make a specific assumption regarding the population distribution. These tests are called **nonparametric** or **distribution-free tests.** The advantage of non-parametric tests is that we make fewer assumptions. The disadvantage is that nonparametric tests do not allow us to analyze data at higher levels of measurement. They are generally appropriate for only nominal and ordinal scales. The binomial test is a nonparametric test. Accordingly, in stating our assumptions we write: *Population Distribution: No assumption made.*

Sampling Method

The third assumption concerns the sampling method used. When we conduct research we want our sample to be a good representation of the population from which it is drawn. Put in statistical terms, we want our study to have high **external validity.**

Let us suppose you are interested in attitudes toward the death penalty. Would a sample of your friends provide an externally valid sample of all Americans? Clearly not, because a sample of only your friends is likely not to include age or ethnic or class differences that typify the U.S. population. Even if we use your friends as a sample of U.S. college students, we can still identify threats to the external validity of your study. Colleges have differing criteria for admission, so it is not likely that one college will be representative of all colleges. Even as a sample of students at your college, your friends may not provide a valid sample. They may be drawn primarily from a specific year of college, or have other characteristics that make them attractive as friends but also mean that they are a poor representation of others in the college.

How can we draw a **representative sample**? The most straightforward approach is to choose cases at random from the population. This type of sampling is called **random sampling.** Random samples are assumed to have high external validity compared with what may be termed **convenience samples.** A convenience sample consists of whatever subjects are readily available to the researcher. Your friends form a convenience sample of students at your college or of all college students.

It is important to note that convenience samples are not always bad samples. For example, if you choose to examine one prison on the basis that it is thought to provide a cross section of the different types of prisoners in the United States, then you might argue that it is a representative sample. However, if you use a convenience sample, such as a single prison, you must always be wary of potential threats to external validity. Convenience samples are prone to systematic biases precisely because they are convenient. The characteristics that make them easy for the researcher to define are likely as well to differentiate them in one way or another from the population the researcher seeks to study.

Statistical tests of significance generally assume that the researcher has used a type of random sampling called **independent random sampling.** An independent random sample not only requires that cases be identified at random, but that the selection of cases be independent. As discussed in the previous chapter, two events are statistically independent when the occurrence of one does not impact upon the occurrence of the other. In sampling, this means that the choice of one case or group of cases will not have any impact upon the choice of another case or group of cases. This is a useful assumption in assuring the external validity of a study because it prevents biases that might be brought into the process of sampling.

For example, suppose you wanted to select 1,000 prisoners from the population of all prisoners in the United States. Each time you select a prisoner for your sample you use a random method of selection. However, prison officials have told you that if you select one prisoner from a cell then you cannot select any other prisoner from that cell. Accordingly, after each selection of a prisoner, you must remove all of his cellmates from your **sampling frame,** or universe of eligible cases. The result is that there are now systematic reasons why you might suspect that your sample is not representative of the population.

In order to ensure independent random sampling, the same population of cases must be used in drawing each case for a sample. If we use the same population each time we select a case, then the choice of one case cannot impact upon the choice of another. For every selection, the sampling frame must remain exactly the same. Although this method ensures independence, it also means that a particular case may be selected more than once. For example, you may choose a particular prisoner as case number five in your sample. Because you must use the same sampling frame each time you select a case, that prisoner is returned to the sampling frame after selection. Later in your study, you might choose that prisoner again.

While **sampling with replacement,** or returning sampled cases to the sampling frame after each selection, makes statistical sense, it often does not make practical sense when carrying out research in the real world. If you are conducting an interview study, for example, independent random sampling would suggest that individuals may be interviewed more than once. It is likely in this regard that subjects would find it strange that they are being reinterviewed using the same interview schedule. Moreover, their responses are likely to be influenced by their knowledge of the survey. If a subject or place is chosen twice in a study that involves a specific treatment or intervention, then by implication, subjects or places should also be given the treatment after each selection. Here there is the difficulty that it may be harmful to provide treatment more than once.

Even when there are no specific practical barriers to sampling with replacement, it is difficult to explain to practitioners, or even many researchers, why it is that an individual may appear twice in the same sample. As a result, many, if not most, criminal justice studies do not replace individuals in the sampling frame once they are selected. Although this represents a formal violation of the assumptions of your test, in most cases its impact on your test result is negligible. This is because samples are generally very small relative to populations, and, thus, in practice there is little chance of selecting a case more than once even when sampling with replacement. If, however, your sample reaches one-fifth or more of the size of your population you may want to include a correction factor in your test.[3]

---

[3] The correction factor adjusts your test to account for the fact that you have not allowed individuals to be selected more than once from the population. When not including a correction factor, you make it more difficult to reject the null hypothesis. That is, the inclusion of a correction factor will make it easier for you to reject the null hypothesis. One problem that criminal justice scholars are likely to face in using a correction factor is that they often want to infer to populations that are beyond their sampling frame. For example, a study of police patrol at hot spots in a particular city may sample 50 of 200 hot spots in the city during a certain month. However, researchers may be interested in making inferences to hot spots generally in the city (and not just those that exist in a particular month) or even to hot spots in other places. For those inferences, it would be misleading to adjust the test statistic based on the small size of the sampling frame. For a discussion of how to correct for sampling without replacement, see Paul S. Levy and Stanley Lemeshow (1991), *Sampling of Populations: Methods and Applications* (New York: Wiley).

For the purposes of our example statistical test we assume that re-searchers in the Jersey City POP study sampled cases randomly from a large population of hot spots during the sample selection month. Because it would not have been practical to implement treatments more than once at any site, the researchers did not sample with re-placement. The binomial test, however, as with most tests of signifi-cance examined in this book, assumes independent random sam-pling. Accordingly, in stating our assumptions, it is important to note both the requirement for this test and our failure to meet that require-ment. Therefore we state our assumption: *Sampling Method: Inde-pendent random sampling (no replacement, sample is small relative to population).*

Throughout this text we state the assumptions of a test and then place any violations of assumptions in parentheses. This is good prac-tice, as it will alert you to the fact that in many studies there are viola-tions of assumptions of one type or another. Some of those violations are not important. For example, not sampling with replacement in this study does not affect the test outcome because the population of hot spots is assumed to be very large relative to the sample. However, you will sometimes find more serious violations of assumptions. In those cases you will have to take a more critical view of the results of the test.

It is good practice to define not only the sampling method used but also the sampling frame of your study. In our example, we can make inferences based on our random sample to the population of hot spots in Jersey City during the month of sample selection. Accord-ingly, we state in our assumptions: *Sampling Frame: Hot spots of vio-lent crime in one month in Jersey City.*

Our sampling frame reminds us of the specific population to which our sample infers. However, researchers usually want to infer beyond the specific population identified by their sampling frame. For exam-ple, the population of interest for the POP study is likely to be hot spots throughout the year, not just those in a specific month. More likely, researchers will want to infer to violent-crime hot spots gener-ally and not just those in Jersey City.

We cannot assume that our sample is a representative sample for these inferences based on our sampling method, since these popula-tions did not constitute our sampling frame. However, we can ask whether our sample is likely to provide valid inferences to those populations. In the case of hot spots in Jersey City, we would need to question whether there is any reason to suspect that hot spots chosen in the month of study were different from those that would be found in other months of the year. For inferences to the population of hot spots in other locations, we would have to assume that Jersey City hot spots are similar to those in other places and would respond similarly to POP interventions. In making any inference beyond your sampling frame you must be cautious to identify all possible threats to external validity.

The Hypotheses

The final assumptions we make in a test of statistical inference refer to the hypotheses of our study. As discussed in chapter 6, hypotheses are developed from the research questions raised in a project. Hypotheses must be stated before the researcher collects outcome data for a study. If hypotheses are stated only after data has been collected and analyzed, the researcher might be tempted to make changes in the hypotheses that unfairly impact the statistical tests of significance that are conducted.

As discussed in chapter 6, the researcher ordinarily begins by defining the research hypothesis. In the problem-oriented policing study, we might state our research hypothesis in three different ways:

Hypothesis 1. Incivilities in treatment hot spots decline relative to incivilities in control hot spots after POP intervention.

Hypothesis 2. Incivilities in treatment hot spots increase relative to incivilities in control hot spots after POP intervention.

Hypothesis 3. The level of incivilities in treatment hot spots relative to incivilities in control hot spots changes after POP intervention.

The first two research hypotheses are called **directional hypotheses** because they specify the direction or type of relationship that is expected. For example, hypothesis 1 is concerned only with whether the POP program is successful in reducing incivilities. If the researcher adopts this hypothesis then he or she is stating that the statistical test employed will not be concerned with the second hypothesis, that the intervention makes matters worse and increases incivilities. The third hypothesis is a **nondirectional hypothesis.** In this case, the researcher is interested in testing the possibility that the intervention improves hot spots or makes them worse.

In the POP study, researchers wanted to assess both positive and negative outcomes. Although they believed that problem-oriented policing should reduce incivilities at violent-crime hot spots, they did not want to preclude a finding at the outset that the program actually made matters worse. Accordingly, they used a nondirectional research hypothesis: "The level of incivilities in treatment hot spots relative to incivilities in control hot spots changes after POP intervention." The null hypothesis is: "The level of incivilities in treatment hot spots does not change relative to incivilities in control hot spots after POP intervention."

In practice, the null hypothesis may be stated in terms of probabilities, just as we could state the coin toss hypothesis in the last chapter in terms of probabilities. In this study, the researchers examine (for each matched pair of hot spots) whether the hot spot that received the problem-oriented policing intervention improved or got worse relative to the control location. The null hypothesis suggests that it is just as likely for either the treatment or control hot spots to improve. Put in terms of probabilities, there is a 0.50 chance of success ($P = 0.50$) for the intervention under the null hypothesis. The research hypothesis represents all other possible outcomes ($P \neq 0.50$). Stating our assumptions we write:

Hypotheses: H_0: The level of incivilities in treatment hot spots does not change relative to incivilities in control hot spots after POP intervention, $P = 0.50$; H_1: The level of incivilities in treatment hot spots relative to incivilities in control hot spots changes after POP intervention, $P \neq 0.50$.

Stating All of the Assumptions
Our assumptions may be stated as follows:

Assumptions:
Level of Measurement: Nominal binary scale

Population Distribution: No assumption made

Sampling Method: Independent random sampling (no replacement, sample is small relative to population)

Sampling Frame: Hot spots of violent crime in one month in Jersey City

Hypotheses:
H_0: The level of incivilities in treatment hot spots does not change relative to incivilities in control hot spots after POP intervention, $P = 0.50$;

H_1: The level of incivilities in treatment hot spots relative to incivilities in control hot spots changes after POP intervention, $P \neq 0.50$.

Selecting a Sampling Distribution

Once the assumptions have been stated, the researcher must define the sampling distribution that will be used to assess the risk of falsely rejecting the null hypothesis. Choosing a sampling distribution is one of the most important decisions that researchers make in statistical inference. As we show in later chapters, there are a number of different types of sampling distributions. If a sampling distribution is used that is inappropriate for the research problem examined, then the conclusion reached will be suspect.

Because our measure is nominal and binary (see assumptions) we have selected the binomial distribution for our test. The specific distribution that we use is based on our null hypothesis and the size of our sample. As illustrated in chapter 7, the binomial distribution provides the likelihood of gaining a particular number of successes (heads in the example of the coin toss) in a fixed number of trials. In order to assess that likelihood, we also need to know what the probability of a success or failure is on any particular trial.

In our example there are 11 trials, or 11 matched comparisons. Our null hypothesis states that the likelihood of a success for any comparison is 0.50. To build our sampling distribution, we would apply the binomial formula to each of the 12 possible outcomes that could be gained in our study under the assumption that $P = 0.50$. The resulting distribution is presented in table 8.2.

Table 8.2   Binomial Distribution of Success or Failure in 11 Trials

OUTCOME OF TRIALS	OVERALL PROBABILITY
0 Successes	0.00049
1 Success	0.00537
2 Successes	0.02686
3 Successes	0.08057
4 Successes	0.16113
5 Successes	0.22559
6 Successes	0.22559
7 Successes	0.16113
8 Successes	0.08057
9 Successes	0.02686
10 Successes	0.00537
11 Successes	0.00049

The Significance Level and Rejection Region

Having selected the distribution that will be used to assess the Type I error, we are ready to define the outcomes that will lead us to reject the null hypothesis. Our first step is to choose the significance level of our test. As described in chapter 6, the significance level of a test is the amount of Type I error we are willing to risk in rejecting the null hypothesis. By convention, criminal justice researchers use a 5 percent significance threshold. But, as discussed in chapter 6, we should consider at the outset whether a more lenient or more stringent significance level is appropriate for our study.

As researchers in the problem-oriented policing study do not present any special reason for altering conventionally accepted levels of significance, we will set a 5 percent significance threshold for our test. In articles or books, the significance level is often expressed by the Greek letter α. For our test, $\alpha = 0.05$. When researchers ask what level of significance corresponds to an observed outcome of a test, they are referring to an observed level of significance, which is commonly called a p value.

The significance level defines the Type I error we are willing to risk in our test. But it does not tell us directly what outcomes in our sample would lead us to reject the null hypothesis. For this, we need to turn to our sampling distribution and define an area within it called a **rejection region.** The rejection region of a test is the area in the sampling distribution that includes those outcomes that would lead to rejection of the null hypothesis. The point at which the rejection region begins is called the critical value. This is because it is the point at which the test becomes critical and would lead the researcher to reject the null hypothesis.

The area covered by the rejection region is equivalent to the significance level of a test. In the problem-oriented policing example, the rejection region includes 5 percent of the sampling distribution. Our initial problem is to define which five percent. Should we define the rejection region in the middle of the distribution represented in table 8.2, for example at 5 or 6 successes in 11 comparisons? Or should we look at only the extreme values on the positive side of the distribution, where there are mostly successes? Or should we include the area on the negative side of the distribution, where there are no successes?

Choosing a One-Tailed
or a Two-Tailed Rejection Region

The answer to our questions comes in part from common sense and in part from our assumptions. It just does not make sense to place the rejection region in the middle of the sampling distribution. We are trying to decide whether the outcomes observed in our sample are very different from the outcomes that would be expected if problem-oriented policing had no impact. Putting the rejection region in the middle of the distribution would place it among those outcomes that are most likely under the null hypothesis. Clearly, we want the rejection region to be on the edges of the distribution, or what statisticians call the **tails of the distribution.** These are the unlikely events, or those that we would not expect if the null hypothesis is true. As indicated in our sampling distribution in table 8.2, we would expect to get 11 successes in a row in about 5 in 10,000 samples if the program had no impact in the population. This is a very unlikely event and one that would lead us to reject the null hypothesis.

But zero successes is also an unlikely event, with the same probability of occurrence as 11 successes. Should we include only one tail of the distribution in our rejection region—the tail that assesses whether the program was a success? Or should we also include the opposite side of the distribution that suggests that the program led to more disorder? Our answer is drawn from the research hypothesis that we stated in our assumptions. We chose a nondirectional research hypothesis, meaning that we are interested in evaluating both the possibility that the experimental sites improved as compared with the control hot spots and the potential outcome that they got worse as compared with the control hot spots. In terms of the sampling distribution, our research hypothesis suggests that the rejection region for our test should be split between both tails of the distribution.

This type of test is called a **two-tailed test of significance.** If we had stated a directional research hypothesis, we would be concerned with outcomes on only one side of the sampling distribution. This is called a **one-tailed test of significance.** For example, if our research hypothesis was that incivilities in treatment hot spots decrease relative to incivilities in control hot spots after POP intervention, we would be concerned only with outcomes on the side of the distribution that shows program success.

The choice of a one-tailed or two-tailed test of significance has important implications for the types of study outcomes that will lead to rejection of the null hypothesis. Because our test is a two-tailed test, the rejection region is divided between both sides of the sampling distribution. This means in practice that only 2.5 percent of the distribution is found in each tail. In our example, an outcome of 0 or 1 success, or 10 or 11 successes, would lead to rejection of the null hypothesis in a two-tailed test. If we add up the probabilities associated with 0, 1, 10, and 11 successes we obtain a value of 0.012, or less than the 0.05 total area defined by our significance level. However, including 2 or 9 successes, which each have a probability value of 0.027, increases this area to 0.066. This area is larger than our rejection region.

But what if we had stated a directional research hypothesis? How would this have impacted upon our rejection region? In this case we would calculate the area of the rejection region on only one side of the sampling distribution. If our research hypothesis was that incivilities in treatment hot spots decline relative to incivilities in control hot spots after POP intervention, we would look at outcomes only on the tail of the distribution that shows program success. Because we are concerned only about these outcomes, all 5 percent of the rejection region is placed on this one tail of the distribution. We do not have to split the area of the rejection region. In this example, outcomes 9, 10, and 11 successes are all within the rejection region, because adding their probabilities results in a value of 0.033, which is less than the 5 percent threshold of our test. Adding the probability of 8 successes puts us above that threshold.

This example reinforces a rule we suggested when discussing hypotheses. It is important to state the research hypothesis before you gain study outcomes. What if the problem-oriented policing hot spots improved relative to control locations in nine comparisons? Using a one-tailed test, the result falls within our rejection region and would lead to rejection of the null hypothesis. Using a two-tailed test, the result is outside our rejection region. The choice of a directional or nondirectional research hypothesis can have an important impact on our conclusions. Merely by stating the research hypothesis a bit differently, we can change the statistical outcome of the test.

A one-tailed test makes it easier to reject the null hypothesis based on outcomes on one side of a sampling distribution because it precludes rejection of the null hypothesis based on outcomes on the opposite side. The price of a larger rejection region in one tail of the sampling distribution is thus no rejection region on the other tail. Similarly, the price of being able to examine outcomes on both sides of the distribution, as is the case with a two tailed test, is that the rejection region will be smaller on each side. The benefit is that you can assess results in both directions. If you already know the outcomes of a test, you might be tempted to adjust the direction of the test according to the observed outcomes of a study. Taking such an approach unfairly adjusts the rejection region to your advantage.

The Test Statistic

In most tests of statistical significance it is necessary to convert the specific outcome of a study to a **test statistic.** A test statistic provides the value of your outcome in units of the sampling distribution employed in your test. For the binomial distribution, the units are simply the number of successes in the total number of trials. The test statistic for our POP intervention example is 10.

Making a Decision

The final step in a statistical test is making a decision. If you have laid out all of the prior steps discussed above, then your choice should be easy. If your test statistic falls within the rejection region, then you reject the null hypothesis. If the test statistic does not fall in the rejection region, you cannot reject the null hypothesis. In our example, the test statistic (10) does fall in the rejection region, which includes 0, 1, 10, and 11 successes. Our decision, then, is to reject the null hypothesis that incivilities in treatment hot spots do not change relative to incivilities in control hot spots after POP intervention. We conclude that the differences observed are **statistically significant.**

But what does this mean? When we say that a result is statistically significant, we are not claiming that it is substantively important. The importance of a result would depend on such issues as whether the research impacts on real-life criminal justice decision making, or whether it contributes new knowledge in a specific area of criminology or criminal justice. We also are not stating that we are certain that the null hypothesis is untrue in the population. Without knowledge of the population parameter we cannot answer this question for sure.

Statistical significance has a very specific interpretation. If an outcome is statistically significant it means that it falls within the rejection region of your test. A statistically significant result is one that is unlikely if the null hypothesis is true for the population. Whenever we make a statement that a result is statistically significant we do it with the recognition that we are risking a certain level of Type I error. In this test, as in most tests of statistical significance in criminal justice, we were willing to take a 5 percent risk of falsely rejecting the null hypothesis.

Chapter Summary

The first stage in a **statistical test of significance** is to state one's **assumptions**. The first assumption is the type of measurement used. The second assumption concerns the shape of the population distribution. A **parametric test** is one that makes assumptions about the shape of the population distribution. A **nonparametric test** makes no such assumptions. Although nonparametric tests have the advantage of making fewer assumptions, they are generally used only for nominal and ordinal scales. The third assumption relates to the sampling method. A **random sample** is generally considered to be more representative, or to have greater **external validity,** than a **convenience sample. Independent random sampling** is the most accepted form of sampling. To ensure the independence of the sampling, it is in theory necessary to return the subject to the **sampling frame** after selection. **Sampling with replacement** creates practical problems, however, and is generally not required if the sample is small relative to the population. The fourth assumption states the null and research hypotheses. Care should be taken in framing them and in deciding whether they should be **directional.**

The second stage is to select an appropriate sampling distribution. The third stage is to select a significance level. The significance level determines the size of the **rejection region** and the location of the critical values of the test. If a test result falls within the rejection region, the researcher is prepared to reject the null hypothesis. If the hypotheses are directional, then the researcher will be concerned only with one **tail of the distribution,** and the entire rejection region will be placed on one side of the distribution (a **one-tailed test of significance**). If the hypotheses are nondirectional, then the researcher is concerned with results on both tails, and the rejection region will be divided equally between both sides of the distribution (a **two-tailed test of significance**).

The fourth stage involves calculating a **test statistic.** The study result is now converted into the units of the sampling distribution. Finally, a decision is made: the null hypothesis will be rejected if the test statistic falls within the rejection region. When such a decision can be made, the results are said to be **statistically significant.**

Key Terms

Assumptions Statements the researcher takes to be true at the outset of a test of statistical significance. These are the foundations upon which the rest of the test is built.

Convenience Sample A sample chosen not at random, but according to criteria of expedience or accessibility to the researcher.

Directional Hypothesis A hypothesis reflecting the concern of the researcher with the results obtained on only one side of the sampling distribution. This may be, for example, whether a program has a positive impact or, alternatively, whether it has a negative impact.

Distribution-Free Tests Another name for nonparametric tests.

External Validity The extent to which a study sample is reflective of the population from which it is drawn. A study is said to have high external validity when the sample used is representative of the population to which inferences are made.

Independent Random Sampling A form of random sampling whereby the fact that one subject is drawn from a population in no way affects the probability of drawing any other subject from that population.

Nondirectional Hypothesis A hypothesis reflecting the concern of the researcher with the results obtained on both sides of the sampling distribution. This may be, for example, whether a program has any impact, positive or negative.

Nonparametric Tests Statistical tests of significance that make no assumptions as to the shape of the population distribution.

One-Tailed Test of Significance A statistical test of significance in which the region for rejecting the null hypothesis falls on only one side of the sampling distribution. One-tailed tests are based on directional research hypotheses.

Parametric Tests Statistical tests of significance that make assumptions as to the shape of the population distribution.

Random Sampling Drawing samples from the population in a manner that ensures every individual in that population has an equal chance of being selected.

Rejection Region The area of a sampling distribution containing the test statistic values that will cause the researcher to reject the null hypothesis.

Representative Sample A sample that reflects the population from which it is drawn.

Sampling Frame The universe of eligible cases from which a sample is drawn.

Sampling with Replacement A sampling method whereby individuals in a sample are returned to the sampling frame after they have been selected. This raises the possibility that certain individuals in a population may appear in a sample more than once.

Statistically Significant A test statistic is deemed statistically significant if it falls within the rejection region defined by the researcher. When such a result is obtained, the researcher is prepared to reject the null hypothesis. In other words, the researcher is prepared to say that the null hypothesis is not true for the population, acknowledging a risk of error that corresponds with the level of significance chosen for the test.

Statistical Test of Significance A step-by-step method that enables the researcher to come to a conclusion about the population parameter based on a sample statistic.

Tails of the Distribution The extremes on either side of a distribution. The events represented in the tails of a sampling distribution are those deemed least likely to occur if the null hypothesis is true for the population.

Test Statistic The outcome of the study expressed in units of the sampling distribution. A test statistic that falls within the rejection region will lead the researcher to reject the null hypothesis.

Two-Tailed Test of Significance A statistical test of significance in which the region for rejecting the null hypothesis falls on both sides of the sampling distribution. Two-tailed tests are based on nondirectional research hypotheses.

Exercises

8.1 Conceptual questions:

a Is it better to have more or fewer assumptions at the beginning of a test of statistical significance? Explain your answer.

b Why is it important to state all of the assumptions at the outset of the test?

c In what sense can stating the null and research hypotheses be seen as making assumptions?

8.2 Gatley University is an elite university of 1,000 students. Nadia, a student of Chinese at the university, wishes to determine the average IQ of students at Gatley. She has decided that her sample size will be 50, and she is considering several different sampling methods. For each method, state the sampling frame and discuss whether the sampling method is "random" and whether it is "independent."

a Nadia chooses 50 names at random from the list of language students at the university.

b Nadia asks 50 of her acquaintances at the university if they would mind doing an IQ test.

c Nadia chooses the first two students from the alphabetical lists of each of the 25 university faculties.

d Nadia takes all 1,000 names and puts them into a hat. She draws out a name, writes it down and then puts it back in the hat and draws again. This procedure is repeated 50 times.

8.3 Hale prison is renowned for its poor internal discipline. The new prison governor wants to tackle this problem and decides to investigate whether removing prisoners' visiting privileges will act as a deterrent against future misbehaving. From 100 prisoners who recently took part in a violent prison riot, he selects the 25 inmates with the worst disciplinary records, removes their visiting privileges, and begins to monitor their progress relative to the others.

a Does this method meet the criteria of independent random sampling?

b Is "independent" sampling possible in this case?

c Can you suggest a more appropriate sampling method?

8.4 For each of the following hypotheses, state whether a one-tailed or a two-tailed test of statistical significance would be appropriate. In each case, explain your choice.

a H_1: Citizens over the age of 50 are more likely to be the victims of assault than citizens under the age of 50.

b H_1: Children raised by adopted parents have rates of delinquency different than those raised by their biological parents.

c H_1: The experience of imprisonment has an impact on the chances of an exconvict reoffending.

d H_1: Women are more likely than men to support increased sentences for rapists.

8.5 In chapter 7, we constructed a binomial distribution showing the chances of success and failure for ten tosses of a fair coin. The distribution was as follows:

0	Heads	0.001
1	Heads	0.010
2	Heads	0.044
3	Heads	0.118
4	Heads	0.206
5	Heads	0.247
6	Heads	0.206
7	Heads	0.118
8	Heads	0.044
9	Heads	0.010
10	Heads	0.001

Consider the following alternative hypotheses:

Alternative 1: H_0: The coin is fair

H_1: The coin is biased

Alternative 2: H_0: The coin is fair

H_1: The coin is biased in favor of heads

a Would a one-tailed or a two-tailed test be more appropriate for a researcher who chose alternative 1? Explain your answer.

b From a sequence of ten throws, what results would cause a researcher operating under the hypotheses listed under alternative 1 to reject the null hypothesis at a significance level of 5 percent?

c What would your answer be had the researcher chosen the hypotheses under alternative 2?

Computer Exercises

1. The UCR measures crime based on reports from participating agencies, that provide data to the FBI voluntarily. What are some possible strengths and weaknesses of this sample? What does it measure well? What important information might be missing from this data?

2. Let's look more closely at the type of police agencies that are reporting to the FBI using the binomial test, which is appropriate for dichotomous variables. Using the Agency Count variable, test the hypothesis that the probability of a reporting agency being a U.S. Park or State Police agency is 0.50 (use a 0.05 level of significance for a two-tailed test). This procedure is found in the Statistics (Non-Parametric) menu.

Chi Square: A Commonly Used Test for Nominal-Level Measures

choosing the chi-square distribution

When Is the Chi-Square Distribution Appropriate?

What Are Degrees of Freedom?

How Do Degrees of Freedom Affect the Distribution?

calculating the chi-square statistic

How Is the Chi-Square Statistic Calculated?

How Does One Interpret a Chi-Square Statistic?

THE BINOMIAL TEST provides a good introduction to the problem of statistical inference because it examines relatively simple statistical decisions. In the context of the binomial we were able to illustrate how statisticians build a sampling distribution from probabilities. But the binomial distribution can be applied only to a single binary variable. In this chapter we examine a more commonly used nonparametric test of significance for nominal-level measures, chi square, which allows the researcher to examine multicategory nominal level variables as well as the relationship between nominal level measures.

We begin our discussion of chi square with an example similar to the coin toss we used to introduce the binomial distribution in chapter 7. In this case we examine the problem of a fair roll of a die. We then turn to two applications of the chi-square test in criminal justice.

Testing Hypotheses Concerning the Roll of a Die

In chapter 7 we examined how you might make a decision about whether to challenge the fairness of a coin used to decide who would gain the ball in a weekly volleyball match. But what if you had the same question regarding a die used in a friendly game of chance at a local club. Each week, you and a few friends go down to the club and play a game of chance that involves the toss of a die. Let us say that the house (i.e., the club) wins whenever you roll a two or a six. You win whenever you roll a three or a four, and no one wins when you roll a one or a five. Over the month you have played the game 60 times. Of the 60 rolls of the die, you have lost with a roll of six 20 times and a roll of two 4 times (see table 9.1). You have won 10 times in total, with a roll of three 6 times and with a roll of four 4 times. The remaining 26 rolls of the die were split, with 16 ones and 10 fives.

Table 9.1   60 Rolls of a Die: A Frequency Distribution

1	No Winner	16
2	You Lose	4
3	You Win	6
4	You Win	4
5	No Winner	10
6	You Lose	20
Total		**60**

As in the coin toss, you and your friends have begun to become suspicious. Does it make sense that there should be such an uneven split in the outcomes of the game if the die is fair? Should you raise this issue with the club and suggest that they change their die? You don't want to appear like a sore sport. Nonetheless, if the distribution of rolls of the die that you observed is a very unlikely one given a fair die, you would be willing to make a protest.

The Chi-Square Distribution

You cannot use the binomial distribution to assess the fairness of the die because the binomial assumes that there are only two potential outcomes for each event, for example a head or tail on each toss of a coin. For the die there are six potential outcomes, a roll of one, two, three, four, five or six. In such cases you can make use of another probability distribution, which is called the **chi square (χ^2) distribution.** Like the binomial distribution, which varies depending on the number of trials conducted, the chi-square distribution also varies from problem to problem. However, the chi-square distribution varies not according to the number of trials that are conducted but according to the number of **degrees of freedom** (df) that are associated with a test. Degrees of freedom refer to how much a mathematical operation is free to vary, or to take on any value, after an agreed-upon set of limitations has been imposed.

In the chi-square distribution, those limitations are associated with the number of categories or potential outcomes examined. To define the degrees of freedom of a chi-square test we ask how many categories would have to be known to us to predict the remaining categories with certainty. For example, if we know that there are 60 rolls of the die and we also know the precise number of events that fall in five of the six categories, we will be able to predict the sixth category simply by subtracting from the total number of events (60) the number in the five known categories (see table 9.2). If two categories are blank, we can predict the total of both, but not the exact split be-

Table 9.2   Frequency Distribution for 60 Rolls of a Die with Information Missing

1	No Winner	16
2	You Lose	4
3	You Win	6
4	You Win	4
5	No Winner	10
6	You Lose	?
Total		**60**

Frequency of category 6 = (total frequency) − (sum of categories 1 to 5)
20 = 60 − 40

tween them. Accordingly, the degrees of freedom for this chi-square example is 5. Once we know the number of events or observations in five categories we can predict the sixth with certainty. More generally you can identify the degrees of freedom for a one variable chi-square distribution using the equation: $df = k - 1$, where k equals the number of categories in your measure (for our example, $6 - 1 = 5$).

In figure 9.1, we show how chi-square distributions vary according to degrees of freedom. The height of the distribution represents the proportion of cases found at any specific value of the **chi-square statistic.** As the number of degrees of freedom grows, the height of the chi-square distribution decreases with a longer and longer tail to the right. This means that the proportion of cases found above higher values of the chi-square statistic grows as degrees of freedom increase. To understand what this means substantively, as well as to illustrate

Figure 9.1   *Chi-Square Distributions for Various Degrees of Freedom*

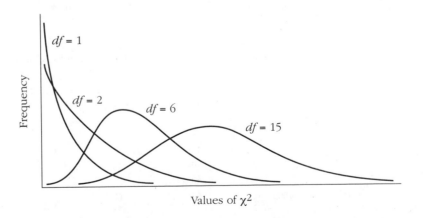

the use of the chi-square distribution in making decisions about hypotheses, it is important to turn to how the chi-square statistic is calculated.

Calculating the Chi-Square Statistic

Equation 9.1

$$\chi^2 = \sum_{i=1}^{k} \frac{(f_o - f_e)^2}{f_e}$$

The formula for the chi-square statistic is presented in equation 9.1. The summation symbol in the body of the equation has an $i = 1$ below it and a k above. This means that we sum the quantity that follows for each category from the first to the kth, or last, category. Since there are six categories in our example, we will have to carry out the same calculation six times, once for each of the six potential outcomes of the roll of a die.

The quantity that follows the summation symbol includes two symbols, f_o and f_e. The symbol f_o represents the frequency of the events observed in a category, or the **observed frequencies.** For example, in 20 of the 60 trials we observed, a six was rolled (see table 9.1). The observed frequency for a roll of six is 20. The symbol f_e represents the **expected frequency** of a category. The expected frequencies are ordinarily defined by the null hypothesis. In our example, they represent the number of events that would be expected in each category in the long run if the die were fair. Because a fair die would mean one in which there is an equal chance of obtaining any of the six potential outcomes, we divide the 60 observations evenly across the six categories. This leads to expected frequencies of 10 for each potential outcome. Table 9.3 shows the observed and expected frequencies for our example.

Table 9.3 Expected and Observed Frequencies for 60 Rolls of a Fair Die

	f_e	f_o
1	10	16
2	10	4
3	10	6
4	10	4
5	10	10
6	10	20
Total	**60**	**60**

Table 9.4   Computation of Chi Square for 60 Rolls of a Die

OUTCOME A	f_o	f_e	$(f_o - f_e)$	$(f_o - f_e)^2$	$\dfrac{(f_o - f_e)^2}{f_e}$
1	16	10	6	36	3.6
2	4	10	−6	36	3.6
3	6	10	−4	16	1.6
4	4	10	−6	36	3.6
5	10	10	0	0	0.0
6	20	10	10	100	10.0

$$\Sigma = 22.4$$

To calculate the chi-square statistic, equation 9.1 tells us first to subtract the expected frequency from the observed frequency in each category. We then square the result, and divide that quantity by the expected frequency of the category. For example, for a roll of six, we would subtract 10 (the expected frequency) from 20 (the observed frequency). We would then square that quantity (to get 100), and divide it by 10. This gives us 10 for a roll of six. After carrying out this computation for each category, as is done in table 9.4, we then add up the results of all six categories to obtain the total chi-square statistic. The resulting chi-square statistic in this example is 22.4.

The chi-square statistic measures how much the observed distribution differs from that expected under the null hypothesis. If the observed frequencies are similar to the expected frequencies, the chi-square statistic is small. If the observed frequencies are the same as the expected frequencies, the chi-square statistic equals 0. In contrast, to the extent that the observed frequencies differ from the expected frequencies, the chi-square statistic will be larger. What does this mean in terms of making a decision about the fairness of the die? For this, we have to turn to a table of probabilities associated with the chi-square distribution.

Linking the Chi-Square Statistic to Probabilities: The Chi-Square Table

In chapters 7 and 8, we used the binomial formula to calculate probabilities associated with each of the possible outcomes in our sample. For other statistical tests, including chi square, we can take advantage of already calculated probability distributions. Appendix 3 presents a table of probabilities associated with chi-square distributions with degrees of freedom of from 1 to 30. The chi-square table does not give us the probabilities associated with every possible outcome, but rather provides probabilities and then lists the chi-square statistics associated with them.

As illustrated in the chi-square table in appendix 3, a larger chi-square statistic is associated with a smaller p value. For example under one degree of freedom, a statistic of 2.706 is associated with a p value of 0.10, a statistic of 3.841 with a p value of 0.05, and a statistic of 10.827 with p value 0.001. This means that the larger the test statistic the less likely it is that the observed distribution is drawn from the expected distribution. This logic makes good common sense. Using our example of the roll of a die, it is reasonable to become more suspicious of the fairness of the die as the number of events that are found among the categories becomes more uneven. If we expect 10 events in each category and actually get one with 20 and one with 16, while two others have only 4, this should begin to make us suspicious. If one or two categories have 25 cases and two or three have none, it would seem even more likely that the die is not a fair one. But if each category had about 10 cases, which is to be expected in the long run with 60 rolls of a fair die, both common sense and chi square give us little reason to suspect a biased die.

Notice in appendix 3 as well that as the number of degrees of freedom gets larger, a larger chi-square statistic is needed to arrive at the same probability value. For example, a chi-square statistic of 3.841 is associated with a p value of 0.05 with one degree of freedom. With 30 degrees of freedom, a statistic of 43.773 is needed to achieve the same threshold. This reflects the difference in the shape of chi-square distributions with different degrees of freedom, and makes good sense if you consider how the chi-square statistic is calculated. A separate addition is made to the chi-square statistic for each possible outcome. Accordingly, it makes sense to demand a larger statistic as the number of categories in the test increases.

What of our decision regarding the roll of the die? Looking at appendix 3, we can see that with five degrees of freedom a chi-square statistic of greater than 11.070 is associated with a p value of less than 0.05. This means that in the long run we would expect to obtain a chi-square statistic greater than 11.070 less than 5 in 100 times if the die is fair. In fact, we obtained a chi-square statistic of 22.4. This number is even larger than that needed for a probability level of 0.001. If the die were fair, the probability of getting a distribution like the one observed in our 60 trials is less than 1 in 1,000. Given this result, we would likely come to the conclusion that the die was not a fair one and call for the club to use a new one.

Relating Two Nominal-Scale Measures in a Chi-Square Test

In criminal justice and criminology, we seldom examine research questions like that of the roll of a die, which are concerned with outcomes of only one measure. More often it is the case that we are interested in describing the relationships among two or more variables. For example, we may want to assess whether men and women are likely to be placed in different types of treatment facilities, or whether different ethnic groups receive different types of sanctions. For each of these examples, two measures must be assessed at the same time. In the former, we examine both gender and type of treatment facility. In the latter, we examine type of sentence and ethnicity. Below we use the example of a study of white-collar criminals to illustrate the use of chi square in making inferences about the relationship between two variables: recidivism and sanction type.

A Substantive Example: Type of Sanction and Recidivism among Convicted White-Collar Criminals

My colleagues and I collected data on reoffending from FBI records for a sample of white-collar offenders over a 10-year period. The sample included offenders from seven U.S. district courts, convicted of eight different white-collar crimes (antitrust violations, securities fraud, mail and wire fraud, false claims and statements, credit and lending institution fraud, bank embezzlement, income tax fraud, and bribery). The sample was chosen randomly without replacement.[1] Our research question concerned whether imprisonment of white-collar offenders impacted upon reoffending.

We compared the likelihood of rearrest for a group of offenders that received a prison sanction with a matched group that did not receive a prison sanction. We found that 33.0 percent of the prison group ($N = 100$) were rearrested during the follow-up period, as contrasted with 28.4 percent of the no-prison group ($N = 67$). What conclusions can we come to concerning white-collar criminals generally?

---

[1] In this case a stratified random sample was selected in order to ensure a broad sampling of white-collar offenders. For our example here we treat the sample as a simple random sample. See also David Weisburd, Elin Waring, and Ellen Chayet (1995), Specific Deterrence in a Sample of Offenders Convicted of White Collar Crimes, *Criminology* 33:587–607.

To answer our research question, we follow the format of a statistical test introduced in chapter 8. We begin by stating the assumptions of our test.

Assumptions:

Level of Measurement: Nominal scales

Population Distribution: No assumption made

Sampling Method: Independent random sampling (no replacement, sample is small relative to population)

Sampling Frame: Offenders from seven federal judicial districts convicted under eight different white-collar crimes.

Hypotheses:

H_0: There is no difference in the likelihood of rearrest among similar white-collar offenders sentenced or not sentenced to prison.

H_1: There is a difference in the likelihood of rearrest among similar white-collar offenders sentenced or not sentenced to prison.

The level of measurement required for a chi-square test is a nominal scale. Our example includes two variables: rearrest and type of sanction. Each is measured as a binary nominal variable. For rearrest, we examine those rearrested versus those not rearrested in the follow-up period. For type of sanction we differentiate between those sentenced to prison and those who did not receive a prison sanction. In regard to the population distribution, chi square is a nonparametric test and therefore requires no specific assumption.

In regard to sampling, our example here is similar to that presented in chapter 8. Although the chi-square test ordinarily requires a fully independent random sample,[2] this sample, like most criminal justice samples, is selected without replacement. At the same time, the population from which the sample is drawn is very large relative to the sample, and thus we have no reason to suspect that this violation of the assumptions will affect our test result.

The sampling frame includes offenders from seven federal judicial districts convicted of eight different white-collar crimes. Accordingly, our inferences relate directly to the population of those offenses and those districts. As discussed in chapter 8, it is necessary to explain why your sample is representative of a broader population of cases if you want to make inferences beyond your sampling frame. In this

---

[2]There are certain specific situations in which the chi-square test does not require sampling with replacement (see B. S. Everitt (1997), *The Analysis of Contingency Tables*, London: Chapman and Hall.)

study, the seven districts examined were seen as providing a sample with geographic spread throughout the United States, and the selected white-collar offenses were defined as offering a "broad sampling of white-collar offenders."

The research hypothesis for our test is nondirectional. It states simply that the two groups (prison and no-prison) differ in terms of likelihood of rearrest during the follow-up period. The null hypothesis states that there is no difference between the prison and no-prison groups.

The Sampling Distribution

Because we examine the relationship between two nominal-scale variables, the chi-square distribution provides an appropriate sampling distribution for our test. However, our decision about degrees of freedom is not as straightforward as that in the example of a roll of a die. In this case, we must take into account the joint distribution of our measures. This is illustrated in table 9.5, which shows two potential outcomes for the prison variable and two potential outcomes for the arrest variable. This leaves us with four **cells,** or four possible combined outcomes—cell A: an offender who received a prison sanction and is arrested in the follow-up period; cell B: an offender who did not receive a prison sanction and is arrested in the follow-up period; cell C: an offender who received a prison sanction and is not arrested in the follow-up period; and cell D: an offender who did not receive a prison sanction and is not arrested in the follow-up period.

If we sum across and down from the cells we gain two row **marginals** and two column marginals. The row marginals represent the totals for the rows, that is 52 for those arrested and 115 for those not arrested. The column marginals represent the totals for the columns ($N = 100$ for the prison group; $N = 67$ for the no-prison group). If you know the row and column marginals, as is assumed in computing the degrees of freedom for chi square, you can predict with certainty

Table 9.5   Recidivism among 167 White-Collar Criminals According to Whether They Did or Did Not Receive Prison Sentences

	IMPRISONED	NOT IMPRISONED	ROW MARGIN
Subsequently Arrested	Cell A 33	Cell B 19	52
Not Subsequently Arrested	Cell C 67	Cell D 48	115
Column Margin	100	67	167

Table 9.6   Predicting the Missing Cells in a Two-Variable Chi Square

			ROW MARGIN
	Cell A	Cell B	
	33	?	52
	Cell C	Cell D	
	?	?	115
Column Margin	100	67	167

Given that cell A = 33:
Cell B = (52 − 33) = 19
Cell C = (100 − 33) = 67
Cell D = (115 − 67) = 48

the remaining cells once the value of any one cell is known (see table 9.6). Degrees of freedom for a two-variable chi square can be gained more simply through the formula: $df = (r - 1)(c - 1)$, where r represents the number of rows and c the number of columns. For our example there are two rows and two columns so: $df = (2 - 1)(2 - 1) = 1$.

Significance Level and Rejection Region

We stated no reason at the outset for choosing a more strict or more lenient significance threshold for our example than is used by convention. Accordingly, we use a significance level of 0.05 for our test. Our rejection region is defined by the chi-square table (see appendix 3). Importantly, the chi-square distribution is not concerned with the direction of outcomes in a test. It tells us to what extent the observed frequencies in our example differ from those that would be expected under the null hypothesis of no difference. Whether they differ in one direction or another, the chi-square statistic will always be positive.

The terms "directional" or "nondirectional" are very tenuous ones in a chi-square test. Chi-square assumes nominal-scale variables, which by definition do not provide information about the order of values in a measure. In turn, if we cannot specify the order of two measures we cannot speak of the direction of their relationship. In most situations a directional hypothesis is not appropriate for a chi-square test. In the special case of two binary variables, however, researchers do sometimes use chi square to examine directional research hypotheses. For example, we might have stated our research hypothesis as: The likelihood of arrest in the follow-up period for white-collar offenders sentenced to prison is lower than that of similar white-collar offenders not sentenced to prison.

However, our research hypothesis is nondirectional, as is the table of chi-square values. To define our rejection region we turn to the row of the table associated with one degree of freedom. Under a probability value of 0.05, we obtain an estimate of 3.841. To reject the null hypothesis our test statistic will have to be greater than or equal to this value.[3]

The Test Statistic

To apply chi square to the two-variable case, we need to adapt our original equation. The formula for the chi-square statistic for relating two measures is presented in equation 9.2.[4]

Equation 9.2

$$\chi^2 = \sum_{r=1}^{r} \sum_{c=1}^{c} \frac{(f_o - f_e)^2}{f_e}$$

The only change we have in equation 9.2 as compared with equation 9.1 is that we have an additional summation symbol. In this case, we do not sum simply across the categories of one measure, but rather across each row (r) and column (c) of the joint distribution of two measures. Accordingly, equation 9.2 reminds us that we must examine the expected and observed frequencies for every potential outcome we can observe, or, in terms of the chi-square equation, for every cell in our table.

For our example, this means we must sum across cells A, B, C, and D. As before, we want to compare the observed to the expected frequencies in each cell. The observed frequencies are those gained in our research. The expected frequencies are defined through the null hypothesis. The null hypothesis states that there is no difference in arrest rates between the prison and no-prison groups. If this is true, then we should expect the same proportion of arrests in both groups. To calculate the expected frequencies, accordingly, we need to first define the overall proportion of offenders arrested in the follow-up period.

---

[3]What if we had defined a directional research hypothesis? In this case we look to the column of the table that is twice the value of the significance level that is desired, since we now have placed all risk of falsely rejecting the null hypothesis in only one direction. For example, for a 0.05 significance level, we turn to the test statistic for a 0.10 level.

[4]When a chi-square test has only one degree of freedom, it is recommended that a correction factor be added if the expected frequencies of any cell fall below 20. The correction provides a more conservative, or smaller, chi-square statistic:

$$\chi^2 = \sum_{r=1}^{r} \sum_{c=1}^{c} \frac{(|f_o - f_e| - 0.5)^2}{f_e}$$

The proportion of offenders arrested overall in the sample in the follow-up period is obtained by dividing the total number of offenders arrested ($N_{cat} = 52$) by the total number of offenders in the sample ($N_{tot} = 167$):

$$Prop. = \frac{N_{cat}}{N_{tot}} = \frac{52}{167} = 0.3114$$

To get the expected frequency for cell A, we multiply this proportion by the marginal total of 100($f_e = 31.14$). For the no-prison group, there is a total of 67 offenders. Applying the proportion for the total sample to this group, we multiply 67 by 0.3114, and get an expected frequency of 20.86 for cell B. In practice, we do not need to compute the expected frequencies for the remaining two cells, C and D. Indeed, we could have assigned all of the cells expected frequencies with the knowledge of only one cell. This is what the degrees of freedom for this example tell us. If you know the number of cases in one cell, you can predict with certainty the rest. The expected and observed frequencies for our example are shown in table 9.7.

Now that we have calculated the observed and expected frequencies for each potential outcome, or cell, we can calculate the chi-square statistic. To do this we first square the difference of the observed and expected frequencies for each cell, and then divide this quantity by the expected frequency of the cell:

$$\frac{(f_o - f_e)^2}{f_e}$$

This is done in table 9.8 for each of the four cells in our problem. Using cell A as an example, we first subtract the expected frequency 31.14 from the observed frequency of 33. We then square this quan-

Table 9.7　The Expected and Observed Frequencies of Recidivism and Nonrecidivism for White-Collar Offenders according to Whether They Received Prison Sentences

	IMPRISONED	NOT IMPRISONED	ROW MARGIN
Subsequently Arrested	Cell A $f_o = 33$ $f_e = 31.14$	Cell B $f_o = 19$ $f_e = 20.86$	52
Not Subsequently Arrested	Cell C $f_o = 67$ $f_e = 68.86$	Cell D $f_o = 48$ $f_e = 46.14$	115
Column Margin	100	67	167

Table 9.8   Computation of Chi Square for 167 White-Collar Criminals

CELL	f_0	f_e	$(f_0 - f_e)$	$(f_0 - f_e)^2$	$\dfrac{(f_0 - f_e)^2}{f_e}$
A	33	31.14	1.86	3.4596	0.1111
B	19	20.86	−1.86	3.4596	0.1658
C	67	68.86	−1.86	3.4596	0.0502
D	48	46.14	1.86	3.4596	0.0750
					$\Sigma = 0.4021$

tity (1.86), obtaining a result of 3.4596. Dividing this result by the expected frequency in the cell (31.14) gives us 0.1111. The sum of all four cells, 0.402, is our test statistic.

The Decision

Our rejection region was defined as including any chi-square statistic greater than 3.841. The test statistic for our example is only 0.402. Accordingly, we choose not to reject the null hypothesis. We conclude that there is no significant difference in the likelihood of recidivism among white-collar offenders who have or have not been sentenced to prison. Our inferences are made directly to the specific offenses and judicial districts defined in the sampling frame.

Extending the Chi-Square Test to Multicategory Variables: The Example of Cell Allocations in Prison

The previous example illustrates the use of chi square in the case of two binary variables. We now turn to an extension of the chi-square test to an example including a multicategory nominal-level variable. Our example is drawn from a study of the relationship between prisoners' race and their cell assignments in a large state prison in the northeastern United States.[5] We examine the placement of non-Hispanic whites and "nonwhite" inmates (including Hispanics) into seven cell blocks. The sample includes all prisoners in the general prison population for a single day. The distribution of cases is presented in table 9.9.

---

[5] See Douglas McDonald and David Weisburd (1991), "Segregation and Hidden Discrimination in Prisons: Reflections on a Small Study of Cell Assignments," in C. Hartchen (ed.), *Correctional Theory and Practice* (Chicago: Nelson Hall).

Table 9.9   Proportions of Non-Hispanic White Prisoners in Seven Cell Blocks

CELL BLOCK	NON-HISPANIC WHITES	NONWHITES	TOTAL
C	48 18.7%	208 81.3%	256 100%
D	17 31.5%	37 68.5%	54 100%
E	28 25.0%	84 75.0%	112 100%
F	32 28.8%	79 71.2%	111 100%
G	37 12.2%	266 87.8%	303 100%
H	34 60.7%	22 39.3%	56 100%
I	44 14.1%	268 85.9%	312 100%
Total	**240** 19.9%	**964** 80.1%	**1,204** 100%

If cell assignments were made on considerations unrelated to race, we would expect to find the proportions of non-Hispanic whites in each cell block roughly equivalent to the proportion of non-Hispanic whites in the general prison population (19.9 percent; see the marginal for non-Hispanic whites in table 9.9). Such equivalence is not evident. In block G, for example, non-Hispanic whites constituted 12.2 percent of the inmates. In block H, they comprised 60.7 percent. Do results for this sample allow us to conclude that there is disparity in cell-block assignments in the prison?

Assumptions:

Level of Measurement: Nominal scales

Population Distribution: No assumption made

Sampling Method: Independent random sampling (the entire sampling frame is examined)

Sampling Frame: All prisoners in the general prison population on a specific day

Hypotheses:

H_0: Cell-block assignment and race are independent.

H_1: Cell-block assignment and race are related.

As in our first example, we assume a nominal level of measurement for our test, and do not make assumptions regarding the form of the population distribution. Prisoner race is measured at the binary nominal level and cell block is a multicategory nominal scale.

The sample includes all cases in the sampling frame. Accordingly, we do not need to use statistical inference to make statements about that population. However, the study was designed not only to describe prison-cell allocations on that day, but to make more general statements about cell allocations in the prison studied throughout the year. This is not an uncommon scenario in criminal justice research, in good part because the realities of the criminal justice system often preclude sampling beyond specific institutions or outside of specific time frames. This means, however, that the researchers seek to make inferences beyond their sampling frame.

If cell allocations on the day examined in this study are representative of cell allocations more generally throughout the year, then the inferences made on the basis of the test will be reliable. If not, then the test will not provide for valid inferences. In our example the investigators argue:

> There was no reason to suspect that the cell assignments of prisoners on that day differed substantially from assignments on other days. Moreover, these cell assignments represented the results of decisions made over the course of months and perhaps years prior to the date of drawing the sample. There was every reason to believe, consequently, that cell assignments on that date constituted a valid representation of cell assignment decisions made during the several months prior to that day.

Our research question asks whether it would be likely to obtain the distribution we observe in our sample if assignment to cell blocks was color blind in the population. Stated in the form of hypotheses, we ask whether race and cell block assignment are independent. If they are independent, as proposed in our null hypothesis, then we would expect about the same proportion of nonwhite and non-Hispanic white prisoners in each cell block. Our research hypothesis is nondirectional. It states that race and cell block assignment are related. In this example, as in most chi-square tests, use of nominal-scale measures, which do not assign order or value to categories, means that one cannot define the direction or order of the research hypothesis.

The Sampling Distribution

Because we are examining the relationship between two nominal measures, one binary and one multicategory, we use the chi-square sampling distribution. Degrees of freedom for our problem are defined as in the previous example:

Working It Out

$$df = (r-1)(c-1)$$
$$= (7-1)(2-1)$$
$$= 6$$

In this case, we have seven categories in our row variable (cell block), and two categories in our column variable (ethnicity). The number of degrees of freedom for our sampling distribution is six.

Significance Level and Rejection Region

As we have no reason to propose more lenient or more strict significance criteria than are used by convention, we will set a 0.05 significance level. To define our rejection region, we turn to the row of the chi-square table associated with six degrees of freedom. Looking under the column 0.05, a chi-square statistic of 12.592 is listed. If the test statistic is greater than or equal to this critical value, then it falls within the rejection region of the test.

The Test Statistic

Calculation of the test statistic in the multicategory example follows that of the two-by-two table examined in the previous section. Our first task is to define the expected frequencies for each cell of the table. We do this, as before, by dividing a marginal of the table by the total proportion of cases. Taking the overall number of non-Hispanic whites in the sample, we obtain a proportion of 0.1993:

Working It Out

$$Prop. = \frac{N_{cat}}{N_{tot}}$$
$$= \frac{240}{1,204}$$
$$= 0.1993$$

To calculate the expected frequencies in each cell in the non-Hispanic white column, we multiply this proportion by the marginal total for each row. So, for example, for cell block C, we multiply 256 by 0.1993, leading to an expected frequency for non-Hispanic whites of 51.021. You would then replicate this procedure for each of the six other cells in the non-Hispanic white column. To calculate the expected frequencies for the nonwhite column, you simply subtract the expected frequency for the non-Hispanic white column from the row marginal. So, for example, for nonwhites in cell block C, the expected frequency would be: 256 (the marginal total) minus 51.021 (the expected frequency for non-Hispanic whites for that cell block), giving an expected frequency of 204.979. Table 9.10 includes the expected and observed frequencies for the 14 cells in our example.

To obtain the test statistic, we use equation 9.2, which may be applied to any two-variable chi-square problem:

$$\chi^2 = \sum_{r=1}^{r} \sum_{c=1}^{c} \frac{(f_o - f_e)^2}{f_e}$$

Again we begin by subtracting the expected from the observed frequencies in each cell and squaring the result. This quantity is then divided by the expected frequency of the cell. The chi-square statistic is gained by summing the result across all 14 cells. The full set of calculations for gaining the test statistic is presented in table 9.11. The chi-square score for our example is 88.2895.

Decision

The outcome of 88.2895 is much greater than the critical value for our test of 12.592. Accordingly, we reject the null hypothesis that race and cell block allocation are independent (using a 5 percent significance level). We conclude that there is a statistically significant relationship between the distribution of prisoners across cell blocks and their race.

Table 9.10 Observed Frequencies and Expected Frequencies for Assignment of Non-Hispanic White and Nonwhite Prisoners in Seven Prison Cells

CELL BLOCK	NON-HISPANIC WHITES	NONWHITES	TOTAL
C	$f_o = 48$ $f_e = 51.020$	$f_o = 208$ $f_e = 204.979$	256
D	$f_o = 17$ $f_e = 10.762$	$f_o = 37$ $f_e = 43.238$	54
E	$f_o = 28$ $f_e = 22.322$	$f_o = 84$ $f_e = 89.678$	112
F	$f_o = 32$ $f_e = 22.122$	$f_o = 79$ $f_e = 88.878$	111
G	$f_o = 37$ $f_e = 60.388$	$f_o = 266$ $f_e = 242.612$	303
H	$f_o = 34$ $f_e = 11.161$	$f_o = 22$ $f_e = 44.839$	56
I	$f_o = 44$ $f_e = 62.182$	$f_o = 268$ $f_e = 249.818$	312
Total	**240**	**964**	**1,204**

Table 9.11   Computation of Chi Square for Assignment of Non-Hispanic White (N-HW) and Nonwhite (N-W) Prisoners in Seven Cell Blocks

CELL BLOCK	ETHNIC GROUP	f_o	f_e	$(f_o - f_e)$	$(f_o - f_e)^2$	$\dfrac{(f_o - f_e)^2}{f_e}$
C	N-HW	48	51.021	−3.021	9.1264	0.1789
C	N-W	208	204.979	3.021	9.1264	0.0445
D	N-HW	17	10.762	6.238	38.1926	3.5488
D	N-W	37	43.238	−6.238	38.1926	0.8833
E	N-HW	28	22.322	5.678	32.2397	1.4443
E	N-W	84	89.678	−5.678	32.2397	0.3595
F	N-HW	32	22.122	9.878	97.5749	4.4108
F	N-W	79	88.878	−9.878	97.5749	1.0979
G	N-HW	37	60.388	−23.388	546.9985	9.0581
G	N-W	266	242.612	23.388	546.9985	2.2546
H	N-HW	34	11.161	22.839	521.6199	46.7359
H	N-W	22	44.839	−22.839	521.6199	11.6332
I	N-HW	44	62.182	−18.182	330.5851	5.3164
I	N-W	268	249.818	18.182	330.5851	1.3233

$$\Sigma = 88.2895$$

The Use of Chi Square When Samples Are Small: A Final Note

The chi-square test is often used by criminal justice researchers. However, it has a very important limitation in its application to studies with small or highly skewed samples. When more than one in five of the cells in your table have expected frequencies of five or less, it is generally considered inappropriate to use a chi-square test. In such situations, it is recommended that you combine categories of your variables until you meet the minimum expected-frequencies requirement.

Chapter Summary

Whereas the binomial distribution is relevant only for binary variables, the **chi-square distribution** can be used to examine a variable with more than two categories.

The shape of the chi-square distribution chosen depends on the **degrees of freedom** associated with the test. The formula for degrees of freedom defines how many categories would have to be known for us to be able to predict the remaining categories with certainty. The greater the degrees of freedom, the flatter is the distribution. In practical terms, as degrees of freedom increase, a larger chi-square statistic is required to reject the null hypothesis.

The chi-square test of statistical significance is a nonparametric test. To calculate the test statistic, the researcher must first identify the **observed frequencies** and the **expected frequencies** of each category. The expected frequencies are those one would expect under the assumption of the null hypothesis. They are distributed in the same proportions as the **marginal** totals. The chi-square formula is then applied for each category, or **cell,** in the table. If the observed frequencies substantially differ from the expected frequencies, then the **chi-square statistic** will be large. If the observed frequencies are similar to the expected frequencies, then the chi-square statistic will be small. If they are the same, the statistic will be 0. The larger the statistic (and the smaller the degrees of freedom), the easier it will be to reject the null hypothesis. The statistic is always positive. Because the chi-square test relies on nominal nonordered data, it is not concerned with the direction of outcomes.

Key Terms

Cell A table is composed of cells, each one identified by a particular row and column. When we use a table to compare two variables, it is convenient to refer to each combination of categories as a cell.

Chi-Square Distribution A probability distribution that is used to conduct statistical tests of significance using binary or multicategory nominal variables. The distribution is nonsymmetrical and varies according to degrees of freedom. All the values in the distribution are positive.

Chi-Square Statistic The test statistic resulting from applying the chi-square formula to the observed and expected frequencies for each cell. This statistic tells us how much the observed distribution differs from that expected under the null hypothesis.

Degrees of Freedom A mathematical index that places a value on the extent to which a particular operation is free to vary after certain limitations have been imposed. Calculating the degrees of freedom for a chi-square test determines which chi-square probability distribution we use.

Expected Frequencies The number of observations one would predict for each cell if the null hypothesis were true.

Marginal The value in the margin of a table that totals the scores for the appropriate columns and rows.

Observed Frequencies The observed results of the study, recorded in each cell.

Symbols and Formulas

χ^2 Chi square.

df   Degrees of freedom.

f_o Observed frequencies.

f_e Expected frequencies.

c Number of columns.

r Number of rows.

k Number of categories.

To determine the degrees of freedom for a chi-square test including only one variable:

$$df = k - 1$$

To determine the degrees of freedom for a chi-square test incuding two variables:

$$df = (r - 1)\,(c - 1)$$

To determine the chi-square statistic for one variable:

$$\chi^2 = \sum_{i=1}^{k} \frac{(f_o - f_e)^2}{f_e}$$

To determine the chi-square statistic for two variables:

$$\chi^2 = \sum_{r=1}^{r} \sum_{c=1}^{c} \frac{(f_o - f_e)^2}{f_e}$$

Exercises

9.1   Sergeant Bob is in charge of the duty roster at Gatley police station. Every week, it is his responsibility to randomly assign the five beat officers, including his son Bob Jr., to patrol in each of the five zones that make up the City of Gatley. Zones A and D are favored by all the officers because they are usually quiet. Of the others, Zone C is notoriously dangerous. The officers have recently begun to suspect Sergeant Bob of favoritism toward his son. In the last 30 weeks, Bob Jr. has been assigned to Zone A 12 times, Zone B and Zone C 2 times each, Zone D 9 times, and Zone E 5 times.

a Do the other officers have reason to believe that Sergeant Bob is not assigning zones in a random manner? Use a 5 percent level of significance and outline each of the steps required in a test of statistical significance.

b Would your answer be any different if a 1 percent level of significance was used?

9.2 In the past 100 years there have been more than 250 successful breakouts from Didsbury prison. Mike is a researcher who has been hired by the prison governor to investigate the phenomenon. Details of the breakouts are available only for those that took place in the past 10 years—a total of 30. Using the records of these 30 breakouts as a sample, Mike decides to break the figures down to see whether breakouts were more common in certain wings of the prison than in others. It transpires that of the 30 breakouts, 4 have been from A-Wing, 8 from B-Wing, 15 from C-Wing, and 3 from D-Wing.

a Does Mike have enough evidence to conclude that, over the 100-year period, breakouts were more (or less) likely to occur from certain wings than they were from others? Use a 5 percent level of significance and outline each of the steps required in a test of statistical significance.

b Would your answer be any different if a 1 percent level of significance was used?

c Are there any problems with Mike's choice of a sample? Explain your answer.

9.3 At a local school, 46 children were accused of cheating on exams in the course of a semester. In a new innovation, the principal decided that every second child accused of cheating would be brought before a "peer jury" to decide guilt or innocence. In all other cases, the decision was taken by the examiners as usual. Of the 30 children who were adjudged "guilty" in the course of the semester, 18 were convicted by the peer jury, and the rest were convicted by the examiners. Of the children who were adjudged "not guilty," 5 were acquitted by their peers.

a The principal is mainly interested in the educational value of the experiment, but he will discontinue it if it becomes clear that the peer jury and the examiners make different decisions to a degree that is statistically significant. He is willing to take a 5 percent risk of error. Should the scheme be continued? Outline each of the steps of a test of statistical significance.

b Could the principal base the test on a directional hypothesis? If so, what would that hypothesis be, and would it make a difference in his final decision?

9.4 Jeremy, a law student, observed a total of 55 cases in the course of a year in which an accused male pleaded guilty to a serious traffic offense. He observed that of the 15 who were sentenced to prison, 6 wore a shirt and tie in court. Of the 40 who were not sentenced to prison, 8 wore a shirt and tie in court.

a Can Jeremy conclude that there is a link between the physical appearance of the accused and whether he is imprisoned? Use a 5 percent level of significance and outline each of the steps required in a test of statistical significance.

b What level of significance would be required for his decision to be reversed?

9.5 Sasha is interested in the extent to which people are prepared to intervene to help a stranger, and whether the race of the stranger is relevant to the likelihood of intervention. She hires four male actors: one of African ancestry, one of Asian ancestry, one of European ancestry, and one of Indian ancestry. The actors are each told to fake a fall in a busy shopping street and to pretend to be in some pain. Sasha observes from nearby and records whether, within five minutes of the actor's fall, anyone has stopped to see if he is okay. Each actor repeats the experiment 40 times.
The results were as follows:

ANCESTRY	✔	✖
African	04	36
Asian	00	40
European	20	20
Indian	08	32

(✔ = Intervention within 5 mins; ✖ = no intervention)

a Can Sasha conclude that there is a link between race of victim and readiness to intervene? Use a 5 percent level of significance and outline each of the steps required in a test of statistical significance.

b Would your answer be any different if a 1 percent level of significance was used?

9.6   Dave takes a random sample of the speeches, interviews, and official statements given by the prime minister and the interior minister of a given country over the course of a given year in which reference is made to "prison policy." He analyzes the content of the statements in his sample and discovers five different types of justification for the government's prison policy. Dave then records each time the prime minister or interior minister refers to any of the five justification types. The results are as follows:

JUSTIFICATION TYPE	PRIME MINISTER	INTERIOR MINISTER
Incapacitation or Protecting Society	06	16
Specific Deterrence	02	14
General Deterrence	04	20
Rehabilitation	00	15
Retribution	13	10

a Is there a statistically significant difference in the policy statements of the prime minister and those of the interior minister? Use a 5 percent level of significance and outline each of the steps required in a test of statistical significance.

b Would your answer be any different if a 1 percent level of significance was used?

9.7   The Television Complaints Board monitors the standard of morality for a nation's TV channels. It has recently set up a telephone hotline for viewers who wish to complain about sex, violence, or foul language on any of the nation's three TV channels. In its first month of operation, the board received the following complaints:

	CHANNEL 1	CHANNEL 2	CHANNEL 3
Sex	02	08	10
Violence	10	12	10
Foul Language	03	10	15

a Which of the following questions would a chi-square test of these results seek to answer?

i. Is there a statistically significant difference between the number of complaints made against each channel?

ii. Is there a statistically significant difference between the number of each type of complaint made?

iii. Is there a statistically significant difference between the types of different complaints received for the three different stations?

b   Answer the question you chose from 9.7a by running a chi-square test at a 5 percent level of significance. Should the null hypothesis be overturned?

Computer Exercises

1.   Expanding on our analysis of the types of agencies that report to the FBI, use the Agency Count variable and the variable you created to identify whether an agency was from your home state to test the hypothesis that there is no difference in the likelihood of an agency being located in your home state among "U.S. Park and State Police" and "Other Agencies." The chi-square test that you need is found in the Statistics (Summarize, Crosstabs) menu. This will also produce a table that tells you how many agencies fall into each category.

An Introduction to Parametric Tests
of Significance

parametric tests of significance: using the normal sampling distribution

How Can We Make Assumptions about an Unknown Population?

What Is the "Central Limit Theorem"?

When Can It Be Used?

parametric tests of significance: two examples

How Can We Define a Sampling Distribution When the Parameters Are Unknown?

What Is the z-Test for Proportions?

What Is the t-Test for Means?

When Can They Be Used?

confidence intervals

What Are They?

How Are They Used?

IN CHAPTERS 8 AND 9, statistical tests were presented that did not make assumptions about the population distribution of the characteristics studied. We now turn to a different type of statistical test of significance in which the researcher must make certain assumptions about the population distribution. These tests are called parametric tests and are widely used in criminal justice and criminology.

We begin the chapter with a basic dilemma. The purpose of statistical inference is to make statements about populations from what is known about samples. However, parametric tests require that we make assumptions about the population at the outset. If population parameters are generally unknown, how can the researcher make assumptions about them? In this chapter, we examine this dilemma in the context of two types of parametric tests that are based on the normal curve introduced in chapter 5.

Applying Normal Sampling Distributions to Nonnormal Populations

In chapter 5 we introduced the normal distribution. By using the example of IQ, we showed how different types of normal distributions could be converted into one general standard normal curve, the z curve. To use the z curve to identify where specific sample scores lie in the distribution of population scores (e.g., comparing the IQ of prisoners with the general population), we assumed that the variable examined was normally distributed in the population.

The normal distribution is also used in inferential statistics as a probability distribution and is the basis for many types of parametric tests. These tests provide an advantage over nonparametric tests of significance in that they allow us to make inferences about interval-level variables. But to make inferences using the normal probability distribution, we must again assume that the population distribution of scores is normal. It seems reasonable to question how we can make such an assumption if characteristics of the population are generally unknown.

Our dilemma is compounded by the fact that the scores of criminal justice variables are rarely distributed normally. With the exception of a few measures that have been developed to take a normal shape, it is very difficult to identify criminal justice variables that meet all of the requirements of a normal distribution. This is not surprising, since a normal distribution is symmetrical and bell-shaped; has the same mean, median and mode; and includes a set proportion of cases a specific distance from the mean in standard deviation units (see chapter 5). Finding true normal distributions in the real world of criminal justice is not an easy task.

How, then, can parametric tests based on the normal distribution be widely used to make statistical inferences? Not only do they demand that we make an assumption about a population we usually know little about, but the assumption we are being asked to make does not make very much sense for criminal justice measures. The answer may be found in an important distinction between sample and population distributions on the one hand, and sampling distributions on the other. While we have every reason to be hesitant in assuming that the population distribution of scores is normal for criminal justice measures, we can assume with a good deal of confidence that the sampling distributions for such measures are approximately normally distributed. By using the toss of a fair coin as an example, we can provide a simple illustration of this fact.

In figure 10.1 we overlay the distribution of scores of 1,000 tosses of a fair coin over the normal distribution. As is apparent, outcomes in a coin toss are not distributed normally. This makes good sense, since there are only two possible scores for the coin toss, heads and tails. No matter what the outcome, it is impossible for a coin toss to approximate the form of the normal distribution.

But let us now turn to a sampling distribution for the coin toss. In this case, we want to know the likelihood of gaining a specific number of heads in a set number of coin tosses. This is the logic we used in developing the binomial probability distribution in chapter 6. In figure 10.2 (see pages 188–189) we present the binomial distribution for different size samples of the coin toss under the null hypothesis that the coin is fair.

For a sample size of 1 (figure 10.2a), the shape of the sampling distribution is the same as the shape of the population distribution of

Figure 10.1   *Distribution of 1,000 Tosses a Fair Coin*
Contrasted to the Normal Distribution

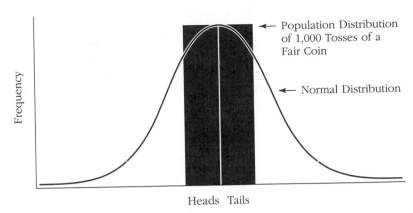

scores. However, notice what happens as the size of the samples used to construct the sampling distributions grow. For a sample of 10 (Figure 10.2b), the histogram for the distribution of scores is still jagged, but it has begun to take a shape similar to the normal distribution. Importantly, for a sample of 10, we do not have two potential outcomes, which would make a normal shape impossible, but 11 potential outcomes (no heads, one head, two heads, three heads, four heads . . . to ten heads). This is the case because we are flipping the coin ten times for each sample. The sampling distribution is telling us the number of times we would expect to gain a specific number of heads in ten tosses of a fair coin in a very large number of trials.

For a sample of 100 flips of a fair coin (Figure 10.2c), the sampling distribution even more closely approximates the normal curve. By the time we get to a sample of 400 flips of the coin (figure 10.2d) the sampling distribution of a fair coin is almost indistinguishable from the normal curve.

The Central Limit Theorem

The distribution of scores for a fair coin is very far from a normal form. Yet the sampling distribution for the same coin begins to approximate the normal distribution as the size of the sample of coin tosses grows. This remarkable fact is summarized in a very important theorem or statement about sampling distributions called the **central limit theorem.** The central limit theorem allows us to overcome our initial dilemma because it says that under many circumstances we can

Figure 10.2

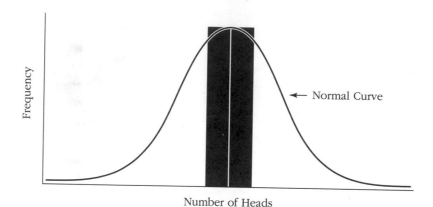

(a) Sampling Distribution for 1 Toss of a Fair Coin

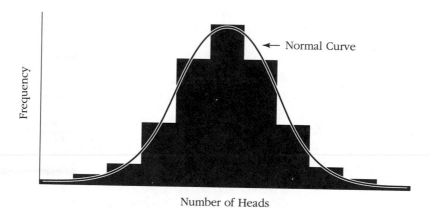

(b) Sampling Distribution for 10 Tosses of a Fair Coin

use a normal sampling distribution for making inferences about a population that is not normal in shape.

Central Limit Theorem
If repeated independent random samples of size N are drawn from a population with mean μ and variance σ^2, then as N grows large, the sampling distribution of sample means will be approximately normal with mean μ and variance σ^2/N.

Figure 10.2   *(continued)*

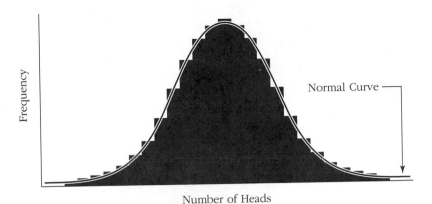

(c) Sampling Distribution for 100 Tosses of a Fair Coin

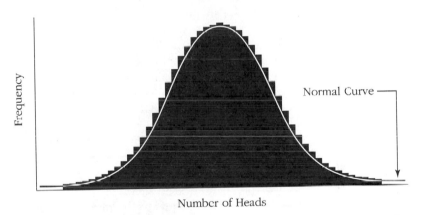

(d) Sampling Distribution for 400 Tosses of a Fair Coin

The central limit theorem tells us that when the number of cases in a sample is large we can assume that the sampling distribution of sample means is approximately normal even if the population distribution itself is not normal. This is what is meant by the statement "then as *N* grows large, the sampling distribution of sample means will be approximately normal." However, the theorem does not provide us with a clear statement about how large the number of cases in a sample must be before we can make this assumption.

One reason for this ambiguity is that the number of cases needed before the sampling distribution begins to approximate normality depends in part on the actual distribution of the measure examined in the population. As can be seen from the example of the coin toss, even when the population distribution departs markedly from the normal distribution, the sampling distribution fits fairly closely to the normal curve with a sample size of 100. For this reason, you will find wide agreement that a normal sampling distribution can be assumed for samples of 100 or more irrespective of the distribution of scores in a population.

There is much less agreement about what to do when a sample is smaller than 100 cases. Some statisticians argue that with 50 cases you can be fairly confident that the central limit theorem applies in most circumstances. Others apply this yardstick to 25 or 30 cases, and still others argue that, under certain circumstances—for example when prior studies suggest a population distribution fairly close to normality—only 15 cases is enough. In conducting research in criminal justice, you should recognize that there is no hard and fast rule regarding sample size and the central limit theorem. In practice, in criminal justice, researchers generally assume that 30 cases is enough for applying the central limit theorem. However, when a distribution strongly departs from normality, as is the case with a proportion, it is safer to require more than 100 cases.

The central limit theorem states that the sampling distribution for a statistical test will be approximately normal when a sample is large irrespective of the shape of the population distribution. This fact removes one barrier to using parametric tests. However, the theorem tells us something else that would seem to raise another difficult barrier to using the normal distribution for making inferences about unknown populations. The theorem states that the mean for the sampling distribution is equal to the mean for the population distribution and that the variance of the sampling distribution is equal to σ^2/N. This means also that the standard deviation, or as it is commonly termed, the **standard error** of the sampling distribution, is equal to the square root of this term or $\sigma/\sqrt{N}$. It would seem that we are back to where we started. In order to define the sampling distribution, we need information about the population parameters (μ and σ).

This information can be gained in part through our test itself. As with the nonparametric tests we have studied, the null hypothesis states the hypothesized value of the population parameter being examined, in this case the mean (μ). Getting an estimate of the standard deviation (σ) of the population distribution is more complex because it is not stated in the null hypothesis. In the following sections, we illustrate two ways in which we can define σ for an unknown population. In the first, illustrated in the next section, we take advantage of the special relationship between the mean and standard deviation of a proportion. In the second, which we turn to afterwards, we estimate the unknown parameter based on information gained in our sample.

Comparing a Sample to an Unknown Population: The z-Test for Proportions

One implication of the central limit theorem is that we can use a normal sampling distribution to test hypotheses involving proportions. This might seem strange at first, since we estimate the shape of a normal distribution through knowledge about its mean and standard deviation. As discussed in chapter 3, the mean and standard deviation are not appropriate statistics to use with a nominal-level measure such as a proportion.

Nonetheless, as illustrated earlier in this chapter, the sampling distribution of a proportion—in our example, the coin toss (see figure 10.2)—begins to approximate a normal distribution when the number of cases for the sample becomes large. The central tendency of this distribution and its dispersion are measured by the mean and standard deviation, just as in distributions that develop from interval-level data. Accordingly, although it would be inappropriate to use the mean and standard deviation to describe a sample or population distribution of a proportion, they are appropriate statistics for describing the normal sampling distribution that is associated with the same proportion.

Computing the Mean and Standard Deviation for the Sampling Distribution of a Proportion

How do we compute the mean and standard deviation of a proportion? One way to do this would be to simply apply the formula for the mean and the standard deviation to the scores associated with a proportion. However, there is a simpler way to arrive at the same result. It turns out that the mean of a proportion is equal to the proportion itself. This is illustrated in table 10.1, which shows an example in which the mean and proportion are calculated for five heads in ten tosses of a coin.

Table 10.1   Calculating the Mean and Proportion of Five Heads in Ten Tosses of a Coin

(a) CALCULATING THE MEAN FOR FIVE HEADS	(b) CALCULATING THE PROPORTION FOR FIVE HEADS
$$\bar{X} = \frac{\sum\limits_{i=1}^{N} X_i}{N} = \frac{1+1+1+1+1+0+0+0+0+0}{10} = 0.5$$	$$Proportion = \frac{N_{successes}}{N_{total}} = \frac{5}{10} = 0.5$$

Note: head = 1; tail = 0

For the numerator of the mean, we sum the scores in the ten trials (five 1s and five 0s) and get 5. The numerator of a proportion is the N of cases in the category of interest. If the category is heads then we also get a result of 5. The denominators for both equations are the same (10), and thus the outcomes are also the same. As a general rule we state that for a proportion: $\mu = P$.

What of the standard deviation of a proportion? It turns out that we can calculate the standard deviation with knowledge of only the proportion itself. This is illustrated in table 10.2. Taking the sum of the squared deviations from the mean and dividing it by N we gain a result of 0.25. But we can gain this same result by multiplying the proportion of heads (P) by the proportion of tails (Q). In our case, by multiplying 0.5 by 0.5. Accordingly, we can substitute $P \cdot Q$ for

$$\sum_{i=1}^{N} (X - \bar{X})^2 / N$$

in the equation for the standard deviation for the mean:

Equation 10.1

$$\sigma = \sqrt{\frac{\sum\limits_{i=1}^{N} (X_i - \bar{X})^2}{N}} = \sqrt{P\,Q}$$

By stating the proportion of successes expected under the null hypothesis, we also state by implication the mean and standard deviation for the population distribution of scores. What this means in practice is that we need not have any a priori knowledge of the shape of the population distribution to construct a sampling distribution for our test of proportions. With a large N, we can assume a normal sampling distribution irrespective of the actual form of the population distribution. Through our null hypothesis, we can define both the mean and the standard deviation or standard error of our sampling distribu-

Table 10.2   Calculating the Standard Deviation of Five Heads in Ten Tosses of a Coin

(a) CALCULATING THE STANDARD DEVIATION FROM THE RAW SCORES	(b) CALCULATING THE STANDARD DEVIATION FROM P AND Q

$$\sigma = \frac{\sqrt{\sum_{i=1}^{N} (X_i - \mu)^2}}{N}$$

$$= \sqrt{\frac{0.25 + 0.25 + 0.25 + 0.25 + 0.25 + 0.25 + 0.25 + 0.25 + 0.25 + 0.25}{10}}$$

$$= \sqrt{0.25} = 0.5$$

$$\sigma = \sqrt{PQ} = \sqrt{(0.5)\,(0.5)} = \sqrt{0.25} = 0.5$$

tion. We are now ready to use the normal distribution to test hypotheses about unknown population parameters.

Testing Hypotheses with the Normal Distribution: The Case of a New Prison Program

Suppose that you were asked to evaluate a new prison education program. The foundation sponsoring the effort sought to achieve a program success rate of 75 percent among the 100,000 prisoners enrolled in the program. Success was defined as completion of a six-month course supported by the foundation. Managers of the program claim that the success rate was actually much greater than the criteria set by the foundation. However, a recent newspaper exposé claims that the success rate of the program is actually much below 75 percent. You are able to collect information on 150 prisoners selected, using independent random sampling. You find that 85 percent of your sample had successfully completed the course. What conclusions can you make about the claims of managers and the newspaper exposé based on your sample results?

Assumptions:
Level of Measurement: Interval scale (program success is measured as a proportion)

Population Distribution: Normal distribution (relaxed because N is large)

Sampling Method: Independent random sampling

Sampling Frame: 100,000 prisoners in the program

Hypotheses:
H_0: The success rate of the program is 0.75. $P = 0.75$.

H_1: The success rate of the program is not 0.75. $P \neq 0.75$.

Because the number of cases in our sample is greater than the threshold of 100 suggested for invoking the central limit theorem in the case of a proportion, we can ignore, or in statistical terms **relax assumptions,** regarding the shape of the population distribution. In the special case of a proportion, we can also relax the assumption of an interval scale of measurement.[1] Our sample, as assumed by our test, is drawn randomly with replacement from the sampling frame of 100,000 prisoners in the program.

Our research hypothesis is nondirectional. Managers of the program claim that the program has a success rate of greater than 0.75 ($P > 0.75$). The newspaper exposé claims that the success rate is much below 75 percent ($P < 0.75$). Accordingly, we want to be able to examine both of these potential outcomes in our test. The null hypothesis is that the rate of success for the program is 0.75 ($P = 0.75$).

The Sampling Distribution

In calculating the mean and standard deviation or standard error for our sampling distribution, we rely on our null hypothesis. Our null hypothesis states that the proportion of successes in the population is 75 percent. This means that the mean of the sampling distribution is also 0.75. We can calculate the standard error of the sampling distribution (σ_{sd}) by taking the square root of the variance as defined in the central limit theorem:

Equation 10.2

$$\sigma_{sd} = \sqrt{\frac{\sigma^2}{N}} = \frac{\sigma}{\sqrt{N}}$$

---

[1] It would not make sense, however, to use a normal distribution test for nominal-scale measures with more than two categories. The normal distribution assumes scores above and below a mean. The sampling distribution of a proportion follows this pattern because it includes only two potential outcomes, which then are associated with each tail of the distribution. In a multicategory nominal-scale measure, we have more than two outcomes, and thus cannot fit each outcome to a tail of the normal curve. Because the order of those outcomes are not defined, we also cannot place them on a continuum within the normal distribution. This latter possibility would suggest that the normal distribution can be applied to ordinal-level measures. However, because we do not assume a constant unit of measurement between ordinal categories, the normal distribution is often considered inappropriate for hypothesis testing with ordinal scales. This issue will be addressed in more detail in the next two chapters. In the case of a proportion, there is a constant unit of measurement between scores simply because there are only two possible outcomes (e.g., success and failure).

For a proportion, based on our knowledge about the relationship between P and the standard deviation, we can rewrite the formula for the standard error as follows:

Equation 10.3

$$\sigma_{sd} = \frac{\sigma}{\sqrt{N}} = \frac{\sqrt{P\,Q}}{\sqrt{N}} = \sqrt{\frac{P\,Q}{N}}$$

Applying this equation to our problem, we obtain a standard error for the normal sampling distribution associated with our null hypothesis of 0.035:

Working It Out

$$\sigma_{sd} = \sqrt{\frac{P\,Q}{N}}$$

$$= \sqrt{\frac{(0.75)\,(0.25)}{150}}$$

$$= \frac{\sqrt{0.1875}}{\sqrt{150}}$$

$$= \frac{0.433}{12.25}$$

$$= 0.0353$$

In order to test our hypothesis we will convert this sampling distribution with mean 0.75 and standard error .035, to the standard normal distribution (or z) which has a mean of 0 and a standard deviation of 1. This calculation is done when we calculate the test statistic below.

Significance Level and Rejection Region

Given that no special concerns have been stated in regard to the risk of either Type I or Type II error, we use a conventional 0.05 significance threshold. As our research hypothesis is nondirectional, we also use a two-tailed test. What this means for our rejection region is illustrated in figure 10.3. On the right-hand side of the distribution are outcomes greater than 0.75 (μ according to H_0), which support the position of the managers. On the left-hand side of the distribution are outcomes less than 0.75, which support the position of the newspaper exposé. Because our research hypothesis is not directional, we split our total rejection region of 5 percent between both tails of the distri-

Figure 10.3   *Showing the Rejection Region on a Normal Frequency Distribution for a 0.05 Two-Tailed Significance Test*

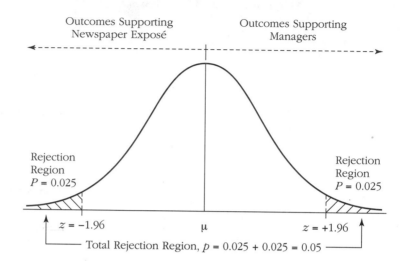

bution. This is represented by the shaded area. Each shaded area represents half the total rejection region, or 0.025.

To define the z-score that corresponds with our rejection region, we must turn to the table of probability values associated with the z distribution (see appendix 1). As discussed in chapter 5, the z table represents only half of the normal curve. We look to the value associated with 0.4750 (1 − 0.0250) in the table, which is 1.96. If we observe a test statistic either greater than or equal to 1.96 or less than or equal to −1.96, we will reject the null hypothesis of our test.

The Test Statistic

We can use the same formula provided for the population distribution of z scores presented in chapter 5 with one change. The standard deviation or standard error (σ_{sd}) of a sampling distribution is not equal to σ, but rather to $\sigma/\sqrt{N}$.

Equation 10.4

$$z = \frac{\overline{X} - \mu}{\sigma_{sd}} = \frac{\overline{X} - \mu}{\sigma/\sqrt{N}}$$

Inserting the values for our problem we obtain the following outcome:

Working It Out

$$z = \frac{\overline{X} - \mu}{\sigma_{sd}} = \frac{\overline{X} - \mu}{\sigma/\sqrt{N}} = \frac{p - P}{\sigma/\sqrt{N}}$$

$$= \frac{0.85 - 0.75}{0.0353}$$

$$= 2.8329$$

The mean of the sample (p) is 0.85, since this is the outcome of the study. The mean of the sampling distribution P(0.75) is taken from our null hypothesis. The standard error of the sampling distribution (σ_{sd}) was calculated earlier based on our null hypothesis that the proportion of successes was 0.75. Our result is a z-score of 2.833.

The Decision

Our test statistic is well within the rejection region of our test (which includes scores greater than or equal to 1.96 or less than or equal to –1.96). We therefore reject the null hypothesis at a 0.05 significance level. We conclude on the side of managers of the program. Our sample results support their position that the overall program has exceeded the criterion for success of the foundation.

Comparing a Sample to an Unknown Population: The *t*-Test for Means

The proportion provides us with a special case in which we can calculate the standard error of our sampling distribution based on our null hypothesis. But this is not possible when our null hypothesis relates to a mean of an interval-level measure. In this case there is not just one specific variance or standard deviation associated with a mean but an infinite number of potential variances or standard deviations.

How, then, can we test hypotheses about unknown parameters in the case of the mean? One obvious method is to simply use the variance of our sample as a "guesstimate" of the variance of the population distribution. The problem with this solution is that the variance of a sample is a somewhat biased estimate of the variance of the population. By this, we mean that the average of repeated observations of the variance (s^2) tends in the long run not to be equivalent to the value of σ^2. We can transform s^2 to a better estimate of σ^2 through a very small correction to the equation for the variance. This new statistic (expressed as $\hat{\sigma}^2$ since it is an estimate of σ^2) is represented in equation 10.5. An estimate of the standard deviation ($\hat{\sigma}$) can be gained by taking the square root of this value.

Equation 10.5

$$\hat{\sigma}^2 = \frac{\displaystyle\sum_{i=1}^{N} (X_i - \overline{X})^2}{N - 1}$$

In order to use this new statistic to test hypotheses, we must also use a slightly different sampling distribution, called the t distribution. It is sometimes called Student's t because its inventor, W. S. Gossett (1876–1936) first described the distribution under the pen name Student in 1908.

The t distribution (appendix 4) is very similar to the z distribution (appendix 1). However, like the chi-square test, the shape of the t distribution is dependent on the number of degrees of freedom. Degrees of freedom for t are defined as $N - 1$. When the number of cases in a sample is greater than 500, then the t and z distributions are virtually identical. However, as the number of cases in a sample gets smaller and smaller, and so accordingly do the number of degrees of freedom, the t distribution becomes flatter and a larger and larger test statistic is needed to reject the null hypothesis.

This fact can be illustrated by looking at the t table in appendix 4. As you can see, the t table lists the critical values associated with six significance thresholds for both one- and two-tailed tests. Let us focus on the fourth column, which is the critical value associated with a two-tailed, 5 percent significance level. When degrees of freedom are 500, the critical value for the t-statistic is the same as for the z distribution, 1.960. At 120, the t value needed to reject the null hypothesis is still almost the same, 1.980. At 100, the value is 1.982, at 50 it is 2.008, and at 25 it is 2.060. The largest differences come for even smaller degrees of freedom.

The t distribution presents a new problem as well in making inferences to unknown populations. It is generally considered more risky to relax the assumption of normality in a t-test as compared with a z-test. This makes good sense because we are now using an estimate of σ rather than the actual population parameter. As the number of cases increases, our confidence in this estimate grows.[2] How large should N be before you are willing to use a t-test? With samples of more than

---

[2] Our statistical problem is that we assume that $\overline{X}$ and s are independent in developing the t distribution. When a distribution is normal, this is indeed the case. However, for other types of distributions we cannot make this assumption, and when N is small, a violation of this assumption is likely to lead to misleading approximations of the statistical significance of a test.

30 cases, your statistical conclusions are not likely to be challenged. However, the *t* distribution is particularly sensitive to outliers. Conclusions based on smaller samples should be checked carefully to make sure that one or two observations are not the cause of a very large statistical outcome.

Testing Hypotheses with the *t* Distribution

We are now ready to turn to a practical example. Suppose that the study described earlier also examined the average test scores for those prisoners who have completed the program. The foundation set a standard of success of 65 on the test. Program managers say that prisoners who have completed the program achieve average scores that are much higher than this. The newspaper exposé again claims that the average scores are considerably lower than those expected by the foundation. In this case you are able to take an independent random sample of 50 prisoners who have completed the test. You find that the test mean for the sample is 60, and the standard deviation is 15. What conclusions about the larger population of prisoners can you come to based on your sample results?

Assumptions:
Level of Measurement: Interval scale

Population Distribution: Normal distribution (relaxed because N is large)

Sampling Method: Independent random sampling

Sampling Frame: Prisoners who have completed the program

Hypotheses:
H_0: The mean test score for prisoners who have completed the program is 65. $\mu = 65$.

H_1: The mean test score for prisoners who have completed the program is not 65. $\mu \neq 65$.

Following the assumptions of our test, we use an interval scale (the mean of test scores) and an independent random sampling method. We relax the assumption of normality because N is larger than the minimum threshold of 30 recommended for interval-level measures. Our research hypothesis is once again nondirectional so that we can examine the positions of both the managers of the program and the newspaper exposé. The null hypothesis is that the mean test score for the population of prisoners completing the program is 65 (the foundation standard), or that $\mu = 65$.

The Sampling Distribution

Because σ is unknown and cannot be deduced from our null hypothesis, we will use the t distribution. The degrees of freedom for our example is defined as $N - 1$, or $50 - 1 = 49$.

The Significance Level and Rejection Region

Again, we have no reason in this example to depart from the 0.05 significance threshold. Because our research hypothesis is not directional, we use a two-tailed test. Turning to the t table, we find that a t-score of 2.01 is associated with a two-tailed, 5 percent significance threshold (at 49 degrees of freedom). This means that we will reject our null hypothesis if we obtain a test statistic greater than or equal to 2.01 or less than or equal to -2.01.

The Test Statistic

The test statistic for the t distribution is similar to that for the distribution z. The only difference is that we now use an estimate of the standard deviation ($\hat{\sigma}$) rather than σ itself.

Equation 10.6

$$t = \frac{\overline{X} - \mu}{\sigma_{sd}} = \frac{\overline{X} - \mu}{\hat{\sigma}/\sqrt{N}}$$

Although we can get an estimate of σ by adjusting the calculation for s, the formula for t may also be written in a way that allows us to calculate t from the unadjusted sample standard deviation.

$$t = \frac{\overline{X} - \mu}{\hat{\sigma}/\sqrt{N}} = \frac{\overline{X} - \mu}{\sqrt{\dfrac{\sum\limits_{i=1}^{N}(X - \overline{X})^2}{N-1}} \Big/ \sqrt{N}}$$

$$= \frac{\overline{X} - \mu}{\sqrt{\dfrac{\sum\limits_{i=1}^{N}(X - \overline{X})^2}{N}} \Big/ \sqrt{N-1}}$$

This means that we can simplify the equation for the t-test as follows:

Equation 10.7

$$t = \frac{\overline{X} - \mu}{s/\sqrt{N-1}}$$

Applying the t formula to our example, we place the mean of the sample, or 60, as $\overline{X}$. μ is defined by the null hypothesis as 65. s is our sample standard deviation of 15, and N is the number of cases for our sample (50).

Working It Out

$$t = \frac{\overline{X} - \mu}{s/\sqrt{N-1}}$$

$$= \frac{60 - 65}{15/\sqrt{50-1}}$$

$$= \frac{-5}{15/7}$$

$$= \frac{-5}{2.1429}$$

$$= -2.3333$$

The Decision

Because the test statistic is smaller than −2.01, we reject the null hypothesis and conclude that the result is significantly different from the goal set by the foundation. In this case, our decision is on the side of the newspaper exposé. We can conclude from our sample (with a 5 percent risk of falsely rejecting the null hypothesis) that the test scores in the population of prisoners who have completed the program are below the foundation goal of 65.

A Note about Confidence Intervals

The logic we have used so far allows us to make a statement about where the parameter is not. When we reject the null hypothesis, we conclude that it is unlikely that the mean or proportion for the population has a specific value (the H_0). However, we can use similar logic to make a very different statement about parameters. In this case we can ask where it is likely that the population parameters are found. In statistics, this is called a **confidence interval,** because we define an interval of values around the sample mean within which we can be fairly confident that the true parameter lies.

Figure 10.4   *Showing the 5% Rejection Region and the 95% Confidence Interval on a Normal Frequency Distribution (where $\overline{X}$ and $\mu = 0$)*

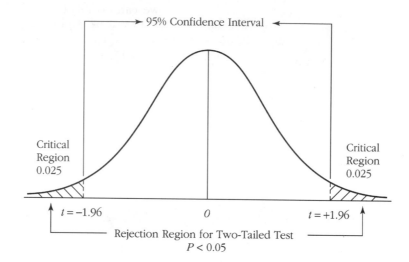

Figure 10.4 illustrates the difference between the logic we use in a test of statistical significance and that which we use in a confidence interval. The figure includes both the rejection region for a two-tailed, 0.05 significance test and the 95 percent confidence interval for the same problem. In this example, the mean of our test statistic ($\overline{X}$) and the mean of the null hypothesis (μ) are equal to 0. This would not likely happen in practice, but it allows us to compare a confidence interval and rejection region in a very straightforward manner.

In this example, the rejection region begins where the confidence interval ends. In other words, the confidence interval includes all of the scores for the distribution that are not included in the rejection region. It is the flip side of our test of significance, or the scores for which we would not reject our null hypothesis. For this reason, when we construct a confidence interval, we are saying that we think it very likely that the true population mean lies somewhere in that interval. The rejection region, in contrast, identifies values that are unlikely given our null hypothesis.

To construct a confidence interval we simply alter our equations to fit our new logic. Remember that the t equation is written as follows:

$$t = \frac{\overline{X} - \mu}{s/\sqrt{N-1}}$$

To construct a confidence interval, we want to adjust this equation so that μ is on the right-hand side and everything else is on the left-hand side of the equal sign. We can do this through simple algebra. Thus we move the denominator of the equation by multiplying both sides of the equation by the denominator. We then add $\overline{X}$ to both sides. Overall, the equation is not equal to μ itself but rather to the confidence limit of μ, which represents the boundary of the confidence interval. Our result is equation 10.8.

Equation 10.8

$$\text{Confidence Limit} = \overline{X} \pm t \left(\frac{s}{\sqrt{N-1}} \right)$$

Since we are interested in a confidence interval both above and below $\overline{X}$ we attach a $-$ to the $+$ in our equation.

The t-value in the equation coincides with the level of confidence we require. Following our logic earlier, this t-value is the flip side of the significance threshold. For a 95 percent confidence interval we use a t value associated with a 0.05 significance level. For a 99 percent confidence interval, we use a t-value associated with a 0.01 significance level.

Taking our example of mean test scores in the foundation prison program, we can now identify a 95 percent confidence interval around our sample mean of 0.60. We place the t-score associated with a 0.05 significance level (2.01) in place of t and then insert s (15) and N (5) for our example in the equation:

Working It Out

$$\text{Confidence Limit} = X \pm t \left(\frac{s}{\sqrt{N-1}} \right)$$

$$= 0.60 \pm 2.01 \left(\frac{15}{\sqrt{50-1}} \right)$$

$$= 0.60 \pm 4.3$$

Our result is $+$ or $-$ 4.3 meaning that the 95 percent confidence interval includes test scores between 55.7 (i.e., $\overline{X} - 4.3$) and 64.3 ($\overline{X} + 4.3$). If the assumptions underlying the t-test are met, we can be fairly confident that the population mean lies somewhere in this interval. Sample statistics similar to those we gained would be expected in only 5 in every 100 samples if the population mean were greater than 64.3 or less than 55.7.

What of our example using proportions? Here we follow the same logic. The z equation may be altered to define the confidence limits in the same way as the t equation:

Equation 10.9   *Confidence Limit* $= \overline{X} \pm z\, \sigma_{sd}$

Below we apply this equation to our earlier example of the proportion of prisoners who have completed the program, using a 99 percent confidence interval. The proportion of prisoners completing the program in our sample is defined as $\overline{X}$ (= 0.85). The z-score in this case is 2.576 (corresponding with an area of 0.005 in each tail) and the standard error of the sampling distribution is 0.035 (as calculated earlier):

Working It Out

$$Confidence\ Limit = \overline{X} \pm z\, \sigma_{sd}$$

$$= 0.85 \pm 2.576\,(0.035)$$

$$= 0.85 \pm 0.09$$

The confidence interval is + or −9 percent. It suggests that we can be very confident based on our sample results that the proportion of prisoners overall who successfully complete the program lies between 76 and 94 percent. If we were to observe repeated samples and calculate a confidence interval for each (in the same manner as above), then only about 1 in 100 would fail to include the true population proportion.

Chapter Summary

Parametric tests of significance allow us to make inferences about a population from samples using interval-level data. In a parametric test, we make certain assumptions about the shape of the population distribution at the outset. How can we make assumptions about the very thing we are trying to determine? The **central limit theorem** provides the solution. According to the theorem, when the number of cases in a sample is large, the sampling distribution will be approximately normal in shape even if the population distribution itself is not. In the field of criminal justice, it is generally assumed that the central limit theorem can be applied where the sample size is 30 or greater. When dealing with proportions, though, it is safer to require a sample size of at least 100. In such circumstances, we may **relax the assumption** of normality. We can now make inferences using a normal sampling distribution, even though the shape of the population distribution is unknown.

In order to define the sampling distribution we need information about the population parameters—information that is not usually available. In the case of a test involving proportions, the null hypothesis can be used to define both the mean and the standard error of the population distribution. Once the population parameters have been defined, we can then apply the formula for the z-test of significance. In the case of a test of means, the null hypothesis cannot be used directly to define the standard error. We may, however, use the t sampling distribution, which relies upon an estimate of the standard error.

By placing a **confidence interval** around a statistic, we are indicating the degree of confidence we have that the true population parameter falls within its boundaries. The boundaries of the confidence interval can be determined by rearranging the equations for the z-test or the t-test.

Key Terms

Central Limit Theorem A theorem that states: "If repeated independent random samples of size N are drawn from a population with mean μ and variance σ^2, then as N grows large, the sampling distribution of sample means will be approximately normal with mean μ and variance σ^2/N." The central limit theorem enables the researcher to make inferences about an unknown population using a normal sampling distribution.

Confidence Interval An interval of values placed around a statistic on a sampling distribution. In placing the interval boundaries on either side of a statistic, we are stating how confident we are that the true parameter falls within these two boundaries.

Relaxing Assumptions When an assumption for a test may be relaxed, we need not be concerned with that assumption. The assumption that a population is normal may be relaxed if the sample size is sufficiently large to invoke the central limit theorem.

Standard Error The standard deviation of a sampling distribution.

Symbols and Formulas

p Proportion of successes (sample).

P Proportion of successes (population).

Q Proportion of failures (population).

σ_{sd} Standard error of sampling distribution.

σ_p Standard deviation of a proportion.

t t-score.

$\wedge$ Estimate.

To determine the standard deviation of a proportion:

$$\sigma_p = \sqrt{P\,Q}$$

To determine the standard error of a sampling distribution:

$$\sigma_{sd} = \frac{\sigma}{\sqrt{N}}$$

To determine the z-score for a sample mean:

$$z = \frac{\overline{X} - \mu}{\sigma_{sd}} = \frac{\overline{X} - \mu}{\sigma/\sqrt{N}}$$

To determine the z-score for a sample proportion:

$$z = \frac{\overline{X} - \mu}{\sigma_{sd}} = \frac{\overline{X} - \mu}{\sigma/\sqrt{N}} = \frac{p - P}{\sqrt{\dfrac{P\,Q}{N}}}$$

To estimate the value of σ from data in a sample:

$$\hat{\sigma} = \sqrt{\frac{\displaystyle\sum_{i=1}^{N} (X - \overline{X})^2}{N - 1}}$$

To determine the value of t:

$$t = \frac{\overline{X} - \mu}{s/\sqrt{N - 1}}$$

To determine the confidence interval from a z distribution:

$$Confidence\ Limit = \overline{X} \pm z\,\sigma_{sd}$$

To determine the confidence interval from a t distribution:

$$Confidence\ Limit = \overline{X} \pm t\ \frac{s}{\sqrt{N-1}}$$

Exercises

10.1 In which of the following circumstances would a researcher be justified in using a normal sampling distribution?

a A sample of 10 subjects is drawn to study a variable known to be normally distributed in the population.

b A sample of 50 subjects is drawn to study a variable known to be normally distributed in the population.

c A sample of 10 subjects is drawn to study a variable. The shape of the distribution of this variable in the population is unknown.

d A sample of 50 subjects is drawn to study a variable. The shape of the distribution of this variable in the population is unknown.

e A sample of 50 subjects is drawn to study a proportion. The shape of the distribution of this proportion in the population is unknown.

Note: In the text, we do not give examples for which the value of σ is known from the outset, for it is rare that a researcher will be interested in making inferences about a population whose parameters are already known. Nonetheless, the following two exercises (10.2 and 10.3) are included to help the student with the basic calculations involved.

10.2 An established test measuring "respect for authority" has a mean among U.S. adults of 73 and a standard error of 13.8. Brenda gives the test to 36 prison inmates and finds the mean score to be 69.

a Is this enough evidence to suggest that the prisoners belong to a population that has significantly less respect for authority than the general U.S. adult population? Remember to outline each of the stages of a statistical test of significance.

10.3 The governor of Stretford prison has a biographical record of all the inmates. The mean age of all the inmates is 22 with a standard deviation of 7.5. A recent survey by a hostile researcher makes damaging criticisms of the educational standards in the prison. The prison governor suspects that the 50 prisoners interviewed for the study were not chosen at random. The mean age of the prisoners chosen was 20.

Can the governor use this finding to cast doubt upon the sampling method of the survey? Remember to outline each of the stages of a statistical test of significance.

10.4   A hundred years ago an anonymous scientist wrote a famous indictment of a notoriously cruel prison somewhere in the United States. Without ever referring to the prison by name, the scientist checked the records of all those who were imprisoned in its 50-year history, and found that 15 percent of those who entered died within. Henry, a historian, is intrigued by the old report and publishes an article in a historical journal in which he states his conviction that the report was referring to Grimsville prison, which existed around about that time. In the subsequent issue of the journal, a rival historian claims that Henry has shown no evidence to support his theory.

Henry finds the records from Grimsville, and from a sample of 80 prisoner records he discovers that 11 percent of them died inside. Can he use this information to substantiate his claim that the object of the report is indeed Grimsville?

10.5   Every pupil at Foggy-Lane College was asked a series of questions, which led to an overall score grading "satisfaction" with the college's discipline procedures. The overall mean score was 65. Roger suspects that the black students at the college feel differently. He takes a random sample of 25 black students from the college and finds that their mean satisfaction score is 61 with a standard deviation of 8.

Are the black students' views on discipline significantly different from those of the general student population?

10.6   A special police unit has spent several years tracking all the members of a large child-abuse ring. In an interview to a daily newspaper, a junior detective on the unit claims that the ringleaders have been tracked down and will shortly be arrested. In response to questions by the interviewer about the makeup of the child-abuse ring, the detective replies, "We have gathered details on every last member of this criminal group—they come from very varied backgrounds and their average age is 36."

X is the chairperson of a charitable club, which is in fact a front for a substantial child-abuse circle. He reads the newspaper article and fears that it might refer to him and his group. He looks through the club's membership files and draws a sample of 50 members, finding an average age of 40 with a standard deviation of 9.

Can X be confident that the detective interviewed in the newspaper was not referring to *his* criminal group?

10.7   Following a revolution, the new leadership of the nation of Kippax intends to hold a national referendum on whether the practice of capital punishment should be introduced. In the buildup to the referendum, a leading army general wishes to gauge how the people are likely to vote so that he can make a public statement in line with popular feeling on the issue. He commissions Greg, a statistician, to carry out a secret poll of how people are expected to vote. The results of Greg's poll are as follows: The sample proportion in favor of introducing capital punishment is 52 percent; the sample had a 95 percent confidence interval of ±10 percent.

How should Greg explain these results to the army general?

10.8   Refer back to exercise 10.5.

a What are the confidence limits of Roger's sample?

b What does this mean in plain English?

Parametric Tests Comparing Means and Proportions in Two Samples

comparing sample proportions

What Is the Two-Sample z-Test?

What Are the Assumptions of the Test?

How Is the Test Carried Out?

comparing sample means

What Is the Two-Sample t-Test?

What Are the Assumptions of the Test?

How Is the Test Carried Out?

What Happens When the Samples Are Not Independent?

$\mathbf{I}$N CHAPTER 10 we introduced parametric significance tests, which compared the mean or proportion of a single sample with a population goal or parameter. In this chapter we turn to a more commonly used application of parametric tests of significance: comparisons between samples. Let us say, for example, that you are interested in whether there is a difference in the mean salary of men and women police officers, or in the proportion of African Americans and others arrested last year. Your question in either of these cases is not whether the population parameters have particular values, but whether the parameters for the groups examined in each case are different. This involves comparisons of means and proportions for two populations. If you take samples from those populations, you can make inferences regarding the differences between them by building upon the z-test and t-test covered in the previous chapter.

Comparing Sample Proportions: The Case of Drug Testing and Pretrial Misconduct

In a study conducted in Maricopa County, Arizona, criminal justice researchers examined whether drug testing of defendants released before trial had an impact on pretrial misconduct.[1] They compared two groups of defendants who were released before trial. The first group was monitored through drug testing two times a week. The second group was released without subsequent drug testing. The sample was chosen over a six-month period. The researchers identified subjects

---

[1]See Chester Britt III, Michael Gottfredson, and John S. Goldkamp (1992), Drug Testing and Pretrial Misconduct: An Experiment on the Specific Deterrent Effects of Drug Monitoring Defendants on Pretrial Release, *Journal of Research in Crime and Delinquency* 29:62–78.

for the study through identification numbers kept in a computerized case-management system. Defendants with odd identification numbers were placed in the drug-testing group. Defendants with even identification numbers were placed in the control, or no drug-testing, group. The drug-testing group had 118 subjects. The control group had 116 subjects.

The researchers followed up on both of these groups of defendants for 90 days. One measure of pretrial misconduct was failure to appear at a hearing during the follow-up period. Thirty-eight percent of the control group and 30 percent of the drug-testing group failed to appear at a hearing during this period. The question the researchers wanted to answer was whether they could infer from this difference between these two samples that there is in fact a difference in pretrial misconduct between the populations these samples represent. An appropriate statistical test to answer this question, as well as other questions comparing group proportions, is the z-test.

Assumptions:

Level of Measurement: Interval scale (failure to appear is measured as a proportion)

Population Distribution: Both populations are normally distributed (relaxed because N is large)

Sampling Method: Independent random sampling (all cases for six months are selected)

Sampling Frame: Defendants released before trial for a six-month period in Maricopa County, Arizona

Hypotheses:

H_0: The two populations do not differ in terms of the proportion who fail to appear for a pretrial hearing: $P_1 = P_2$.

H_1: The two populations do differ in terms of the proportion who fail to appear for a pretrial hearing: $P_1 \neq P_2$.

The **two-sample z-test** includes assumptions similar to the single-sample test. It requires an interval level of measurement, as well as a normal population distribution for each of the two samples examined. The actual level of measurement for our example (as stated in parentheses in our assumptions) is nominal—we compare two proportions. As with the single-sample test of proportions, when the sample sizes are large we can relax assumptions regarding the level of measurement used and the shape of the populations examined. Because we have two samples and not just one, the central limit theorem will apply only when both samples are large. The definition of how large samples must be to invoke the central limit theorem is again a matter of debate. However, when each sample includes more than 100 cases, as is true for the Arizona study, there will be little argument regarding the use of this parametric test for proportions.

For a two-sample test, we must assume that both samples are independent random samples. In practice, researchers do not ordinarily use separate sampling procedures to identify the samples representing each population of interest. Rather, they draw a random sample from all members of a population, and then assume that specific samples within the larger sample are also independent and random. For example, researchers interested in attitudes toward crime in the United States would generally draw an independent random sample of all U.S. residents. They may, however, also have an interest in comparing men and women, or college graduates and non–college graduates in terms of their attitudes. If the larger sample had been drawn as an independent random sample, the subsamples are also independent random samples.[2]

The one practical difficulty here develops when the number of subjects in a particular subpopulation is small. For example, when surveys are taken of U.S. residents, a very small group of Jews or Moslems is likely to be sampled using a simple independent random sample. Thus, even though such samples will still be independent and random (if the larger sample is independent and random), you may not end up with many cases because such groups represent a small proportion of the U.S. population. When there is interest in a subpopulation that is small, researchers will often identify such groups for special attention and attempt to draw larger samples from them.

In our example, researchers did not draw an independent random sample either for the drug-testing group or the control group. Rather, as was the case with the cell allocation study we examined in chapter 9, they sampled all defendants released before trial in Maricopa County for a specific period of time, in this case six months. In order to create the two samples, the researchers assigned the defendants to the groups according to their identification numbers: even numbered

---

[2]The logic here follows simple common sense. If you select each case independently and randomly from a population, on each selection you have an equal probability of choosing any individual, whether a male or female, someone college educated or not, and so on. From the perspective of a particular group, for example, males, each time you have chosen a man, the method can be seen as independent and random. That is, the likelihood of choosing any male from the sample is the same each time a case is drawn. Of course, sometimes you will draw a female. However, for the population of males, each male has an equal chance of selection on each draw in the sample. And if the sampling method is independent, then each male has an equal chance of being selected every time a case is selected.

subjects were assisgned to the control group and odd numbered subjects to the drug-testing group.

In making statistical inferences, the researchers were clearly interested in inferring beyond their sampling frame (defendants released before trial during the six-month period) not only to other time periods in Maricopa County, but also to other jurisdictions and other programs that are similar to the one they studied.[3] They argued that their findings were likely to apply to other "sophisticated and experienced pretrial services agencies." They also noted that it "is reasonable to assume that the programs that were implemented are comparable to the programs that are likely to be implemented in similar agencies." When drawing conclusions from this research, we would have to consider whether the sample used can in fact be seen as representative of these larger populations.

Our final assumptions relate to our hypotheses. In a two-sample test, we generally do not try to define the exact value of the parameters of interest. Rather, we question whether the two populations under study are similar or different. The null hypotheses, as in earlier tests, is that there is no difference. It assumes that those monitored through drug testing and those not (the control group) will have the same proportion of defendants who fail to appear. Another way of expressing this is just to note that the proportion of failures in the drug-tested population (P_1) of released defendants is the same as that in the population that is not drug tested (or P_2), or that $P_1 = P_2$. The research hypothesis is that the two populations are different in the proportion that fail to appear, or $P_1 \neq P_2$. The researchers chose a nondirectional research hypothesis because they wanted to consider both the possibility that drug testing would increase compliance, and thus reduce pretrial misconduct, and that drug testing might lead to less compliance, and thus increase pretrial misconduct.

The Sampling Distribution

Because N is large for both samples, we can use a z distribution as our sampling distribution for testing the difference between proportions. But in applying the z-test to two samples, we are faced with questions similar to those we asked in developing single-sample tests. First, what is the mean of our sampling distribution? Second, how do we define the standard error of this sampling distribution?

The first question is answered in good part simply by stating what it is we are examining in this test. We want to know whether the dif-

---

[3]In fact, although we do not examine their findings here, Britt et al. conducted their study in two Arizona counties.

ference observed (0.30 for the drug-testing group versus 0.38 for the control group—a difference of 0.08) can lead us to reliably reject the null hypothesis that there is no difference between the two populations. Accordingly, our sampling distribution should allow us to contrast the observed difference in our samples, 0.08, with the expected difference according to the null hypothesis of 0 (or no difference). The mean of our sampling distribution is $P_1 - P_2$, or simply 0, because the null hypothesis states that the two population proportions are the same.

Defining the standard deviation or standard error of our sampling distribution takes a bit more work. In the one sample case, the central limit theorem told us that the variance of a sampling distribution of a population with variance σ^2 is σ^2/N. With two samples, we take into account the variances of two populations in constructing the standard error of our sampling distribution. Accordingly, the standard error of a sampling distribution of the difference of proportions is the square root of the sum of the two sample variances.

$$\sigma_{sd} = \sqrt{\frac{\sigma_1^2}{N_1} + \frac{\sigma_2^2}{N_2}}$$

Although we want to take into account the fact that we are looking at two populations in our sampling distribution, in fact, according to our null hypothesis, the two populations have the same variance and standard deviation. This follows directly from the null hypothesis that $P_1 = P_2$ and the fact that the standard deviation in the case of any proportion is equal to the square root of the product of P and Q (defined as $1 - P$):

$$\sigma = \sqrt{PQ}$$

But how do we define the value of P? Our null hypothesis states that the proportion of defendants who fail to appear at hearings in the two populations is the same. It does not, however, tell us what that common value is. Accordingly, we must choose a value for P from the information that we have available to us. We do this by taking a weighted estimate of the observed values in the two samples. Equation 11.1 provides a mathematical method for gaining a value of P that gives more weight to the sample that has the most cases:

Equation 11.1 $$\hat{P} = \frac{N_1 p_1 + N_2 p_2}{N_1 + N_2}$$

The calculation for our example is carried out step-by-step below. The weighted estimate of $\hat{P}$ is 0.34. $\hat{Q}$ then is $1 - 0.34$, or 0.66.

Working It Out

$$\hat{P} = \frac{N_1 p_1 + N_2 p_2}{N_1 + N_2}$$

$$= \frac{(118)\,(0.30) + (116)\,(0.38)}{116 + 118}$$

$$= 0.3397$$

Now that we have estimates of P and Q for the two populations, we can estimate the standard deviation ($\hat{\sigma}$) for the population distribution, as shown in equation 11.2:

Equation 11.2

$$\hat{\sigma} = \sqrt{\hat{P}\hat{Q}}$$

For our sample, the result is 0.474.

Working It Out

$$\hat{\sigma} = \sqrt{\hat{P}\hat{Q}}$$

$$= \sqrt{(0.34)\,(0.66)}$$

$$= \sqrt{0.2244}$$

$$= 0.4737$$

Using this estimate of σ, we can define the standard error of the sampling distribution, represented as $\sigma_{sd(P_1 - P_2)}$. Earlier we defined the standard error as the combination of the standard errors from the two samples. But we can simplify this equation because the standard deviations of the two populations are assumed to be the same under the null hypothesis. This simplification process is performed in table 11.1. Using the simplified equation in table 11.1, we obtain an estimate for the standard error of our sampling distribution of 0.062:

Working It Out

$$\hat{\sigma}_{sd(p_1 - p_2)} = \hat{\sigma}\sqrt{\frac{N_1 + N_2}{N_1 N_2}}$$

$$= 0.474\sqrt{\frac{118 + 116}{(118)\,(116)}}$$

$$= 0.474\sqrt{0.017095}$$

$$= 0.0620$$

Table 11.1   Simplification of the Equation for the Standard Error
for the Sampling Distribution for Two Samples $(\sigma_1 = \sigma_2)$

$$\hat{\sigma}_{sd(p_1 - p_2)} = \sqrt{\frac{\hat{\sigma}_1^2}{N_1} + \frac{\hat{\sigma}_2^2}{N_2}}$$

$$= \hat{\sigma}\sqrt{\frac{1}{N_1} + \frac{1}{N_2}}$$

$$= \hat{\sigma}\sqrt{\frac{N_1 + N_2}{N_1 N_2}}$$

Significance Level and Rejection Region

The researchers in the Maricopa County study decided to use "conventional levels" of statistical significance—that is, a rejection region of $p \leq 0.05$. Following their research hypothesis, they also used a two-tailed test of statistical significance. To define the z-values that correspond with that rejection region, we must turn to the table of probability values associated with the z distribution (appendix 1). As discussed in chapter 10, the z table provides critical values in reference to one side of the normal distribution. In this case, we are looking for a value of 0.475, since the total rejection region on each tail of the distribution is 0.025. The z-score associated with 0.475 is 1.96. If our test statistic is either greater than or equal to 1.96 or less than or equal to −1.96, we will reject the null hypothesis that there is no difference between the drug-testing and non–drug-testing populations.

The Test Statistic

To define the z-score appropriate for our test we must alter equation 10.4 to take into account the fact that we are now comparing two samples. First, we must adjust the numerator to reflect the fact that the differences observed in our study are compared with those defined in the null hypothesis. Second, we must adjust the denominator to reflect the standard error of the difference between proportions.

Equation 11.3 provides the adjusted z-test for proportions. In the numerator we have two quantities. The first is the difference between the two sample proportions $(p_1 - p_2)$. The second is the difference between the two populations as defined by the null hypothesis $(P_1 - P_2)$. Because the null hypothesis states that the two populations are equal, this quantity is equal to 0. For the denominator we have simply replaced the standard error used for a sampling distribution when comparing a sample to a population with the standard error used when comparing sample means drawn from two populations. This quantity was defined in our discussion of the sampling distribution.

Equation 11.3

$$z = \frac{(p_1 - p_2) - (P_1 - P_2)}{\hat{\sigma} \sqrt{\dfrac{N_1 + N_2}{N_1 N_2}}}$$

The z-score calculated for our problem is -1.290.

Working It Out

$$z = \frac{(p_1 - p_2) - (P_1 - P_2)}{\hat{\sigma} \sqrt{\dfrac{N_1 + N_2}{N_1 N_2}}}$$

$$= \frac{(0.3 - 0.38) - 0}{0.474 \sqrt{\dfrac{118 + 116}{(118)(116)}}}$$

$$= \frac{-0.08}{0.0620}$$

$$= -1.2903$$

The Decision

Because our test statistic falls between the two critical values of -1.96 and $+1.96$, we fail to reject the null hypothesis that there is no difference in failure to appear at hearings for the drug testing and control populations. Based on these and other similar results, the researchers in this study concluded that "systematic drug testing and monitoring in the pretrial setting, in programs such as those described above [i.e., examined in this research], is not likely to achieve significant" change in pretrial misconduct.

Comparing Sample Means: The Case of Anxiety among Police Officers and Firefighters

In a study conducted by University of Washington researchers, police officers were compared to firefighters in terms of the amount of stress and anxiety they felt on the job.[4] One measure they used was derived by creating an interval scale index from questions about the occur-

[4]Michael Pendleton, Ezra Stotland, Philip Spiers and Edward Kirsch (1989), Stress and Strain among Police, Firefighters, and Government Workers: A Comparative Analysis, *Criminal Justice and Behavior* 16:196–210.

rence on the job of symptoms of anxiety, such as sweating and "the jitters." The researchers drew a sample of police officers by going to police stations and asking officers to be paid participants in their study. For firefighters, the researchers randomly selected subjects. Their final sample, all drawn from one city, included 127 firefighters and 197 police officers. They found in their sample that the mean anxiety-on-the-job score for police officers was 12.8 ($s_1 = 2.76$), whereas that for firefighters was 8.8 ($s_2 = 2.85$). What conclusions can the researchers come to regarding the larger populations of firefighters and police officers from these sample statistics?

For this question, as other problems involving comparisons between the means of two groups, we turn again to the t-test introduced in chapter 10.

Assumptions:

Level of Measurement: Interval scale

Population Distribution: Both populations are normally distributed (relaxed because N is large)

Sampling Method: Independent random sampling (A nonrandom sampling technique was used for police officers. Random sampling without replacement was used for firefighters.)

Sampling Frame: All police officers and firefighters in one city.

Hypotheses:

H_0: The mean anxiety-on-the-job score for the population of police officers is the same as that for the population of firefighters: $\mu_1 = \mu_2$.

H_1: The mean anxiety-on-the-job score for the population of police officers is different than that for the population of firefighters: $\mu_1 \neq \mu_2$.

As required in the **two-sample t-test,** the level of measurement for anxiety on the job is interval. However, we must rely on the central limit theorem to relax the second assumption—that the population distribution of anxiety on the job is normal for police and for firefighters. As with the test of differences between proportions, the number of cases needed to invoke the central limit theorem applies to each sample. In chapter 10 we noted that a sample of 30 or more was generally large enough to apply the central limit theorem in a test for means. For a two-sample test, you will need a minimum of 30 cases in each sample. In our example, both samples include a much larger number of subjects, and thus we can relax the assumption of normality.

As with other tests we have examined, we are also required to use an independent random sampling method. For firefighters, the researchers used a random sampling method, although they did not sample with replacement. This violation of assumptions is not serious because the sample of firefighters drawn was small relative to the number of subjects in the sampling frame. The method of sampling for police officers provides a more serious violation of the assumptions of our test. The researchers did not draw a random sample. Nonetheless, they argue that their sample is still representative of the population of police officers in the city:

> Participant officers were compared with those of the nonparticipant officers on available data (which were acquired by the police department independently of the study). These data included entrance psychological tests, current departmental physical fitness tests, age, sex, and so on. . . . The participant and non-participant groups did not differ significantly on 25 comparison variables.

The validity of our inferences to the larger population of police officers in the city depends on how persuasive we view the researchers' claims that their sample is representative. But irrespective of the generalizeability of these samples to the population of officers in the city, the researchers also want to infer their findings beyond their sampling frame to police officers and firefighters more generally. For this conclusion to be justified, the researchers would have to explain why this city's firefighters and police officers are representative of firefighters and police officers in other cities.

The null hypothesis for a difference of means test will generally be that there is no difference, and this is the case in the University of Washington research. The null hypothesis states simply that the mean anxiety-on-the-job score for the populations of police officers (μ_1) and firefighters (μ_2) is the same ($\mu_1 = \mu_2$). The research hypothesis is that there is a difference ($\mu_1 \neq \mu_2$). The researchers do not define the direction of this difference. Their research hypothesis allows the possibility that police officers experience more anxiety at work than firefighters as well as the option that firefighters experience more anxiety at work than police officers.

The Sampling Distribution

For a difference of means test we use the t sampling distribution. The degrees of freedom for the distribution is obtained by adding the number of cases in the two samples and subtracting 2: $df = N_1 + N_2 - 2$. For our example the degrees of freedom is 322.

$$df = N_1 + N_2 - 2$$
$$= 197 + 127 - 2$$
$$= 322$$

The mean of the sampling distribution is defined, as in the case of a difference of proportions test, by the null hypothesis. It is represented by $\mu_1 - \mu_2$, or the hypothesized difference between the means of the two populations studied. Since the null hypothesis states that $\mu_1 = \mu_2$, this means that the mean of the sampling distribution is 0.

In calculating the standard error for the sampling distribution, we can use either of two different options. The first follows the process used in the difference of proportions test. Again, we add the variances of the two populations together and take the square root of the result to obtain the standard error of the sampling distribution of the difference of means. This is represented in equation 11.4.

Equation 11.4

$$\sigma_{sd(\overline{X}_1 - \overline{X}_2)} = \sqrt{\frac{\sigma_1^2}{N_1} + \frac{\sigma_2^2}{N_2}}$$

Because σ_1^2 and σ_2^2 are unknown, we use s_1^2 and s_2^2 to gain an estimate of $\sigma_{sd(\overline{X}_1 - \overline{X}_2)}$. However, as in chapter 10, the variances of our samples are not considered unbiased estimates of the variances of the population distributions. Accordingly, in order to gain an unbiased estimate of the standard error using this method, we need once more to adjust the equations, as was done in chapter 10. Our result is represented in equation 11.5.

Equation 11.5

$$\hat{\sigma}_{sd(\overline{X}_1 - \overline{X}_2)} = \sqrt{\frac{\sigma_1^2}{N_1 - 1} + \frac{\sigma_2^2}{N_2 - 1}}$$

We can now calculate the standard error for the sampling distribution of the difference of means based on the sample variances of police officers and firefighters, arriving at a standard error of 0.321:

Working It Out

$$\hat{\sigma}_{sd(\overline{X}_1 - \overline{X}_2)} = \sqrt{\frac{s_1^2}{N_1 - 1} + \frac{s_2^2}{N_2 - 1}}$$

$$= \sqrt{\frac{(2.76)^2}{197 - 1} + \frac{(2.85)^2}{127 - 1}}$$

$$= 0.3214$$

This method of obtaining the standard error for a difference of means test is generally called the **separate variance** method. It is more straightforward than the second option, which is generally defined as the "pooled" variance method.

The **pooled variance** method assumes that the population variances, and accordingly the standard deviations of the two groups, are the same. This assumption is often stated as a requirement of **homoscedasticity** (from the Greek for "same scatter (or spread)"), which may be written in mathematical form as:

$$\sigma_1 = \sigma_2 = \sigma \quad \text{or} \quad \sigma_1^2 = \sigma_2^2 = \sigma^2$$

Using the pooled variance method, we first must define the standard deviation shared by the two populations under study. To do this we weight the two sample variances by the N of cases in each sample. This is only fair because the larger sample is likely to provide a better estimate of the joint standard deviation than the smaller. We also include our correction for bias of the sample variances directly in our estimate of σ by subtracting 2 (1 for each sample) in the denominator of the equation. This is illustrated in equation 11.6.

Equation 11.6

$$\hat{\sigma} = \sqrt{\frac{N_1 \, s_1^2 + N_2 \, s_2^2}{N_1 + N_2 - 2}}$$

Applying this equation to our samples, we arrive at a weighted, pooled standard deviation of 2.804.

Working It Out

$$\hat{\sigma} = \sqrt{\frac{N_1 \, s_1^2 + N_2 \, s_2^2}{N_1 + N_2 - 2}}$$

$$= \sqrt{\frac{(197) \, (2.76)^2 + (127) \, (2.85)^2}{197 + 127 - 2}}$$

$$= \sqrt{\frac{2532.22}{322}}$$

$$= \sqrt{7.86405}$$

$$= 2.8043$$

Having obtained an estimate of the common standard deviation for the two populations, we can then use this estimate to calculate the standard error. To do this, we can return to the estimate of the standard error of the difference of proportions test, because in this case—as with the earlier test—we have only one joint estimate of the standard deviation ($\hat{\sigma}$):

$$\hat{\sigma}_{sd(\bar{X}_1 - \bar{X}_2)} = \hat{\sigma} \sqrt{\frac{N_1 + N_2}{N_1 N_2}}$$

Applying this formula to our example, we estimate the standard error for the sampling distribution to be 0.319.

Working It Out

$$\hat{\sigma}_{sd(\bar{X}_1 - \bar{X}_2)} = \hat{\sigma} \sqrt{\frac{N_1 + N_2}{N_1 N_2}}$$

$$= 2.804 \sqrt{\frac{197 + 127}{(197)(127)}}$$

$$= 2.804 \sqrt{0.01295}$$

$$= 0.3191$$

As you can see, the result using the pooled variance estimate (0.319) is very similar to that found using the separate variance estimate (0.321). This will usually be the case, especially when samples are relatively large or evenly divided between the two groups.

Why, then, would one use the pooled variance method if it generally provides results similar to the separate variance method? We have already discussed the importance of meeting assumptions in a statistical test. In the second method we have added an additional assumption, that of homoscedasticity, thus allowing the possibility that we might violate it.

One advantage of the pooled variance method is that you will generally gain a more efficient estimate of the standard error of your sampling distribution. One disadvantage of the separate variance method is that in studies with very small samples or where one sample is much larger than another, the simple estimate of degrees of freedom noted above will have to be corrected. The correction commonly used involves a good deal of computation.[5] For our problem, which involves large samples of relatively similar size, it is unnecessary to take this approach.

The separate variance method should be used in most circumstances. As a general rule, it is better to make fewer assumptions, be-

---

[5]See H. M. Blalock (1979), *Social Statistics* (New York: McGraw-Hill), 231.

cause then you have less potential for violating them and coming to a mistaken conclusion. Nonetheless, sometimes your sample results or prior research suggests strongly that an assumption of equal variances can be made. For example, if there is little difference in the standard deviations you find in your sample, you may be able to conclude with confidence that the population standard deviations do not differ.[6] If, in turn, prior studies show that the standard deviations between the groups studied are very similar, this might also lead you to apply this assumption in your test. Most statistical analysis computer programs today provide test outcomes for both of these options with the correct degrees of freedom applied.

Significance Level and Rejection Region

The University of Washington researchers used a 0.05 significance threshold and a two-tailed significance test. The two-tailed test is based on their nondirectional research hypothesis, which states simply that there is a difference in anxiety on the job between firefighters and police officers.

The t table (see appendix 4) shows that a t value of about 1.97 is associated with a two-tailed 5 percent significance threshold (with between 120 and 500 degrees of freedom). This means that a test statistic greater than or equal to 1.97 or less than or equal to -1.97 is needed to reject the null hypothesis.

The Test Statistic

To define the t-score for our test, we must again, as in the difference of proportions test, alter the equation used in chapter 10 (equation 10.7) to take into account the fact that we are now comparing two samples. First, we must adjust the numerator to reflect our comparisons of the differences in the means observed in our study with those defined in the null hypothesis. Second, we must adjust the denominator to reflect the standard error of the difference between means. Because we now have two methods for defining the standard error of the sampling distribution, we provide two separate equations below. The first reflects the difference of means test using a separate variance estimate (11.7a). The second illustrates the test using a pooled variance estimate (11.7b).

---

[6]A test of statistical significance may be performed to assess differences in variances. It is based on the F distribution, which is discussed in detail in the next chapter. The test takes a ratio of the two variances examined:

$$F = \hat{\sigma}^2_{\text{larger variance}} \, / \, \hat{\sigma}^2_{\text{smaller variance}}.$$

Equation 11.7a
Separate
variance
method

$$t = \frac{(\overline{X}_1 - \overline{X}_2) - (\mu_1 - \mu_2)}{\sqrt{\dfrac{s_1^2}{N_1 - 1} + \dfrac{s_2^2}{N_2 - 1}}}$$

Equation 11.7b
Pooled
variance
method

$$t = \frac{(\overline{X}_1 - \overline{X}_2) - (\mu_1 - \mu_2)}{\hat{\sigma} \sqrt{\dfrac{N_1 + N_2}{N_1 N_2}}}$$

In both equations we have two quantities in the numerator. The first is the difference between the two sample means (represented by $\overline{X}_1 - \overline{X}_2$). The second is the difference between the two population means $(\mu_1 - \mu_2)$ as defined by the null hypothesis. Because the null hypothesis is that the two populations are equal, this quantity is equal to 0.

For the denominator in each equation, we have simply replaced the standard error used for a sampling distribution when comparing a sample mean to a population mean with the standard error used when comparing sample means drawn from two populations. This quantity was defined in our discussion of the sampling distribution.

The t-score for this problem is 12.461 using the separate variance estimate and 12.539 using the pooled estimate. As recommended (although the differences are small in this case), in making our decision we use the separate variance method.

Working It Out
Separate
variance

$$t = \frac{(\overline{X}_1 - \overline{X}_2) - (\mu_1 - \mu_2)}{\sqrt{\dfrac{s_1^2}{N_1 - 1} + \dfrac{s_2^2}{N_2 - 1}}}$$

$$= \frac{(12.8 - 8.8) - 0}{\sqrt{\dfrac{(2.76)^2}{197 - 1} + \dfrac{(2.85)^2}{127 - 1}}}$$

$$= \frac{4}{0.321}$$

$$= 12.4611$$

Working It Out
Pooled
variance

$$t = \frac{(\overline{X}_1 - \overline{X}_2) - (\mu_1 - \mu_2)}{\hat{\sigma}\sqrt{\dfrac{N_1 + N_2}{N_1 N_2}}} \qquad \hat{\sigma} = \sqrt{\frac{N_1 s_1^2 + N_2 s_2^2}{N_1 + N_2 - 2}}$$

$$t = \frac{(\overline{X}_1 - \overline{X}_2) - (\mu_1 - \mu_2)}{\sqrt{\dfrac{N_1 s_1^2 + N_2 s_2^2}{N_1 + N_2 - 2}} \; \sqrt{\dfrac{N_1 + N_2}{N_1 N_2}}}$$

$$= \frac{(12.8 - 8.8) - 0}{\sqrt{\dfrac{(197)\,(2.76)^2 + (127)\,(2.85)^2}{197 + 127 - 2}} \; \sqrt{\dfrac{197 + 127}{(197)\,(127)}}}$$

$$= \frac{4}{0.319}$$

$$= 12.5392$$

The Decision

Because our test statistic of 12.461 is larger than the critical value of our rejection region of 1.97, we reject the null hypothesis that there is no difference in on-the-job anxiety between the populations of police officers and firefighters to which our test infers.

The *t*-Test for Dependent Samples

Sometimes criminal justice researchers examine samples that are not independent. For example, subjects may be matched and placed in like pairs based on such characteristics as social status, education, gender, age, and IQ. Dependent samples will also be gained when a researcher takes measurements on the same subject over time. For example, researchers may examine the attitudes of juvenile delinquents before and after participation in a specific program. Sometimes the same individuals are compared at different ages or stages in their development. Even though the researcher has two samples of observations—for example, before and after the program—the samples are not independent.

The **_t_-test for dependent samples** is commonly used in such situations. It focuses on the differences between the pairs in developing the sampling distribution of the test statistic. Each pair in a _t_-test for dependent samples is considered a single observation.

As an example, let us suppose that a police department took an independent random sample of 35 high-crime addresses from all high-crime addresses in a city. They then assigned a police officer to walk the beat on each block where an address was located for a full month. Assume we are asked to assess whether the strategy was effective in reducing calls for police service. We have data on the number of emergency calls for police service for the month before the officer walked the beat and for the month the officer walked the beat. These data are represented in table 11.2. The mean number of calls for service the month before was 30, and the mean for the month when the officer walked the beat was 20. Can we conclude from this that the program would be effective in reducing calls for service if applied generally to high-crime addresses?

Table 11.2   Emergency Calls to Police for the Month before and the Month during which the Officer Walked the Beat

LOCATION	CALLS BEFORE	CALLS DURING	LOCATION	CALLS BEFORE	CALLS DURING
1	29	14	19	18	22
2	50	28	20	27	24
3	14	8	21	42	16
4	16	6	22	31	14
5	11	20	23	51	30
6	31	17	24	28	8
7	33	4	25	26	11
8	37	22	26	14	19
9	21	20	27	29	21
10	40	27	28	39	26
11	30	29	29	40	20
12	22	30	30	30	20
13	30	18	31	26	11
14	36	20	32	30	28
15	30	22	33	27	13
16	29	26	34	33	20
17	24	19	35	35	34
18	41	33	Σ	1050	700
			$\bar{X}$	30	20
			s	9.21	7.52

Assumptions:

Level of Measurement: Interval scale

Population Distribution: Population differences are normally distributed (relaxed because N is large)

Sampling Method: Indepedent random sampling

Sampling Frame: All high-crime addresses in the city

Hypotheses:

H_0: There is no difference in the number of calls for service at high-crime addresses whether an officer walks the beat or not: $\mu_1 = \mu_2$.

H_1: There are fewer calls for service at high-crime addresses when an officer walks the beat: $\mu_1 > \mu_2$.

Calls for service is an interval scale measure as required by our test. The test also requires that the population of differences between pairs be normally distributed. Because our sample is large (greater than 30), we are able to relax this assumption for our test.

A *t*-test for dependent samples requires that the pairs examined be selected randomly and independently from the target population of pairs. Accordingly, although the scores for the subjects in the pairs are dependent (i.e., they are related one to another), the pairs themselves are independent one from another. In our case, because we began with an independent random sample of high-crime addresses, we can assume that the paired observations taken before and during the police intervention are random and independent.

Our null hypothesis states that there is no difference in the number of calls for police service at high-crime addresses whether a police officer walks the beat or not. Because the police department is concerned only with whether the presence of a police officer walking the beat is effective in reducing emergency calls for service, we include a directional research hypothesis. It states that the number of calls for police service will be lower when a police officer walks the beat.

The Sampling Distribution

The degrees of freedom for a *t*-test for dependent samples is obtained by taking the number of pairs studied and subtracting 1: $df = N - 1$. In our example, which involves paired observations for the same subjects over two time periods, the degrees of freedom are $35 - 1$, or 34. If we had examined subjects that were matched by common traits, the degrees of freedom would be obtained by taking the number of pairs of subjects and subtracting 1.

The mean of the sampling distribution is defined by the null hypothesis. It is represented by μ_d, or the mean of the population of differences between crime calls when a police officer is or is not walking the beat. Because the null hypothesis states that there is no difference in crime calls during these periods, this means that μ_d for the sampling distribution is 0.

The estimated standard error of the sampling distribution $(\hat{\sigma}_{sd})$ is gained through the same equation we used for a single sample test of means, except that we replace the variance for the single sample with the variance (s_d^2) for the differences between the two sets of observations (see table 11.3). This is done in equation 11.8.

Table 11.3 Calculation of the Standard Deviation for the Differences between the Two Sets of Dependent Observations

LOCATION	DURING	BEFORE	DIFFERENCE X_i	$(X_i - \bar{X}_d)^2$	LOCATION	DURING	BEFORE	DIFFERENCE X_i	$(X_i - \bar{X}_d)^2$
1	14	29	−15	25	19	22	18	+4	196
2	28	50	−22	144	20	24	27	−3	49
3	8	14	−6	16	21	16	42	−26	256
4	6	16	−10	0	22	14	31	−17	49
5	20	11	+9	361	23	30	51	−21	121
6	17	31	−14	16	24	8	28	−20	100
7	4	33	−29	361	25	11	26	−15	25
8	22	37	−15	25	26	19	14	+5	225
9	20	21	−1	81	27	21	29	−8	4
10	27	40	−13	9	28	26	39	−13	9
11	29	30	−1	81	29	20	40	−20	100
12	30	22	+9	361	30	20	30	−10	0
13	18	30	−12	4	31	11	26	−15	25
14	20	36	−16	36	32	28	30	−2	64
15	22	30	−8	4	33	13	27	−14	16
16	26	29	−3	49	34	20	33	−13	9
17	19	24	−5	25	35	34	35	−1	81
18	33	41	−8	4	Σ Totals			**−350**	**2,586**

$$\bar{X}_d = \frac{\sum\limits_{i=1}^{N} X_i}{N}$$

$$= \frac{-350}{35}$$

$$\bar{X}_d = -10$$

$$s_d^2 = \frac{\sum\limits_{i=1}^{N} (X_i - \bar{X}_d)^2}{N}$$

$$= \frac{2586}{35}$$

$$s_d^2 = 73.8857$$

Equation 11.8

$$\hat{\sigma}_{sd} = \sqrt{\frac{s_d^2}{N-1}}$$

The estimated standard error for our problem is 1.474.

$$\hat{\sigma}_{sd} = \sqrt{\frac{s_d^2}{N-1}}$$

$$= \sqrt{\frac{73.8857}{35-1}}$$

$$= 1.4741$$

Significance Level and Rejection Region

Following conventional norms, we use a 0.05 level of statistical significance. However, our research hypothesis suggests a directional test, which means that we place the entire rejection region on one side of the t distribution. Because the research hypothesis states that the period with a police officer walking the beat will have a lower number of crime calls, we are interested in the negative area of the t distribution below the mean. Looking at the t table (appendix 4) under a one-tailed significance test, with 34 degrees of freedom, we see that a critical value of $t \leq -1.691$ is needed to place our score in the rejection region.

The Test Statistic

To define the t-score appropriate for our test, we alter equation 10.7 used for the single sample test of means in chapter 10 to take into account the fact that we are now concerned with the mean difference between pairs of observations. Accordingly, instead of comparing the mean of one sample to the hypothesized population parameter $(\overline{X} - \mu)$, we now compare the mean of the observed differences between the pairs with the hypothesized difference between the pairs based on the null hypothesis $(\overline{X}_d - \mu_d)$. As discussed in the section on the sampling distribution, the hypothesized difference is 0. We also adjust the denominator of the equation to reflect the standard error of the differences between the pairs. The revised test is presented in equation 11.9.

Equation 11.9

$$t = \frac{\overline{X}_d - \mu_d}{\sqrt{\dfrac{s_d^2}{N-1}}}$$

Substituting the values from our example, we obtain a *t*-score of −6.784.

Working It Out

$$t = \frac{\overline{X}_d - \mu_d}{\sqrt{\dfrac{s_d^2}{N-1}}}$$

$$= \frac{-10 - 0}{\sqrt{\dfrac{73.8857}{35-1}}}$$

$$= -6.7836$$

The Decision

Because our test statistic of −6.784 is less than the critical value of our rejection region of −1.691, we reject the null hypothesis of our test. We can conclude that there is a statistically significant decrease in the number of crime calls at high-crime addresses when a police officer is walking the beat.

A Note on Using *t*-Tests for Ordinal Scales

Ordinal scales create a special problem in conducting tests of statistical significance. Most tests we have examined so far assume either a nominal or interval level of measurement. There are nonparametric tests for ordinal-level measures; however, these generally assume that the researcher can rank order all scores in a distribution.[7] In the general case of ordinal measures, where there are a limited number of ordinal categories and many observations, such tests are not appropriate.

---

[7] See chapter 12 for an example of a rank-order test (the Kruskal-Wallis one-way analysis of variance).

There is no simple solution for deciding which test to use for ordinally scaled variables. In practice, when there are a number of categories in an ordinal scale, researchers use the t-test for means to calculate statistical significance. When N is large and the number of categories is more than five, this approach is generally accepted. When the number of categories is less than five, it may be better to use the chi-square statistic introduced in chapter 9.

Chapter Summary

The **two-sample z-test** is a parametric test of statistical significance that may be used to test for equality of two population proportions. Although the test requires an interval level of measurement and normal population distributions, the test will nonetheless be appropriate when N is sufficiently large for both samples. As with other tests of statistical significance, it requires independent random sampling. The null hypothesis states that the population proportions for the two groups studied are the same. A critical value for the test is identified on the z sampling distribution. The mean of the sampling distribution is defined—as with the single-sample z-test—by referring to the null hypothesis. To calculate the standard error of the sampling distribution, the researcher must first obtain a weighted estimate of P. The test statistic is calculated by applying the z-test equation, adjusted to allow for two samples.

The **two-sample t-test for means** follows the same logic as the two-sample z-test. It is used to determine whether, based on the difference observed between the means of two samples, the researcher can conclude that there are differences between the means of the populations from which they are drawn. The assumptions are identical to those in the two-sample z-test. A critical value for the test is identified on the t sampling distribution, after first determining the degrees of freedom. The mean of the sampling distribution is again defined with reference to the null hypothesis. There are two options for calculating the standard error of the sampling distribution. The first is termed the **separate variance** method, because it assumes that the variances between the two populations are different. The second is called the **pooled variance** method, which provides a more efficient statistical estimate, but requires an additional assumption of **homoscedasticity**—that the standard deviations of the two groups are the same.

When the two samples examined are not independent, the **t-test for dependent samples** should be used. The calculation of this statistic is based on the mean difference between pairs of samples and the standard deviation of the differences between the pairs.

Key Terms

Homoscedasticity A statement that the variances/standard deviations of multiple populations are the same.

Pooled Variance A method of obtaining the standard error of the sampling distribution for a difference of means test. The pooled variance method requires an assumption of homoscedasticity.

Separate Variance A method of obtaining the standard error of the sampling distribution for a difference of means test. The separate variance method does not require an assumption of homoscedasticity.

Two-Sample t-Test for Means A test of statistical significance that examines the difference observed between the means of two samples.

Two-Sample z-Test A test of statistical significance that may be used to test the difference between proportions when N is sufficiently large.

t-Test for Dependent Samples A test of statistical significance that is used when two samples are not independent.

Symbols and Formulas

$\hat{P}$ Weighted proportion estimate.

$\hat{\sigma}$ Estimate of the standard deviation of a population.

$\hat{\sigma}_{sd}$ Estimate of the standard error of a sampling distribution.

To calculate a weighted proportion from two sample proportions:

$$\hat{P} = \frac{N_1 p_1 + N_2 p_2}{N_1 + N_2}$$

To estimate the standard deviation of the population distribution for a test of proportions:

$$\hat{\sigma} = \sqrt{\hat{P}\hat{Q}}$$

To estimate the standard error of the sampling distribution for a two-sample z-test of proportions:

$$\hat{\sigma}_{sd(p_1 - p_2)} = \hat{\sigma} \sqrt{\frac{N_1 + N_2}{N_1 N_2}}$$

To calculate the two-sample z-test statistic for proportions:

$$z = \frac{(p_1 - p_2) - (P_1 - P_2)}{\hat{\sigma} \sqrt{\dfrac{N_1 + N_2}{N_1 N_2}}}$$

To calculate degrees of freedom for the two-sample t-test of means:

$$df = N_1 + N_2 - 2$$

To calculate an unbiased estimate of the standard error for the sampling distribution in a two-sample t-test of means (separate variance method):

$$\hat{\sigma}_{sd(\bar{X}_1 - \bar{X}_2)} = \sqrt{\frac{s_1^2}{N_1 - 1} + \frac{s_2^2}{N_2 - 1}}$$

To estimate a pooled joint standard deviation of two populations for the pooled variance method:

$$\hat{\sigma} = \sqrt{\frac{N_1 s_1^2 + N_2 s_2^2}{N_1 + N_2 - 2}}$$

To estimate the standard error for the sampling distribution in a two-sample t-test of means (pooled variance method):

$$\hat{\sigma}_{sd(\bar{X}_1 - \bar{X}_2)} = \hat{\sigma} \sqrt{\frac{N_1 + N_2}{N_1 N_2}}$$

To calculate the two-sample t-test statistic for means (separate variance method):

$$t = \frac{(\bar{X}_1 - \bar{X}_2) - (\mu_1 - \mu_2)}{\sqrt{\dfrac{s_1^2}{N_1 - 1} + \dfrac{s_2^2}{N_2 - 1}}}$$

To calculate the two-sample t-test statistic for means (pooled variance method):

$$t = \frac{(\overline{X}_1 - \overline{X}_2) - (\mu_1 - \mu_2)}{\hat{\sigma} \sqrt{\dfrac{N_1 + N_2}{N_1 N_2}}}$$

To calculate the two-sample t-test statistic for means of dependent samples:

$$t = \frac{\overline{X}_d - \mu_d}{\sqrt{\dfrac{s_d^2}{N - 1}}}$$

Exercises

11.1 After a long political campaign, certain categories of prisoners in Rainy State have been given the right to vote in the forthcoming local election. Carolyn wishes to know whether there is any difference in the proportion of eligible prisoners and the proportion of eligible non-prisoners in Rainy State who will take advantage of their right to vote. She draws two random independent samples—one of 125 prisoners, and the other of 130 nonprisoners. The samples are drawn from the entire eligible prisoner and nonprisoner populations of Rainy State. She finds that 60 percent of her prisoner sample and 44 percent of her nonprisoner sample intend to vote.

a Why is a statistical test of significance necessary here?

b Carry out a test of statistical significance, remembering to outline each stage carefully. Can Carolyn conclude that the two populations are different in terms of their respective members' intentions to vote?

11.2 Eric takes a random sample of 200 offenders convicted of bribery and a random sample of 200 offenders convicted of robbery over the past five years in Sunny State. By checking court records, he finds that 9 percent of the bribery offenders and 1 percent of the robbery offenders in his samples have university educations.

a By using a two-tailed test with a significance level of 0.01, can Eric conclude that the differences he observes are statistically significant?

b   What steps would you recommend Eric take if he wishes to extend his conclusions to the prisoner population of neighboring Rainy State?

11.3   Greg wishes to investigate whether there is any difference in the amount of violent crowd behavior that supporters of two soccer teams report having seen in one season. He distributes questionnaires at random to season-ticket holders at United and at City. The mean number of matches at which the sample of 110 United fans remember seeing violent incidents is 15 ($s = 4.7$). For the sample of 130 City fans, the mean is 8 matches ($s = 4.2$).

a   Can Greg conclude that there are differences in the amounts of observed violent crowd behavior between the two populations of season-ticket holders? Outline all the steps required in the test of statistical significance. Choose an appropriate level of significance and calculate the t-test statistic according to the separate variance method.

b   Would Greg's conclusion be any different if he were to use the pooled variance method?

c   Which of the two methods is preferred in this case?

11.4   An independent random sample is drawn from the 1,000 police officers in Bluesville who graduated from the police academy 10 years previously, to see if there is truth in the claim by a prominent graduate of the academy that white officers are awarded more promotions than African American officers. For the 42 white officers sampled, the mean number of promotions that each had received in the 10 years since graduation was 3.2 ($s = 0.8$). For the 20 African American officers sampled, the sample mean was 2.8 ($s = 0.65$).

a   From these figures can you conclude that white officers who graduated 10 years ago have been awarded more promotions than have African American officers? Use the separate variance method and set a 5 percent significance level.

b   Would your answer be any different if you used a pooled variance method?

c   If the level of significance had been set at 1 percent, would there be any difference in the decisions you make based on the separate variance and the pooled variance methods?

d   Does the size of the samples have any relevance to the extent to which you can rely on the results?

11.5   Three hundred prisoners, all convicted of violent crimes against persons, have enrolled for a six-month course in anger control. A random sample of 41 are chosen to complete the same questionnaire on two separate occasions—once during the first lesson and once during the last lesson. The questionnaire measures how likely prisoners are to resort to violence to solve problems. The results are translated into an index from 0 to 10, with the higher scores indicating a higher tendency to seek nonviolent solutions to problems. The 41 prisoners' scores are shown in the table below.

SUBJECT	FIRST LESSON	LAST LESSON	SUBJECT	FIRST LESSON	LAST LESSON
1	1	2	22	6	6
2	2	4	23	4	4
3	1	6	24	9	6
4	3	2	25	9	7
5	4	5	26	0	1
6	7	9	27	1	4
7	6	6	28	1	4
8	4	3	29	3	3
9	4	7	30	2	2
10	1	1	31	2	4
11	2	1	32	1	1
12	3	4	33	0	3
13	4	9	34	4	5
14	6	7	35	4	5
15	7	8	36	6	7
16	2	2	37	6	6
17	2	7	38	7	7
18	3	3	39	3	6
19	1	4	40	1	1
20	6	4	41	1	2
21	2	4			

a What is the mean change in scores?

b What is the standard deviation for the differences between scores?

c Can you reject the null hypothesis for your test on the basis of the differences observed? Carry out a test of statistical significance, remembering to outline all of the steps required by the test.

Computer Exercises

1. Let us examine the relative danger of working in different types of police agencies using a difference of means test. Remember, our Agency Count variable separates U.S. Park and State Police from Other Agencies. Using a two sample t-test, test the null hypothesis that the mean

number of officers assaulted in 1994 was the same for U.S. Park and State Police as it was for officers in other agencies. Use the Independent Samples *t*-Test command in the Statistics (Compare Means) menu. Note that SPSS produces the *t* statistic for both the separate variance and pooled variance methods. Which do you think is more appropriate? (Levene's test may help you decide.)

2. To fully understand the difference in assaults on officers working for different agencies, we should examine the number of offenses reported. Test the null hypothesis that the mean number of actual offenses reported to the FBI in 1994 was the same for U.S. Park and State Police as it was for officers in other agencies. Use the Independent Samples *t*-Test command (as you did in question 1). Notice that SPSS produces a 95 percent confidence interval by default, which corresponds to a two-tailed test with a 0.05 level of significance.

analysis of variance (ANOVA)

What Is the Logic Underlying ANOVA?

What Are the Assumptions of the Test?

How Is the Test Carried Out?

How Can the Strength of the Relationship Be Defined?

How Does One Make Comparisons between the Groups?

kruskal-wallis test

When Is the Test Used?

How Is the Test Carried Out?

IN CHAPTER 11 we used the t and z distributions to test hypotheses about means drawn from two independent samples. But what if we are interested in looking at more than two samples at a time? This is a common problem in criminology and criminal justice, where many important questions can be raised across a number of different samples. For example, race forms a central concern in criminal justice and criminology. But it often does not make sense to restrict comparisons involving race to just two groups. Similarly, in many criminal justice studies, a number of interventions are compared simultaneously. In such cases, you will want to compare not just two but often three or more means in the context of one statistical test.

Analysis of variance (ANOVA) is a commonly used parametric test that allows the researcher to compare multiple groups on specific characteristics. ANOVA also provides an opportunity to introduce several important statistical concepts used in more complex types of analysis. We examine the concept of explained and unexplained variation in this chapter, and consider how these relate to the total variation found in a specific measure. The chapter also introduces a non parametric test, the Kruskal-Wallis test, that can be used for comparisons across multiple groups when the assumptions underlying ANOVA are difficult to meet.

Analysis of Variance

Analysis of variance is based on a simple premise. As the differences between the means in samples become larger relative to the variability of scores within each sample our confidence in making inferences will also grow. Why is this the case? Certainly the first part of this logic makes good sense. When the means between samples differ more from one sample to another, it provides stronger evidence to support the position that there are differences between the population means. All else being equal, the larger the differences between the samples the more confident you would likely be in rejecting the position that the population means are equal.

But we are faced with a problem in making such an inference. How much confidence can we place in the observed means of our samples? As we have stated many times in this book, sample estimates vary from sample to sample. If the sample means are likely to vary considerably in our example, then we would want to be cautious in drawing strong conclusions from our study. If the sample means are not likely to vary greatly, we will have more confidence in drawing conclusions from the observed means.

In previous chapters we have used the standard errors of our sampling distributions as a method of estimating how much variability, or noise, exists in the problem we examine. Analysis of variance uses the variability within the observed samples to come to conclusions about this variability. Suppose, for example, that you were examining two separate studies, each including three samples. However, in the first study the scores are widely dispersed around the mean for each group. In contrast, in the second study, the scores are tightly clustered around the group means.

If you take the variability you observe in these studies as an indication of variability in the populations from which they are drawn, you are likely to have more confidence in estimates gained from the second than from the first. There is a good deal more noise, or error, in the first than in the second. In making statistical inferences, you will want to take into account variability within the groups examined.

This is precisely the approach taken in analysis of variance. The variability between the groups studied is contrasted with the variability within those groups to produce a ratio:

$$\frac{Variability\ between\ groups}{Variability\ within\ groups}$$

The larger this ratio, the larger the differences between the groups relative to the variability within them, and the more confidence we can have in a conclusion that the population means are not equal. When the contrast is smaller, meaning that the differences between the groups are small relative to the variability within them, we would have less reason to conclude that differences exist in the populations to which we want to infer.

Developing Estimates of Variance between and within Groups

The first step in analysis of variance is to define the variability between and within the groups studied. To make this process more concrete, we use a hypothetical study of depression among 12 prison inmates drawn from high-, moderate-, and low-security prisons (see table 12.1).

Between-group variability is measured first by subtracting the **grand mean** or **overall mean** of the three samples from the mean of each sample. This score must then be adjusted to take into account the number of observations in each sample. Equation 12.1 represents this process in mathematical language. In this case the sample (or category) means are defined as $\overline{X}_c$, the overall mean (or grand mean) is defined as $\overline{X}_g$; N_c represents the number of cases in each category; and the summation sign

$$\sum_{c-1}^{k}$$

tells us to sum the results from the first sample or category mean ($c = 1$) to the last sample, or category, mean k:

Equation 12.1

$$\sum_{c=1}^{k} \left[N_c \left(\overline{X}_c - \overline{X}_g \right) \right]$$

Table 12.1   Depression Scores for 12 Prison Inmates Drawn from High-, Moderate-, and Low-Security Prisons

LOW SECURITY (GROUP 1)	MODERATE SECURITY (GROUP 2)	HIGH SECURITY (GROUP 3)
3	9	9
5	9	10
4	8	7
4	6	10
$\Sigma = 16$	$\Sigma = 32$	$\Sigma = 36$
$\overline{X} = 4$	$\overline{X} = 8$	$\overline{X} = 9$

To calculate the Grand Mean:

$$\overline{X}_g = \frac{\sum_{i=1}^{N} X_i}{N} = \frac{84}{12} = 7$$

As illustrated in table 12.1, the overall mean is gained by adding up all scores in the three samples and dividing by the total number of cases ($N = 12$). In calculating the amount of between-group variability, we have just three quantities in our example: the mean depression score of high-security inmates ($\overline{X} = 9$) minus the overall mean; the mean depression score of moderate-security inmates ($\overline{X} = 8$) minus the overall mean; and the mean depression score of low-security inmates ($\overline{X} = 4$) minus the overall mean—each one multiplied by its sample size.

Within-group variability is identified by summing the difference between each subject's score and the mean of the sample in which the subject is found. In equation 12.2, X_i represents each subject from all three samples, and, as before, $\overline{X}_c$ represents the mean for each sample. In this case we sum from $i = 1$ to N, meaning from the first to the last case in the overall study.

Equation 12.2

$$\sum_{i=1}^{N} (X_i - \overline{X}_c)$$

For within-group variability, we have four calculations to conduct for each group. For the first subject in the low-security prison sample, for example, we subtract from the subject's score of 3 the mean score of low-security inmates in the study (4). The same is done for each of the three other members of this sample. In the case of the moderate-security sample we repeat the process, starting with the first subject with a score of 9 and using the mean of 8 for the group as a whole. The same is done for the high-security prison sample.

When we add up the deviations between the groups, or those within them, as is done in tables 12.2 and 12.3, we find that the result is 0. This does not mean that there is an absence of variability either within or between the samples we examine, but rather reflects a rule we stated in chapter 3: the sum of the deviations from a mean equal 0. Clearly, we cannot use the sum of the deviations from the mean as an indicator of variation. As in other similar problems, it makes sense

Table 12.2 Summing the Deviations of the Group Means from the Grand Mean of the Three Groups in the Inmate Depression Study

$\overline{X}_c$	$\overline{X}_g$	$(\overline{X}_c - \overline{X}_g)$	$N_c(\overline{X}_c - \overline{X}_g)$
4	7	−3	−12
8	7	1	4
9	7	2	8
		$\Sigma = 0$	$\Sigma = 0$

Table 12.3   Summing the Deviations of Each Score from the Group Means within the Three Groups in the Inmate Depression Study

X_i	$\overline{X}_c$	$(X_i - \overline{X}_c)$
3	4	−1
5	4	1
4	4	0
4	4	0
9	8	1
9	8	1
8	8	0
6	8	−2
9	9	0
10	9	1
7	9	−2
10	9	1
		$\Sigma = 0$

to square the deviations we observe from the mean. The squares of all the deviations from the mean will then be positive or 0.

The result when we square these quantities is commonly referred to as **sums of squares**. The variability measured in this way between the groups is called the **between sums of squares (BSS)**. It is calculated by taking the sum of the squared deviation of each sample mean $(\overline{X}_c)$ from the overall mean $(\overline{X}_g)$ multiplied by the number of cases (N_c) in each sample.

Equation 12.3

$$BSS = \sum_{c=1}^{k} \left[N_c \, (\overline{X}_c - \overline{X}_g)^2 \right]$$

The between-groups sums of squares for our hypothetical problem is calculated by the same approach as shown in table 12.2. The one difference is that after we subtract the overall mean from a category mean, we square the result. Our final result is 56.

Working It Out

$$BSS = \sum_{c=1}^{k} \left[N_c \, (\overline{X}_c - \overline{X}_g)^2 \right]$$

$$= 4(4 - 7)^2 + 4(8 - 7)^2 + 4(9 - 7)^2$$

$$= 56$$

When we measure variability within the groups using this method, it is defined as the **within sums of squares (WSS).** The within-groups sums of squares is obtained by taking the sum of the squared deviations of each score from its category mean. This is represented in equation 12.4. As before, we first take the score for each subject and subtract from it the group or sample mean. However, before adding the scores together we square each deviation. The within-groups sums of squares in our hypothetical example is equal to 14.

Equation 12.4

$$WSS = \sum_{i=1}^{N} (X_i - \overline{X}_c)^2$$

Working It Out

$$WSS = \sum_{t=1}^{N} (X_i - \overline{X}_c)^2$$

$$= (3-4)^2 + (5-4)^2 + (4-4)^2 + (4-4)^2 + (9-8)^2 + (9-8)^2$$
$$+ (8-8)^2 + (6-8)^2 + (9-9)^2 + (10-9)^2 + (7-9)^2 + (10-9)^2$$
$$= 14$$

Partitioning Sums of Squares

We can also calculate a third type of variability for our example, the **total sums of squares (TSS).** The total sums of squares takes into account all of the variability in our three samples. It is calculated by taking the sum of the squared deviations of each score from the overall mean of scores for the three groups, as in equation 12.5.

Equation 12.5

$$TSS = \sum_{i=1}^{N} (X_i - \overline{X}_g)^2$$

In practice this means that we first take the deviation of a score from the overall mean and then square it. For example, the first subject in the low-security prison sample has a score of 3. We subtract from this score the overall mean of 7, and then square the result (-4) to obtain a value of 16. To arrive at the total sums of squares we do this for each of the 12 subjects in the sample and then sum the result.

Working It Out

$$TSS = \sum_{i=1}^{N} (X_i - \overline{X}_g)^2$$

$$= (3-7)^2 + (5-7)^2 + (4-7)^2 + (4-7)^2 + (9-7)^2 + (9-7)^2$$

$$+ (8-7)^2 + (6-7)^2 + (9-7)^2 + (10-7)^2 + (7-7)^2 + (10-7)^2$$

$$= 70$$

The quantity obtained is equivalent to the sum of the between- and within-groups sums of squares. That is, the total variability across all of the cases is made up of the variability between the samples and the variability within the samples. More generally, the three types of variability discussed so far may be expressed in terms of a simple formula that partitions the total sum of squares into its two component parts: the between sums of squares and the within sums of squares.

Equation 12.6

Total sums of squares = between sums of squares
+ within sums of squares

(for our example: 70 = 56 + 14)

Another way to express the relationship among the three types of sums of squares is to partition the total sums of squares into explained and unexplained components:

Equation 12.7

Total sums of squares = explained sums of squares
+ unexplained sums of squares

In this case, the between sums of squares is represented by the **explained sums of squares (ESS).** This is because the between sums of squares represents the part of the total variability that is accounted for by the differences between the groups. In the case of our hypothetical example, this is the proportion of the total variability in depression that is "explained" by the type of prison examined.

The within sums of squares is represented by, in this case, the unexplained variability or **unexplained sums of squares (USS).** This is the part of the total variability that differences between our samples do not explain. We usually do not know the cause of this variability. For this reason, we term this type of sums of squares as the unexplained sums of squares.

Developing Estimates of Population Variances

So far we have defined the sums of squares associated with between and within variability. But analysis of variance, as its name implies, is concerned with variance and not just variability. Accordingly, we have to adjust our scores by the appropriate number of degrees of freedom. In chapter 4, when we developed estimates of variance, we divided the squared deviations from the mean by the number of cases in the sample or population. For analysis of variance we divide the between and within sums of squares by the appropriate degrees of freedom.

For the between-group variance estimate, we define degrees of freedom as $k - 1$, where k is the number of categories or samples examined. If we compare three sample means, the degrees of freedom associated with the between-group estimate of variance would thus be 2. As illustrated by equation 12.8, an estimate of the between-group variance ($\hat{\sigma}^2_{bg}$) is obtained by dividing the between-groups sums of squares by $k - 1$.

Equation 12.8

$$\hat{\sigma}^2_{bg} = \frac{\sum_{c=1}^{k} \left[N_c \, (\overline{X}_c - \overline{X}_g)^2 \right]}{k - 1}$$

The degrees of freedom for the within-group estimate of variance is $N - k$, or the number of cases in the sample minus the number of categories or samples examined. The within-group variance estimate ($\hat{\sigma}^2_{wg}$) is calculated by dividing the within-group sums of squares by $N - k$ (see equation 12.9).

Equation 12.9

$$\hat{\sigma}^2_{wg} = \frac{\sum_{i=1}^{N} (X_i - \overline{X}_c)^2}{N - k}$$

A Substantive Example: Age and White-Collar Crimes

Now that we have defined the two types of variance that are compared in analysis of variance, let us look at a substantive problem. Table 12.4 presents data from three samples of offenders convicted of

Table 12.4   Ages of 30 White-Collar Criminals Convicted of Three Different Offenses

OFFENSE 1 BANK EMBEZZLEMENT	OFFENSE 2 BRIBERY	OFFENSE 3 ANTITRUST
19	28	35
21	29	46
23	32	48
25	40	53
29	42	58
30	48	61
31	58	62
35	50	62
42	64	62
49	68	75
$\bar{X} = 30.4$	$\bar{X} = 46.7$	$\bar{X} = 56.2$
$s = 8.98$	$s = 13.99$	$s = 10.54$

Grand mean $(\bar{X}_g) = 1333/30 = 44.43$

white-collar crimes in seven federal district courts.[1] The first sample is drawn from offenders convicted of bank embezzlement, the second from offenders convicted of bribery, and the third from offenders convicted under criminal antitrust statutes. Ten subjects were drawn randomly from the population of each category over a three-year period. The values listed in table 12.4 represent the ages of the sampled offenders. The mean age of bank embezzlers is 30.4 years; of bribery offenders, 46.7 years; and of antitrust offenders, 56.2 years. Can we conclude from the differences found among our samples that there are differences among the means of the populations from which these samples are drawn?

Assumptions:

Level of Measurement: Interval scale

Population Distribution: Normal populations for each sample compared (the shape of the population distribution is unknown and the sizes of the samples examined are small)

---

[1]The data are drawn from S. Wheeler, D. Weisburd, and N. Bode (1988), *Sanctioning of White Collar Crime, 1976–1978: Federal District Courts* (Ann Arbor, Mich.: Inter-University Consortium for Political and Social Research).

Sampling Method: Independent random sampling (no replacement, sample is small relative to population)

Sampling Frame: All white-collar offenders convicted of the crimes examined in seven federal judicial districts over a three-year period

Population variances are equal: $\sigma_1^2 = \sigma_2^2 = \sigma_3^2$

Hypotheses:

H_0: Population means of age for bank embezzlers, bribery offenders, and antitrust offenders are equal: $\mu_1 = \mu_2 = \mu_3$

H_1: Population means of age for bank embezzlers, bribery offenders, and antitrust offenders are not equal.

As with other parametric tests, analysis of variance requires an interval-scale level of measurement for the scores examined. Our example meets this assumption because age is an interval measure. Some statisticians add an assumption of nominal measurement because a comparison of means across samples requires that we define categories (or samples) for comparison. For example, in the case of age and white-collar crime, the three samples represent three categories of offenses. Our interest in this case is with the relationship between age—an interval-scale variable—and category of crime—a nominal-scale variable. In the hypothetical example brought earlier, we were interested in the relationship between depression (measured at an interval level) and type of prison (a nominal-scale variable).

Analysis of variance also requires that the populations underlying the samples examined be normally distributed. For our example, this is our most troubling assumption. We do not have evidence from prior studies that age is distributed normally within categories of crime. Nor are our samples large enough to invoke the central limit theorem. In ANOVA, as for the two-sample *t*-test, we want to have at least 30 cases per sample before relaxing the normality assumption. Because the computations for analysis of variance are complex, 10 cases in each group provides a good example for learning about ANOVA. However, our test will provide valid results only if the population distributions we infer to are in fact normally distributed.

As in the *t*-test, we must assume that the samples compared are drawn randomly and independently. In this study, random samples were drawn independently from each category of crime. However, the researchers did not sample with replacement. Because the sample drawn is very small relative to the population of offenders in the districts studied, we can assume that this violation of assumptions is not serious.

For analysis of variance, we must also assume that the population variances of the three groups are equal. This assumption of homoscedasticity is similar to that introduced for the t-test (using the pooled variance method) in chapter 11. However, in contrast to the t-test, there is not an alternative test if we cannot assume equal variances between the groups. Although this seems at first to be an important barrier to using analysis of variance, in practice it is generally accepted that violations of this assumption must be very large before the results of a test come into question.[2]

One reason why researchers, as opposed to statisticians, are not very concerned about the assumption of equal variances is that even large violations will affect the estimates of statistical significance to only a small degree. Sometimes it is suggested that you simply define a more conservative level of statistical significance when you are concerned with a serious violation of the homoscedasticity assumption.[3] Accordingly, you might select a 1 percent significance threshold as opposed to the more conventional 5 percent threshold. In general, large deviations in variance are not likely to occur across all of the groups studied. In such cases, you might choose to conduct your test (and compare your results) both including the group that is very different from others and excluding it. In our example, the variances do not differ widely one from another (see table 12.4).

Our final assumptions relate to the null and research hypotheses. For analysis of variance, the null hypothesis is that the means of the groups are the same. In our example, the null hypothesis is that the mean ages for offenders in the populations of the three crime categories examined are equal. Our research hypothesis is that the means

---

[2]For example, see G. Hornsnell (1954), The Effect of Unequal Group Variances on the F test for Homogeneity of Group Means, *Biometrika* 40:128–136; G. E. P. Box (1954), Some Theorems on Quadratic Forms Applied in the Study of Analysis of Variance Problems. I. Effect of Inequality of Variance in the One Way Classification, *Annuals of Mathematical Statistics* 25:290–302.

[3]Most packaged statistical programs today provide a test for equivalence of variances as an option with their ANOVA program. However, be careful not to automatically reject use of analysis of variance on the basis of a statistically significant result. In smaller studies, with samples of less than 50 per group, a finding of a statistically significant difference should make you cautious in using analysis of variance. In this case, you may want to adjust the significance level, as suggested earlier, or consider alternative nonparametric tests (discussed later in this chapter). In larger samples, a statistically significant result at conventional significance levels should not necessarily lead to any adjustments in your test. For such adjustments to be made, the differences should be highly significant and reflect large actual differences among variance estimates.

are not equal. As in ANOVA more generally, our research hypothesis is nondirectional. If we are making inferences to three or more means, it is not possible to define the direction of the differences among them.[4]

The Sampling Distribution

The sampling distribution used for making decisions about hypotheses in analysis of variance is called the F distribution, after R. A. Fisher, the statistician who first described it. The shape of the F distribution varies, depending on the degrees of freedom of the variance estimates being compared. In our problem, the degrees of freedom are represented by $k - 1$ for the between-group variance and $N - k$ for the within-group variance:

Working It Out

df for between-group variance $= k - 1 = 3 - 1 = 2$

df for within-group variance $\quad = N - k = 30 - 3 = 27$

Because we need to take into account two types of degrees of freedom at the same time, a different table of probability estimates is given for each significance threshold. Accordingly, in appendix 5, we provide F tables for 0.05, 0.01, and 0.001 significance levels.

Each table provides the F-scores, adjusted for degrees of freedom, that correspond with the specific significance threshold identified. Thus, for example, in the table for $p = 0.05$, the values given are the critical values of the test. You will need to obtain an F-score greater than this value to reject the null hypothesis of equal means. Looking at the table for $p = 0.05$ we can also identify two specific characteristics of the F distribution.

First, it is unidirectional, consisting only of positive values. Consistent with the fact that the research hypothesis in analysis of variance with three or more means states simply that the means are not equal, the F distribution is concerned only with the absolute size of the statistic obtained.

---

[4]However, in the special case of analysis of variance with only two sample means, the researcher can use a directional research hypothesis. This will sometimes be done in experimental studies when the researcher seeks to examine differences across samples, taking into account additional factors (e.g., see L. W. Sherman and D. Weisburd (1995), General Deterrent Effects of Police Patrol in Crime "Hot Spots": A Randomized Study, *Justice Quarterly* 12:625–648).

Second, as the number of degrees of freedom associated with the within-group variance grows, the F-value needed to reject the null hypothesis gets smaller. Remember that the degrees of freedom for the within-group variance is equal to "$N - k$." Accordingly, as the number of cases in the sample gets larger, the degrees of freedom also gets larger. Why should the F-value needed to reject the null hypothesis be related to the size of the sample? As was true for the t distribution, as the number of cases increases so also does our confidence in the estimate that is obtained from the F-test.[5]

Significance Level and Rejection Region

Given that no special concerns have been stated in regard to the risk of either Type I or Type II error, we use a conventional 0.05 significance threshold. By looking at the F table for $p = 0.05$ (appendix 5), with 2 and 27 degrees of freedom, respectively, we find a score of 3.35. This means that we need an F-score greater than or equal to 3.35 to reject our null hypothesis of no difference between the population means.

The Test Statistic

To calculate the F-ratio, we must compute our estimates of the between- and within-group population variances on the basis of our three samples. Computing the between-group variance is relatively easy. As noted earlier, the formula for between-group variance (σ_{bg}^2) is

$$\hat{\sigma}_{bg}^2 = \frac{\sum_{c=1}^{k} \left[N_c \, (\overline{X}_c - \overline{X}_g)^2 \right]}{k - 1}$$

Applying this formula to our example, we would first take the mean for each group, subtract from it the overall mean of the sample (44.43), square the result, and multiply it by 10—the number of observations in each sample. This process would be repeated for each of the three groups. The totals are then added together and divided by the between-group variance degrees of freedom (2). These calculations are illustrated below. The between sums of squares for our problem is 3405.267. Dividing this by the number of degrees of freedom (2), results in a between-group variance estimate of 1702.634.

---

[5]Indeed, note that the values of F with one degree of freedom for the between sums of squares are simply the values of t squared.

$$\hat{\sigma}^2_{bg} = \frac{\sum\limits_{c=1}^{k} \left[N_c \, (\overline{X}_c - \overline{X}_g)^2 \right]}{k - 1}$$

$$= \frac{10 \, (30.4 - 44.43)^2 + 10 \, (46.7 - 44.43)^2 + 10 \, (56.2 - 44.43)^2}{3 - 1}$$

$$= \frac{3405.267}{2}$$

$$= 1702.6335$$

It is practically more difficult to apply the formula for within-group variance, in good part because in its raw form the calculation for within-group sums of squares demands a good deal of computation even for small samples. For that reason, some texts provide an alternative estimating technique for the within-group sums of squares. However, it is probably safe to assume that in conducting research in the future you will turn to statistical computing packages. Because the purpose here is to gain a better understanding of analysis of variance, we focus on the raw computation. Although cumbersome, it illustrates more directly the logic behind ANOVA.

As discussed earlier, the formula for within-group variance is:

$$\hat{\sigma}^2_{wg} = \frac{\sum\limits_{i=1}^{N} (X_i - \overline{X}_c)^2}{N - k}$$

For our problem, as illustrated in table 12.5, we would first take each individual's score and subtract from it that individual's category mean $(X - \overline{X}_c)$. We would then square this quantity: $(X - \overline{X}_c)^2$. This is done for all 30 observations, which are then summed. The within-group sum of squares is 3874.1. When we divide this quantity by the correct degrees of freedom ($N - k$, or 27), we obtain a within-group variance estimate of 143.485.

To obtain the F statistic for our example, we simply have to calculate the ratio of the between- and within-group variances (see equation 12.10) to get 11.866.

Equation 12.10

$$F = \frac{Between \ Group \ Variance}{Within \ Group \ Variance}$$

Table 12.5   Calculating the Within-Group Sum of Squares

OFFENSE 1 BANK EMBEZZLEMENT $\bar{X} = 30.4$			OFFENSE 2 BRIBERY $\bar{X} = 46.7$			OFFENSE 3 ANTITRUST $\bar{X} = 56.2$		
X	$X_i - \bar{X}_c$	$(X_i - \bar{X}_c)^2$	X	$X_i - \bar{X}_c$	$(X_i - \bar{X}_c)^2$	X	$X_i - \bar{X}_c$	$(X_i - \bar{X}_c)^2$
19	−11.4	129.96	28	−18.7	349.69	35	−21.2	449.44
21	−9.4	88.36	29	−17.7	313.29	46	−10.2	104.04
23	−7.4	54.76	32	−14.7	216.09	48	−8.2	67.24
25	−5.4	29.16	40	−6.7	44.89	53	−3.2	10.24
29	−1.4	1.96	42	−4.7	22.09	58	1.8	3.24
30	−0.4	0.16	48	1.3	1.69	61	4.8	23.04
31	0.6	0.36	58	11.3	127.69	62	5.8	33.64
35	4.6	21.16	58	11.3	127.69	62	5.8	33.64
42	11.6	134.56	64	17.3	299.29	62	5.8	33.64
49	18.6	345.96	68	21.3	453.69	75	18.8	353.44
							Σ	3,874.1

Working It Out

$$F = \frac{Between\ Group\ Variance}{Within\ Group\ Variance}$$

$$F = \frac{1702.6335}{143.4852}$$

$$= 11.8663$$

The Decision

Because our test statistic (11.866) is larger than 3.35, the critical value of our rejection region, our result is statistically significant at the 0.05 level. Accordingly we reject the null hypothesis of no difference between the sample means, and conclude (with a conventional level of risk of falsely rejecting the null hypothesis) that the average age of offenders differs across the three crime types examined. However, given our concern about violating assumptions of normality, our final results are suspect. Our conclusions will be valid only if age is indeed normally distributed in the three populations studied.

Defining the Strength of the Relationship Observed

Even though analysis of variance is concerned with comparing means from independent samples, in practice those samples are usually defined as representing a multicategory nominal-level variable. For example, as noted earlier, in comparing three samples of white-collar offenders, we could define each as one category in a nominal-scale measure of types of white-collar crime. Similarly, if we had examined the differences between racial groups in terms of age, we might have created separate categories, or samples, for whites, Hispanics, African Americans, and others. Nonetheless, our main concern in comparing the means among these groups is likely to be whether the average age of offenders differs by race.

Accordingly, one question we might ask after finding a statistically significant result is: "How strong is the relationship we have identified?" The simplest way to answer this question is to look at the differences between the means in the samples. With just three samples, you can get a pretty good sense of the strength of a relationship using this method. But even with three samples, it is difficult to summarize the extent of the relationship observed because you must look at three separate comparisons (that between group 1 and group 2, that between group 2 and group 3, and that between group 3 and group 1). In the case of four groups, the number of potential comparisons is 6; for seven samples there are 21 possible comparisons. Clearly, it is useful, especially as the number of samples or categories grows, to have a single statistic for establishing the strength of the observed relationship.

A commonly used measure of association for ANOVA is a statistic called **eta** (η). Eta relies on the partialling of sums of squares identified earlier to establish the relationship, or **correlation,** between the interval-level variable in ANOVA and the nominal-level variable. To calculate η, we simply take the square root of the ratio of the between sums of squares to the total sums of squares (see equation 12.11).

Equation 12.11

$$\eta = \sqrt{\frac{BSS}{TSS}}$$

Although it might not seem so at first glance, this measure makes very good sense. To show this, however, it will be easier if we square this measure to gain a statistic, **eta squared** (η^2), which is sometimes referred to as the **percent of variance explained** (see equation 12.12).

Equation 12.12

$$\eta^2 = \frac{BSS}{TSS}$$

Eta squared is the proportion of the total sums of squares that is accounted for by the between sums of squares. We previously noted that the between sums of squares is also defined as the explained sums of squares because it represents the part of the total variation that is accounted for by the differences between the samples. Eta squared thus identifies the proportion of the total sums of squares that is accounted for by the explained sums of squares; thus, its identification as the percent of variance explained.

The larger the proportion of total variance that is accounted for by the between-groups sums of squares, the stronger the relationship between the nominal- and interval-level variables examined. When the means of the groups studied are the same, eta squared will be 0. In this case there is no relationship between the nominal- and interval-level measures examined. The largest value of eta squared is 1, meaning that all of the variability in the samples is accounted for by the between sums of squares. In practice, as eta squared increases in value between 0 and 1, the relationship examined gets stronger.

The square root of eta squared provides a measure more sensitive to smaller relationships. For example, a value of eta squared of 0.04, is equal to a value of eta of 0.20, and a value of eta squared of 0.1 is equivalent to a value of eta of 0.32, as shown in table 12.6. In criminal justice, where the relationships examined are often not very large, measures such as this one, which allow us to distinguish relatively smaller values more clearly, are particularly useful.

Table 12.6   Comparing Eta Squared with Eta

η^2	η
0.00	0.00
0.01	0.10
0.02	0.14
0.03	0.17
0.04	0.20
0.05	0.22
0.10	0.32
0.25	0.50
0.50	0.71
0.75	0.87
1.00	1.00

Turning to our example of age and white collar crime, we can see that the differences between the groups account for a good deal of the variability in the total sums of squares. Taking the between sums of squares for our problem and dividing it by the total sums of squares leaves us with a value of eta squared of 0.468.

Working It Out

$$\eta^2 = \frac{BSS}{TSS}$$

$$BSS = 3405.267$$

$$TSS = BSS + WSS$$

$$= 3405.267 + 3874.100$$

$$= 7279.367$$

$$\eta^2 = \frac{3405.267}{7279.367}$$

$$= 0.4678$$

By taking the square root of this value, we obtain a correlation coefficient (η) of 0.684.

Working It Out

$$\eta = \sqrt{\frac{BSS}{TSS}} = \sqrt{\frac{3405.267}{7279.367}}$$

$$= \sqrt{0.4678}$$

$$= 0.6840$$

Is this a large or small relationship? In part, large and small is a matter of value and not statistics. We might decide whether this value is large or small based on results from other studies in other areas of criminal justice, or perhaps in comparison to similar studies that draw different samples. There is no clear yardstick for making this decision. One psychologist suggests that a large effect for eta is any value greater than 0.371.[6] A moderate-size effect is represented as a value of 0.243. In this context we would define the relationship between age and type of white-collar crime as very strong. However, in this exam-

---

[6]See Jacob Cohen (1988), *Statistical Power Analysis for the Behavioral Sciences* (Hillsdale, N.J.: Lawrence Erlbaum), 285–287.

ple we should be cautious about relying upon the results obtained. In smaller samples, the values of eta obtained through these estimates are not considered very reliable.[7]

Making Pairwise Comparisons between the Groups Studied

Once you have established that there is a statistically significant difference between the samples studied through an analysis of variance, you may want to look at differences between specific groups examined. In this case, you will make comparisons between two sample means at a time. Such comparisons within an analysis of variance are often called **pairwise comparisons.**

It would seem, at first glance, that you could simply apply the two-sample *t*-test discussed in chapter 11 to test hypotheses related to these comparisons. However, you are faced with a very important statistical problem. If you run a number of *t*-tests at the same time, you are unfairly increasing your odds of obtaining a statistically significant finding along the way. For example, let us say that you conducted an analysis of variance comparing seven samples, or categories, and you obtained a statistically significant result. You now want to look at the pairwise comparisons to see which of the specific samples are different one from another. There are a total of 21 separate comparisons for you to make (see table 12.7). For each test you set a significance level of 0.05, which means that you are willing to take a 1 in 20 chance of falsely rejecting the null hypothesis. That is, if you run 20 tests, you might expect to get at least one statistically significant result just by chance.

In this case, a finding of a significant result could simply be attributed to the fact that you have run a large number of tests. Accordingly, to be fair, you will want to adjust your tests to take into account the change in the probabilities that results from looking at a series of pairwise comparisons. There are a number of different tests that allow you to do this, many of which are provided in standard statistical

---

[7]Once again, there is no universally accepted definition of what is "small." There will be little question regarding the validity of your estimate of eta if your samples meet the 30 cases per group minimum defined for invoking the central limit theorem. Some statisticians suggest that you will gain relatively reliable estimates even for samples as small as 10.

Table 12.7   The 21 Separate Pairwise Comparisons That Can Be Made for an Analysis of Variance with Seven Samples or Categories

SAMPLE	1	2	3	4	5	6	7
1							
2	✔						
3	✔	✔					
4	✔	✔	✔				
5	✔	✔	✔	✔			
6	✔	✔	✔	✔	✔		
7	✔	✔	✔	✔	✔	✔	

packages.[8] One commonly used test is the **honestly significant difference (HSD)** test developed by John Tukey (see equation 12.13).

Equation 12.13

$$HSD = P_{\text{crit}} \sqrt{\frac{Variance_{\text{wg}}}{N_c}}$$

HSD defines the value of the difference between the pairwise comparisons that are required to reject the null hypothesis at a given level of statistical significance.

For the white-collar crime example with a conventional 5 percent significance threshold, we would first identify the critical value (P_{crit}) associated with that significance threshold by looking at appendix 6. With three groups and 27 degrees of freedom in the within sums of squares estimate, the critical value is about 3.51. We then multiply this value by the square root of the within-group variance ($Variance_{\text{wg}}$) divided by the *N* of each sample (N_c)—in our example, 10.[9] Our result is 13.296, meaning that the absolute value of the difference in mean age between the pairwise comparisons must be greater than 13.296 to reject the null hypothesis of no difference (using a 5 percent significance threshold).

Working It Out

$$HSD = P_{\text{crit}} \sqrt{\frac{Variance_{\text{wg}}}{N_c}}$$

$$= 3.51 \sqrt{\frac{143.49}{10}}$$

$$= 13.2959$$

---

[8]For a discussion of pairwise comparison tests, see A. J. Klockars and G. Sax (1986), *Multiple Comparison*s (Quantitative Applications in the Social Sciences Vol. 61), London: Sage.

[9]The HSD test requires equal sample sizes in the groups studied.

Table 12.8   Results of the Pairwise Comparison Tests

	OFFENSE 1 BANK EMBEZZLEMENT	OFFENSE 2 BRIBERY	OFFENSE 3 ANTITRUST
Offense 1 Bank Embezzlement			
Offense 2 Bribery	16.300*		
Offense 3 Antitrust	25.800*	9.500	

$*p < 0.5$

Table 12.8 shows the absolute differences found for the three comparisons between means. Two of the three comparisons are statistically significant at the 5 percent level (i.e., they are greater than 13.296). This was true for the difference between bank embezzlers and bribery offenders, and between bank embezzlers and antitrust offenders. However, for the difference between bribery and antitrust offenders our result just misses the value needed to reject the null hypothesis. In this case, we would have to conclude that our sample results do not provide persuasive evidence for stating that the mean age of bribery and antitrust offenders is different in the larger population of cases in these two groups.

The comparisons we have made so far were carried out on the basis of a statistically significant result for our ANOVA overall. Should such comparisons be made if the overall differences between the means are not statistically significant? In general, it is not a good idea to look for pairwise comparisons if the overall analysis of variance is not statistically significant. This is a bit like going fishing for a statistically significant result. However, sometimes one or another of the pairwise comparisons is of particular interest. Such interest should come before you develop your analyses. However, if you do start off with a strong hypothesis for a pairwise comparison, it is acceptable to examine it irrespective of the outcomes of the larger test. In such cases it is also acceptable to use a simple two-sample t-test to examine group differences.

A Nonparametric Alternative: The Kruskal-Wallis Test

In cases such as our example, where you cannot meet the parametric assumptions of the analysis of variance test, you may want to consider a nonparametric **rank-order test.** In a rank-order test you lose some crucial information because you focus only on the order of scores and not on the differences in the values between them. However, such tests have the advantage of not requiring assumptions about the population distribution.

One such test is the **Kruskal-Wallis test.** As a nonparametric test it does not require a normal distribution nor equal variances between the groups. The test asks simply whether the distribution of ranks of scores in the three groups is what you would expect under a null hypothesis of no difference. When the number of cases in each group is greater than 5, the sampling distribution of the Kruskal-Wallis test score, denoted H, is approximately chi square.

As an illustration, let us examine whether this nonparametric test also suggests significant differences across the white-collar crime categories in terms of age.

Assumptions:

Level of Measurement: Ordinal scale

Sampling Method: Independent random sampling (no replacement, sample is small relative to population)

Sampling Frame: All white-collar offenders convicted of the crimes examined in seven federal judicial districts over a three-year period.

Hypotheses:

H_0: The distribution of ranked scores in the three populations are identical.

H_1: The distribution of ranked scores differs across the three populations.

In this test we use an ordinal-level measure, the rank order of ages in the sample. To obtain this measure we simply rank the 30 subjects studied according to age, with the youngest offender given a rank of 1 and the oldest a rank of 30 (see table 12.9). In the case of ties, subjects share a rank. For example, the two subjects aged 29, share the rank of 6.5 (the average of ranks 6 and 7), and the three subjects aged 62 share a rank of 26 (the average of ranks 25, 26, and 27).

Assumptions regarding our sampling method are similar. However, we no longer compare means in our null hypothesis. Our null hypothesis is that the distribution of ranked scores in the three populations are identical. Our research hypothesis is that they are not identical.

Table 12.9   White-Collar Offenders Ranked according to Age

OFFENSE 1 BANK EMBEZZLEMENT		OFFENSE 2 BRIBERY		OFFENSE 3 ANTITRUST	
AGE	RANK	AGE	RANK	AGE	RANK
19	1	28	5	35	11.5
21	2	29	6.5	46	16
23	3	32	10	48	17.5
25	4	40	13	53	20
29	6.5	42	14.5	58	22
30	8	48	17.5	61	24
31	9	58	22	62	26
35	11.5	58	22	62	26
42	14.5	64	28	62	26
49	19	68	29	75	30
	$\Sigma\,78.5$		$\Sigma\,167.5$		$\Sigma\,219$

Sampling Distribution

The sampling distribution H is distributed approximately according to chi square because the number of cases in each group is greater than 5. The degrees of freedom for the distribution is defined as $k - 1$. In our case, because there are three samples examined, the degrees of freedom for the chi-square distribution is $3 - 1$, or 2.

Significance Level and Rejection Region

Following our earlier choice of a 0.05 significance threshold, we turn to the 0.05 value of the chi-square table with 2 degrees of freedom (see appendix 3). The critical value identified is 5.991.

The Test Statistic

The formula for H given in equation 12.14 looks complex. However, it is relatively simple to compute when broken into pieces.

Equation 12.14

$$H = \left[\left(\frac{12}{N(N+1)} \right) \sum_{c=1}^{k} \frac{\left(\sum_{i=1}^{N_c} R_i \right)^2}{N_c} \right] - 3(N+1)$$

There is only one complex term in the equation. This is

$$\sum_{c=1}^{k} \frac{\left(\sum_{i=1}^{N_c} R_i \right)^2}{N_c}$$

This term tells us to take the sum of the ranks in each sample, square it and then divide it by the number of cases in the sample, and sum these values for all the samples.[10] The H value obtained for our problem is 13.038.

Working It Out

$$H = \left[\left(\frac{12}{N(N+1)} \right) \left(\sum_{c=1}^{k} \frac{\left(\sum_{i=1}^{N_c} R_i \right)^2}{N_c} \right) \right] - 3(N+1)$$

$$= \left(\frac{12}{30(31)} \right) \left(\frac{(78.5)^2}{10} + \frac{(167.5)^2}{10} + \frac{(219)^2}{10} \right) - 3(31)$$

$$= \left(\frac{12}{930} \right) 8217.95 - 3(31)$$

$$= 13.0381$$

The Decision

As in the F-test, our H-score exceeds the critical value needed to reject the null hypothesis of no difference. By using the Kruskal-Wallis test, we also can conclude that there is a statistically significant relationship between type of white-collar crime and age of offenders. In this case, however, we can have more confidence in our findings because the assumptions of the test are met more strictly.

---

[10]Most statistical computing packages provide an alternative calculation that adjusts for ties. In practice, the differences using this correction procedure and the unadjusted test are generally small. In our example, where there are a large number of ties relative to the sample size (14/30), the difference in calculated statistical significance is only 0.0001.

Chapter Summary

ANOVA is a parametric test that allows the researcher to compare specific characteristics across more than two groups. It takes into account variability not only between groups, but also within groups. The larger the differences between the groups relative to the variability within them, the more confidence we can have in a conclusion that differences exist in the populations' means. Between-group variability is measured by the **between sums of squares** (or **explained sums of squares**). Within-group variability is measured by the **within sums of squares** (or **unexplained sums of squares**). The **total sum of squares** is equal to the sum of the between and the within sums of squares. To develop estimates of population variances, the sums of squares are divided by the appropriate degrees of freedom. ANOVA requires the following assumptions: interval scales, normal population distributions, independent random sampling, and homoscedasticity. The sampling distribution for ANOVA is denoted as F. The F-value needed to reject the null hypothesis gets smaller as within-group degrees of freedom grows. The F-statistic is calculated by dividing the between-group variance by the within-group variance.

The strength of the relationship observed is measured by the statistic **eta squared,** or the **percent of variance explained.** Eta squared is the ratio of the between sums of squares and the total sum of squares. An eta squared value of 0 indicates that there is no relationship between the nominal and the interval variables (i.e., the means are the same). An eta squared of 1 represents a perfect relationship between the interval and nominal variables. The correlation coefficient eta is obtained by taking the square root of eta squared.

A researcher who wishes to compare two specific sample means within a larger test makes a **pairwise comparison.** Running a series of two-sample t-tests, however, will unfairly increase the odds of getting a statistically significant result. The **honestly significant difference (HSD)** test corrects for this bias.

When the assumptions underlying ANOVA are difficult to meet, the researcher may choose a nonparametric alternative—the **Kruskal-Wallis test.** This test does not require assumptions of normal population distributions, nor homoscedasticity. As a **rank-order test,** however, it does not use all of the information available from interval-level data.

Key Terms

Analysis of Variance (ANOVA) A parametric test of statistical significance that assesses whether differences in the means of several sampled groups can lead the researcher to reject the null hypothesis that the means of the populations from which they are drawn are the same.

Between Sums of Squares (BSS) A measure of the variability between groups. The between sums of squares is calculated by taking the sum of the squared deviation of each sample mean from the grand mean multiplied by the number of cases in each sample.

Correlation A measure of the strength of a relationship between two variables.

Eta A measure of the degree of correlation between an interval-level and a nominal-level variable.

Eta Squared The proportion of the total sums of squares that is accounted for by the between sums of squares.

Explained Sums of Squares (ESS) Another name for between sums of squares. The explained sums of squares is the part of the total variability that can be explained by visible differences between the groups.

Grand Mean The overall mean of every single case across all of the samples.

Honestly Significant Difference (HSD) A parametric test of statistical significance, adjusted for making pairwise comparisons. The HSD statistic defines the difference between the pairwise comparisons required to reject the null hypothesis.

Kruskal-Wallis Test A nonparametric test of statistical significance for multiple groups requiring at least an ordinal scale of measurement.

Overall Mean See grand mean.

Pairwise Comparisons Comparisons made between two sample means extracted from a larger statistical analysis.

Percent of Variance Explained The proportion of the total sums of squares that is accounted for by the explained sums of squares (See also eta squared).

Rank-Order Test A test of statistical significance that uses information relating to the relative order or rank of variable scores.

Sums of Squares The sum of squared deviations of scores from a mean or set of means.

Total Sums of Squares (TSS) A measure of the total amount of variability across all of the groups examined. The total sums of squares is calculated by summing the squared deviation of each score from the grand mean.

Unexplained Sums of Squares (USS) Another name for the within sums of squares. The unexplained sums of squares is the part of the total variability that cannot be explained by visible differences between the groups.

Within Sums of Squares (WSS) A measure of the variability within groups. The within sums of squares is calculated by summing the squared deviation of each score from its sample mean.

Symbols and Formulas

X_i Individual subject.

$\overline{X}_c$ Sample or category mean.

$\overline{X}_g$ Grand mean.

N_c Number of cases in each sample.

k Number of categories or samples.

P_{crit} Critical value for HSD test.

R_i Individual rank of score.

To calculate the between sums of squares:

$$BSS = \sum_{\iota - 1}^{k} \left[N_c \, (\overline{X}_c - \overline{X}_g)^2 \right]$$

To calculate the within sums of squares:

$$WSS = \sum_{i=1}^{N} (X_i - \overline{X}_c)^2$$

To calculate the total sums of squares:

$$TSS = \sum_{i=1}^{N} (X_i - \overline{X}_g)^2$$

To partition the total sums of squares:

Total sums of squares = between sums of squares
+ within sums of squares

$$TSS = BSS + WSS$$

To estimate between-group variance:

$$\hat{\sigma}^2_{bg} = \frac{\sum\limits_{c=1}^{k} \left[N_c (\overline{X}_c - \overline{X}_g)^2 \right]}{k-1}$$

To estimate within-group variance:

$$\hat{\sigma}^2_{wg} = \frac{\sum\limits_{i=1}^{N} (X_i - \overline{X}_c)^2}{N-k}$$

To calculate F:

$$F = \frac{Between\ Group\ Variance}{Within\ Group\ Variance}$$

To calculate eta:

$$\eta = \sqrt{\frac{BSS}{TSS}}$$

To calculate eta squared:

$$\eta^2 = \frac{BSS}{TSS}$$

To calculate the HSD test:

$$HSD = P_{crit} \sqrt{\frac{Variance_{wg}}{N_c}}$$

To calculate the Kruskal-Wallis test:

$$H = \left[\left(\frac{12}{N(N+1)} \right) \sum\limits_{c=1}^{k} \frac{\left(\sum\limits_{i=1}^{N_c} R_i \right)^2}{N_c} \right] - 3(N+1)$$

Exercises

12.1 Dawn, a criminal justice researcher, gives 125 pretrial defendants a score based on a questionnaire assessing their ability to understand the court process. The defendants were selected from five separate counties. Dawn took an independent random sample of 25 defendants from each. The scores for the five populations are normally distributed. Dawn runs an ANOVA test for her results, which produces a test statistic of 3.35.

a Would Dawn be able to reject her null hypothesis that there is no difference between the populations in their ability to comprehend the court process if she were to set a 5 percent significance level?

b Would she be able to reject the null hypothesis using a 1 percent significance level?

c Would either of your answers for 12.1a and 12.1b be different if Dawn's sample had consisted of 5 equally sized groups of 200 subjects?

12.2 Listed below is a set of data outlining the previous convictions for any offense of 40 inmates serving prison sentences for robbery, rape, murder, and drug dealing

ROBBERY	RAPE	MURDER	DRUG DEALING
1	1	0	5
0	1	0	3
2	1	0	7
6	0	6	4
4	0	2	8
5	2	7	0
3	2	1	6
1	1	4	2
5	0	2	1
3	2	3	4

Calculate the following values:

a $\overline{X}_g$

b df (between-group)

c df (within-group)

d the four values of $\overline{X}_c$

e the between sums of squares

12.3 Convicted drug dealers in Grimsville Prison are divided into cell blocks A, B, and C according to their city of origin. Danny (who has little knowledge of statistics) was once an inmate in the prison himself. Now released, he still bears a grudge against the prison authorities. Danny wishes to make up a series of statistics to show that the convicts in the various blocks are being treated differently. According to his fictitious sample, the mean hours of exercise per week given to the inmates is 10 hours for block A offenders, 20 hours for block B offenders, and 30 hours for block C offenders. Shown below are two fictitious sets of results.

Fictitious study 1:

BLOCK A	BLOCK B	BLOCK C
9	21	30
10	19	29
9	20	31
11	19	29
11	21	31
$\overline{X} = 10$	$\overline{X} = 20$	$\overline{X} = 30$

Fictitious study 2:

BLOCK A	BLOCK B	BLOCK C
18	16	37
16	18	36
10	2	7
2	31	41
4	33	29
$\overline{X} = 10$	$\overline{X} = 20$	$\overline{X} = 30$

a From simply looking at the numbers, without running any statistical tests, which of the two fictitious studies would you expect to provide the strongest backing for Danny's claim? Explain your answer.

b Calculate the between sums of squares and the within sums of squares for study 1.

c Calculate the between sums of squares and the within sums of squares for study 2.

d Calculate the value of eta for the two studies. How do you account for the difference?

12.4   A researcher takes three independent random samples of young pick-
pockets and asks them how old they were when they first committed
the offense. The researcher wishes to determine whether there are
any differences among the three populations from which the samples
are drawn—those who have no siblings, those who have one or two
siblings, and those with three or more siblings.

Age of first theft:

0 SIBLINGS	1, 2 SIBLINGS	3+ SIBLINGS
10	14	15
8	15	15
16	15	10
14	13	13
7	12	16
8	9	15

a Show that the total sums of squares is equal to the between sums of
squares plus the within sums of squares.

b What is the value of eta?

c Can the researcher reject the null hypothesis on the basis of the differences observed? Run an F-test using a 5 percent significance level. Remember to outline all of the stages of a test of statistical significance,
including any violations of assumptions.

12.5   Using independent random sampling, Sophie draws samples from
three different populations: psychologists, police, and factory workers. She gives each subject a hypothetical case study of a drug dealer
who has been found guilty and awaits sentence. The subjects are
then asked to suggest how many years in prison the drug dealer
should serve. The results are represented below:

PSYCHOLOGISTS	POLICE	FACTORY WORKERS
2	3	5
1	2	6
0	3	4
0	3	8
1	4	7
2.5	1	7
2	1.5	6
1.5	0	2
4	0.5	3
1	7	2

a Can Sophie conclude that the three populations are different in terms of their attitudes toward punishing convicted drug dealers? Run an *F*-test using a 5 percent significance level. Remember to outline all of the stages of a test of statistical significance, including any violations of assumptions.

b Would Sophie's decision be any different if she chose a 1 percent or a 0.1 percent level of significance?

c Calculate the value of eta for the results above. Is the relationship a strong one?

12.6   Using the data in exercise 12.4, run a Kruskal-Wallis test using a 5 percent level of statistical significance. Remember to outline all of the stages of a test of statistical significance, including any violations of assumptions.

a Are you able to reject the null hypothesis?

Computer Exercises

1.   Continuing our analysis of the patterns of crime, test the null hypothesis that the population means of the Number of Homicides Cleared by Arrest are equal in different areas of the United States (use the Region variable). Following the age and white-collar crime example in the text, discuss the assumptions for the ANOVA procedure and run the analysis. You can use either the Means command or the ANOVA command in the Statistics (Compare Means) menu to obtain a one-way ANOVA. The Means command allows you to select the ANOVA table and the eta statistic. The ANOVA command has a large variety of statistics available for more in-depth analysis. Run the analysis both ways. What decision would you make regarding the null hypothesis? How strong is the relationship between the Number of Homicides Cleared by Arrest and Region?

2.   Your text discusses the nonparametric Kruskal-Wallis test. Using the K Independent Samples command in the Statistics (Nonparametric) menu, obtain this test statistic for the hypothesis presented in question 1. Begin by rewriting the hypothesis so that it is appropriate for this nonparametric test. Compare these results to those from question 1. Was the Kruskal-Wallis test necessary? What is the cost of using a nonparametric test in this example?

Statistical Power: Avoiding Studies That Are Designed for Failure

statistical power

How Is It Defined?

How Can It Be Maximized?

What Is a Suitable Sample Size for a Powerful Study?

$\mathbf{I}$N CHAPTERS 7 THROUGH 12 we focused attention on statistical significance and its concern with clearly specifying and calculating the Type I error of a study. In this chapter we focus on the related concept of statistical power, which is concerned with the second type of error in hypothesis testing—Type II error. A Type II error occurs when the researcher fails to reject the null hypothesis when it is false.

In research we want to minimize both of these types of error. On the one hand, we do not want to develop a study that is biased toward the research hypothesis. Accordingly, we set our significance threshold strictly enough to guard against too high a level of Type I error. But neither do we want our study to err too strongly in favor of the null hypothesis. To avoid this error, we try to develop statistically powerful studies. In this chapter we introduce the idea of statistical power and explain why it is important for the researcher to be concerned with statistical power in designing research studies. We also examine the different factors that impact upon statistical power and the methods used to increase the power of a test.

Statistical Power

The most common way to assess the risk of Type II error in a study is to measure its level of **statistical power.** Statistical power may be defined as "$1 - P$ (Type II error)," or one minus the probability of falsely accepting the null hypothesis. In contrast to statistical significance—which identifies for the researcher the risk of stating that factors are related when they are not—statistical power questions how often one would fail to identify a relationship that in fact exists in the population.

As the statistical power of a study gets higher, the risk of making a Type II error, or failing to identify a relationship, gets smaller. For example, a test with a statistical power level of 0.90 would be one in which there was only a 10 percent probability of accepting the null hypothesis when it is false. Conversely, as the power level of a study gets lower, the risk of making a Type II error gets larger. A study, for example, in which the statistical power level is only 0.10, would have a 90 percent probability of accepting the null hypothesis when it is false.

Sometimes statistical power is defined as the probability that a test will lead to rejection of the null hypothesis. If the power of a test is high, then it is very likely that the researcher will reject the null hypothesis and conclude that there is a statistically significant finding. If the power of a test is very low, it is unlikely to yield a statistically significant finding. Studies with very low statistical power are sometimes described as being "designed for failure." This is because a study that is underpowered is unlikely to yield a statistically significant result even when the outcomes observed are consistent with the research hypothesis.

It is generally recommended that a statistical test have a power level greater than 0.50, meaning that it is more likely to show a significant result than not if the null hypothesis is false in the populations under study. But it is generally accepted that the most powerful studies seek a power level of 0.80 or above. Such studies are highly likely to evidence a significant finding. One might assume that researchers in criminal justice work very hard to develop statistically powerful studies because such studies are more likely to support the research hypothesis proposed by the researcher. In fact, however, statistical power is often ignored by criminal justice researchers, and thus criminal justice studies are often highly likely to make a Type II error.[1]

Clearly, the researcher should try to design a study in a such a way as to minimize the probability of Type II error. However, the methods that we have so far discussed for minimizing statistical error in a test of hypotheses present a dilemma for the researcher. The Type II error can be minimized, but at the expense of increasing the level of Type I error.

[1] See S. E. Brown (1989), Statistical Power and Criminal Justice Research, *Journal of Criminal Justice* 17:115–122. However, criminal justice researchers are not very different from researchers in other areas of social science (see also D. Weisburd (1991), Design Sensitivity in Criminal Justice Experiments, *Crime and Justice* 17:337–379).

Statistical Significance and Statistical Power

In previous chapters we have adjusted the levels of statistical significance that are used to take into account both Type I and Type II errors in our statistical tests (see chapter 6). Indeed, the most straightforward way to increase the statistical power of a test is to change the significance level used.

A significance level of 0.05 results in a more powerful test than a significance level of 0.01 because it is easier to reject the null hypothesis using a more lenient significance criteria than a more strict one. A 0.20 level of significance would, of course, make it even easier to reject the null hypothesis, as illustrated in table 13.1. Using the z test, it would take a z value greater than 1.282 or less than -1.282 to reject the null hypothesis in a two-tailed test with $p < 0.20$, a z value greater than 1.960 or less than -1.960 with $p < 0.05$, and a z value greater than 2.576 or less than -2.576, with $p < 0.01$. Clearly, it is much easier to reject the null hypothesis with a 0.20 significance threshold than a 0.01 significance threshold.

This method for increasing statistical power is direct, but it means that any benefit we gain in reducing the risk of a Type II error is offset by an increase in the risk of a Type I error. By setting a less strict significance threshold, we do indeed gain a more statistically powerful research study. However, the level of statistical significance of our test also declines. Moreover, as pointed out throughout the book, norms concerning statistical significance are strongly established in criminal justice. Generally, a 0.05 significance level is expected in research. When significance thresholds that make it easier to reject the null hypothesis are used, the researcher is expected to carefully explain this departure from established convention.

A related method for increasing the statistical power of a study is to limit the direction of the research hypothesis. A one-tailed test provides greater power than a two-tailed test for the same reason that a less stringent level of statistically significance provides more power than a more stringent one. By choosing a one-tailed test, the researcher reduces the value of the test statistic needed to reject the null

Table 13.1 The z-Score Needed to Reject H_0 in a Two-Tailed Significance Test at Different Levels of Statistical Significance

p	0.20	0.10	0.05	0.01	0.001
z	1.282	1.645	1.960	2.576	3.291

Table 13.2   The z-Score Needed to Reject H_0 in One-Tailed
and Two-Tailed Tests of Significance

p	0.20	0.10	0.05	0.01	0.001
z-Score One-Tailed Test	0.842	1.282	1.645	2.326	3.090
z-Score Two-Tailed Test	1.282	1.645	1.960	2.576	3.260

hypothesis. Once again, we can see this in practice by referring to the z-test.

Table 13.2 lists the z-values needed to reject the null hypothesis using one- and two-tailed tests for five different levels of statistical significance. At each level, as in other statistical tests, the test statistic required to reject the null hypothesis is smaller in the case of a one-tailed test. For example, at the 0.05 level, a z-value greater than or equal to 1.960 or less than or equal to −1.960 is needed to reject the null hypothesis in a two-tailed test, whereas in a one-tailed test z need only be greater than or equal to 1.645. At the 0.01 level, a z-value greater than or equal to 2.576 or less than or equal to −2.576 is needed to reject the null hypothesis in a two-tailed test, whereas in a one-tailed test z need only be greater than or equal to 2.326. As discussed in earlier chapters, in a one-tailed test all of the rejection region is on one side of the sampling distribution; thus, the rejection region is larger and it is easier to reject the null hypothesis.

Although the researcher can increase the statistical power of a study by using a directional, as opposed to a nondirectional, research hypothesis, as discussed in earlier chapters there is a price for shifting the rejection region to one side of the sampling distribution. Once a one-directional test is defined, a finding in the direction opposite to that originally predicted cannot be recognized. To do otherwise brings into question the integrity of the findings.

Effect Size and Statistical Power

Effect size is a component of statistical power that is unrelated to the criteria for statistical significance used in a test. Effect size measures the difference between the actual parameters in the population and those hypothesized in the null hypothesis. Its relationship to statistical power is clear. When the population parameters differ more strongly from the null hypothesis, you are more likely to observe a significant difference in a particular sample.

In defining effect size, statisticians often take into account both the raw differences between scores and the degree of variability found in the measures examined. Taking into account variability in effect size is a method of standardization that allows the comparison of effects between studies that use different types of measures. Generally, effect size (*ES*) is defined as in equation 13.1.

Equation 13.1

$$ES = \frac{Parameter - H_0}{\sigma}$$

Effect size will increase either as the difference between the actual parameter and the hypothesized parameter under the null hypothesis increases, or as the variability in the measure examined decreases. As an example, for a difference of means test, effect size is calculated by first subtracting the difference between the true means in the population $(\mu_1 - \mu_2)$—usually unknown—from the population difference as stated in the null hypothesis $(H_0 \, \mu_1 - H_0 \, \mu_2)$. Taking the case in which we assume that the standard deviations of the two populations are equal (see discussion of pooled variances in chapter 11), this value is then divided by the common standard deviation for the two populations studied (see equation 13.2).

Equation 13.2

$$ES = \frac{(\mu_1 - \mu_2) - (H_0 \, \mu_1 - H_0 \, \mu_2)}{\sigma}$$

Because the null hypothesis for a difference of means test is ordinarily that the two population means are equal, we can simplify this formula and simply include the difference between the actual population parameters. Thus, *ES* for a difference of means test may be defined simply as the raw difference between the two population parameters, divided by their common standard deviation, as shown in equation 13.3.

Equation 13.3

$$ES = \frac{\mu_1 - \mu_2}{\sigma}$$

As equation 13.3 illustrates, when the difference between the means is greater, *ES* for a difference of means test will be larger. Also, as the variability of the scores of the parameters grows, as represented by the standard deviation of the estimates, *ES* will get smaller. This same logic underlies the concept of effect size in other statistical tests.

Table 13.3 shows the relationship between effect size and statistical power in practice. It presents the number of statistically significant outcomes expected in 100 *t*-tests (using a 0.05 significance threshold and a nondirectional research hypothesis, $\sigma_1 = \sigma_2$), each of 100 cases per sample under six different scenarios. In the first three scenarios, the mean differences between groups are varied and the standard deviations for the populations are the same. In the second three, the mean differences are the same and the standard deviations differ.

As table 13.3 shows, the largest number of statistically significant outcomes is expected in either the comparisons with the largest differences between mean scores or the comparisons with the smallest standard deviations. As the differences between the means grow (scenarios 1, 2, and 3), so too does the likelihood of obtaining a statistically significant result. Conversely, as the standard deviations of the comparisons get larger (scenarios 4, 5, and 6), the expected number of signficant outcomes decreases.

As this exercise illustrates, there is a direct relationship between the two components of effect size and statistical power. Studies with a larger effect size, all else being equal, have a higher level of statistical power. Importantly, the relationship between effect size and statistical power is unrelated to the significance criteria we use in a test. In this sense, effect size allows the possibility for increasing the statistical power of a study (and thus reducing the risk of Type II error), while

Table 13.3   Number of Statistically Significant Outcomes Expected in 100 Two-Sample t-Tests ($\sigma_1 = \sigma_2$), Each Including 100 Cases per Sample, Using a 0.05 Significance Threshold and a Nondirectional Research Hypothesis in Six Different Scenarios

GROUP A: MEANS DIFFER; STANDARD DEVIATIONS HELD CONSTANT				
SCENARIO	μ_1	μ_2	σ	EXPECTED SIGNIFICANT OUTCOMES
1	0.3	0.5	2	10
2	0.3	0.9	2	56
3	0.3	1.3	2	94

GROUP B: MEANS HELD CONSTANT; STANDARD DEVIATIONS DIFFER				
SCENARIO	μ_1	μ_2	σ	EXPECTED SIGNIFICANT OUTCOMES
4	0.3	0.5	0.5	80
5	0.3	0.5	1	29
6	0.3	0.5	2	10

minimizing the risk of Type I error (through the establishment of rigorous levels of statistical significance).

Even though effect size is often considered the most important component of statistical power,[2] it is generally very difficult for the researcher to manipulate effect size in a specific study. A study is ordinarily initiated in order to determine the type of relationship that exists in a population. In many cases the researcher has no influence at all over the raw differences, or the variability of the scores of the measures examined. For example, if the researcher is interested in identifying whether men and women police officers have different attitudes toward corruption, the nature of those attitudes or their variability is a "given" that the researcher does not influence.

Nonetheless, particularly in evaluation research—in which the study attempts to evaluate a specific program or intervention—the researcher can influence the effect size of a study and thus minimize the risk of making a Type II error. There is a growing recognition, for example, of the importance of ensuring the strength and integrity of criminal justice interventions.[3] Many criminal justice evaluations fail to show a statistically significant result simply because the interventions that are brought are too weak to have the desired impact or the outcomes are too variable to allow a statistically significant finding.

Statistical power suggests that evaluation researchers should be very concerned with the effect size of their studies if they want to develop a fair test of the research hypothesis. First, the interventions that are brought should be strong enough to lead to the expected differences in the populations under study. Of course, the larger the differences expected, the greater the statistical power of an investigation. Second, interventions should be administered in ways that maximize the homogeneity of outcomes. For example, interventions applied differently to each subject will likely increase the variability of outcomes and thus the standard deviation of scores. Finally, researchers should recognize that the heterogeneity of the subjects studied will often influence the statistical power of their tests. Different types of people or different types of places are likely to respond in different ways to treatment or interventions. If they do, the variability of outcomes in a study will be larger, and thus the likelihood of making a Type II error will grow.

---

[2]See M. W. Lipsey (1990), *Design Sensitivity: Statistical Power for Experimental Research* (Newbury Park, Calif.: Sage).

[3]For example, see J. Petersilia (1989), Randomized Experiments: Lessons from BJA's Intensive Supervision Project, *Evaluation Review* 13:435–458; and D. Weisburd (note 1).

Sample Size and Statistical Power

The method used most often to manipulate statistical power in social science research is to change sample size. As with effect size, sample size can be manipulated without altering the risk of a Type I error in a test. In contrast to effect size, in most circumstances the number of subjects included in an investigation is under the control of the researcher.

The relationship between statistical power and sample size is straightforward. Larger samples, all else being equal, provide more stable estimates than do smaller samples. As discussed in chapter 7, this makes intuitive sense. One would not be too surprised to throw a successive run of heads in three tosses of an honest coin. However, getting 25 heads in 25 coin tosses would lead even the most trusting person to doubt the fairness of the coin. In statistics, we have a more formal measure for assessing the reliability of results in a study—the standard error. When the standard error is smaller, reliability is greater. Importantly, as the number of cases studied increases, the standard error of the sampling distribution used in a test decreases.

This relationship can be illustrated simply by looking at the calculation for the standard error in the single-sample t-test:

$$\sigma_{sd} = \frac{\sigma}{\sqrt{N}}$$

The standard error for this distribution is obtained by dividing the standard deviation of the population parameter, or our estimate of that parameter, by the square root of N. As N gets larger, irrespective of the value of the standard deviation itself, the standard error of the estimate gets smaller. For example, when the standard deviation is 10, table 13.4 shows that the standard error with 25 cases is twice as large as it is with a sample of 100.

As the standard error of a test declines, the likelihood of achieving statistical significance grows. This is the case because the test statistic for statistical tests of significance is calculated by taking the ratio of the observed difference from the null hypothesis to the standard error of that difference. For example, in the t-test for two independent samples (see equation 13.4), the value of the t-statistic is obtained by dividing the difference between the observed means minus the difference between the population means under the null hypothesis (generally 0) by the standard error of the estimates ($\hat{\sigma}_{sd(\bar{X}_1 - \bar{X}_2)}$).

Table 13.4   Changes in the Standard Error of the Sampling Distribution for the Single Sample t-Test as Sample Size Increases, $\sigma = 10$

SAMPLE SIZE	STANDARD ERROR OF SAMPLING DISTRIBUTION
10	3.16
25	2.00
75	1.15
100	1.00
200	0.71
500	0.45

Equation 13.4
$$t = \frac{(\overline{X}_1 - \overline{X}_2) - (\mu_1 - \mu_2)}{\hat{\sigma}_{sd(\overline{X}_1 - \overline{X}_2)}}$$

For the difference of means test, as for other statistical tests of significance, as the standard error gets smaller the test statistic will grow. Accordingly, there is a relationship between sample size and statistical power because larger samples lead to smaller standard errors, and smaller standard errors lead to larger test statistics. Of course, a larger test statistic will lead to a larger likelihood of rejecting the null hypothesis.

Table 13.5 illustrates the relationship between sample size and statistical power in practice. The number of statistically significant outcomes expected in 100 two-sample t-tests in which there is a mean difference of two arrests between groups ($\sigma = 1$) is examined for four different scenarios (using a 5 percent significance threshold and a two tailed test). In the first scenario, the sample size for each group is only 35 cases; in the second scenario, the sample size is 100; in the third, 200; and in the fourth, fully 1,000. Table 13.5 shows that the likelihood of rejecting the null hypothesis changes greatly in each of these scenarios, even though the population parameters remain the same. Under the first scenario, we would expect only about 13 statistically significant outcomes in 100 tests. In the second scenario, 29 significant outcomes would be expected; and in the third, 51. In the final scenario of samples of 1,000, nearly every test (99 out of 100) would be expected to lead to a significant result.

Because sample size is (1) directly related to statistical power, (2) it is a factor usually under the control of the researcher, and (3) it can be manipulated without altering the criteria for statistical significance of a study, it is often a primary concern in statistical power analysis.

Table 13.5   Number of Statistically Significant Outcomes Expected
in 100 Two-Sample *t*-Tests Using a 0.05 Significance Threshold
and a Nondirectional Research Hypothesis in Four Different Scenarios in
which the Parameters Are Held Constant but the Sample Size Varies

SCENARIO	SAMPLE SIZE (PER GROUP)	$\mu_1 - \mu_2$	σ	EXPECTED SIGNIFICANT OUTCOMES
1	35	0.2	1	13
2	100	0.2	1	29
3	200	0.2	1	51
4	1,000	0.2	1	99

In most cases, researchers maximize the statistical power of a study by increasing sample size. However, sometimes adding cases to a study can have unanticipated consequences on other factors that influence statistical power.[4] This is most likely to occur in evaluation research.

For example, let us say that a researcher has developed a complex and intensive method for intervening with high-risk youth. The impact of the treatment is dependent on the subjects receiving the full "dosage" of the treatment for a six-month period. If the researcher were to increase the sample size of this study, it might become more difficult to deliver the treatments in the way they were intended. More generally, when increasing the sample size of a study you should be careful not to decrease the integrity or dosage of the interventions that are applied.[5]

---

[4]For a review of this issue in criminal justice experiments, see D. Weisburd (note 1).

[5]Increasing the size of a sample may also impact upon the variability of study estimates in other ways. For example, it may become more difficult to monitor implementation of treatments as a study grows. It is one thing to make sure 100 people or places receive a certain intervention, but quite another to ensure consistency of interventions across hundreds or thousands of subjects. Also, studies are likely to include more heterogenous groups of subjects as sample size increases. For example, in one intensive probation study, eligibility requirements were continually relaxed in order to meet project goals regarding the number of participants (see J. Petersilia, note 3). As noted earlier, as the heterogeneity of treatments or subjects in a study grows, it is likely that the standard deviations of the outcomes examined will also get larger. This, in turn, leads to a smaller effect size for the study, and thus a lower level of statistical power.

Parametric versus Nonparametric Tests

Before turning to methods for calculating the statistical power of a test, it is important to note that the type of statistical test used in a study can also affect its statistical power. The differences in power of various tests (assuming that the tests are equally appropriate for making statistical inferences from the data examined) are usually relatively small. However, in the case of one general group of comparisons, differences can often be more meaningful. As a general rule, parametric tests are more statistically powerful than are nonparametric tests. This is one reason why researchers generally prefer to use parametric tests, even though they require more assumptions than do their nonparametric counterparts.

Why do parametric tests lead to a smaller risk of Type II error? The answer lies in a principle we stated much earlier in the book. Statistics that take advantage of more information are better statistics, all else being equal, than those that use less information. This is why interval-level measures are generally preferred over ordinal measures, and ordinal measures over nominal measures. Parametric tests generally involve comparisons among interval-level measures. Nonparametric tests make comparisons based on nominal or ordinal data, for example, groupings or rankings in a distribution. Because parametric tests take into account more information in coming to a decision about the statistical significance of findings, they are more statistically powerful or more sensitive tests of hypotheses.

Estimating Statistical Power:
What Size Sample Is Needed
for a Statistically Powerful Study?

In recent years, a number of texts have been written that provide detailed tables for defining the statistical power of a study.[6] You can also calculate the statistical power of specific examples by hand, although this can be a very tedious exercise. Calculation of specific power esti-

---

[6]For example, see Jacob Cohen (1988), *Statistical Power Analysis for the Behavioral Sciences* (Hillsdale, N.J.: Lawrence Erlbaum); M. W. Lipsey (note 2); H. C. Kraemer and S. Thiemann (1987), *How Many Subjects: Statistical Power Analysis in Research* (Newbury Park, Calif.: Sage). There also are software packages for computing statistical power; for example, see M. Borenstein and J. Cohen (1988), *Statistical Power Analysis: A Computer Program* (Hillsdale, N.J.: Lawrence Erlbaum).

mates is beyond the scope of this text. Nonetheless, it is possible to develop some basic rules for statistical power analysis that rely on standardized estimates of effect size.

Statistical power analysis is generally used to define the sample size needed to achieve a statistically powerful study. We have already noted that sometimes increasing the size of a sample can impact upon other features of statistical power. Thus, in using increased sample size to minimize Type II error, we must consider the potential consequences that larger samples might have on the nature of interventions or subjects studied. Nonetheless, sample size remains the most used tool for adjusting the power of studies, because it can often be manipulated by the researcher and it does not require changes in the significance criteria of a test.

Of course, we must conduct power analyses before a study is begun to define how many cases should be included. To define the sample size needed for a powerful study, we must first define clearly each of the components of statistical power other than sample size. These include:

1. the statistical test

2. the significance level

3. the research hypothesis (whether directional or nondirectional)

4. the effect size

The first three of these elements are familiar and based on our assumptions in developing tests of hypotheses. The statistical test is chosen based on the type of measurement and the extent to which the study can meet certain assumptions. For example, if we want to compare three sample means, we are likely to use analysis of variance as our test. If we are comparing means from two samples, we are likely to use a two-sample t-test.

To calculate statistical power, we must also define the significance level of a test and its research hypothesis. By convention we generally use a 0.05 significance threshold, and thus we are likely to compute statistical power estimates based on this criterion. The research hypothesis defines whether a test is directional or nondirectional. Again, in most circumstances, we choose a nondirectional test to take into account the different types of outcomes that can be found in a study.

The fourth element, defining effect size, is more difficult. How can we estimate the effect size in the population before conducting a study? The answer is that we conduct a power analysis to define the number of cases needed to identify a particular size effect. This is one of the reasons that statistical power is sometimes defined as **design**

sensitivity. The purpose of statistical power is to see whether the study we have designed has been developed in such a way that if the effect in the population is of a certain size we are likely to be able to detect it.

Statisticians have made our task easier here by defining broad categories of effect size. That is, they have developed a general scale for comparing effect size within and across studies. Jacob Cohen, a psychologist from New York University, has suggested one widely used measure that simply divides effect size into small, medium, and large effects.[7] Using the example of a proportion, Cohen defines a difference of 0.50 versus 0.40 between the two populations under study as a small effect,[8] a difference of 0.65 versus 0.40 as a medium effect, and a difference of 0.78 versus 0.40 as a large effect. Cohen has developed similar estimates for other statistical tests, trying to use a similar standard in each of the cases. A more detailed statistical explanation of his logic is presented in his text; he states generally, regarding these standardized estimates of effect size:

> Although arbitrary, the proposed conventions will be found to be reasonable by reasonable people. An effort was made in selecting these operational criteria to use levels of ES which accord with a subjective average of effect sizes such as are encountered in behavioral sciences. "Small" effect sizes must not be so small that seeking them amidst the inevitable operation of measurement and experimental bias and lack of fidelity is a bootless task, yet not so large as to make them fairly perceptible to the naked observational eye. . . . In contrast, large effects must not be defined as so large that their quest by statistical methods is wholly a labor of supererogation, or to use Tukey's delightful term "statistical sanctification." That is, the difference in size between apples and pineapples is of an order which hardly requires an approach via statistical analysis. (p. 13)

Put simply, Cohen suggests that his estimates make good common sense. As we have emphasized throughout this text, common sense is at the root of most statistics.

---

[7]Jacob Cohen (note 6).

[8]The example of a proportion is a very simple one because its standard deviation is simply a function of the split of scores in the population. Remember that the standard deviation of a proportion is equal to the square root of PQ.

Table 13.6 Sample Size per Group Required to Achieve a Statistical Power Level of 0.80 for a Two-Sample *t*-Test of Means

EFFECT SIZE	SMALL ES	MEDIUM ES	LARGE ES
Required Sample Size	393	64	25

Significance level set at 5 percent.
Two-tailed test.

These standardized estimates of effect size allow us identify the size sample needed to achieve a statistically powerful study, given a specific set of assumptions. They also illustrate the importance of sample size in statistical power. Table 13.6 provides the sample size needed to achieve a statistical power level of 0.80 or above, under assumptions of small, medium, and large effect size. Table 13.6 is based on a two-sample *t*-test of means, with a 5 percent significance threshold and a nondirectional research hypothesis.

If we define the effect size for the test as large, it does not take a very large sample to achieve a power level of 0.80. Only 25 cases are needed in each group. To achieve the same threshold with a moderate effect size, we must have 64 cases in each group. If the effect size in the population is small, then fully 393 cases are needed in each group. This example shows how important effect size is in statistical power. When effects are assumed to be large, it is relatively easy to design a powerful study. However, if we seek to identify a relationship with a small effect size, a very large number of cases will be required.

Table 13.7 provides similar statistical power estimates for some commonly used tests. In each case we use a 0.05 significance threshold and a nondirectional test. For each test, table 13.7 provides the

Table 13.7 Overall Sample Size Required to Achieve a Statistical Power Level of 0.80 for Selected Statistical Tests

EFFECT SIZE	SMALL ES	MEDIUM ES	LARGE ES
Binomial	783	85	30
Chi Square*	964	107	39
Two-Sample *z*-Test[†]	784	126	50
Two-Sample *t*-Test[†]	786	128	50
ANOVA (3 Groups)[†]	945	156	63

* *df* = 2 (e.g., a 3 × 2 table).
[†] Equal group sizes assumed.

Significance level set at 5 percent.
Two-tailed test.

number of cases needed for achieving a statistical power level of 0.80. This is the threshold generally used for defining a powerful study. Estimates are given for small, medium, and large effects.

You can get a general sense of the requirements of sample size from table 13.7, although you should use caution in applying it to specific cases. In general, if you are trying to identify small effects, your overall sample will have to be very large. For example, in a two-sample t-test you will need 786 cases (393 cases per group) to achieve a statistical power level of 0.80. In a chi square with 3 columns and 2 rows (2 df) you will need more than 960 cases in your total sample to achieve the same level effect. In contrast, for large effects you can generally use very small samples and still have a statistically powerful study. For example, only 50 cases (25 per group) would be required in a t-test for means. The sample sizes needed for a statistically powerful study for medium effect size do not fall midway between the estimates for large and small effect size, but are generally much closer to the sample size required for small effects. For the difference of means test, for example, 128 cases (64 per group) would be required, and for the chi square test (with 2 degrees of freedom), 107 cases would be required.

Summing Up: Avoiding Studies Designed for Failure

Statistical power can be compared to a radiation meter. A very sensitive meter will be able to identify even the smallest deposits of radioactivity. A meter that is not very sensitive will often miss such small deposits, although it likely will detect very large radiation signals from areas rich in radioactivity. Similarly, a statistically sensitive study will be able to identify even small effects. This is usually the case because the researcher has increased the sample size of the study to make it more statistically powerful. Conversely, a study that has little sensitivity is unlikely to yield a statistically significant result even when relatively large differences or program impacts are observed. Such studies may be seen as "designed for failure," not because of inadequacies in the theories or programs evaluated, but because the investigator had failed to consider statistical power at the outset of the study.

You might question why we would even bother to define the size sample needed for statistically powerful studies. Why not just collect a thousand or more cases in every study, and then you can usually be assured of a statistically powerful result. The simple answer is that although you should try to sample as many cases as you can in a study, there are generally constraints in developing samples. These may be monetary, related to time, or associated with access to subjects. It is often important to know the minimum number of cases that are needed to achieve a certain threshold of statistical power so that you can try, within the constraints faced, to reach an adequate level of statistical power in your study.

Chapter Summary

A statistically powerful test is one for which there is a low risk of making a Type II error. **Statistical power** can be defined as 1 minus the probability of falsely accepting the null hypothesis. A test with a statistical power of 0.9 is one for which there is only a 10 percent probability of making a Type II error. If the power of a test is 0.1, the probability of type II error is 90 percent. A minimum statistical power level of at least 0.50 is recommended; it is generally accepted that in better studies, the level of statistical power will be at least 0.80. A study with a low level of statistical power can be described as "designed for failure"—it is unlikely to produce a statistically significant result even if the outcomes observed are consistent with the research hypothesis.

There are several ways in which statistical power can be maximized. First, we may raise the significance threshold. Doing so, however, also increases the risk of Type I error. Second, we may limit the direction of the research hypothesis and conduct a one-tailed test. Doing so, though, will necessarily ignore outcomes in the opposite direction. Third, we may try to maximize the **effect size.** The greater the difference between the null hypothesis and the population parameters, and the smaller the variability within a measure, the larger will be the effect size. Effect size, however, is usually beyond the control of the researcher. Fourth, we may increase the sample size. A larger sample produces a smaller standard error for the sampling distribution, and a larger test statistic. The larger the sample, all else being equal, the greater the chance of rejecting the null hypothesis.

Sample size is generally the most useful tool for maximizing statistical power. A power analysis before beginning a study will define the number of cases needed to identify a particular size effect—small, medium, or large. To identify a small effect size, the overall sample must be very large. For a large effect size, a much smaller sample will suffice.

Key Terms

Design Sensitivity The statistical power of a research study. In a sensitive study design, statistical power will be maximized, and the statistical test employed will be more capable of identifying an effect.

Effect Size A standardized measure of the extent to which the actual parameters differ from the hypothesized parameters of a test. It is generally calculated by taking the difference between the actual value and the hypothesized value of the parameter and

dividing this by the estimated population standard deviation. The larger the effect size expected in a study, the greater will be the statistical power of that study, all else being equal.

Statistical Power One minus the probability of a Type II error. The greater the statisical power of a test, the less chance there is that a researcher will mistakenly fail to reject the null hypothesis.

Symbols and Formulas

ES Effect size.

To calculate effect size:

$$ES = \frac{Parameter - H_0}{\sigma}$$

To calculate the effect size for a difference of means test:

$$ES = \frac{(\mu_1 - \mu_2) - (H_0\,\mu_1 - H_0\,\mu_2)}{\sigma}$$

Exercises

13.1   Emma wishes to run a series of statistical tests comparing samples drawn from two different populations. She devises four scenarios:

Scenario 1   One-tailed test, 0.01 significance level,

Sample size = 100 each

$\mu_1 = 15$, $\mu_2 = 10$, $\sigma = 2$

Scenario 2   One-tailed test, 0.05 significance level,

Sample size = 100 each

$\mu_1 = 15$, $\mu_2 = 10$, $\sigma = 2$

Scenario 3   Two-tailed test, 0.01 significance level,

Sample size = 100 each

$\mu_1 = 15$, $\mu_2 = 10$, $\sigma = 2$

Scenario 4   Two-tailed test, 0.05 significance level,

Sample size = 100 each

$\mu_1 = 15$, $\mu_2 = 10$, $\sigma = 2$

a   What is the effect size for each of the four scenarios?

b   In which of these scenarios would the test have the highest level of statistical power? Explain your answer.

13.2   A joint Swedish–U.S. research foundation wishes to sponsor research to investigate whether parents in the two countries have different ways of disciplining their children. Four researchers, Anna, Bert, Christina, and Dave, have each submitted a proposal. The researchers intend to run a two-tailed test of statistical significance, except for Anna, who proposes a one-tailed test. The researchers intend to set a 5 percent level of significance, except for Dave, who proposes a 1 percent level. Anna and Bert propose samples of 400 Swedish parents and 400 U.S. parents, Christina proposes samples of 70 each, and Dave proposes samples of 40 each. Each of the researchers expects a moderate size effect from their test.

a   Do any of these proposals appear to you to be "designed for failure"? Explain your answer.

b   Which researcher's proposal would you recommend for acceptance? Explain your answer.

13.3   Fiona wishes to run a series of statistical tests comparing samples drawn from two different populations. She devises four scenarios.

Scenario 1   Two-tailed test, 0.05 significance level,

Sample size = 100 each

$\mu_1 = 15$, $\mu_2 = 14$, $\sigma = 5$

Scenario 2   Two-tailed test, 0.05 significance level,

Sample size = 100 each

$\mu_1 = 13$, $\mu_2 = 16$, $\sigma = 5$

Scenario 3   Two-tailed test, 0.05 significance level,

Sample size = 100 each

$\mu_1 = 8$, $\mu_2 = 10$, $\sigma = 5$

Scenario 4   Two-tailed test, 0.05 significance level,

Sample size = 100 each

$\mu_1 = 11.5$, $\mu_2 = 9$, $\sigma = 5$

a What is the effect size for each of the four scenarios?

b In which of these scenarios would the test have the highest level of statistical power? Explain your answer.

13.4 Philip is studying the attitudes of members of a newly formed police precinct toward drug offenders. He has prepared a 45-minute film in which offenders talk frankly about their backgrounds and how they came to be involved in crime, as well as a questionnaire, which should take about 15 minutes to complete. He has been given permission to show the film and distribute the questionnaire in a one-hour lunch break on a specific day only, in a lecture room that holds no more than 25 people.

For the planned study Philip intends to draw two independent random samples of 25 officers. Both groups will be asked to complete a questionnaire assessing their attitudes toward drug offenders. One group (the research group) will have seen the film, and the other (the control group) will not. The researcher plans to check for differences between the research and control groups by running a two-sample *t*-test and making a decision about his null hypothesis on the basis of a two-tailed test of statistical significance, setting the significance threshold at 0.05. He is worried, however, about the statistical power of the test.

Philip's assistant suggests three different ways of increasing the statistical power of the test. Discuss the merits and pitfalls of each suggestion.

a To run a one-tailed test of statistical significance instead of a two-tailed test.

b To increase the size of the rejection region by changing the significance threshold from 0.05 to 0.1.

c To double the size of each sample to 50. Because of limitations on time and space, the film will have to be shown in two sittings. The research group will have to be split into two subgroups of 25. Each subgroup will watch the first 20 minutes of the 45-minute film and then spend 10 minutes filling in the questionnaire.

13.5   Caroline wishes to run a series of statistical tests comparing samples drawn from two different populations. She devises four scenarios.

Scenario 1   Two-tailed test, 0.05 significance level,

Sample size = 50 each

$\mu_1 = 16$, $\mu_2 = 10$, $\sigma = 2$

Scenario 2   One-tailed test, 0.05 significance level,

Sample size = 150 each

$\mu_1 = 16$, $\mu_2 = 10$, $\sigma = 2$

Scenario 3   Two-tailed test, 0.05 significance level,

Sample size = 150 each

$\mu_1 = 16$, $\mu_2 = 10$, $\sigma = 2$

Scenario 4   Two-tailed test, 0.05 significance level,

Sample size = 100 each

$\mu_1 = 16$, $\mu_2 = 10$, $\sigma = 2$

a What is the standard error of the sampling distribution for each of the four scenarios?

b In which of these scenarios would the test have the highest level of statistical power? Explain your answer.

13.6   Robert draws an independent random sample of 100 men and 100 women from Chaos Town and questions them about their fear of crime, scoring each one on an index from 0 to 20, and then comparing the sample means using a two-sample t-test.

A few months later he decides to repeat the experiment, but comparing instead a random sample of youngsters under the age of 18 with a random sample of adults aged 18 or older.

Assume that for his first experiment the population mean for men was 11 and for women, 14 (with a common standard deviation of 6), and that for his second experiment, the population mean for the youngsters was 10 and for the adults, 14 (with a common standard deviation of 8).

a If the sample sizes in the second experiment were the same as those for the first experiment, would the statistical power of the two tests be the same?

b How large would the samples need to be in the second experiment for the standard error of the sampling distributions in both tests to be the same?

Computer Exercise

1. This chapter discusses statistical power. One way to adjust statistical power is to adjust the significance level of your tests. Another is to use a one-tailed test rather than a two-tailed test. In chapter 11, you tested the hypothesis that the mean number of officers assaulted in 1994 was the same for U.S. Park and State Police as it was for officers in other agencies. Run this test again, but use the Options subcommand to specify a 98 percent confidence interval. Note that the t statistic, the degrees of freedom, and the two-tailed significance don't change. With this confidence interval, what significance level are you using for your two-tailed test? How would you interpret the results for a one-tailed test (what significance level would be indicated by the confidence interval)?

chapter fourteen

Introduction to Correlation and Regression

the linear correlation coefficient

What Does a Correlation Coefficient Describe?

What Are the Characteristics of Pearson's r?

When Might Pearson's r Provide Misleading Results?

What Are the Characteristics of Spearman's r?

the regression coefficient

What Does a Regression Coefficient Describe?

How Is the Regression Coefficient, b, Expressed?

testing for statistical significance

What Is the Test of Statistical Significance for Pearson's r and the Regression Coefficient b?

What Is the Test of Statistical Significance for Spearman's r?

THE DESCRIPTIVE STATISTICS we have examined so far have allowed us to compare different samples or categories one to another. For example, we have looked at the relationship between different types of crime and age, or between categories of race and assignments to cell blocks. In these cases we have measured the relationship between two nominal-level variables, or between a nominal- and interval-level variable. This chapter introduces a new group of descriptive statistics that enable the researcher to describe the relationship between two interval-level measures.

This circumstance is encountered often in criminal justice research. For example, researchers may want to establish whether number of prior arrests is related to age, or education, or monthly income. Similarly, it is common in criminal justice research to ask whether the severity of a sanction measured as an interval scale (e.g., number of years sentenced to imprisonment or amount of a fine) is related to variables such as the amount stolen in an offense or the number of prior arrests or convictions of a defendant.

In this chapter, we examine two types of descriptive statistics for relating interval-level measures. Although these statistics are computationally similar, they describe the relationship between variables in different ways. The first, the linear correlation coefficient, describes the strength of a relationship using a standardized unit of measurement. The second, the regression coefficient, describes how two variables relate with respect to their specific units of measurement.

Measuring Association between Two Interval-Level Variables

In previous chapters we described the association between two variables by providing the mean or proportion of cases found in specific categories. For example, we compared the mean anxiety level of police officers and firefighters in chapter 11. In chapter 9, we examined the relationship between prison and reoffending in a sample of white-collar offenders by looking at the proportion of those in each category who were rearrested.

A similar approach cannot be taken when examining the relationship between two interval-level variables. Suppose, for example, that we are presented with the data provided in table 14.1. For each of 15 young offenders in our sample, we have information regarding age and number of prior arrests. The mean age of the sample overall is 17.067 years. The mean number of arrests is 4.867. These statistics describe the characteristics of our sample overall, but they do not tell us anything about the relationship between age and prior arrests in our study.

One way to do this would be to divide one of these measures into a categorical variable. For example, we might divide the offenders into a group under age 18 and a group aged 18 and older. Then we could use the same approach taken in earlier chapters, and simply compare the means for the younger and older groups, as shown in table 14.2. On average, the older offenders appear to have more arrests than the younger offenders ($\bar{X} = 7.571$ versus $\bar{X} = 2.500$). Similarly, we could divide prior arrests into categories and compare the mean age

Table 14.1   Age and Number of Prior Arrests for 15 Young Offenders

SUBJECT	PRIOR ARRESTS	AGE
1	0	14
2	1	13
3	1	15
4	2	13
5	2	14
6	3	14
7	3	17
8	4	19
9	4	21
10	6	19
11	8	16
12	9	18
13	9	20
14	10	21
15	11	22
$\bar{X} =$	4.8667	17.0667

Table 14.2 Mean Number of Prior Arrests for Offenders Aged
under 18 versus Those Aged 18 and Older

PRIOR ARRESTS AGED UNDER 18	PRIOR ARRESTS AGED 18 AND OLDER
0	4
1	4
1	6
2	9
2	9
3	10
3	11
8	
$\overline{X} = 2.5000$	$\overline{X} = 7.5714$

of offenders in each category. For example, table 14.3 divides prior
arrests into three categories: low arrests (less than 3), moderate arrests
(3–8), and high arrests (9 and above). On average, older offenders
have more arrests than younger ones. In this case the mean age for
the high-arrest group was 20.250, and that for the moderate- and low-
arrest groups was 17.667 and 13.800, respectively.

Although this approach has allowed us to come to a general conclusion regarding the relationship between age and prior arrests in
our sample, it has forced us to take one measure in each case and
convert it from an interval- to a nominal-level variable. In each example, we have had to take a step down the ladder of measurement,
which means that we have not used all of the information provided
by our data. This, of course, violates one of the general principles

Table 14.3 Mean Ages for Offenders with Low, Moderate,
and High Number of Prior Arrests

LOW PRIOR ARRESTS (0–2)	MODERATE PRIOR ARRESTS (3–8)	HIGH PRIOR ARRESTS (9+)
14	14	18
13	17	20
15	19	21
13	21	22
14	19	
	16	
$\overline{X} = 13.8000$	$\overline{X} = 17.6667$	$\overline{X} = 20.2500$

raised early in the text: statistics based on more information are generally preferred over those based on less information.

But how can we describe the relationship between two interval-level variables without converting one to a nominal scale? A logical solution to this dilemma is provided in a coefficient named after Karl Pearson, a noted British statistician who died in 1936. **Pearson's _r_** estimates the correlation or relationship between two measures by comparing how specific individuals stand relative to the mean of each. **Pearson's correlation coefficient** (_r_) has become one of the most widely used measures of association in the social sciences.

Pearson's Correlation Coefficient

Pearson's _r_ is based on a very simple idea. If we use the mean of each distribution as a starting point, we can then see how specific individuals in the sample stand on each measure relative to mean. If, in general, people who are above average on one trait are also above average on another, we can say that there is a generally positive relationship between the two traits. That is, being high on average on one trait is related to being high on average on the other. If, in contrast, people who are higher than average on one trait tend to be lower than average on another, then we would conclude that there is a negative relationship between those traits.

To illustrate these relationships, let us use the ages and number of prior arrests presented in table 14.1. If we put a plus next to each subject whose average age or number of arrests is above the mean for the sample overall, and a minus for those whose average is below, a pattern begins to emerge (see table 14.4). When a subject is above average in number of arrests, the subject is also generally above average in age. This is true for five of the six subjects above average in number of arrests (subjects 10, 12, 13, 14, and 15). Conversely, when a subject is below average in number of arrests, the subject is generally below the mean age for the sample. This is true for seven of the nine subjects below average in number of arrests (subjects 1 through 7).

Accordingly, for this sample, subjects generally tend to stand in the same relative position to the mean for both age and arrests. When someone in the sample has a relatively high number of arrests, they also tend to be relatively older. When they have fewer arrests, they tend to be younger than average for the sample. A simple mathematical way to express this relationship is to take the product of the signs. By doing this, we find that in 12 of the 15 cases the result is a positive

Table 14.4   Age and Number of Prior Arrests for 15 Young Offenders Relative to the Means—A Positive Relationship

SUBJECT	PRIOR ARRESTS	ABOVE OR BELOW THE MEAN?	AGE	ABOVE OR BELOW THE MEAN?	PRODUCT OF THE SIGNS
1	0	−	14	−	+
2	1	−	13	−	+
3	1	−	15	−	+
4	2	−	13	−	+
5	2	−	14	−	+
6	3	−	14	−	+
7	3	−	17	−	+
8	4	−	19	+	−
9	4	−	21	+	−
10	6	+	19	+	+
11	8	+	16	−	−
12	9	+	18	+	+
13	9	+	20	+	+
14	10	+	21	+	+
15	11	+	22	+	+
$\bar{X}$	4.8667		17.0667		

value (see table 14.4). Put simply, 12 of the cases move in the same direction relative to the mean. The relationship observed in this case is generally positive.

A generally "negative" relationship can be illustrated by reversing the scores for arrests in table 14.4. In this case, the first subject would not have 0 arrests but rather 11, the second not 1 arrest but 10, and so forth. If we now indicate each subject's placement relative to the mean, we would obtain the set of relationships listed in table 14.5. In this example, subjects who are above average in number of arrests are generally below average in age, and subjects below average in number of arrests are generally above average in age. The products of these signs are mostly negative. Put differently, the scores generally move in opposite directions relative to the mean. There is still a relationship between age and number of arrests, but in this case the relationship is negative.

This is the basic logic that underlies Pearson's r. However, we need to take into account two additional pieces of information to develop this correlation coefficient. The first is the value of scores. Using plus and minus divides the scores into categories, but it does not take full advantage of the information provided by interval-level measures. Ac-

Table 14.5 Age and Number of Prior Arrests for 15 Young Offenders Relative to the Means—A Negative Relationship

SUBJECT	PRIOR ARRESTS	ABOVE OR BELOW THE MEAN?	AGE	ABOVE OR BELOW THE MEAN?	PRODUCT OF THE SIGNS
1	11	+	14	−	−
2	10	+	13	−	−
3	9	+	15	−	−
4	9	+	13	−	−
5	8	+	14	−	−
6	6	+	14	−	−
7	4	−	17	−	+
8	4	−	19	+	−
9	3	−	21	+	−
10	3	−	19	+	−
11	2	−	16	−	+
12	2	−	18	+	−
13	1	−	20	+	−
14	1	−	21	+	−
15	0	−	22	+	−
$\overline{X}$	4.8667		17.0667		

cordingly, instead of taking the product of the signs, we take the product of the difference between the actual scores and the sample means. This is termed the **covariation** of scores and is expressed mathematically in equation 14.1.

Equation 14.1

$$\text{Covariation of Scores} = \sum_{i=1}^{N} (X_{1i} - \overline{X}_1)(X_{2i} - \overline{X}_2)$$

Table 14.6 illustrates what we gain by including the value of the scores. We now not only have a measure of the placement of subjects on both variables relative to the mean—the sign of the relationship— we also have an estimate for how strongly the scores vary from the mean. In general, for this distribution, the stronger the deviation from the mean on one variable, the stronger the deviation on the second. For example, if we look at the scores most distant from the mean in value in terms of prior arrests, we also find the scores most distant in terms of age. Those subjects with either zero or one arrest are not just younger on average than other subjects, they are among the

Table 14.6   Covariation of Prior Arrests (X_1) and Age (X_2) for 15 Young Offenders

SUBJECT	PRIOR ARRESTS X_1	$X_{1i} - \bar{X}_1$	AGE X_2	$X_{2i} - \bar{X}_2$	$(X_{1i} - \bar{X}_1)(X_{2i} - \bar{X}_2)$
1	0	−4.8667	14	−3.0667	14.9247
2	1	−3.8667	13	−4.0667	15.7247
3	1	−3.8667	15	−2.0667	7.9913
4	2	−2.8667	13	−4.0667	11.6580
5	2	−2.8667	14	−3.0667	8.7913
6	3	−1.8667	14	−3.0667	5.7246
7	3	−1.8667	17	−0.0667	0.1245
8	4	−0.8667	19	1.9333	−1.6760
9	4	−0.8667	21	3.9333	−3.4090
10	6	1.1333	19	1.9333	2.1910
11	8	3.1333	16	−1.0667	−3.3430
12	9	4.1333	18	0.9333	3.8576
13	9	4.1333	20	2.9333	12.1242
14	10	5.1333	21	3.9333	20.1908
15	11	6.1333	22	4.9333	30.2574

$\bar{X}_1 = 4.8667$ $\qquad$ $\bar{X}_2 = 17.0667$

$$\sum_{i=1}^{N} (X_{1i} - \bar{X}_1)(X_{2i} - \bar{X}_2) =$$

125.1321

youngest offenders overall in the sample. Similarly, those with the most arrests (10 or 11) are also the oldest members of the sample (ages 21 and 22).

The covariation of scores provides an important piece of information for defining Pearson's r. However, the size of the covariation between two measures depends on the units of measurement used. To make it possible to compare covariation across variables with different units of measurement, we must standardize the covariation between the two variables according to the variability within each. This is done by taking the square root of the product of the sums of the squared deviations from the mean of each variable. Pearson's r is then the ratio between the covariation of scores and this value (see equation 14.2). The numerator of the equation is the sum of the covariations of the two variables. The denominator of the equation standardizes this outcome according to the square root of the product of the variability found in each of the two distributions, again summed across all subjects.

Equation 14.2

$$\text{Pearson's } r = \frac{\displaystyle\sum_{i=1}^{N}(X_{1i} - \overline{X}_1)(X_{2i} - \overline{X}_2)}{\sqrt{\left(\displaystyle\sum_{i=1}^{N}(X_{1i} - \overline{X}_1)^2\right)\left(\displaystyle\sum_{i=1}^{N}(X_{2i} - \overline{X}_2)^2\right)}}$$

This ratio will be positive when the covariation between the variables is positive (i.e., when subjects' scores vary in the same direction relative to the mean). It will be negative when the covariation between the variables is negative (i.e.,when the subjects' scores vary in opposite directions relative to the mean). The ratio will be largest when there is a good deal of covariation of the variables and when the variability of scores around each mean are small. The ratio will be smallest when there is little covariation, and a good deal of variability in the measures. The range of possible values of r is between -1 and $+1$.

The Calculation

Calculating Pearson's r by hand takes a good deal of work. For that reason, you will probably prefer to enter data into a computer and then use a packaged statistical program to calculate correlation coefficients in the future. Nonetheless, it will help you to understand r better if we take the time to calculate an actual example. We use the data on prior arrests and age presented in table 14.1. The calculations to be used for Pearson's r are shown in table 14.7.

To calculate the numerator of equation 14.2, we must first take the simple deviation of each subject's score from the mean of prior arrests (table 14.7, column 3) and then multiply it by the deviation of the subject's age from the mean age of the sample (column 6). The result, the covariation between the measures, is presented in column 8 of table 14.7. So for the first subject the product of the deviations from the means is 14.9247, for the second it is 15.7247, and so on. The covariation for our problem, 125.1321, is gained by summing these fifteen products.

To obtain the denominator of the equation, we again begin with the deviations of subjects' scores from the mean. However, in this case we do not multiply the two scores for each subject. Rather, we first square the deviations from each mean (columns 4 and 7), and then sum the squared deviations for each variable. The sum of the squared deviations of each score from the mean of prior arrests is equal to 187.7338; the sum of the squared deviations of each score

Table 14.7 Calculations for the Correlation of Prior Arrests (X_1) and Age (X_2) for 15 Young Offenders

SUBJECT	2 PRIOR ARRESTS X_1	3 $X_{1i} - \bar{X}_1$	4 $(X_{1i} - \bar{X}_1)^2$	5 AGE X_2	6 $X_{2i} - \bar{X}_2$	7 $(X_{2i} - \bar{X}_2)^2$	8 $(X_{1i} - \bar{X}_1)(X_{2i} - \bar{X}_2)$
1	0	-4.8667	23.6848	14	-3.0667	9.4046	14.9247
2	1	-3.8667	14.9514	13	-4.0667	16.5380	15.7247
3	1	-3.8667	14.9514	15	-2.0667	4.2712	7.9913
4	2	-2.8667	8.2180	13	-4.0667	16.5380	11.6580
5	2	-2.8667	8.2180	14	-3.0667	9.4046	8.7913
6	3	-1.8667	3.4846	14	-3.0667	9.4046	5.7246
7	3	-1.8667	3.4845	17	-0.0667	0.0044	0.1245
8	4	-0.8667	0.7512	19	1.9333	3.7376	-1.6760
9	4	-0.8667	0.7512	21	3.9333	15.4708	-3.4090
10	6	1.1333	1.2844	19	1.9333	3.7376	2.1910
11	8	3.1333	9.8176	16	-1.0667	1.1378	-3.3430
12	9	4.1333	17.0842	18	0.9333	0.8710	3.8576
13	9	4.1333	17.0842	20	2.9333	8.8042	12.1242
14	10	5.1333	26.3508	21	3.9333	15.4708	20.1908
15	11	6.1333	37.6174	22	4.9333	24.3374	30.2574

$\bar{X}_1 = 4.8667$

$\sum_{i=1}^{N} (X_{1i} - \bar{X}_1)^2 =$ $\bar{X}_2 = 17.0667$

187.7538

$\sum_{i=1}^{N} (X_{2i} - \bar{X}_2)^2 =$

139.1326

$\sum_{i=1}^{N} (X_{1i} - \bar{X}_1)(X_{2i} - \bar{X}_2) =$

125.1321

from the mean age is equal to 139.1326. Now we take the product of those deviations, and finally the square root of that product:

Working It Out

$$\sqrt{\left(\sum_{i=1}^{N} (X_{1i} - \overline{X}_1)^2\right)\left(\sum_{i=1}^{N} (X_{2i} - \overline{X}_2)^2\right)}$$

$$= \sqrt{(187.7338)\,(139.1326)}$$

$$= \sqrt{26119.892}$$

$$= 161.6165$$

This leaves us with a value of 161.6165 for the denominator of our equation.

We are now ready to calculate Pearson's r for our example. We simply take the covariation of 125.1321 and divide it by 161.6165 to get 0.7743.

Working It Out

$$\text{Pearson's } r = \frac{\sum_{i=1}^{N} (X_{1i} - \overline{X}_1)\,(X_{2i} - \overline{X}_2)}{\sqrt{\left(\sum_{i=1}^{N} (X_{1i} - \overline{X}_1)^2\right)\left(\sum_{i=1}^{N} (X_{2i} - \overline{X}_2)^2\right)}}$$

$$= \frac{125.1321}{\sqrt{(187.7338)\,(139.1326)}}$$

$$= \frac{125.1321}{161.6165}$$

$$= 0.7743$$

Our correlation is about 0.77, meaning that the correlation between age and arrests is a positive one. As arrests increase so does the average age of the offenders in our sample. But what is the strength of this relationship? Is it large or small? As discussed in chapter 12, when we examined the correlation coefficient eta, whether something is large or small is in good measure a value judgment. The answer depends in part on how your result compares to other research in the same area of criminal justice. For example, if other studies produce correlations that are generally much smaller, you might conclude that the relationship in your sample is a very strong one. Using the standard measures of effect size discussed in chapter 13, a correlation of 0.10 may be defined as a small relationship, a correlation of 0.30 a medium relationship, and 0.50 a large relationship.[1] Using this yardstick, the relationship observed in our example is a very strong one.

Nonlinear Relationships and Pearson's *r*

Pearson's *r* allows us to assess the correlation between two interval-level measures taking into account the full amount of information that those measures provide, but it assesses the strength of only a **linear relationship**. If the correlation between two variables is not linear, then Pearson's *r* will give very misleading results.

A simple way to illustrate this is to look at **scatterplots,** or **scatter diagrams,** representing different types of relationships. A scatterplot positions subjects according to their scores on both variables examined. Figure 14.1 represents the subjects in our example of age and prior arrest. The first case (age = 14, prior arrests = 0) is identified with a 1 next to the dot representing this case. The overall relationship in this example is basically linear and positive. That is, the dots move together in a positive direction (as age increases so too do arrests). A scatterplot of the example in which we switched arrests around so that the highest number of arrests is found among younger rather than older subjects (see table 14.5) is presented in figure 14.2. In this case the scatterplot shows a negative relationship (as age increases arrests decrease).

But what would happen if there were a **curvilinear relationship** between age and arrests? That is, what if the number of arrests for both younger and older subjects was high, and the number for those of average age was low. This relationship is illustrated in figure 14.3 (page 309). Here, there is a clear relationship in this scatterplot: the number of arrests declines until age 17 and then increases. However, Pearson's *r* associated with these data is close to 0. If there is a relationship, why does this happen? Table 14.8 (page 310) shows why. Subjects who are either much above or much below the mean in terms of age have large numbers of arrests. The covariance for these subjects is accordingly also very high. However, for those below the mean in age the covariance is positive, and for those above the mean, the covariance is negative. If we add these scores together, they sim-

---

[1] See Jacob Cohen (1988), *Statistical Power Analysis for the Behavioral Sciences* (Hillsdale, N.J.: Lawrence Erlbaum), 79–80.

Figure 14.1 *Scatterplot Showing a Positive Relationship between Age and Number of Prior Arrests for 15 Subjects*

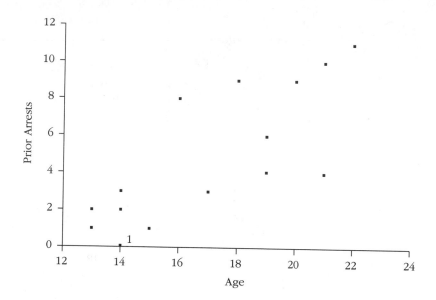

Figure 14.2 *Scatterplot Showing a Negative Relationship between Age and Number of Prior Arrests for 15 Subjects*

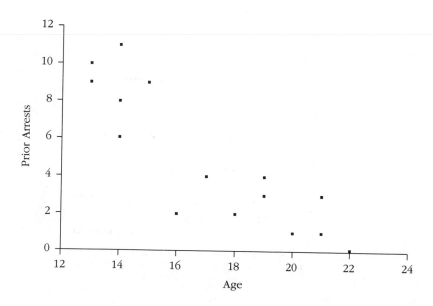

Figure 14.3   *Scatterplot Showing a Curvilinear Relationship between Age and Number of Prior Arrests for 15 Subjects*

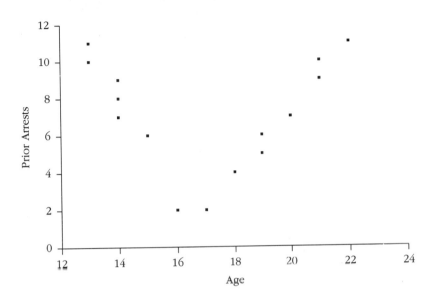

ply cancel each other out. As a result, Pearson's *r* for this example is close to 0:

Working It Out

$$\text{Pearson's } r = \frac{\sum\limits_{i=1}^{N} (X_{1i} - \overline{X}_1)(X_{2i} - \overline{X}_2)}{\sqrt{\left(\sum\limits_{i=1}^{N} (X_{1i} - \overline{X}_1)^2\right)\left(\sum\limits_{i=1}^{N} (X_{2i} - \overline{X}_2)^2\right)}}$$

$$= \frac{0.8655}{\sqrt{(123.7698)(139.1326)}}$$

$$= 0.0066$$

Pearson's *r* will provide good estimates of correlation when the relationship between two variables is approximately linear. However, a strong nonlinear relationship will lead to a misleading correlation coefficient. Figure 14.4 (page 311) provides examples of a number of nonlinear relationships. These examples illustrate why it is important to look at the scatterplot of the relationship between two interval-

Table 14.8 Curvilinear Relationship: Calculations for the Correlation of Prior Arrests (X_1) and Age (X_2) for 15 Young Offenders

SUBJECT	PRIOR ARRESTS X_1	$X_{1i} - \bar{X}_1$	$(X_{1i} - \bar{X}_1)^2$	AGE X_2	$X_{2i} - \bar{X}_2$	$(X_{2i} - \bar{X}_2)^2$	$(X_{1i} - \bar{X}_1)(X_{2i} - \bar{X}_2)$
1	9	1.8666	3.4842	14	-3.0667	9.4046	-5.7243
2	11	3.8666	14.9506	13	-4.0667	16.5380	-15.7243
3	6	-1.1344	1.2869	15	-2.0667	4.2712	2.3445
4	10	2.8666	8.2174	13	-4.0667	16.5380	-11.6576
5	8	0.8666	0.7510	14	-3.0667	9.4046	-2.6576
6	7	-0.1344	0.0181	14	-3.0667	9.4046	0.4122
7	2	-5.1344	26.3621	17	-0.0667	0.0044	0.3425
8	5	-2.1344	4.5557	19	1.9333	3.7376	-4.1264
9	9	1.8666	3.4842	21	3.9333	15.4708	7.3419
10	6	-1.1344	1.2869	19	1.9333	3.7376	-2.1931
11	2	-5.1344	26.3621	16	-1.0667	1.1378	5.4769
12	4	-3.1344	9.8245	18	0.9333	0.8710	-2.9253
13	7	-0.1344	0.0181	20	2.9333	8.8042	-0.3942
14	10	2.8666	8.2174	21	3.9333	15.4708	11.2752
15	11	3.8666	14.9506	22	4.9333	24.3374	19.0751

$\bar{X}_1 = 7.1334$

$\sum_{i=1}^{N}(X_{1i} - \bar{X}_1)^2 =$ 123.7698

$\bar{X}_2 = 17.0667$

$\sum_{i=1}^{N}(X_{2i} - \bar{X}_2)^2 =$ 139.1326

$\sum_{i=1}^{N}(X_{1i} - \bar{X}_1)(X_{2i} - \bar{X}_2) =$ 0.8655

Figure 14.4   *Examples of Nonlinear Relationships*

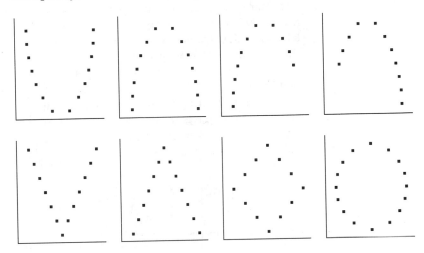

level measures to establish that it is linear before examining the Pearson's correlation coefficient. Linear relationships are much more common in criminal justice than nonlinear ones, but you would not want to conclude that there was a very small relationship between two variables, based on *r*, when in fact there was a very strong nonlinear correlation between them.

What can you do if the relationship is nonlinear? Sometimes the solution is simply to break up the distribution of scores. For example, figure 14.3 shows a nonlinear relationship that results in an *r* of 0.007. If we break this distribution at the point where it changes direction, we can calculate two separate Pearson's correlations, each for a linear relationship. The first would provide an estimate of the relationship for younger offenders (which is positive), and the second for older ones (which is negative).

For some nonlinear relationships you may want to consider using alternative statistics. For example, it may be worthwhile to break up your sample into a number of groups, or categories, and then to look at the means for each. In some cases, it may be possible to change the form of the variables and in doing so increase the linearity of the relationship examined. Although such transformations are beyond the scope of this text, you should be aware that they provide one solution to problems of nonlinearity.[2]

---

[2] For a discussion of this issue, see J. Fox (1994), *Linear Statistical Models and Related Methods* (New York: Wiley).

Beware of Outliers

For Pearson's r, as for other statistics based on deviations from the mean, outliers can have strong impacts on your results. For example, let us say that we added one subject to our study of age and arrests (from table 14.1) who was very young (12) but nonetheless had an extremely large number of prior arrests (25), as shown in the scatterplot in figure 14.5. If we take the covariation for this one relationship (see subject 16 in table 14.9), we see that it is very large relative to that of other subjects in our analysis. Because it is negative, it cancels out the positive covariation produced by the general group of cases. Indeed, the correlation with this subject included decreases from 0.77 to 0.10:

Working It Out

$$\text{Pearson's } r = \frac{\sum_{i=1}^{N}(X_{1i} - \overline{X}_1)(X_{2i} - \overline{X}_2)}{\sqrt{\left(\sum_{i=1}^{N}(X_{1i} - \overline{X}_1)^2\right)\left(\sum_{i=1}^{N}(X_{2i} - \overline{X}_2)^2\right)}}$$

$$= \frac{29.5000}{\sqrt{(567.7496)(163)}}$$

$$= 0.0970$$

Figure 14.5   *Scatterplot Showing the Relationship between Age and Number of Prior Arrests for 16 Subjects Including 1 Outlier*

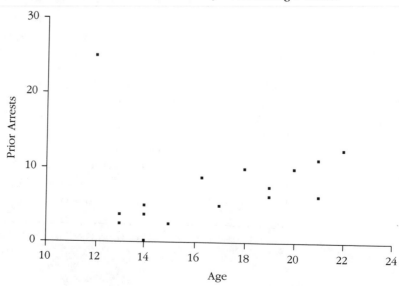

Table 14.9 Calculations for the Correlation of Prior Arrests (X_1) and Age (X_2) for 16 Young Offenders

SUBJECT	PRIOR ARRESTS X_1	AGE X_2	$X_{1i} - \bar{X}_1$	$(X_{1i} - \bar{X}_1)^2$	$X_{2i} - \bar{X}_2$	$(X_{2i} - \bar{X}_2)^2$	$(X_{1i} - \bar{X}_1)(X_{2i} - \bar{X}_2)$
1	0	14	-6.1250	37.5156	-2.7500	7.5625	16.84375
2	1	13	-5.1250	26.2656	-3.7500	14.0625	19.21875
3	1	15	-5.1250	26.2656	-1.7500	3.0625	8.96875
4	2	13	-4.1250	17.0156	-3.7500	14.0625	15.46875
5	2	14	-4.1250	17.0156	-2.7500	7.5625	11.34375
6	3	14	-3.1250	9.7656	-2.7500	7.5625	8.59375
7	3	17	-3.1250	9.7656	0.2500	0.0625	-0.78125
8	4	19	-2.1250	4.5156	2.2500	5.0625	-4.78125
9	4	21	-2.1250	4.5156	4.2500	18.0625	-9.03125
10	6	19	-0.1250	0.0156	2.2500	5.0625	-0.28125
11	8	16	1.8750	3.5156	-0.7500	0.5625	-1.40625
12	9	18	2.8750	8.2656	1.2500	1.5625	3.59375
13	9	20	2.8750	8.2656	3.2500	10.5625	9.34375
14	10	21	3.8750	15.0156	4.2500	18.0625	16.46875
15	11	22	4.8750	23.7656	5.2500	27.5625	25.59375
16	25	12	18.8750	356.2656	-4.7500	22.5625	-89.65625

$\bar{X}_1 = 6.1250 \qquad \bar{X}_2 = 16.500$

$$\sum_{i=1}^{N} (X_{1i} - \bar{X}_1)^2 = 567.7496$$

$$\sum_{i=1}^{N} (X_{2i} - \bar{X}_2)^2 = 163.0000$$

$$\sum_{i=1}^{N} (X_{1i} - \bar{X}_1)(X_{2i} - \bar{X}_2) = 29.5000$$

What should you do when faced with outliers? If you have just a few deviant cases in your sample, the best decision may be to exclude them from your analysis. If you take this approach, it is important to clearly state that certain cases have been excluded and to explain why. Before excluding outliers, however, you should compare the correlations with and without them. When samples are large, deviant cases may have a relatively small impact, and thus including them may not lead to misleading results.

When there are a relatively large number of outliers that follow the general pattern of relationships in your data, it may be better to choose an alternative correlation coefficient rather than to exclude such cases. For example, let us add three different subjects to our study of age and prior arrests, in which the relationships were similar to those noted here, but the number of arrests and the average age of the offenders was much higher (see subjects 16, 17, and 18 in table 14.10). These data are illustrated in the scatterplot in figure 14.6 (page 316). For such situations Pearson's r is likely to give a misleading view of the relationship between two variables. For our example, the correlation changes from 0.77 to 0.98.

Working It Out

$$\text{Pearson's } r = \frac{\sum_{i=1}^{N} (X_{1i} - \overline{X}_1)(X_{2i} - \overline{X}_2)}{\sqrt{\left(\sum_{i=1}^{N} (X_{1i} - \overline{X}_1)^2\right)\left(\sum_{i=1}^{N} (X_{2i} - \overline{X}_2)^2\right)}}$$

$$= \frac{3472.222}{\sqrt{(4065.6116)(3065.5068)}}$$

$$= 0.9835$$

In such situations, you may want to use a rank-order correlation coefficient called **Spearman's r**, or r_s. Spearman's r is a correlation coefficient used for ordinally scaled variables. It does not take into account the actual scores in a distribution but only the ranks of the scores. Pearson's r is generally more appropriate for interval-level data. However, where a number of outliers are found in the distribution, Spearman's rank-order correlation coefficient can provide a useful alternative.

Table 14.10 Calculations for the Correlation of Prior Arrests (X_1) and Age (X_2) for 18 Offenders

SUBJECT	PRIOR ARRESTS X_1	AGE X_2	$(X_{1i} - \bar{X}_1)^2$	$x_{1i} - \bar{X}_1$	$x_{2i} - \bar{X}_2$	$(X_{2i} - \bar{X}_2)^2$	$(X_{1i} - \bar{X}_1)(X_{2i} - \bar{X}_2)$
1	0	14	127.1888	-11.2778	-8.5556	73.1983	96.4883
2	1	13	105.6332	-10.2778	-9.5556	91.3095	98.2105
3	1	15	105.6332	-10.2778	-7.5556	57.0871	77.6550
4	2	13	86.0776	-9.2778	-9.5556	91.3095	88.6550
5	2	14	86.0776	-9.2778	-8.5556	73.1983	79.3771
6	3	14	68.5220	-8.2778	-8.5556	73.1983	70.8215
7	3	17	68.5220	-8.2778	-5.5556	30.8647	45.9881
8	4	19	52.9664	-7.2778	-3.5556	12.6423	25.8770
9	4	21	52.9664	-7.2778	-1.5556	2.4199	11.3213
10	6	19	27.8552	-5.2778	-3.5556	12.6423	18.7657
11	8	16	10.7440	-3.2778	-6.5556	42.9759	21.4879
12	9	18	5.1884	-2.2778	-4.5556	20.7535	10.3767
13	9	20	5.1884	-2.2778	-2.5556	6.5311	5.8211
14	10	21	1.6328	-1.2778	-1.5556	2.4199	1.9877
15	11	22	0.0772	-0.2778	-0.5556	0.3087	0.15435
16	36	40	611.1872	24.7222	17.4444	304.3071	431.2640
17	40	50	824.9648	28.7222	27.4444	753.1951	788.2636
18	54	60	1825.1854	42.7222	37.4444	1402.0831	1599.7071

$\bar{X}_1 = 11.2778$

$\bar{X}_2 = 22.5556$

$$\sum_{i=1}^{N} (X_{1i} - \bar{X}_1)^2 = 4065.6116$$

$$\sum_{i=1}^{N} (X_{2i} - \bar{X}_2)^2 = 3065.5068$$

$$\sum_{i=1}^{N} (X_{1i} - \bar{X}_1)(X_{2i} - \bar{X}_2) = 3472.2220$$

Figure 14.6   *Scatterplot Showing the Relationship between Age and Number of Prior Arrests for 18 Subjects, Including 3 Outliers Who Follow the General Pattern*

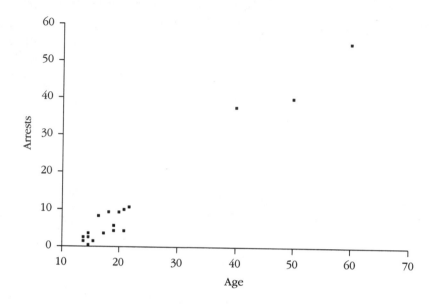

Spearman's *r*

Spearman's *r* compares the rank order of subjects on each measure rather than the relative position of each subject to the mean. Like Pearson's *r*, its range of possible values is between −1 and +1. It is calculated using equation 14.3.

Equation 14.3

$$r_s = 1 - \frac{6 \sum\limits_{i=1}^{N} D_i^2}{N(N^2 - 1)}$$

Let us calculate r_s for our example of age and prior arrests with 15 cases (from table 14.1), and for the example with the additional three outliers (from table 14.10). To carry out the calculation, we must first rank order the cases, as shown in tables 14.11 and 14.12 (page 318). We then take the squared difference in ranks for each subject on the two measures and sum that difference across all the cases in our example. This value is multiplied by six, and then divided by $N(N^2 - 1)$. The final figure is then subtracted from 1.

**Working It Out
(No Outliers)**

$$r_s = 1 - \frac{6\sum_{i=1}^{N} D_i^2}{N(N^2 - 1)}$$

$$= 1 - \frac{(6)(98)}{(15)(224)}$$

$$= 1 - \frac{588}{3360}$$

$$= 1 - 0.1750$$

$$= 0.8250$$

**Working It Out
(With Outliers)**

$$r_s = 1 - \frac{6\sum_{i=1}^{N} D_i^2}{N(N^2 - 1)}$$

$$= 1 - \frac{(6)(98)}{(18)(323)}$$

$$= 1 - \frac{588}{5814}$$

$$= 1 - 0.1011$$

$$= 0.8989$$

In this case the correlation coefficients for our two distributions are similar. In the case without the outliers, $r_s = 0.83$, in the case with them, $r_s = 0.90$. The outliers here do not have as much of an impact because Spearman's correlation coefficient does not take into account the actual values of the scores but only their ranks in the distribution. Note that the correlation coefficient obtained here for the 15 cases, $r_s = 0.83$, is a bit larger, although similar, to $r = 0.77$. Which is the better estimate of the correlation between these two variables? In the case without outliers, Pearson's r is preferred because it takes into account more information (order as well as value). In the case with outliers, however, Spearman's r_s would be preferred because it is not affected by the extreme values of the three outliers but only by their relative positions in the distributions.

Table 14.11   Calculation of "D" for Spearman's r for 15 Young Offenders

SUBJECT	PRIOR ARRESTS	RANK ARRESTS Rk_1	AGE	RANK AGE Rk_2	D $(Rk_1 - Rk_2)$	D^2
1	0	1	14	4	−3	9
2	1	2.5	13	1.5	1	1
3	1	2.5	15	6	−3.5	12.25
4	2	4.5	13	1.5	3	9
5	2	4.5	14	4	0.5	0.25
6	3	6.5	14	4	2.5	6.25
7	3	6.5	17	8	−1.5	2.25
8	4	8.5	19	10.5	−2	4
9	4	8.5	21	13.5	−5	25
10	6	10	19	10.5	−0.5	0.25
11	8	11	16	7	4	16
12	9	12.5	18	9	3.5	12.25
13	9	12.5	20	12	0.5	0.25
14	10	14	21	13.5	0.5	0.25
15	11	15	22	15	0	0

$\bar{X}_1 = 4.8667$ $\bar{X}_2 = 17.0667$

$$\sum_{i=1}^{N} D_i^2 = 98$$

Table 14.12   Calculation of "D" for Spearman's r for 18 Offenders

SUBJECT	PRIOR ARRESTS	RANK ARRESTS Rk_1	AGE	RANK AGE Rk_2	D $(Rk_1 - Rk_2)$	D^2
1	0	1	14	4	−3	9
2	1	2.5	13	1.5	1	1
3	1	2.5	15	6	−3.5	12.25
4	2	4.5	13	1.5	3	9
5	2	4.5	14	4	0.5	0.25
6	3	6.5	14	4	2.5	6.25
7	3	6.5	17	8	−1.5	2.25
8	4	8.5	19	10.5	−2	4
9	4	8.5	21	13.5	−5	25
10	6	10	19	10.5	−0.5	0.25
11	8	11	16	7	4	16
12	9	12.5	18	9	3.5	12.25
13	9	12.5	20	12	0.5	0.25
14	10	14	21	13.5	0.5	0.25
15	11	15	22	15	0	0
16	36	16	40	16	0	0
17	40	17	50	17	0	0
18	54	18	60	18	0	0

$\bar{X}_1 = 11.2778$ $\bar{X}_2 = 22.5556$

$\Sigma D^2 = 98$

Estimating the Influence of One Variable on Another: The Regression Coefficient

By making only a slight change to equation 14.2 for Pearson's correlation coefficient, we can construct a second statistic that estimates how much one variable influences another—the **regression coefficient.** But in using this measure, we make a very important assumption about the relationship between the interval variables examined. We assume that one variable, termed the **independent variable,** predicts the second, termed the **dependent variable.**

In practice, we often make this assumption in relating one variable to another. For example, in examining the relationship between imprisonment and reoffending in chapter 9, it was logical to assume that if there was a relationship it was prison that influenced reoffending and not vice versa. Although we did not explicitly state that age affects prior arrests in this chapter, it clearly would not make much sense to assume that prior arrests impact upon a person's age. In these examples, we might have defined one variable examined as an independent, or predictor variable, and the second as a dependent, or influenced variable. What sets regression apart from the statistics we have studied so far is not that we *can* make this choice, but that we *must* in order to calculate the regression coeffcient.

The regression coefficient, *b*, asks how much impact one variable (the independent variable) has on another (the dependent variable). It answers this question not in standardized units, but in the specific units of the variables examined. The specific interpretation of a regression coefficient will depend on the units of measurement used. Nonetheless, *b* has a general interpretation in terms of *X*, the symbol for the independent variable, and *Y*, the symbol for the dependent variable:

A change of one unit in *X* produces a change of *b* units in the estimated value of *Y*.

Let us take a concrete example. Suppose that you were studying the relationship between education and reoffending. You assume that education impacts reoffending and thus define years of education as the independent variable *X* and number of rearrests as the dependent variable *Y*. You calculate your regression coefficient and find it has a value of −2. You can interpret this coefficient as meaning that a one year change (or increase) in education produces on average a two-unit change, in this case reduction, in number of rearrests. If *b* had been positive, we would have concluded that a one-year increase in education produces on average an increase of two rearrests.

Calculating the Regression Coefficient

The calculation for the regression coefficient *b* (equation 14.4) is very similar to that for the correlation coefficient *r* (equation 14.2). In the numerator is once again the covariation between the two variables examined, although the two variables are expressed as *X* and *Y* rather than X_1 and X_2. The difference is in the denominator of the equation. Instead of standardizing this value according to the variability found in both measures, we now contrast the covariation of the relationship of *X* and *Y* with the variability found only in *X*.

Equation 14.4

$$ b = \frac{\sum_{i=1}^{N} (X_i - \overline{X})(Y_i - \overline{Y})}{\sum_{i=1}^{N} (X_i - \overline{X})^2} $$

By taking the example of age and number of prior arrests from table 14.1, we can see how a regression coefficient is calculated in practice (see table 14.13). We must first define *X* and *Y*, in this case that age is the independent variable (*X*) and arrests the dependent variable (*Y*). As noted earlier, it would not make sense to argue that prior arrests produce a change in age. As with the correlation coefficient, we first calculate the covariation between age (*X*) and arrests (*Y*). Our result (see table 14.13, column 6) is the same as that for the correlation coefficient, 125.1321. The calculation for the denominator, however, involves less work than before. In this case, we simply take the sum of the squared deviations of each subject's age from the mean of age. This is calculated in column 3 of table 14.13, and leads to a result of 139.1326. Our regression coefficient is obtained by dividing these two values.

Working It Out

$$ b = \frac{\sum_{i=1}^{N} (X_i - \overline{X})(Y_i - \overline{Y})}{\sum_{i=1}^{N} (X_i - \overline{X})^2} $$

$$ = \frac{125.1321}{139.1326} $$

$$ = 0.8994 $$

Table 14.13 Calculations for the Regression Coefficient of Age and Prior Arrests for 15 Young Offenders

1 AGE X	2 $X_i - \bar{X}$	3 $(X_i - \bar{X})^2$	4 ARRESTS Y	5 $Y_i - \bar{Y}$	6 $(X_i - \bar{X})(Y_i - \bar{Y})$
14	−3.067	9.4046	0	−4.8667	14.9247
13	−4.067	16.538	1	−3.8667	15.7247
15	−2.067	4.2712	1	−3.8667	7.9913
13	−4.067	16.538	2	−2.8667	11.658
14	−3.067	9.4046	2	−2.8667	8.7913
14	−3.067	9.4046	3	−1.8667	5.7246
17	−0.067	0.0044	3	−1.8667	0.1245
19	1.9333	3.7376	4	−0.8667	−1.676
21	3.9333	15.4708	4	−0.8667	−3.409
19	1.9333	3.7376	6	1.1333	2.191
16	−1.067	1.1378	8	3.1333	−3.343
18	0.9333	0.871	9	4.1333	3.8576
20	2.9333	8.8042	9	4.1333	12.1242
21	3.9333	15.4708	10	5.1333	20.1908
22	4.9333	24.3374	11	6.1333	30.2574

$\bar{X} = 17.0667$ $\quad\quad\quad\quad \sum_{i=1}^{N} (X_i - X)^2 =$ $\quad \bar{Y} = 4.8667 \quad\quad\quad\quad \sum_{i=1}^{N} (X_i - \bar{X})(Y_i - \bar{Y}) =$

$\quad\quad\quad\quad\quad\quad\quad\quad\quad\quad\quad\quad 139.1326 \quad\quad\quad\quad\quad\quad\quad\quad\quad\quad\quad\quad\quad\quad\quad\quad\quad 125.1321$

Our result of 0.899 can be interpreted as meaning that a one-year increase in age produces, on average, a 0.899 increase in number of prior arrests.

Statistical Significance for Correlation and Regression Coefficients

Our emphasis in this chapter has not been on statistical inference but rather on statistical description. Our concern has been to describe the strength or nature of the relationship between two interval-level variables. Nonetheless, it is important here, as before, to define whether the differences observed in our samples can be inferred to the populations from which they are drawn.

Testing the Statistical Significance of r or b
The same statistical test of significance may be used for r and b. It is based on the t distribution introduced in chapter 10.

Assumptions:

Level of Measurement: Interval scale

Population Distribution: Normal distribution of Y around each value of X (must be assumed because N is not large)

Homoscedasticity

Sampling Method: Independent random sampling

Sampling Frame: Youth in one U.S. city

Linearity

Hypotheses:

H_0: There is no linear relationship between age and prior arrests in the population; $r_p = 0$; $B = 0$.

H_1: There is a linear relationship between age and prior arrests in the population; $r_p \neq 0$; $B \neq 0$.

It is assumed for both regression and correlation that the variables examined are measured at an interval scale. This is the case for our problem. In practice, researchers sometimes use ordinal-scale measures for calculating these coefficients. Although estimates of regression and correlation coefficients often provide reliable estimates of relationships between ordinal-scale measures, or between ordinal- and interval-scale measures, the smaller the spread of scores in such measures, the more questionable are the outcomes observed. You should not use correlation or regression coefficients when defining the relationship between two variables in which either or both are measured as nominal scales.

Because this is a parametric test of significance, we must also make assumptions regarding the population distribution. For tests of statistical significance with r and b, we must assume that for each value of X the scores of Y are normally distributed around the regression line. We must also assume that the variances of the distribution of Y scores around each value of X are equal. This is the assumption of homoscedasticity. In general, for regression and correlation, researchers use the central limit theorem to relax assumptions of normality. As with analysis of variance, we are generally concerned only with marked violations of the homoscedasticity assumption.

To visualize these assumptions, it is useful to look at a scatterplot. Suppose figure 14.7 represents the scatterplot of the population of scores for age and prior arrests in the city examined. The relationship, as in our sample, is linear. But notice how the points in the scatterplot are distributed. If we put an imaginary line through the scatter of

Figure 14.7 *Scatterplot Showing the Relationship between Age and Number of Prior Arrests: Normal Distribution and Homoscedasticity*

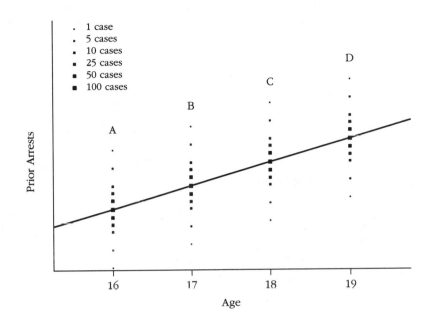

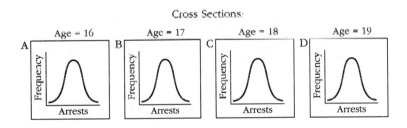

points, we can see that there is a clustering of points close to the line. Farther from the line, there are fewer points. This distribution is basically normal in that there is a bell shape of points for every value of X that is highest on the imaginary line and then slopes down in normal form away from the line. This is illustrated in the cross sections for each age group.

Also, there are about equal variances for the points around the line. That is, the spread of the scores around each X in this distribution is about equal, whether we look at the cases associated with the youngest subjects (to the left of the scatterplot), those associated with average age subjects (in the middle of the scatterplot), or those associated with the oldest offenders (on the right of the scatterplot).

In contrast, the scatterplot in figure 14.8 shows a case that violates rather than meets the assumptions for our t-test. In this scatterplot, the points are not clustered in the center of the distribution (as represented by our imaginary line). Indeed, they represent a type of bimodal distribution with peaks above and below the line (see cross sections for each age group). **Heteroscedasticity,** or unequal variances, rather than homoscedasticity, is also represented in the scatterplot of figure 14.8. For subjects aged 17 and 19, the scores are scattered widely around our imaginary line. For subjects aged 16 and 18, however, the scores are tightly clustered. If this were the population distribution of the variables under study, you would want to be very cautious in applying the t-test to your regression or correlation coefficient.

One problem in drawing conclusions about these assumptions is that they relate to the population and not to the sample. Because the population distribution is usually unknown, we generally cannot come to solid conclusions regarding our assumptions. In the case of an assumption of normality, the researcher is most often aided by the central limit theorem. When the number of cases in a sample is greater than 30, the central limit theorem can be safely invoked. For our example, we cannot invoke the central limit theorem. Accordingly, our test results cannot be relied upon unless the assumption of a normal distribution of Y around each value of X is true for the population to which we infer.

With regard to the assumption of homoscedasticity, researchers generally use the scatterplot of sample cases as an indication of the form of the population distribution. Because we are concerned only with large violations of this assumption, such violations should also appear in the scatterplot of sample observations.

Correlation and regression add one new assumption to our test, that of linearity. Our null hypothesis for both coefficients is simply that there is no linear relationship, or that the population correlation coefficient (r_p) and the population regression coefficient (B) are equal to 0. The research hypothesis is nondirectional. However, we might have proposed a directional research hypothesis, for example that there is a positive relationship between age and arrests in the population (for correlation, $r_p > 0$; for regression, $B > 0$).

Figure 14.8 *Scatterplot Showing the Relationship between Age and Number of Prior Arrests: Nonnormal Distribution and Heteroscedasticity*

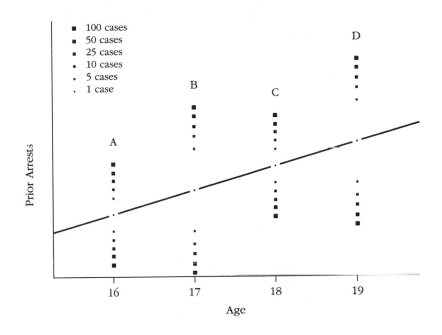

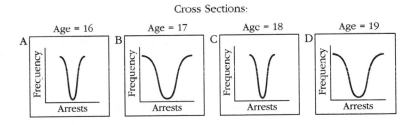

Cross Sections:

The Sampling Distribution
The sampling distribution is t, with $N - 2$ degrees of freedom. For our example, $df = 15 - 2 = 13$.

Significance Level and Rejection Region
Using a two-tailed 0.05 significance threshold, the critical value for the t-test (with 13 degrees of freedom) is 2.160 (see appendix 4). We will reject the null hypothesis if the t-score is greater than or equal to 2.160 or less than or equal to −2.160.

The Test Statistic

It is important to note that there is more than one way to test statistical significance for r and b. Equation 14.5 provides an estimate of t, based only on our calculation of r.

Equation 14.5

$$t = r \sqrt{\frac{n-2}{1-r^2}}$$

By inserting our sample estimates, we calculate that the t statistic for both r and b is 4.412.

Working It Out

$$t = r \sqrt{\frac{n-2}{1-r^2}}$$

$$= 0.7743 \sqrt{\frac{15-2}{1-(0.7743)^2}}$$

$$= 0.7743 \sqrt{32.462708}$$

$$= 4.4117$$

The Decision

As 4.412 is greater than our critical value of t (2.160), we reject the null hypothesis and conclude that there is a statistically significant relationship between age and number of prior arrests. However, because we cannot strongly support the assumption of normality in this test, nor relax that assumption because N is large, we cannot place strong reliance on our test result.

Testing the Statistical Significance of r_s

For Spearman's r_s, we use a nonparametric statistical test. With $N \le 30$, we use an exact probability distribution constructed for the distribution of differences between ranked pairs (see appendix 7). For larger samples, a normal approximation of this test is appropriate. It is constructed by taking the difference between the observed value of r_s and the parameter value under the null hypothesis (r_{sp}). This value is then divided by 1 divided by the square root of $N - 1$:

Equation 14.6

$$z = \frac{r_s - r_{sp}}{\dfrac{1}{\sqrt{N-1}}}$$

Because we examine less than 15 cases we will use the exact probability table presented in appendix 7.

Assumptions:
Level of Measurement: Ordinal scale

Sampling Method: Independent random sampling

Sampling Frame: Youth in one U.S. city

Hypotheses:
H_0: There is no linear relationship between the rank order of scores in the population: $r_{sp} = 0$.

H_1: There is a linear relationship between the rank order of scores in the population: $r_{sp} \neq 0$.

Because we use a nonparametric test we do not need to make assumptions regarding the population distribution. The null hypothesis is the same as for the correlation coefficient r; however, it is concerned with ranks rather than raw scores.

The Sampling Distribution

Because N is small, we use the exact probability distribution constructed for Spearman's r_s in appendix 7.

Significance Level and Critical Region

As earlier, we use the conventional 0.05 significance threshold. As our research hypothesis is not directional, we use a two-tailed rejection region. From appendix 7, under a 0.05, two-tailed probability value and an N of 15, we find that an r_s greater than or equal to 0.525 or less than or equal to −0.525 is needed to reject the null hypothesis.

The Test Statistic

In the case of the exact probability distribution, the test statistic is simply the value of r_s. As calculated earlier in this chapter (see table 14.11), r_s equals 0.825.

The Decision

Because the observed r_s is larger than 0.525, we reject the null hypothesis and conclude that there is a statistically significant linear relationship between ranks of age and prior arrests in the population.

Chapter Summary

Linear correlation coefficients describe the relationship between two interval-level measures, telling us how strongly the two are associated. **Pearson's *r*** is a widely used linear correlation coefficient. It examines the placement of subjects on both variables relative to the mean, and estimates how strongly the scores move together or in opposite directions relative to the mean. The **covariation,** which is the numerator of the Pearson's *r* equation, is positive when both scores vary in the same direction relative to the mean, and negative when they vary in opposite directions. Dividing the covariation by the denominator of the Pearson's *r* equation serves to standardize the coefficient so that it varies between –1 and +1. Pearson's *r* will produce a misleading correlation coefficient if there is a nonlinear relationship between the variables.

Outliers have a strong impact on Pearson's *r*. If there are several outliers that follow the general pattern of relationships in the data, an alternative measure, **Spearman's *r*,** may provide less misleading results. Spearman's *r* also varies between –1 and +1. It compares the rank order of subjects on each measure. It is generally more appropriate for ordinally scaled variables.

The **regression coefficient,** *b*, tells us how much one variable (the **independent variable,** *X*) influences another variable (the **dependent variable,** *Y*). The regression coefficient is expressed in specific units of the dependent variable and is interpreted as follows: a change of one unit in *X* produces a change of *b* units in the estimated value of *Y*.

The *t* distribution may be used to test significance for the coefficients *r* and *b*. It is assumed that the variables examined are measured at an interval scale. There is also an assumption of normality and a requirement of homoscedasticity. These assumptions relate to the distribution of *Y* around each value of *X*. The researcher must also assume linearity. For Spearman's *r*, a nonparametric test of statistical significance is used.

Key Terms

Covariation The extent to which two variables vary together relative to their respective means. The covariation between the two variables serves as the numerator for the equations to calculate both Pearson's *r* and the regression coefficient *b*.

Curvilinear Relationship An association between two variables whose values may be represented as a curved line when plotted on a scatter diagram.

Dependent Variable (Y) The variable assumed by the researcher to be influenced by one or more independent variables.

Heteroscedasticity A situation in which the variances of scores are not equal. Heteroscedasticity violates one of the assumptions of the parametric test of statistical significance for the regression or correlation coefficients.

Independent Variable (X) A variable assumed by the researcher to impact upon the value of the dependent variable, Y.

Linear Relationship An association between two variables whose joint distribution may be represented in linear form when plotted on a scatter diagram.

Pearson's Correlation Coefficient See Pearson's r.

Pearson's r A commonly used measure of association between two variables. Pearson's r measures the strength and direction of linear relationships on a standardized scale from −1 to +1.

Regression Coefficient (b) A statistic used to assess the influence of an independent variable, X, on a dependent variable, Y. b is interpreted as the estimated change in Y that is associated with a one unit change in X.

Scatter Diagram See Scatterplot.

Scatterplot A graph whose two axes are defined by two variables, and upon which a point is plotted for each subject in a sample according to its score on the two variables.

Spearman's r (r_s) A measure of association between two ordinally scaled variables. Spearman's r measures the strength and direction of linear relationships on a standardized scale between −1 and +1. It is used mainly for rank-ordered data.

Symbols and Formulas

r	Pearson's correlation coefficient.
r_s	Spearman's correlation coefficient.
b	Regression coefficient.
B	Regression coefficient for the population.
X	Independent variable.
Y	Dependent variable.
D	Difference in rank of a subject for two variables.

To calculate the covariation of scores for two variables:

$$\text{Covariation of Scores} = \sum_{i=1}^{N} (X_{1i} - \overline{X}_1)(X_{2i} - \overline{X}_2)$$

To calculate Pearson's correlation coefficient:

$$\text{Pearson's } r = \frac{\displaystyle\sum_{i=1}^{N}(X_{1i} - \overline{X}_1)(X_{2i} - \overline{X}_2)}{\sqrt{\left(\displaystyle\sum_{i=1}^{N}(X_{1i} - \overline{X}_1)^2\right)\left(\displaystyle\sum_{i=1}^{N}(X_{2i} - \overline{X}_2)^2\right)}}$$

To calculate Spearman's correlation coefficient:

$$r_s = 1 - \frac{6\displaystyle\sum_{i=1}^{N} D_i^2}{N(N^2 - 1)}$$

To calculate the regression coefficient, b:

$$b = \frac{\displaystyle\sum_{i=1}^{N}(X_i - \overline{X})(Y_i - \overline{Y})}{\displaystyle\sum_{i=1}^{N}(X_i - \overline{X})^2}$$

To test statistical significance for Pearson's r or for b:

$$t = r\sqrt{\frac{n-2}{1-r^2}}$$

To test statistical significance for Spearman's r where N is large:

$$z = \frac{r_s - r_{sp}}{\dfrac{1}{\sqrt{N-1}}}$$

Exercises

14.1 A researcher draws four random samples of 10 offenders, aged between 30 and 35 years, all of whom are currently serving out a term of imprisonment and all of whom have been in prison before. For each sample, he compares the subjects on the following pairs of variables:

SAMPLE 1	1	2	3	4	5	6	7	8	9	10
X_1: Number of Convictions	3	5	1	7	6	2	4	9	10	8
X_2: Average Sentence	2	2.5	0.5	3	3	1	2	4.5	5	3.5

SAMPLE 2	1	2	3	4	5	6	7	8	9	10
X_1: Years of Education	9	12	17	16	9	14	10	17	17	9
X_2: Age on First Offense	14	17	14	16	10	17	16	10	12	12

SAMPLE 3	1	2	3	4	5	6	7	8	9	10
X_1: Age on First Offense	13	17	10	16	14	11	18	19	15	12
X_2: Number of Convictions	7	3	10	4	6	9	1	1	6	8

SAMPLE 4	1	2	3	4	5	6	7	8	9	10
X_1: Age on First Offense	11	16	18	12	15	17	13	20	20	13
X_2: Average Sentence	3	5	1.5	1	1	4	4.5	5	3	2.5

a Calculate the mean scores of both variables for samples 1, 2, 3, and 4.

b Display the data for each of the four samples in four frequency distribution tables. For each score, add a positive or negative sign to indicate the direction in which the score differs from the mean (as is done in tables 14.4 and 14.5 in the text). Add an extra column in which you record a plus or a minus for the product of the two signs.

c Draw four scatterplots, one for each sample distribution, and for each one, state whether it shows a positive relationship, a negative relationship, a curvilinear relationship, or no relationship between the two variables.

d Would you advise against using Pearson's correlation coefficient as a measure of association for any of the four samples? Explain your answer.

14.2 Jeremy, a police researcher, is concerned that police officers may not be assigned to areas where they are needed. He wishes to check whether there is a connection between the number of police officers assigned to a particular block, and the number of violent incidents reported on that block during the preceding week. For ten different blocks (designated A through J), the number of patrolling officers assigned and the number of prior violent incidents reported are as follows:

	A	B	C	D	E	F	G	H	I	J
X_1: Violent Incidents	7	10	3	9	8	0	4	4	2	8
X_2: Officers Assigned	6	9	3	10	8	1	4	5	2	7

   a Calculate the covariance for the data recorded above.

   b Calculate the value of Pearson's r for the data recorded above.

   c On an 11th block—block K—there are no police officers patrolling, yet in the previous week 11 violent incidents were reported there. What effect would it have on Pearson's r if Jeremy were to include block K in his calculations?

   d How do you explain this difference?

14.3   Seven subjects of different ages are asked to complete a questionnaire measuring attitudes about criminal behavior. Their answers are coded into an index with scores ranging from 1 to 15. The subjects' scores are as follows:

X_1: Age	12	22	10	14	18	20	16
X_2: Score	6	3	3	9	9	6	13

   a Calculate Pearson's correlation coefficient for the two variables listed above.

   b Illustrate the sample distribution on a scatterplot.

   c Divide the scatterplot into two sections as you feel appropriate and calculate the value of Pearson's r for each section.

   d Explain the difference in r values you obtained in exercises 14.3a and 14.3c.

14.4   Eight homeowners in the inner-city neighborhood of Moss Tide are asked how long they have been living in the neighborhood, and how many times during that period their house has been burglarized. The results for the eight subjects are listed below:

X_1: Years in Neighborhood	2	1.5	3.5	28	1	5	20	3
X_2: Number of Burglaries	2	1	5	55	0	4	10	3

a Calculate Pearson's r for the two variables recorded above.

b Calculate Spearman's r for the same data.

c Illustrate the sample distribution on a scatterplot.

d Which of the two correlation coefficients is more appropriate, in your opinion, for this case? Refer to the scatterplot in explaining your answer.

14.5 A researcher carries out a series of regression analyses for different studies. The results in three of the studies are listed below. In each case, explain what they mean in plain English:

a X = number of prior driving offenses; Y = fine in dollars imposed by magistrate; b = 72.

b X = number of times a household has been broken into prior to purchase of first burglar alarm; Y = amount of money in dollars spent by homeowner on first burglar alarm; b = 226.

c X = number of times subject has been involved in a car accident; Y = estimated average speed of subject when driving on a freeway in miles per hour; b = –8.5.

14.6 Refer to the data in exercise 14.2.

a Calculate the regression coefficient for the initial set of data (10 street blocks).

b Calculate the regression coefficient for the set of data including block K from exercise 14.2c (11 street blocks).

14.7 Refer to the data in exercise 14.4.

a Calculate the regression coefficient and explain what it means in plain English.

b Run a test of statistical significance on the result obtained from your calculation of Pearson's r. Be sure to list all of the assumptions and state clearly any violations of them. Can you reject the null hypothesis that Pearson's r is different from 0 for the population?

c Run a nonparametric test of statistical significance on the result obtained from Spearman's r, remembering to list all assumptions and any violations of them. Is your decision in this case any different?

Computer Exercises

1. Many people believe that an area that has a high rate of one type of crime is likely to have high rates of other types of crime. Examine the relationship between the number of crimes of different types by choosing four of the types of crimes (cleared by arrest) that are included in our data. Examine the strength of the relationships between these crimes by using the Bivariate command in the Statistics (Correlate) menu. This procedure includes Pearson's r and Spearman's r statistics. Request both and discuss the differences. Which two crimes are most strongly correlated? Which are the least?

2. To check the appropriateness of using linear correlation coefficients for the relationships you assessed in question 1, produce scatterplots of each relationship you found using the Simple command in the Graphs (Scatter) menu. Is the assumption of a linear relationship met in each case? Is the Pearson's r or Spearman's r statistic more appropriate? Save these graphs for later use.

3. Using the graphs you produced in question 2, graph the linear regression line by checking the Total box in the Fit Line Command in the Chart Options menu of the Chart Editor. Does it make sense to use these variables in a regression equation? Do the data meet the required assumptions? Can one type of crime cause another type of crime?

4. Some criminologists have suggested that high rates of less serious crime lead to high rates of more serious crime. Test this hypothesis using one of the theft measures in the data base and one of the measures of violent crime. Use the Statistics (Regression, Linear) command to do this. Interpret the regression coefficient (the Unstandardized B) and discuss its statistical significance.

and Multivariate Regression Modeling

prediction: building the regression line

How Can We Predict the Value of Y?

How Is the Regression Line Built?

What Are the Limits of Prediction?

evaluation: evaluating the regression line

What Is the R^2 Statistic?

What Is the F-test for the Overall Regression?

specification: building a multivariate model

What Is a Correctly Specified Model?

How Does the Researcher Try to Correctly Specify the Model?

multicolinearity

When Does it Arise?

How Is it Diagnosed?

How Is it Treated?

ONE OF THE MOST COMMONLY USED statistical tools in criminal justice and criminology is regression modeling. A regression model allows the researcher to take a much broader approach to criminological research problems. It is based not simply on understanding the relationships among variables, but on specifying why changes occur and the factors that are directly responsible for these changes. In a regression model, the researcher seeks to predict values of the dependent variable based on knowledge about one or more independent variables. The researcher also tries to disentangle the various potential causes of change in the dependent variable, in order to provide an accurate picture of which variables are in fact most important in causing change.

This chapter provides a basic introduction to regression modeling. Our discussion focuses on how regression analysis is used to create a prediction model, and the statistics that researchers use to evaluate such models. We also discuss why it is generally important to take into account more than just one independent variable in building regression models. Previous chapters have focused on bivariate statistical analysis, in which we relate two variables—whether nominal, ordinal, or interval—one to another. This chapter introduces multivariate analysis, in which the researcher can take into account a series of independent variables at one time.

Prediction in Regression: Building the Regression Line

The regression coefficient introduced in chapter 14 provides a method for estimating how change in an independent variable influences change in a dependent variable. However, it does not allow the researcher to predict the actual values of the dependent variable. For example, we found in chapter 14 that a one-year increase in age in our sample of young offenders was associated with a 0.8994 increase in the number of prior arrests. Accordingly, based on our analysis, we would predict that a 14-year-old would have about 0.9 more arrests than a 13-year-old. Someone 15 years old would be expected to have about 1.8 more arrests than someone 13 years old. This is because our regression coefficient suggests that for each year of age, we can expect about 0.9 more arrests.

But this still does not tell us how many arrests overall a person 13, 14, or 15 years old would be expected to have. To answer this question, we need another piece of information. We need to have a starting point from which to calculate change. That starting point is provided by a statistic called the Y-intercept.

The Y-Intercept

The **Y-intercept,** or b_0,[1] is the expected value of Y when X equals 0. It is calculated by subtracting the product of b and the mean of X, from the mean of Y (equation 15.1).

Equation 15.1

$$b_0 = \overline{Y} - b\overline{X}$$

For example, we would obtain the value of b_0 for the regression example calculated in chapter 14 by first taking the product of b (0.8994) and the mean of age (17.0667; see table 14.1), and then subtracting that value (15.3498) from 4.8667, the mean for prior arrests in the sample. The result is −10.483.

Working It Out

$$b_0 = \overline{Y} - b\overline{X}$$
$$= 4.8667 - (0.8994)(17.0667)$$
$$= 4.8667 - 15.3498$$
$$= -10.4831$$

The Regression Line

By looking at a scatterplot, we can see how the Y-intercept helps in developing predictions of Y from X (see figure 15.1). If we put the value −10.483 on the line where the value of age is 0, we can then use the regression coefficient b to draw a line of prediction, called the

---

[1]Note that there is no single accepted convention for representing the Y-intercept. Some researchers use the symbol α (alpha), and others prefer to use a.

Figure 15.1   *Scatterplot and Regression Line Showing the Relationship between Age and Number of Prior Arrests for 15 Subjects*

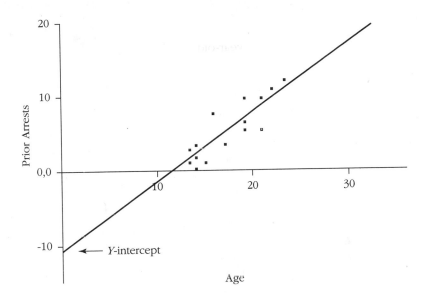

regression line. The regression coefficient tells us that for each increase of one year in age, there is a corresponding increase of 0.899 arrests. That means that when age is about 1, then prior arrests should be b_0 (−10.483) + 0.899, or −9.584. For two years of age the number of prior arrests should be b_0 + 0.899 + 0.899, and so forth. By plotting these values, we can draw the regression line for our example. This is done in figure 15.1, which also includes the scatterplot of the 15 sample scores (from table 14.1).

The predicted values of Y, designated $\hat{Y}$, can also be found through a simple equation. In this case, $\hat{Y}$ is equivalent to the Y-intercept plus the regression coefficient times the value of X (equation 15.2).

Equation 15.2 $\hat{Y} = b_0 + bX$

For our example this equation may be represented as in equation 15.3.

Equation 15.3   Predicted prior arrests = −10.483 + (0.8994) (age)

We now have a method for predicting the number of prior arrests based on the age of subjects in our sample. Looking at our regression line, we would, for example predict that someone 12 years old would not have any prior arrests. To obtain the exact prediction, we would simply put age 12 in equation 15.3. The result is 0.3098:

Working It Out

$$\text{Predicted prior arrests} = -10.4831 + (0.8994)\,(\text{age})$$
$$= -10.483 + (0.8994)\,(12)$$
$$= 0.3098$$

For someone 16 years old, we predict about four prior arrests.

Working It Out

$$\text{Predicted prior arrests} = -10.483 + (0.8994)\,(\text{age})$$
$$= -10.483 + (0.8994)\,(16)$$
$$= 3.9074$$

For someone 20 years old, we predict between seven and eight arrests.

Working It Out

$$\text{Predicted prior arrests} = -10.483 + (0.8994)\,(\text{age})$$
$$= -10.483 + (0.8994)\,(20)$$
$$= 7.5050$$

Choosing the Best Line of Prediction Based on Regression Error

One question we might ask is whether this particular line is the best one that could be drawn, given the data available to us. In order to answer this question we must first decide upon the criteria that we would use for defining the best line. In regression, as in many of the statistical techniques we have examined, we use the criterion of minimizing error.

Regression error (or **residual error,** designated e) is defined as the difference between the actual values of Y and the predicted values of Y ($\hat{Y}$) (equation 15.4).

Equation 15.4

$$e = Y - \hat{Y}$$

In table 15.1 the actual values of Y and the predicted values ($\hat{Y}$) are contrasted for the 15 subjects in our example. Subject 8, for example, has four prior arrests. But the predicted value for prior arrests based on our regression equation is 6.6056. The error in this case is −2.6056. In other words, the actual value of Y is made up of both our predic-

Table 15.1 Contrast of the Predicted Values for Y ($\hat{Y}$) and the Actual Values for Y

SUBJECT	AGE X	PRIOR ARRESTS Y	$\hat{Y}$	$Y_i - \hat{Y}$
1	14	0	2.1086	−2.1086
2	13	1	1.2092	−0.2092
3	15	1	3.0080	−2.0080
4	13	2	1.2092	+0.7908
5	14	2	2.1086	−0.1086
6	14	3	2.1086	+0.8914
7	17	3	4.8068	−1.8068
8	19	4	6.6056	−2.6056
9	21	4	8.4044	−4.4044
10	19	6	6.6056	−0.6056
11	16	8	3.9074	+4.0926
12	18	9	5.7062	+3.2938
13	20	9	7.5050	+1.495
14	21	10	8.4044	+1.5956
15	22	11	9.3038	+1.6962

$$\sum_{i=1}^{N} (Y_i - \hat{Y}) = 0.0*$$

*Due to rounding error, the actual value of $Y_i - \hat{Y}$ in our example is slightly less than 0.

tion and some amount of error. The equation form of this relation gives the basic **regression model** for our example. The value of Y in this case is equal to the Y-intercept plus the regression coefficient times the age of the individual plus the error:

$$Y = b_0 + (b) \,(\text{age}) + e$$

By looking at one of our 15 subjects, we can see this relationship in practice. Subject 3's age is 15. The difference between the predicted value for arrests and the actual number of arrests, or the error (e), for subject 3 is −2.008. If we add the Y-intercept, the subject's age times the coefficient b, and the error, we obtain a value of 1.

Working It Out

$$Y = b_0 + (b) \,(\text{age}) + e$$
$$= -10.483 + 0.8994(15) + (-2.008)$$
$$= -10.483 + 13.491 + (-2.008)$$
$$= 1$$

As we see from table 15.1, this is also this subject's actual value for Y (one prior arrest).

In using error as a criterion for choosing the best line, we are forced to base our decision not on the sum of errors in our equation, but on the sum of the squared errors. This is the case because the deviations above and below the regression line cancel each other out. Indeed, in regression the sum of the deviations of $\hat{Y}$ from Y are always equal to 0. Squaring the deviations of $\hat{Y}$ from Y provides estimates with only positive signs and allows us to assess the amount of error found. The regression line we have constructed is the best line using the criteria of squared deviations of $\hat{Y}$ from Y. Put in mathematical language, the regression line is the line for which the sum of the squared errors is at a minimum (equation 15.5).

Equation 15.5

$$\sum_{i=1}^{N} (Y_i - \hat{Y})^2 = \text{minimum}$$

For this reason, we call this approach **ordinary least squares regression analysis,** or OLS regression.

Predictions beyond the Distribution Observed in a Sample

Even though OLS regression provides the best line under these criteria, our data illustrate a very important limitation of regression modeling. You should be very cautious about predicting beyond the distribution observed in your sample. For example, our regression line provides very misleading predictions of prior arrests for very young offenders. Below the age of 12, our predictions are negative, leading to predicted values much below 0 (see figure 15.1). OLS regression provides good estimates for the range of offenders in our sample; however, it does not provide a solid basis for predictions beyond that range.

Evaluating the Regression Model

Having illustrated that OLS regression provides the best line using the least squares criteria for error, we may still ask how well this line predicts the dependent variable. Does the regression model add to our ability to predict prior arrests in our sample? Researchers commonly use a measure called the **percent of variance explained,** or R^2, to answer this question.

Percent of Variance Explained

The percent of variance explained in regression is analogous to eta squared in analysis of variance. In eta squared, we examined the proportion of the total sums of squares that was accounted for by the between (or "explained") sums of squares. In the case of regression, the explained sums of squares (ESS) is the difference between the predicted value of Y ($\hat{Y}$) and the mean of Y ($\overline{Y}$). The total sums of squares (TSS) is represented by the difference between Y and the mean of Y ($\overline{Y}$). R^2 for regression, as for analysis of variance, is the ratio of the explained to the total sums of squares (equation 15.6).

Equation 15.6

$$R^2 = \frac{ESS}{TSS} = \frac{\sum_{i=1}^{N} (\hat{Y}_i - \overline{Y})^2}{\sum_{i=1}^{N} (Y_i - \overline{Y})^2}$$

Why do we define the explained and total sums of squares in terms of the mean? If we did not have our regression model, but only the raw data in our sample, our best single prediction of Y would be the mean of Y ($\overline{Y}$). The question asked by R^2 is how much knowledge we have gained by developing the regression line. This is illustrated in figure 15.2, where we take one subject from our sample, subject 13, and plot that subject's score relative to the regression line and the mean of Y. The distance between the predicted value of Y and the mean of Y represents the explained deviation ($\hat{Y} - \overline{Y}$). The distance from the mean of Y to the actual score for the subject is the total deviation from the mean ($Y - \overline{Y}$). The explained deviation thus represents the improvement in predicting Y that the regression line provides over the mean.

To calculate the explained sums of squares in our example, we simply take the difference of the predicted score for arrests for each subject and the mean for arrests, square that value, and sum the outcomes across the 15 subjects. This is done in column 5 of table 15.2, where our final result is 112.3861. For the total sums of squares, we subtract the mean of arrests for the sample from each subject's actual number of arrests. This value is squared, and the 15 outcomes are

Figure 15.2   *The Explained, Unexplained, and Total Deviations from the Mean for Subject 13 (Age = 20; Prior Arrests = 9)*

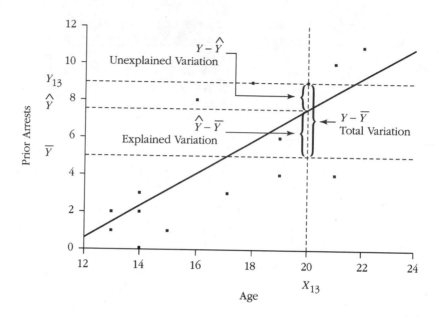

added together (see table 15.2, column 7). The total sums of squares for our example is 187.7338.

To gain the percent of variance explained, or R^2, we take the ratio of these two values. The percent of variance explained beyond the mean in our regression model or R^2 is 0.59.

Working It Out

$$R^2 = \frac{ESS}{TSS} = \frac{\sum\limits_{i=1}^{N} (\hat{Y}_i - \overline{Y})^2}{\sum\limits_{i=1}^{N} (Y_i - \overline{Y})^2}$$

$$= \frac{112.3861}{187.7338}$$

$$= 0.5986$$

Is this value large or small? As we noted in earlier chapters, determining whether an effect is large or small inevitably involves a value judgment. In deciding on the strength of your prediction, you would likely compare your results to that of other research on the same or related topics. As a general rule in criminal justice, regression models seldom result in R^2 values greater than 0.40. If your R^2 is larger than 0.40, you can usually assume that your prediction model is a powerful one. The percent of variance explained in our model accordingly suggests a very high level of prediction. Conversely, when the percent of variance explained is less than 0.15 or 0.20, the model is likely to be viewed as relatively weak in terms of prediction.

The *F*-Test for the Overall Regression

The logic used for developing the measure of percent of variance explained also provides for another regression statistic. So far, we have asked how much our model improves our predictions beyond what can be learned from the mean. But another question is whether we

Table 15.2   Calculations for R^2 Value for 15 Young Offenders

1 SUBJECT	2 Y	3 $\hat{Y}$	4 $\hat{Y}_i - \bar{Y}$	5 $(\hat{Y}_i - Y)^2$	6 $Y_i - \bar{Y}$	7 $(Y_i - \bar{Y})^2$
1	0	2.1086	−2.7581	7.6071	−4.8667	23.6848
2	1	1.2092	−3.6575	13.3773	−3.8667	14.9514
3	1	3.0080	−1.8587	3.4548	−3.8667	14.9514
4	2	1.2092	−3.6575	13.3773	−2.8667	8.2180
5	2	2.1086	−2.7581	7.6071	−2.8667	8.2180
6	3	2.1086	−2.7581	7.6071	−1.8667	3.4846
7	3	4.0060	−0.0599	0.0036	−1.8667	3.4846
8	4	6.6056	1.7389	3.0238	−0.8667	0.7512
9	4	8.4044	3.5377	12.5153	−0.8667	0.7512
10	6	6.6056	1.7389	3.0238	1.1333	1.2844
11	8	3.9074	−0.9593	0.9203	3.1333	9.8176
12	9	5.7062	0.8395	0.7048	4.1333	17.0842
13	9	7.5050	2.6383	6.9606	4.1333	17.0842
14	10	8.4044	3.5377	12.5153	5.1333	26.3508
15	11	9.3038	4.4371	19.6879	6.1333	37.6174

$\bar{Y} = 4.8667$

$$\sum_{i=1}^{N} (\hat{Y}_i - \bar{Y})^2 =$$

$$\sum_{i=1}^{N} (Y_i - \bar{Y})^2 =$$

112.3861

187.7338

can conclude from our sample R^2 that R^2 is in fact different from 0 in the population. This is the test of statistical significance for the regression model overall. The assumptions for this test are the same as those given for the regression coefficient in chapter 14.

To test this hypothesis we use analysis of variance, which was introduced in chapter 13. Again, the F-test is a ratio of the explained and unexplained variance. The explained and unexplained variance estimates are obtained by dividing the explained sums of squares (*ESS*) and unexplained sums of squares (*USS*) by their appropriate degrees of freedom (equation 15.7).

Equation 15.7

$$F = \frac{ESS/df}{USS/df}$$

The explained sums of squares was discussed above. The unexplained sums of squares is simply the sum of the squared error of the regression or

$$\sum_{i=1}^{N} (Y_i - \hat{Y})^2$$

The total sums of squares can be partitioned into its explained and unexplained components. The total sums of squares for our 15 cases is 187.7338. This is equivalent to the sum of the explained sums of squares (112.3861) plus the unexplained sums of squares or error sums of squares of the regression (75.3477).

Working It Out

$$TSS = ESS + USS$$

$$\sum_{i=1}^{N} (Y_i - \overline{Y})^2 = \sum_{i=1}^{N} (\hat{Y}_i - \overline{Y})^2 + \sum_{i=1}^{N} (Y_i - \hat{Y})^2$$

$$187.7338 = 112.3861 + 75.3477$$

The degrees of freedom for the ESS is k, or the number of variables in the regression. In our example the regression includes only one independent variable—age, and thus the degrees of freedom for the ESS is 1. For the USS, the number of degrees of freedom is equal to $N - k - 1$. In our case this is equal to $15 - 1 - 1$, or 13. The F-statistic for our regression is thus calculated by taking the ratio of the explained variance (112.3861/1) to that of the unexplained variance (75.3477/13), obtaining $F = 19.390$.

Working It Out

$$F = \frac{ESS/df}{USS/df}$$

$$= \frac{112.3861/1}{75.3477/13}$$

$$= \frac{112.3861}{5.7960}$$

$$= 19.3903$$

Setting a 5 percent significance threshold, we can see in the F table in appendix 5 that the critical value associated with 1 and 13 degrees of freedom is 4.67. Our test statistic of 19.39 is much larger than this value, and thus we would reject the null hypothesis that the percent of variance explained by the regression line in the population to which we infer is 0.[2]

The Importance of Correct Model Specification

The most important assumption that we make in regression modeling is that the model we have estimated is specified correctly. A **correctly specified** regression model is one in which the researcher has taken into account all of the relevant predictors of the dependent variable and has measured them correctly. This requirement of regression modeling is the most difficult one that researchers face. Its importance is linked both to prediction and to correct estimation of regression coefficients.

Errors in Prediction

Predictions of Y in regression are based on the factors that are included in a regression model. So far, we have examined **bivariate regression** models, in which one independent variable is used to predict values of Y. But in the real world it is unlikely that only one variable will influence the dependent measure you examine. Most often it will be necessary for you to take into account a number of independent variables. Regression analysis that takes into account more than one independent variable is called **multivariate regression** analysis. The regression model we have discussed so far can be ex-

---

[2]At the same time, as noted in chapter 14, we have likely violated the normality assumption of our test. This is because we do not have knowledge about the shape of the joint distribution of age and prior arrests in the population, and $N = 15$ cases is not enough to safely invoke the central limit theorem ($N > 30$).

tended to the multivariate case simply by adding terms for each new variable. For example, if we include years of education in the model predicting arrests presented earlier, we would express our regression equation as follows:

$$Y_{arrests} = b_0 + b_{age} \text{ (age)} + b_{education} \text{ (education)} + e$$

In theory, you could define all relevant predictors of Y and include them in your regression model. This correctly specified model would also provide the most accurate predictions of Y. Conversely, a misspecified model, or one that does not include all relevant predictors, will provide biased predictions of Y.

Correctly Estimating the Effect of *b*

Failure to correctly specify a regression model may also lead the researcher to present biased estimates of the effects of specific independent variables. Suppose, for example, that a bivariate regression is defined in which number of years of prison is identified as influencing number of arrests after prison:

$$Y_{rearrests} = b_0 + b_{yrs.\ pris.} \text{ (YrsPrison)} + e$$

In estimating this relationship from the data presented in table 15.3, we find that the regression coefficient based on this model is 1.709. That is, every additional year of imprisonment produces about a 1.709 increase in our prediction of number of subsequent arrests.

Working It Out

$$b = \frac{\displaystyle\sum_{i=1}^{N} (X_i - \overline{X})(Y_i - \overline{Y})}{\displaystyle\sum_{i=1}^{N} (X_i - \overline{X})^2}$$

$$= \frac{31.7}{18.55}$$

$$= 1.7089$$

Our model for subsequent arrests states that the only causal factor that influences arrests is years of imprisonment. This, of course, is a highly problematic statement, because common sense would tell us that this model is not correctly specified. There are certainly other factors that influence arrests. Some of those factors, in turn, may also be

Table 15.3   Number of Rearrests (Y) and Years Spent in Prison (X) for 20 Former Inmates

SUBJECT	REARRESTS Y	$Y_i - \bar{Y}$	YEARS IN PRISON X	$X_i - \bar{X}$	$(X_i - \bar{X})^2$	$(X_i - \bar{X})(Y_i - \bar{Y})$
1	0	−3.1	2	−1.15	1.3225	3.565
2	0	−3.1	3	−0.15	0.0225	0.465
3	1	−2.1	1	−2.15	4.6225	4.515
4	1	−2.1	2	−1.15	1.3225	2.415
5	1	−2.1	3	−0.15	0.0225	0.315
6	1	−2.1	3	−0.15	0.0225	0.315
7	2	−1.1	4	0.85	0.7225	−0.935
8	2	−1.1	2	−1.15	1.3225	1.265
9	2	−1.1	2	−1.15	1.3225	1.265
10	3	−0.1	3	−0.15	0.0225	0.015
11	3	−0.1	3	−0.15	0.0225	0.015
12	3	−0.1	3	−0.15	0.0225	0.015
13	4	0.9	3	−0.15	0.0225	-0.135
14	4	0.9	4	0.85	0.7225	0.765
15	4	0.9	4	0.85	0.7225	0.765
16	4	0.9	4	0.85	0.7225	0.765
17	5	1.9	4	0.85	0.7225	1.615
18	6	2.9	4	0.85	0.7225	2.465
19	7	3.9	5	1.85	3.4225	7.215
20	9	5.9	4	0.85	0.7225	5.015

$$\bar{Y} = 3.1 \qquad \bar{X} = 3.15$$

$$\sum_{i=1}^{N} (X_i - \bar{X})^2 = 18.55 \qquad \sum_{i=1}^{N} (X_i - \bar{X})(Y_i - \bar{Y}) = 31.7$$

Bivariate Regression Model:

Dependent Variable: Subsequent rearrests
Independent Variable: Years in prison
Regression coefficient: b (Years in Prison)   = 31.7 / 18.55
                                                       = 1.7089

related to the number of years that an offender serves in prison. If this is true—that there are relevant factors omitted from the model that are related to years of imprisonment—then the regression coefficient may provide a very misleading estimate of the effect of imprisonment on arrests.

Judges, for example, are likely to impose longer prison sentences on offenders with more serious prior records. This is illustrated in our

Table 15.4   Number of Rearrests, Years Spent in Prison, and Number of Prior Arrests for 20 Former Inmates

SUBJECT	REARRESTS	YEARS IN PRISON	PRIOR ARRESTS
1	0	2	4
2	0	3	2
3	1	1	2
4	1	2	3
5	1	3	3
6	1	3	2
7	2	4	3
8	2	2	3
9	2	2	1
10	3	3	2
11	3	3	3
12	3	3	3
13	4	3	4
14	4	4	3
15	4	4	4
16	4	4	5
17	5	4	4
18	6	4	5
19	7	5	5
20	9	4	6
	$\overline{Y} = 3.1$	$\overline{X} = 3.15$	$\overline{X} = 3.35$
	$s = 2.300$	$s = 0.9631$	$s = 1.2360$

sample data (see table 15.4) by looking at the correlations among these three variables (see table 15.5). The number of prior arrests is strongly related ($r = 0.63$) to the length of prison term served. Prior record is even more strongly related to subsequent arrests ($r = 0.76$). This suggests, first of all, that prior record is a relevant factor that should be included if our model is to be correctly specified. But it also raises a very important concern: How do we know that our finding that years in prison increase reoffending is not simply a result of the fact that those who serve longer prison terms generally have more serious prior records of offending?

In an ideal world, our comparisons of the impacts of imprisonment would be made for subjects that are otherwise similar. That is, we would want to be sure that the offenders who have longer and shorter prison sentences were comparable on other characteristics such as the seriousness of their prior records. In this case there would

Table 15.5 Correlation Coefficients for the Variables Years Imprisonment, Prior Arrests, and Subsequent Rearrests Based on Data from 20 Former Inmates

	Years in Prison	Prior Arrests
Years in Prison		
Prior Arrests	$r = 0.6280$	
Subsequent Rearrests	$r = 0.7156$	$r = 0.7616$

be no relationship between prior record and the length of imprisonment, and thus we would not have to be concerned with the possibility that length of imprisonment is actually reflecting the influence of prior record on reoffending.

In criminal justice, this approach is taken in the development of **randomized experiments.**[3] A randomized study of the impacts of length of imprisonment on reoffending would be one in which the researcher took a sample of offenders and then assigned them different sentences at random. The advantage of this approach is that the researcher can now assume that those offenders who receive shorter or longer prison sentences are not systematically different. By definition, through randomization, the researcher has scattered such traits as the seriousness of prior record, as well as any other factors that differentiate subjects one from another, randomly. Our problem in criminal justice is that it is often impractical to develop experimental research designs. For example, it is highly unlikely that judges would allow a researcher to randomly allocate prison sanctions. The same is true for many other research problems relating to crime and justice.

Fortunately for criminal justice researchers, a correctly specified regression model will take into account and control for relationships that exist among the independent variables included in the model. So, for example, the inclusion of both length of imprisonment and prior record in one regression model will provide regression coefficients that reflect the specific impacts of each variable once the impacts of the second have been taken into account. This can be illustrated by looking at equation 15.8, which describes the calculation for a multivariate regression coefficient in the case of two independent variables (X_1 and X_2). Equation 15.9 simply applies equation 15.8 to the specific

---

[3]For a discussion of experimental methods in criminal justice, see E. Babbie and M. Maxfield (1995), *The Practice of Social Research in Criminal Justice* (Belmont, Calif.: Wadsworth).

example of the multivariate regression coefficient for length of imprisonment in our example.

Equation 15.8

$$b_{(X_1)} = \left(\frac{r_{Y,X_1} - (r_{Y,X_2} \, r_{X_1,X_2})}{1 - r_{X_1,X_2}^2} \right) \left(\frac{s_Y}{s_{X_1}} \right)$$

Equation 15.9

$$b_{(X_1)} = \left(\frac{r_{Y,LP} - (r_{Y,PA} \, r_{LP,PA})}{1 - r_{LP,PA}^2} \right) \left(\frac{s_Y}{s_{LP}} \right)$$

In these equations the bivariate correlations among the three measures examined, as well as the standard deviations of length of prison and rearrests, are used to calculate the multivariate regression coefficients. The three correlations for our specific example are: (1) $r_{Y,LP}$, or the correlation between subsequent arrests and length of prison; (2) $r_{Y,PA}$, or the correlation between subsequent arrests and prior arrests; and (3) $r_{LP,PA}$, or the correlation between length of imprisonment and prior arrests.

What is most important to note in looking at equation 15.9 is that the numerator (in the first part) takes into account the product of the relationship between prior arrests and length of imprisonment, and prior arrests and subsequent arrests. This relationship is subtracted from the simple correlation between length of imprisonment and arrests. In this way, multivariate regression provides an estimate of b that takes into account the fact that some of the impact of length of imprisonment may be due to the fact that longer prison terms are associated with more serious prior records. This estimate is now purged of the bias that was introduced when prior record was not included in the regression model. The multivariate regression coefficient for length of imprisonment when prior record is included in the regression model (0.936) is considerably smaller than the estimate calculated earlier in the bivariate regression (1.709).

Working It Out

$$b_{(X_1)} = \left(\frac{r_{Y,LP} - (r_{Y,PA} \, r_{LP,PA})}{1 - r_{LP,PA}^2} \right) \left(\frac{s_Y}{s_{LP}} \right)$$

$$= \left(\frac{0.7156 - [(0.7616)\,(0.6280)]}{1 - (0.6280)^2} \right) \left(\frac{2.36}{0.988} \right)$$

$$= \left(\frac{0.2373152}{0.605616} \right) (2.388664)$$

$$= 0.9361$$

The difference in regression coefficients suggests that the bivariate regression coefficient was indeed biased in that it provided an estimate of the effect of length of imprisonment that was much too high. This difference also reflects a change in the interpretation of multivariate regression coefficients as contrasted with bivariate regression coefficients. In the bivariate case, the regression coefficient represents the estimated change in Y that is produced by a one-unit change in X. In the multivariate case, b represents the estimated change in Y associated with a unit change in X when *all other independent variables in the model are held constant*. Holding prior record constant leads to a reduction in the impact of length of imprisonment. This difference may be seen as the bias introduced by misspecifying the regression model through the exclusion of prior record.

Correctly Specifying the Regression Model

In the previous section we illustrated the importance of a correctly specified regression model. If a regression model is not correctly specified, then the predictions that are made and the coefficients that are estimated may provide misleading results for the researcher. This makes model specification an extremely important task. How then should you begin?

Defining Relevant Independent Variables

Importantly, model specification does not begin with your data. Rather it should start with theory and a visit to the library or other information systems. To build a regression model, you should first identify what is already known about the dependent variable you have chosen to study. If your interest, for example, is in the factors that influence involvement in criminality, you will need to carefully research what others have said or found regarding the causes of criminality. Your regression model should take into account the main theories and perspectives that have been raised by others.

If you do not take prior research and theory into account, then those reviewing your work will argue that your predictions or your estimates of variable effects are biased in one way or another. Just as the exclusion of prior record from our example led to a misleading estimate of the impacts of imprisonment, so too the exclusion of relevant causal factors in other models may also lead to bias. The only way to refute this potential criticism is to include such variables in your regression model.

Taking into account the theories and perspectives of others is a first step in building a correctly specified regression model. However, in most research we seek to add something new to existing knowledge. In regression modeling, this usually involves the addition of new variables. Sometimes such new variables are drawn from an innovative change in theory. Sometimes, they involve improvements in measurement. Often the finding that these new or transformed variables have an independent impact above and beyond those variables traditionally examined by researchers provides for important advances in the development of criminal justice theory and policy.

It is important to note in this regard that multivariate regression is a very flexible statistical approach. In the context of multivariate regression, you can take into account many different types of variables. We have noted so far that in a bivariate regression it is assumed that the independent variable examined is an interval-scale measure. However, in multivariate regression, you may take into account not only interval-level variables, but ordinal and nominally scaled measures as well.[4] The one criterion is that you include at least one interval-level independent variable. Even though regression analysis assumes linear relationships, theories that involve nonlinear associations can also be tested in a regression context.[5]

The Problem of Multicolinearity

In trying to build correctly specified regression models, researchers are faced with an ironic statistical problem. Even though multivariate regression is developed in part to take into account the interrelationships among variables that predict Y, when independent variables in a regression model are too strongly related one to another, then the regression estimates that are obtained become unstable. This problem is called **multicolinearity.**

---

[4]For a straightforward discussion of the use of nominal-level variables in multivariate regression, as well as regression modeling generally, see M. S. Lewis Beck (1990), *Applied Regression: An Introduction* (Newbury Park, Calif.: Sage).

[5]See J. Fox (1994), *Linear Statistical Models and Related Methods* (New York: Wiley).

In criminal justice, the independent variables examined are generally multicolinear, or correlated one to another. Indeed, this is one of the reasons it is so important to use multivariate techniques in criminal justice. When variables are intercorrelated, as is the case with our example of length of imprisonment and prior record, it is important to control for the potential confounding influences of one on the other. To fail to do so is likely to lead to bias in your estimates of the effects of specific regression coefficients. However, the irony of multicolinearity is that when variables become too correlated one to another, or highly multicolinear, the regression estimates become unreliable.

Multicolinearity can be identified in one of two ways. A common method is to look at the intercorrelations among the independent variables included in your model. Very high correlations between independent variables are likely to lead to multicolinearity problems. What is considered a very high correlation? As with many other definitions in statistics, there is no absolute number at which multicolinearity is considered serious. As a general rule, a correlation between two independent variables of greater than 0.80 should be seen as a warning that serious multicolinearity may be evident in your model.

Multicolinearity between two variables occurs less often than multicolinearity across a series of variables. To diagnose this type of multicolinearity, we use a statistic that is usually defined as **tolerance.** Tolerance measures the extent of the intercorrelations of each independent variable with all other independent variables. It is defined as one minus the percent of variance explained in X by the other independent variable examined (equation 15.10).

Equation 15.10 $\text{Tolerance} = 1 - R_X^2$

Tolerance is generally provided as an option in standard statistical computing packages, but it also can be calculated by taking each independent variable as the dependent variable in a regression that includes all other independent variables. This value is then subtracted from 1. For example, let us say that we defined a model for explaining arrests that included three independent variables:

$$Y_{\text{rearrests}} = b_0 + b_{\text{age}} \, (\text{age}) + b_{\text{age first arrest}} \, (\text{age at first arrest})$$
$$+ \, b_{\text{ed.}} \, (\text{education}) + e$$

R_x^2 would be estimated for age by calculating a regression in which age is the dependent variable and education and age at first arrest are the independent variables. You would then take this R^2 and subtract it from 1. Similarly, to get R_x^2 for education, you would regress age and age at first arrest on education and then take the R^2 that results and subtract it from 1.

When the tolerance statistic is very small, then your model is likely to include a high level of multicolinearity. Again, there is no clear yardstick for defining a level of tolerance that is likely to lead to estimation problems. In general, however, a tolerance level of less than 0.20 should be taken as a warning that serious multicolinearity may exist in your model.

Beyond these diagnostic procedures for multicolinearity, there are warning signs that can be observed in the regressions that are estimated. Sometimes when multicolinearity is present, the percent of explained variance in a model is high, but the regression coefficients overall fail to reach conventional thresholds of statistical significance. Sometimes multicolinearity inflates the size of coefficients to unrealistic sizes, or produces coefficients in a direction that is contrary to conventional wisdom. One problem in diagnosing multicolinearity is that it may have such varied effects in your model that it will be difficult to distinguish a misleading result that is due to multicolinearity and one that represents a new and interesting finding.

When there are indications of serious multicolinearity, you can take a number of alternative corrective measures. The simplest is to exclude the variable or variables that are contributing most to multicolinearity. The drawback of this approach is that the exclusion of such measures is likely to lead to model mispecification and may result in biased estimates of other regression coefficients that remain in the model. This approach makes sense only when one or more independent variables are measuring the same concept or theory.

An approach that achieves a similar result, without excluding specific measures, is to create new indices from clusters of variables that are multicolinear. For example, if a series of measures all relating to social status are multicolinear, you may decide to create a new composite measure, which is defined as social status.

The Limits of Criminal Justice Theory

Multicolinearity provides a statistical barrier to correct model specification because it may restrict the number or type of variables that can be included in your regression model. However, a more serious barrier to correct model specification—and one for which there is no clear correction—develops from the state of criminal justice knowledge and theory.

In criminal justice we can seldom say with assurance that the models that we develop include all relevant predictors of the dependent variables examined. The problem is often that our theories are not powerful enough to clearly define the factors that influence criminal justice questions. Criminal justice is still a young science, and our theories for explaining crime and justice questions are often not well specified. This fact has important implications for the use of criminal justice research in developing public policy. When our predictions are weak, they do not form a solid basis upon which to inform criminal justice policies.[6]

One implication of our failure to develop strongly predictive models in criminal justice is that it is likely that our estimates of variable effects include some degree of bias. We have stressed in this chapter the importance of controlling for relevant predictors in regression modeling. The cost of leaving out important causes is not just weaker prediction, but estimates of variable effects that include potentially spurious components. This fact should make you cautious in reporting regression analyses and critical in evaluating the research of others. Just because regression coefficients are reported to the fifth decimal point on a computer printout does not mean that the estimates so obtained are solid ones.

The fact that our regression models often include some degree of misspecification should not lead you to the conclusion that the regression approach is not useful for criminal justice researchers. As in any science, the task is to continue to build on the knowledge that is presently available. The researcher's task in developing regression models is to improve on models that were developed before. With each improvement, the results we gain provide a more solid basis for making decisions about criminal justice theory and policy.

---

[6]Mark Moore of Harvard University has argued, for example, that legal and ethical dilemmas make it difficult to base criminal justice policies about crime control on models that still include a substantial degree of statistical error. See M. Moore (1986), "Purblind Justice: Normative Issues in the Use of Prediction in the Criminal Justice System," in A. Blumstein, J. Cohen, A. Roth, and C. A. Visher (eds.), *Criminal Careers and "Career Criminals,"* Vol. 2 (Washington, D.C.: National Academy Press).

Chapter Summary

A researcher cannot predict values of Y using the regression coefficient alone. The additional piece of information required is the **Y-intercept (b_0).** The b_0 coefficient may be interpreted as the expected value of Y when $X = 0$. The predicted value of Y for other values of X can be calculated by adding b_0 to the product of the regression coefficient and X. **Regression error** is the difference between the predicted and the actual values of Y. The **regression line** is the line for which the sum of the squared error is at a minimum—hence the name, **ordinary least squares regression (OLS).** OLS is a solid basis for prediction within, but not beyond, the sample range.

The **R^2** statistic is the proportion of the total sums of squares $(Y - \overline{Y})^2$ accounted for by the explained sums of squares $(\hat{Y} - \overline{Y})^2$. This proportion represents the improvement in predicting Y that the regression line provides over the mean. The F-test for the overall regression tests whether the researcher can conclude from the sample R^2 that R^2 is different from 0 in the population.

In a **bivariate regression model,** there is only one independent variable, and it must be an interval measure. Importantly, the researcher can rarely be sure that the change observed in the dependent variable is due to one independent variable alone. **Randomized experiments,** which scatter different traits at random, offer a solution, but they are often impractical for criminal justice. A different solution is to create a correctly specified multivariate regression model. In a **multivariate regression model** there may be several independent variables of which only one need be interval. Such a model considers the effect of each independent variable while holding all the other variables constant. A model is **correctly specified** if the researcher has taken into account and correctly measured all of the relevant predictors of the dependent variable. Existing literature and prior research are suitable places to start.

Multicolinearity occurs when independent variables in a regression model are too strongly related. It leads to unstable results. The problem may be diagnosed by checking the bivariate correlations between the variables and by measuring **tolerance.** Multicolinearity may be dealt with either by excluding specific variables altogether or by merging several similar variables into one combined index.

Key Terms

Bivariate Regression A technique for predicting change in a dependent variable using one independent variable.

Correctly Specified Description for a regression model for which the researcher has taken into account all of the relevant predictors of the dependent variable and has measured them correctly.

Multicolinearity A condition in a mutivariate regression model in which independent variables examined are very strongly intercorrelated. The condition leads to unstable regression coefficients.

Multivariate Regression A technique for predicting change in a dependent variable using more than one independent variable.

Ordinary Least Squares (OLS) Regression Analysis A type of regression analysis in which the sum of squared errors from the regression line is at a minimum.

Percent of Variance Explained (R^2) A measure for evaluating how well the regression model predicts values of Y. It represents the improvement in predicting Y that the regression line provides over the mean.

Randomized Experiment A type of study in which the effect of one variable can be examined in isolation through random allocation of subjects to treatment and control groups.

Regression Error (e) The difference between the predicted value of Y and the actual value of Y.

Regression Line The line predicting values of Y. The line is plotted from knowledge of the Y-intercept and the regression coefficient.

Regression Model The hypothesized statement by the researcher of the combined factors that define the value of the dependent variable, Y. The model is normally expressed in equation form.

Residual Error See Regression Error.

Tolerance A measure of the extent of the intercorrelations of each independent variable with all other independent variables. It may be used to test for multicolinearity in a multivariate regression model.

Y-intercept (b_0) The expected value of Y when $X = 0$. The Y-intercept is used in predicting values of Y.

Symbols and Formulas

b_0 The Y-intercept.

e Error.

ESS Explained sums of squares.

USS Unexplained sums of squares.

TSS Total sums of squares.

k Number of variables in the overall regression model.

r_{Y,X_1} The correlation coefficient for Y and X_1.

r_{Y,X_2} The correlation coefficient for Y and X_2.

r_{X_1,X_2} The correlation coefficient for X_1 and X_2.

s_Y The standard deviation for Y.

s_{X_1} The standard deviation for X_1.

R_x^2 The R^2 obtained when treating an independent variable as a dependent one in a test for tolerance.

To determine the value of the Y-intercept:
$$b_0 = \bar{Y} - b\bar{X}$$

To predict values of the independent variable, Y:
$$\hat{Y} = b_0 + bX$$

To identify the residual error in a prediction:
$$e = Y - \hat{Y}$$

To show that the sum of squared error in an OLS regression line is a minimum:
$$\sum_{i=1}^{N} (Y_i - \hat{Y})^2 = \text{minimum}$$

A bivariate regression model:
$$Y = b_0 + bX + e$$

A multivariate regression model with three independent variables:
$$Y = b_0 + b_1X_1 + b_2X_2 + b_3X_3 + e$$

To calculate the percent of explained variance:

$$R^2 = \frac{ESS}{TSS} = \frac{\sum_{i=1}^{N} (\hat{Y}_i - \overline{Y})^2}{\sum_{i=1}^{N} (Y_i - \overline{Y})^2}$$

To calculate the value of F for the overall regression:

$$F = \frac{ESS/df}{USS/df} = \frac{\sum_{i=1}^{N} (\hat{Y}_i - \overline{Y})^2/k}{\sum_{i=1}^{N} (Y_i - \hat{Y})^2/N - k - 1}$$

To calculate a multivariate regression coefficient for two independent variables:

$$b_{(X_1)} = \left(\frac{r_{Y,X_1} - (r_{Y,X_2} \, r_{X_1,X_2})}{1 - r_{X_1,X_2}^2} \right) \left(\frac{s_Y}{s_{X_1}} \right)$$

To calculate tolerance:

$$\text{Tolerance} = 1 - R_X^2$$

Exercises

15.1   Ten police officers are asked how many promotions they have received and how many years they have served on the force. The results are recorded below:

X: Years on the Force	7	1	5	3	12	2	4	1	9	6
Y: Number of Promotions	5	1	3	1	8	1	2	0	7	2

a Calculate the regression coefficient, b.

b Calculate the value of the Y-intercept, b_0.

c How many promotions would you predict for an officer who had served 10 years on the force?

d What is the regression error in predicting the number of promotions expected for the officer who has served 12 years on the force?

15.2   Joan consults prison records and, for the last 10 convicts released from Wilmslow prison, records the percentage of their initial sentence from which they were excused. She also records the number of times that each convict was called before a disciplinary committee over the course of his sentence. The scores of each subject for these two variables are listed below:

X: Disciplinary Hearings	0	5	2	1	6	4	4	0	5	3
Y: Percentage of Sentence Not Served	33	5	18	32	0	10	5	30	0	17

a Calculate the regression coefficient, b.

b Calculate the value of the Y-intercept, b_0.

c Using the data set above, show that the sum of the error on either side of the regression line equals 0.

$$\left[\sum_{i=1}^{N} (Y_i - \hat{Y}) = 0 \right]$$

d Using the data set above, show that

$$\sum_{i=1}^{N} (Y_i - \hat{Y})^2$$

is less than

$$\sum (Y_i - \bar{Y})^2$$

e Explain in plain English the meaning of what you have shown in exercise 15.2d for the regression model.

15.3   George is running a small pilot study for a large-scale future research project and takes data on the average number of monthly homicides for five U.S. cities. While he is looking for a good predictor of the different homicide rates, he stumbles across the following set of data on the number of theaters in each of the cities:

X: Number of Theaters	1	3	6	7	8
Y: Monthly Homicides	10	14	23	26	32

a Calculate the regression coefficient, b.

b Calculate the value of the Y-intercept, b_0.

c According to this regression model, how many homicides would a city with 10 theaters expect per month?

d Why is this model misleading?

15.4 Lee is investigating six recent cases of vandalism in the local shopping mall. She compares the amount of damage done in each case with the number of vandals who were involved in each incident. Her findings are as follows:

X: Number of Vandals	3	2	6	4	1	2
Y: Damage Done ($)	1,100	1,850	3,800	3,200	250	1,200

a Calculate the regression coefficient, b.

b Calculate the value of the Y-intercept, b_0.

c Plot the scores on a scatterplot and draw where you think the regression line should go.

d Calculate the value of R^2. What does this tell you about the model?

15.5 A researcher has built a multivariate regression model to predict the effect of prior offenses and years of education on the length of sentence received by 100 convicted burglars. He feeds the data into a computer package and obtains the following readout:

Dependent Variable (Y):   Length of Sentence

Independent Variable (X_1): Number of Prior Offenses

Independent Variable (X_2): Years of Education

F sig   = 0.018

R^2 = 0.16

X_1: $b = + 0.4$ Sig $t = 0.023$

X_2: $b = -0.3$ Sig $t = 0.310$

Evaluate the results, taking care to explain the meaning of each of the statistics produced by the computer.

15.6 Refer to the data from exercise 15.4.

a Calculate the unexplained sums of squares.

b Run an *F*-test for the overall regression. Remember to outline all of the steps required in a test of statistical significance, including any violations of your assumptions. Can you conclude that the percent of explained variance (R^2) is different from 0 for the population?

15.7 Danny has obtained figures on the amount of drugs seized per month at a seaport over the course of two years. He wishes to explain variations in the amount of drugs seized per month and runs a regression analysis to check the effect of his independent variable—the total number of customs officers on duty for each month—on the quantity of drugs seized. The resulting regression coefficient is +4.02.

Danny is worried, however, that his bivariate model might not be correctly specified, and he decides to add a further variable—the number of ships that arrive at the port each month. He calculates the correlations between the three pairs of variables, and the results are as follows:

Y (drugs seized), X_1 (customs officers):   +0.55

Y (drugs seized), X_2 (ships arriving):   +0.60

X_1 (customs officers), X_2 (ships arriving): +0.80

The standard deviations for the three variables are: 20 kg (quantity of drugs seized per month), 1.6 (number of customs officers on duty), and 22.5 (number of ships arriving).

a Calculate the regression coefficient for customs officers.

b Calculate the regression coefficient for ships arriving at the port.

c How do you account for the difference between your answer to exercise 15.7a and the regression coefficient of +4.02 that Danny obtained earlier.

15.8 Consider the following regression model, which purports to predict the length of sentence given to convicted thieves:

Y = Length of sentence

X = Number of prior sentences

$Y = b_0 + bX + e$

a List the variables you might wish to include in a more comprehensive model.

b Present your model in equation form.

15.9 Rachel collects police data on a series of burglaries and wishes to determine the factors that influence the amount of property stolen in each case. She creates a multivariate regression model and runs tests of tolerance for each one of the independent variables. Her results are as follows:

Y = Amount of property stolen ($)

	INDEPENDENT VARIABLE	SCALE	TOLERANCE
X_1	Time of robbery (AM or PM)	Nominal	0.98
X_2	Accessibility of property	Ordinal	0.94
X_3	Number of rooms in house	Interval	0.12
X_4	Size of house	Interval	0.12
X_5	Joint income of family	Interval	0.46

Do you advise that Rachel make any changes to her model? Explain your answer.

Computer Exercises

1. Repeat the exercise in chapter 14, question 4 using a different measure of theft and a different measure of violent crime. Write out the regression equation. Next, interpret the R square, the F statistic in the ANOVA table, the Unstandardized B, and its corresponding t statistic.

2. Add Population I as an independent variable to the regression model used in question 1, above. This variable measures the total population of the jurisdiction. Would you expect heavily populated areas to have more or less crime? Write out the regression formula and interpret R square, F, B, and t. Is this regression model better than that calculated in question 1? If so, why?

appendix 1

Areas of the Standard Normal Distribution

The entries in this table are the proportion of cases in a standard normal distribution that lie between 0 and z.

	SECOND DECIMAL PLACE IN z									
z	0.00	0.01	0.02	0.03	0.04	0.05	0.06	0.07	0.08	0.09
0.0	0.0000	0.0040	0.0080	0.0120	0.0160	0.0199	0.0239	0.0279	0.0319	0.0359
0.1	0.0398	0.0438	0.0478	0.0517	0.0557	0.0596	0.0636	0.0675	0.0714	0.0753
0.2	0.0793	0.0832	0.0871	0.0910	0.0948	0.0987	0.1026	0.1064	0.1103	0.1141
0.3	0.1179	0.1217	0.1255	0.1293	0.1331	0.1368	0.1406	0.1443	0.1480	0.1517
0.4	0.1554	0.1591	0.1628	0.1664	0.1700	0.1736	0.1772	0.1808	0.1844	0.1879
0.5	0.1915	0.1950	0.1985	0.2019	0.2054	0.2088	0.2123	0.2157	0.2190	0.2224
0.6	0.2257	0.2291	0.2324	0.2357	0.2389	0.2422	0.2454	0.2486	0.2517	0.2549
0.7	0.2580	0.2611	0.2642	0.2673	0.2704	0.2734	0.2764	0.2794	0.2823	0.2852
0.8	0.2881	0.2910	0.2939	0.2967	0.2995	0.3023	0.3051	0.3078	0.3106	0.3133
0.9	0.3159	0.3186	0.3212	0.3238	0.3264	0.3289	0.3315	0.3340	0.3365	0.3389
1.0	0.3413	0.3438	0.3461	0.3485	0.3508	0.3531	0.3554	0.3577	0.3599	0.3621
1.1	0.3643	0.3665	0.3686	0.3708	0.3729	0.3749	0.3770	0.3790	0.3810	0.3830
1.2	0.3849	0.3869	0.3888	0.3907	0.3925	0.3944	0.3962	0.3980	0.3997	0.4015
1.3	0.4032	0.4049	0.4066	0.4082	0.4099	0.4115	0.4131	0.4147	0.4162	0.4177
1.4	0.4192	0.4207	0.4222	0.4236	0.4251	0.4265	0.4279	0.4292	0.4306	0.4319
1.5	0.4332	0.4345	0.4357	0.4370	0.4382	0.4394	0.4406	0.4418	0.4429	0.4441
1.6	0.4452	0.4463	0.4474	0.4484	0.4495	0.4505	0.4515	0.4525	0.4535	0.4545
1.7	0.4554	0.4564	0.4573	0.4582	0.4591	0.4599	0.4608	0.4616	0.4625	0.4633
1.8	0.4641	0.4649	0.4656	0.4664	0.4671	0.4678	0.4686	0.4693	0.4699	0.4706
1.9	0.4713	0.4719	0.4726	0.4732	0.4738	0.4744	0.4750	0.4756	0.4761	0.4767

SECOND DECIMAL PLACE IN z

z	0.00	0.01	0.02	0.03	0.04	0.05	0.06	0.07	0.08	0.09
2.0	0.4772	0.4778	0.4783	0.4788	0.4793	0.4798	0.4803	0.4808	0.4812	0.4817
2.1	0.4821	0.4826	0.4830	0.4834	0.4838	0.4842	0.4846	0.4850	0.4854	0.4857
2.2	0.4861	0.4864	0.4868	0.4871	0.4875	0.4878	0.4881	0.4884	0.4887	0.4890
2.3	0.4893	0.4896	0.4898	0.4901	0.4904	0.4906	0.4909	0.4911	0.4913	0.4916
2.4	0.4918	0.4920	0.4922	0.4925	0.4927	0.4929	0.4931	0.4932	0.4934	0.4936
2.5	0.4938	0.4940	0.4941	0.4943	0.4945	0.4946	0.4948	0.4949	0.4951	0.4952
2.6	0.4953	0.4955	0.4956	0.4957	0.4959	0.4960	0.4961	0.4962	0.4963	0.4964
2.7	0.4965	0.4966	0.4967	0.4968	0.4969	0.4970	0.4971	0.4972	0.4973	0.4974
2.8	0.4974	0.4975	0.4976	0.4977	0.4977	0.4978	0.4979	0.4979	0.4980	0.4981
2.9	0.4981	0.4982	0.4982	0.4983	0.4984	0.4984	0.4985	0.4985	0.4986	0.4986
3.0	0.4987	0.4987	0.4987	0.4988	0.4988	0.4989	0.4989	0.4989	0.4990	0.4990
3.1	0.4990	0.4991	0.4991	0.4991	0.4992	0.4992	0.4992	0.4992	0.4993	0.4993
3.2	0.4993	0.4993	0.4994	0.4994	0.4994	0.4994	0.4994	0.4995	0.4995	0.4995
3.3	0.4995	0.4995	0.4995	0.4996	0.4996	0.4996	0.4996	0.4996	0.4996	0.4997
3.4	0.4997	0.4997	0.4997	0.4997	0.4997	0.4997	0.4997	0.4997	0.4997	0.4998
3.5	0.4998	0.4998	0.4998	0.4998	0.4998	0.4998	0.4998	0.4998	0.4998	0.4998
3.6	0.4998	0.4998	0.4999	0.4999	0.4999	0.4999	0.4999	0.4999	0.4999	0.4999
3.7	0.4999									
4.0	0.49997									
4.5	0.499997									
5.0	0.4999997									

Source: R. Johnson, *Elementary Statistics* (Belmont, Calif.: Duxbury Press, 1996).

Factorials

1!	=	1
2!	=	2
3!	=	6
4!	=	24
5!	=	120
6!	=	720
7!	=	5,040
8!	=	40,320
9!	=	362,880
10!	=	3,628,800
11!	=	39,916,800
12!	=	479,001,600
13!	=	6,227,020,800
14!	=	87,178,291,200
15!	=	1,307,674,368,000
16!	=	20,922,789,888,000
17!	=	355,687,428,096,000
18!	=	6,402,373,705,728,000
19!	=	121,645,100,408,832,000
20!	=	2,432,902,008,176,640,000
21!	=	51,090,942,171,709,440,000
22!	=	1,124,000,727,777,607,680,000
23!	=	25,852,016,738,884,976,640,000
24!	=	620,448,401,733,239,439,360,000
25!	=	15,511,210,043,330,985,984,000,000

Critical Values of χ^2 Distribution

df	.20	.10	.05	.02	.01	.001
1	1.642	2.706	3.841	5.412	6.635	10.827
2	3.219	4.605	5.991	7.824	9.210	13.815
3	4.642	6.251	7.815	9.837	11.341	16.268
4	5.989	7.779	9.488	11.668	13.277	18.465
5	7.289	9.236	11.070	13.388	15.086	20.517
6	8.558	10.645	12.592	15.033	16.812	22.457
7	9.803	12.017	14.067	16.622	18.475	24.322
8	11.030	13.362	15.507	18.168	20.090	26.125
9	12.242	14.684	16.919	19.679	21.666	27.877
10	13.442	15.987	18.307	21.161	23.209	29.588
11	14.631	17.275	19.675	22.618	24.725	31.264
12	15.812	18.549	21.026	24.054	26.217	32.909
13	16.985	19.812	22.362	25.472	27.688	34.528
14	18.151	21.064	23.685	26.873	29.141	36.123
15	19.311	22.307	24.996	28.259	30.578	37.697
16	20.465	23.542	26.296	29.633	32.000	39.252
17	21.615	24.769	27.587	30.995	33.409	40.790
18	22.760	25.989	28.869	32.346	34.805	42.312
19	23.900	27.204	30.144	33.687	36.191	43.820
20	25.038	28.412	31.410	35.020	37.566	45.315
21	26.171	29.615	32.671	36.343	38.932	46.797
22	27.301	30.813	33.924	37.659	40.289	48.268
23	28.429	32.007	35.172	38.968	41.638	49.728
24	29.553	33.196	36.415	40.270	42.980	51.179
25	30.675	34.382	37.652	41.566	44.314	52.620
26	31.795	35.563	38.885	42.856	45.642	54.052
27	32.912	36.741	40.113	44.140	46.963	55.476
28	34.027	37.916	41.337	45.419	48.278	56.893
29	35.139	39.087	42.557	46.693	49.588	58.302
30	36.250	40.256	43.773	47.962	50.892	59.703

α column spans: .20, .10, .05, .02, .01, .001

Source: From Table IV of R. A. Fisher and F. Yates, Statistical Tables for Biological, Agricultural and Medical Research (London: Longman Group Ltd., 1974). (Previously published by Oliver & Boyd, Edinburgh.) Reprinted by permission of Addison-Wesley Longman Ltd.

Critical Values of Student's *t* Distribution

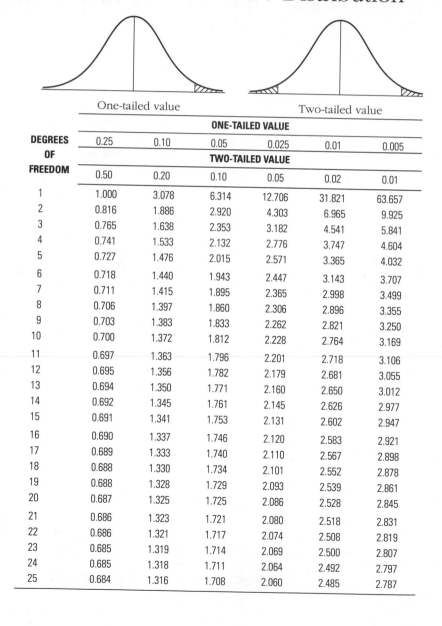

	One-tailed value		Two-tailed value		
	ONE-TAILED VALUE				
DEGREES	0.25	0.10	0.05	0.025	0.01	0.005
OF	**TWO-TAILED VALUE**				
FREEDOM	0.50	0.20	0.10	0.05	0.02	0.01
1	1.000	3.078	6.314	12.706	31.821	63.657
2	0.816	1.886	2.920	4.303	6.965	9.925
3	0.765	1.638	2.353	3.182	4.541	5.841
4	0.741	1.533	2.132	2.776	3.747	4.604
5	0.727	1.476	2.015	2.571	3.365	4.032
6	0.718	1.440	1.943	2.447	3.143	3.707
7	0.711	1.415	1.895	2.365	2.998	3.499
8	0.706	1.397	1.860	2.306	2.896	3.355
9	0.703	1.383	1.833	2.262	2.821	3.250
10	0.700	1.372	1.812	2.228	2.764	3.169
11	0.697	1.363	1.796	2.201	2.718	3.106
12	0.695	1.356	1.782	2.179	2.681	3.055
13	0.694	1.350	1.771	2.160	2.650	3.012
14	0.692	1.345	1.761	2.145	2.626	2.977
15	0.691	1.341	1.753	2.131	2.602	2.947
16	0.690	1.337	1.746	2.120	2.583	2.921
17	0.689	1.333	1.740	2.110	2.567	2.898
18	0.688	1.330	1.734	2.101	2.552	2.878
19	0.688	1.328	1.729	2.093	2.539	2.861
20	0.687	1.325	1.725	2.086	2.528	2.845
21	0.686	1.323	1.721	2.080	2.518	2.831
22	0.686	1.321	1.717	2.074	2.508	2.819
23	0.685	1.319	1.714	2.069	2.500	2.807
24	0.685	1.318	1.711	2.064	2.492	2.797
25	0.684	1.316	1.708	2.060	2.485	2.787

DEGREES OF FREEDOM	ONE-TAILED VALUE					
	0.25	0.10	0.05	0.025	0.01	0.005
	TWO-TAILED VALUE					
	0.50	0.20	0.10	0.05	0.02	0.01
26	0.684	1.315	1.706	2.056	2.479	2.779
27	0.684	1.314	1.703	2.052	2.473	2.771
28	0.683	1.313	1.701	2.048	2.467	2.763
29	0.683	1.311	1.699	2.045	2.462	2.756
30	0.683	1.310	1.697	2.042	2.457	2.750
31	0.682	1.309	1.696	2.040	2.453	2.744
32	0.682	1.309	1.694	2.037	2.449	2.739
33	0.682	1.308	1.692	2.035	2.445	2.733
34	0.682	1.307	1.691	2.032	2.441	2.728
35	0.682	1.306	1.690	2.030	2.438	2.724
40	0.681	1.303	1.684	2.021	2.423	2.704
45	0.680	1.301	1.680	2.014	2.412	2.690
50	0.680	1.299	1.676	2.008	2.403	2.678
55	0.679	1.297	1.673	2.004	2.396	2.669
60	0.679	1.296	1.671	2.000	2.390	2.660
70	0.678	1.294	1.667	1.994	2.381	2.648
80	0.678	1.293	1.665	1.989	2.374	2.638
90	0.678	1.291	1.662	1.986	2.368	2.631
100	0.677	1.290	1.661	1.982	2.364	2.625
120	0.677	1.289	1.658	1.980	2.358	2.617
>500	0.674	1.282	1.645	1.960	2.326	2.576

Source: "Table D, The *t* Table" adapted from SCIENTIFIC TABLES, published by Ciba-Geigy, in WAYS AND MEANS OF STATISTICS by Leonard Tashman and Kathleen Lamborn, Copyright © 1979 by Harcourt Brace & Company, reprinted by permission of Harcourt Brace & Company.

appendix 5

Critical Values of the F Statistic

NUMERATOR DEGREES OF FREEDOM

df_2 \ df_1	1	2	3	4	5	6	8	12	24	∞
1	161.4	199.5	215.7	224.6	230.2	234.0	238.9	243.9	249.0	254.3
2	18.51	19.00	19.16	19.25	19.30	19.33	19.37	19.41	19.45	19.50
3	10.13	9.55	9.28	9.12	9.01	8.94	8.84	8.74	8.64	8.53
4	7.71	6.94	6.59	6.39	6.26	6.16	6.04	5.91	5.77	5.63
5	6.61	5.79	5.41	5.19	5.05	4.95	4.82	4.68	4.53	4.36
6	5.99	5.14	4.76	4.53	4.39	4.28	4.15	4.00	3.84	3.67
7	5.59	4.74	4.35	4.12	3.97	3.87	3.73	3.57	3.41	3.23
8	5.32	4.46	4.07	3.84	3.69	3.58	3.44	3.28	3.12	2.93
9	5.12	4.26	3.86	3.63	3.48	3.37	3.23	3.07	2.90	2.71
10	4.96	4.10	3.71	3.48	3.33	3.22	3.07	2.91	2.74	2.54
11	4.84	3.98	3.59	3.36	3.20	3.09	2.95	2.79	2.61	2.40
12	4.75	3.88	3.49	3.26	3.11	3.00	2.85	2.69	2.50	2.30
13	4.67	3.80	3.41	3.18	3.02	2.92	2.77	2.60	2.42	2.21
14	4.60	3.74	3.34	3.11	2.96	2.85	2.70	2.53	2.35	2.13
15	4.54	3.68	3.29	3.06	2.90	2.79	2.64	2.48	2.29	2.07
16	4.49	3.63	3.24	3.01	2.85	2.74	2.59	2.42	2.24	2.01
17	4.45	3.59	3.20	2.96	2.81	2.70	2.55	2.38	2.19	1.96
18	4.41	3.55	3.16	2.93	2.77	2.66	2.51	2.34	2.15	1.92
19	4.38	3.52	3.13	2.90	2.74	2.63	2.48	2.31	2.11	1.88
20	4.35	3.49	3.10	2.87	2.71	2.60	2.45	2.28	2.08	1.84
21	4.32	3.47	3.07	2.84	2.68	2.57	2.42	2.25	2.05	1.81
22	4.30	3.44	3.05	2.82	2.66	2.55	2.40	2.23	2.03	1.78
23	4.28	3.42	3.03	2.80	2.64	2.53	2.38	2.20	2.00	1.76
24	4.26	3.40	3.01	2.78	2.62	2.51	2.36	2.18	1.98	1.73
25	4.24	3.38	2.99	2.76	2.60	2.49	2.34	2.16	1.96	1.71
26	4.22	3.37	2.98	2.74	2.59	2.47	2.32	2.15	1.95	1.69
27	4.21	3.35	2.96	2.73	2.57	2.46	2.30	2.13	1.93	1.67
28	4.20	3.34	2.95	2.71	2.56	2.44	2.29	2.12	1.91	1.65
29	4.18	3.33	2.93	2.70	2.54	2.43	2.28	2.10	1.90	1.64
30	4.17	3.32	2.92	2.69	2.53	2.42	2.27	2.09	1.89	1.62
40	4.08	3.23	2.84	2.61	2.45	2.34	2.18	2.00	1.79	1.51
60	4.00	3.15	2.76	2.52	2.37	2.25	2.10	1.92	1.70	1.39
120	3.92	3.07	2.68	2.45	2.29	2.17	2.02	1.83	1.61	1.25
>500	3.84	2.99	2.60	2.37	2.21	2.09	1.94	1.75	1.52	1.00

DENOMINATOR DEGREES OF FREEDOM

$(\alpha = 0.01)$
NUMERATOR DEGREES OF FREEDOM

df_2 \ df_1	1	2	3	4	5	6	8	12	24	∞
1	4052	4999	5403	5625	5764	5859	5981	6106	6234	6366
2	98.49	99.01	99.17	99.25	99.30	99.33	99.36	99.42	99.46	99.50
3	34.12	30.81	29.46	28.71	28.24	27.91	27.49	27.05	26.60	26.12
4	21.20	18.00	16.69	15.98	15.52	15.21	14.80	14.37	13.93	13.46
5	16.26	13.27	12.06	11.39	10.97	10.67	10.27	9.89	9.47	9.02
6	13.74	10.92	9.78	9.15	8.75	8.47	8.10	7.72	7.31	6.88
7	12.25	9.55	8.45	7.85	7.46	7.19	6.84	6.47	6.07	5.65
8	11.26	8.65	7.59	7.01	6.63	6.37	6.03	5.67	5.28	4.86
9	10.56	8.02	6.99	6.42	6.06	5.80	5.47	5.11	4.73	4.31
10	10.04	7.56	6.55	5.99	5.64	5.39	5.06	4.71	4.33	3.91
11	9.65	7.20	6.22	5.67	5.32	5.07	4.74	4.40	4.02	3.60
12	9.33	6.93	5.95	5.41	5.06	4.82	4.50	4.16	3.78	3.36
13	9.07	6.70	5.74	5.20	4.86	4.62	4.30	3.96	3.59	3.16
14	8.86	6.51	5.56	5.03	4.69	4.46	4.14	3.80	3.43	3.00
15	8.68	6.36	5.42	4.89	4.56	4.32	4.00	3.67	3.29	2.87
16	8.53	6.23	5.29	4.77	4.44	4.20	3.89	3.55	3.18	2.75
17	8.40	6.11	5.18	4.67	4.34	4.10	3.79	3.45	3.08	2.65
18	8.28	6.01	5.09	4.58	4.25	4.01	3.71	3.37	3.00	2.57
19	8.18	5.93	5.01	4.50	4.17	3.94	3.63	3.30	2.92	2.49
20	8.10	5.85	4.94	4.43	4.10	3.87	3.56	3.23	2.86	2.42
21	8.02	5.78	4.87	4.37	4.04	3.81	3.51	3.17	2.80	2.36
22	7.94	5.72	4.82	4.31	3.99	3.76	3.45	3.12	2.75	2.31
23	7.88	5.66	4.76	4.26	3.94	3.71	3.41	3.07	2.70	2.26
24	7.82	5.61	4.72	4.22	3.90	3.67	3.36	3.03	2.66	2.21
25	7.77	5.57	4.68	4.18	3.86	3.63	3.32	2.99	2.62	2.17
26	7.72	5.53	4.64	4.14	3.82	3.59	3.29	2.96	2.58	2.13
27	7.68	5.49	4.60	4.11	3.78	3.56	3.26	2.93	2.55	2.10
28	7.64	5.45	4.57	4.07	3.75	3.53	3.23	2.90	2.52	2.06
29	7.60	5.42	4.54	4.04	3.73	3.50	3.20	2.87	2.49	2.03
30	7.56	5.39	4.51	4.02	3.70	3.47	3.17	2.84	2.47	2.01
40	7.31	5.18	4.31	3.83	3.51	3.29	2.99	2.66	2.29	1.80
60	7.08	4.98	4.13	3.65	3.34	3.12	2.82	2.50	2.12	1.60
120	6.85	4.79	3.95	3.48	3.17	2.96	2.66	2.34	1.95	1.38
>500	6.64	4.60	3.78	3.32	3.02	2.80	2.51	2.18	1.79	1.00

DENOMINATOR DEGREES OF FREEDOM

(Appendix 5: Critical Values of the F Statistic, cont'd)

(α = 0.001)
NUMERATOR DEGREES OF FREEDOM

df_2 \ df_1	1	2	3	4	5	6	8	12	24	∞
1	405284	500000	540379	562500	576405	585937	598144	610667	623497	636619
2	998.5	999.0	999.2	999.2	999.3	999.3	999.4	999.4	999.5	999.5
3	167.5	148.5	141.1	137.1	134.6	132.8	130.6	128.3	125.9	123.5
4	74.14	61.25	56.18	53.44	51.71	50.53	49.00	47.41	45.77	44.05
5	47.04	36.61	33.20	31.09	29.75	28.84	27.64	26.42	25.14	23.78
6	35.51	27.00	23.70	21.90	20.81	20.03	19.03	17.99	16.89	15.75
7	29.22	21.69	18.77	17.19	16.21	15.52	14.63	13.71	12.73	11.69
8	25.42	18.49	15.83	14.39	13.49	12.86	12.04	11.19	10.30	9.34
9	22.86	16.39	13.90	12.56	11.71	11.13	10.37	9.57	8.72	7.81
10	21.04	14.91	12.55	11.28	10.48	9.92	9.20	8.45	7.64	6.76
11	19.69	13.81	11.56	10.35	9.58	9.05	8.35	7.63	6.85	6.00
12	18.64	12.97	10.80	9.63	8.89	8.38	7.71	7.00	6.25	5.42
13	17.81	12.31	10.21	9.07	8.35	7.86	7.21	6.52	5.78	4.97
14	17.14	11.78	9.73	8.62	7.92	7.43	6.80	6.13	5.41	4.60
15	16.59	11.34	9.34	8.25	7.57	7.09	6.47	5.81	5.10	4.31
16	16.12	10.97	9.00	7.94	7.27	6.81	6.19	5.55	4.85	4.06
17	15.72	10.66	8.73	7.68	7.02	6.56	5.96	5.32	4.63	3.85
18	15.38	10.39	8.49	7.46	6.81	6.35	5.76	5.13	4.45	3.67
19	15.08	10.16	8.28	7.26	6.61	6.18	5.59	4.97	4.29	3.52
20	14.82	9.95	8.10	7.10	6.46	6.02	5.44	4.82	4.15	3.38
21	14.59	9.77	7.94	6.95	6.32	5.88	5.31	4.70	4.03	3.26
22	14.38	9.61	7.80	6.81	6.19	5.76	5.19	4.58	3.92	3.15
23	14.19	9.47	7.67	6.69	6.08	5.65	5.09	4.48	3.82	3.05
24	14.03	9.34	7.55	6.59	5.98	5.55	4.99	4.39	3.74	2.97
25	13.88	9.22	7.45	6.49	5.88	5.46	4.91	4.31	3.66	2.89
26	13.74	9.12	7.36	6.41	5.80	5.38	4.83	4.24	3.59	2.82
27	13.61	9.02	7.27	6.33	5.73	5.31	4.76	4.17	3.52	2.75
28	13.50	8.93	7.19	6.25	5.66	5.24	4.69	4.11	3.46	2.70
29	13.39	8.85	7.12	6.19	5.59	5.18	4.64	4.05	3.41	2.64
30	13.29	8.77	7.05	6.12	5.53	5.12	4.58	4.00	3.36	2.59
40	12.61	8.25	6.60	5.70	5.13	4.73	4.21	3.64	3.01	2.23
60	11.97	7.76	6.17	5.31	4.76	4.37	3.87	3.31	2.69	1.90
120	11.38	7.31	5.79	4.95	4.42	4.04	3.55	3.02	2.40	1.56
>500	10.83	6.91	5.42	4.62	4.10	3.74	3.27	2.74	2.13	1.00

DENOMINATOR DEGREES OF FREEDOM

Source: From Table IV of R. A. Fisher and F. Yates, *Statistical Tables for Biological, Agricultural and Medical Research* (London: Longman Group Ltd., 1974). (Previously published by Oliver & Boyd, Edinburgh.) Reprinted by permission of Addison-Wesley Longman Ltd.

appendix 6

Critical Value for P (P_{crit}), Tukey's HSD Test

LEVEL OF SIGNIFICANCE ($\alpha = 0.05$)
k = THE NUMBER OF MEANS OR
NUMBER OF STEPS BETWEEN ORDERED MEANS

df_w	2	3	4	5	6	7	8	9	10	12	15	20
1	17.97	26.98	32.82	37.08	40.41	43.12	45.40	47.36	49.07	51.96	55.36	59.56
2	6.08	8.33	9.80	10.88	11.74	12.44	13.03	13.54	13.99	14.75	15.65	16.77
3	4.50	5.91	6.82	7.50	8.04	8.48	8.85	9.18	9.46	9.95	10.52	11.24
4	3.93	5.04	5.76	6.29	6.71	7.05	7.35	7.60	7.83	8.21	8.66	9.23
5	3.64	4.60	5.22	5.67	6.03	6.33	6.58	6.80	6.99	7.32	7.72	8.21
6	3.46	4.34	4.90	5.30	5.63	5.90	6.12	6.32	6.49	6.79	7.14	7.59
7	3.34	4.16	4.68	5.06	5.36	5.61	5.82	6.00	6.16	6.43	6.76	7.17
8	3.26	4.04	4.53	4.89	5.17	5.40	5.60	5.77	5.92	6.18	6.48	6.87
9	3.20	3.95	4.41	4.76	5.02	5.24	5.43	5.59	5.74	5.98	6.28	6.64
10	3.15	3.88	4.33	4.65	4.91	5.12	5.30	5.46	5.60	5.83	6.11	6.47
11	3.11	3.82	4.26	4.57	4.82	5.03	5.20	5.35	5.49	5.71	5.98	6.33
12	3.08	3.77	4.20	4.51	4.75	4.95	5.12	5.27	5.39	5.61	5.88	6.21
13	3.06	3.73	4.15	4.45	4.69	4.88	5.05	5.19	5.32	5.53	5.79	6.11
14	3.03	3.70	4.11	4.41	4.64	4.83	4.99	5.13	5.25	5.46	5.71	6.03
15	3.01	3.67	4.08	4.37	4.59	4.78	4.94	5.08	5.20	5.40	5.65	5.96
16	3.00	3.65	4.05	4.33	4.56	4.74	4.90	5.03	5.15	5.35	5.59	5.90
17	2.98	3.63	4.02	4.30	4.52	4.70	4.86	4.99	5.11	5.31	5.54	5.84
18	2.97	3.61	4.00	4.28	4.49	4.67	4.82	4.96	5.07	5.27	5.50	5.79
19	2.96	3.59	3.98	4.25	4.47	4.65	4.79	4.92	5.04	5.23	5.46	5.75
20	2.95	3.58	3.96	4.23	4.45	4.62	4.77	4.90	5.01	5.20	5.43	5.71
24	2.92	3.53	3.90	4.17	4.37	4.54	4.68	4.81	4.92	5.10	5.32	5.59
30	2.89	3.49	3.85	4.10	4.30	4.46	4.60	4.72	4.82	5.00	5.21	5.47
40	2.86	3.44	3.79	4.04	4.23	4.39	4.52	4.63	4.73	4.90	5.11	5.36
60	2.83	3.40	3.74	3.98	4.16	4.31	4.44	4.55	4.65	4.81	5.00	5.24
120	2.80	3.36	3.68	3.92	4.10	4.24	4.36	4.47	4.56	4.71	4.90	5.13
∞	2.77	3.31	3.63	3.86	4.03	4.17	4.29	4.39	4.47	4.62	4.80	5.01

Source: From *Comprehending Behavioral Statistics,* by R. T. Hurlburt, Copyright © 1994, Brooks/Cole Publishing Company, Pacific Grove, CA 93950, a division of International Thomsom Publishing Inc. By permission of the publisher. Adapted from *Biometrika Tables for Statisticians,* vol. 1, 3rd. ed., E. S. Pearson and H. O. Hartley (eds.). Copyright © 1966, Cambridge University Press for Biometrika Trust. By permission of the Biometrika Trust.

Critical Values for Spearman's Rank-Order Correlation Coefficient

	LEVEL OF SIGNIFICANCE FOR ONE-TAILED TEST			
	.05	.025	.01	.005
	LEVEL OF SIGNIFICANCE (p) FOR TWO-TAILED TEST			
n	.10	.05	.02	.01
5	.900	—	—	—
6	.829	.886	.943	—
7	.714	.786	.893	.929
8	.643	.738	.833	.881
9	.600	.700	.783	.833
10	.564	.648	.745	.794
11	.536	.618	.709	.818
12	.497	.591	.703	.780
13	.475	.566	.673	.745
14	.457	.545	.646	.716
15	.441	.525	.623	.689
16	.425	.507	.601	.666
17	.412	.490	.582	.645
18	.399	.476	.564	.625
19	.388	.462	.549	.608
20	.377	.450	.534	.591
21	.368	.438	.521	.576
22	.359	.428	.508	.562
23	.351	.418	.496	.549
24	.343	.409	.485	.537
25	.336	.400	.475	.526
26	.329	.392	.465	.515
27	.323	.385	.456	.505
28	.317	.377	.448	.496
29	.311	.370	.440	.487
30	.305	.364	.432	.478

Source: From *Comprehending Behavioral Statistics*, by R. T. Hurlburt, Copyright © 1994, Brooks/Cole Publishing Company, Pacific Grove, CA 93950, a division of International Thomsom Publishing Inc. By permission of the publisher.

Glossary

Analysis of Variance (ANOVA) A parametric test of statistical significance that assesses whether differences in the means of several sampled groups can lead the researcher to reject the null hypothesis that the means of the populations from which they are drawn are the same.

Arrangements The different ways, or specific ordering of events, that result in a single outcome. For example, there is only one arrangement for gaining the outcome of ten heads in ten tosses of a coin. There are, however, ten ways, or ten different arrangements, for gaining the outcome nine heads in ten tosses of a coin.

Assumptions Statements the researcher takes to be true at the outset of a test of statistical significance. These are the foundations upon which the rest of the test is built.

Between Sums of Squares (BSS) A measure of the variability between groups. The between sums of squares is calculated by taking the sum of the squared deviation of each sample mean from the grand mean multiplied by the number of cases in each sample.

Binomial Distribution The probability distribution for an event that has only two possible outcomes.

Binomial Formula The means of determining the probability that a given set of binomial events will occur in all its possible arrangements.

Bivariate Regression A technique for predicting change in a dependent variable using one independent variable.

Cell A table is composed of cells, each one identified by a particular row and column. When we use a table to compare two variables, it is convenient to refer to each combination of categories as a cell.

Central Limit Theorem A theorem that states: "If repeated independent random samples of size N are drawn from a population with mean μ and variance σ^2, then as N grows large, the sampling distribution of sample means will be approximately normal with mean μ and variance σ^2/N." The central limit theorem enables the researcher to make inferences about an unknown population using a normal sampling distribution.

Chi-Square Statistic The test statistic resulting from applying the chi-square formula to the observed and expected frequencies for each cell. This statistic tells us how much the observed distribution differs from that expected under the null hypothesis.

Chi-Square Distribution A probability distribution that is used to conduct statistical tests of significance using binary or multicategory nominal variables. The distribution is nonsymmetrical and varies according to degrees of freedom. All the values in the distribution are positive.

Classification The process whereby data are organized into categories or groups.

Coefficient of Relative Variation A measure of dispersion calculated by dividing the standard deviation by the mean.

Confidence Interval An interval of values placed around a statistic on a sampling distribution. In placing the interval boundaries on either side of a statistic, we are stating how confident we are that the true parameter falls within these two boundaries.

Convenience Sample A sample chosen not at random, but according to criteria of expedience or accessibility to the researcher.

Correctly Specified Description for a regression model for which the researcher has taken into account all of the relevant predictors of the dependent variable and has measured them correctly.

Correlation A measure of the strength of a relationship between two variables.

Covariation The extent to which two variables vary together relative to their respective means. The covariation between the two variables serves as the numerator for the equations to calculate both Pearson's r and the regression coefficient b.

Curvilinear Relationship An association between two variables whose values may be represented as a curved line when plotted on a scatter diagram.

Data Information used to answer a research question.

Degrees of Freedom A mathematical index that places a value on the extent to which a particular operation is free to vary after certain limitations have been imposed. Calculating the degrees of freedom for a chi-square test determines which chi-square probability distribution we use.

Dependent Variable (Y) The variable assumed by the researcher to be influenced by one or more independent variables.

Design Sensitivity The statistical power of a research study. In a sensitive study design, statistical power will be maximized, and the statistical test employed will be more capable of identifying an effect.

Deviation from the Mean The extent to which each individual score differs from the mean of all the scores.

Directional Hypothesis A hypothesis reflecting the concern of the researcher with the results obtained on only one side of the sampling distribution. This may be, for example, whether a program has a positive impact or, alternatively, whether it has a negative impact.

Distribution-Free Tests Another name for nonparametric tests.

Effect Size A standardized measure of the extent to which the actual parameters differ from the hypothesized parameters of a test. It is generally calculated by taking the difference between the actual value and the hypothesized value of the parameter and dividing this by the estimated population standard deviation. The larger the effect size expected in a study, the greater will be the statistical power of that study, all else being equal.

Eta Squared The proportion of the total sums of squares that is accounted for by the between sums of squares.

Eta A measure of the degree of correlation between an interval-level and a nominal-level variable.

Expected Frequencies The number of observations one would predict for each cell if the null hypothesis were true.

Explained Sums of Squares (ESS) Another name for between sums of squares. The explained sums of squares is the part of the total variability that can be explained by visible differences between the groups.

External Validity The extent to which a study sample is reflective of the population from which it is drawn. A study is said to have high external validity when the sample used is representative of the population to which inferences are made.

Factorial The product of a number and all the positive whole numbers lower than it.

Frequency Distribution An arrangement of scores in order from the lowest to the highest that shows the number of times each score occurs.

Grand Mean The overall mean of every single case across all of the samples.

Heteroscedasticity A situation in which the variances of scores are not equal. Heteroscedasticity violates one of the assumptions of the parametric test of statistical significance for the regression or correlation coefficients.

Histogram A bar graph used to represent a frequency distribution.

Homoscedasticity A statement that the variances/standard deviations of multiple populations are the same.

Honestly Significant Difference (HSD) A parametric test of statistical significance, adjusted for making pairwise comparisons. The HSD statistic defines the difference between the pairwise comparisons required to reject the null hypothesis.

Independent Two events are statistically independent when the occurrence of one does not impact upon the occurrence of the other.

Independent Random Sampling A form of random sampling whereby the fact that one subject is drawn from a population in no way affects the probability of drawing any other subject from that population.

Independent Variable (X) A variable assumed by the researcher to impact upon the value of the dependent variable, Y.

Index of Qualitative Variation A measure of dispersion calculated by dividing the sum of the possible pairs of observed scores by the sum of the possible pairs of scores expected (when cases are equally distributed across categories).

Interval Scale A scale of measurement that uses a common and standard unit and, in addition to categorizing and ordering data, enables the researcher to calculate exact differences between scores.

Kruskal-Wallis Test A nonparametric test of statistical significance for multiple groups requiring at least an ordinal scale of measurement

Least Squares Property A characteristic of the mean whereby the sum of all the squared deviations from the mean is a minimum—it is lower than the sum of the squared deviations from any other fixed point.

Levels of Measurement Types of measurement that make use of progressively increasing amounts of information.

Linear Relationship An association between two variables whose joint distribution may be represented in linear form when plotted on a scatter diagram.

Marginal The value in the margin of a table that totals the scores for the appropriate columns and rows.

Mean A measurement of central tendency calculated by dividing the sum of the scores by the number of cases.

Mean Deviation A measure of dispersion calculated by adding the absolute deviations of each score from the mean and then dividing the sum by the number of cases.

Measurement The assignment of numerical values to objects, characteristics, or events in a systematic manner.

Median A measurement of central tendency calculated by identifying the value or category of the score that occupies the middle position in the spread of scores.

Mode A measurement of central tendency calculated by identifying the score or category that occurs most frequently.

Multicolinearity A condition in a mutivariate regression model in which independent variables examined are very strongly intercorrelated. The condition leads to unstable regression coefficients.

Multiplication Rule The means for determining the probability that a series of events will jointly occur.

Multivariate Regression A technique for predicting change in a dependent variable using more than one independent variable.

Nominal Scale A scale of measurement that assigns each piece of information to an appropriate category without suggesting any order for the categories created.

Nondirectional Hypothesis A hypothesis reflecting the concern of the researcher with the results obtained on both sides of the sampling distribution. This may be, for example, whether a program has any impact, positive or negative.

Nonparametric Tests Statistical tests of significance that make no assumptions as to the shape of the population distribution.

Normal Curve A normal frequency distribution represented on a graph by a continuous line.

Normal Frequency Distribution A frequency distribution, bell shaped and symmetrical in form. Its mean, mode, and median are always the same.

Null Hypothesis A statement that reduces the research question to a simple assertion to be tested by the researcher. The null hypothesis normally suggests that there is no relationship or no difference.

Observed Frequencies The observed results of the study, recorded in each cell.

One-Tailed Test of Significance A statistical test of significance in which the region for rejecting the null hypothesis falls on only one side of the sampling distribution. One-tailed tests are based on directional research hypotheses.

Ordinal Scale A scale of measurement that categorizes information and places it in an order of magnitude without using a standard scale of equal intervals.

Ordinary Least Squares (OLS) Regression Analysis A type of regression analysis in which the sum of squared errors from the regression line is at a minimum.

Outlier(s) A single or small number of exceptional cases that substantially deviate from the general pattern of scores.

Overall Mean See grand mean.

Pairwise Comparisons Comparisons made between two sample means extracted from a larger statistical analysis.

Parameter A characteristic of the population, for example, the mean number of previous convictions for all U.S. prisoners.

Parametric Tests Statistical tests of significance that make assumptions as to the shape of the population distribution.

Pearson's Correlation Coefficient See Pearson's r.

Pearson's r A commonly used measure of association between two variables. Pearson's r measures the strength and direction of linear relationships on a standardized scale from −1 to +1.

Percent of Variance Explained The proportion of the total sums of squares that is accounted for by the explained sums of squares (See also eta squared).

Percent of Variance Explained (R^2) A measure for evaluating how well the regression model predicts values of Y. It represents the improvement in predicting Y that the regression line provides over the mean.

Percentage The relation between two numbers for which the whole is accorded a value of 100, and the other is given a numerical value corresponding to its share of the whole. Calculating what percentage of the cases are found in the modal category serves as a simple measure of dispersion.

Pooled Variance A method of obtaining the standard error of the sampling distribution for a difference of means test. The pooled variance method requires an assumption of homoscedasticity.

Population The universe of cases that the researcher seeks to study. The population of cases is fixed at a particular time (e.g., the population of the United States). However, populations usually change across time.

Population Distribution The frequency distribution of a particular variable within a population.

Probability Distribution A theoretical distribution, consisting of the probabilities expected in the long run for each possible outcome of an event.

Proportion The relation between two numbers for which the whole is accorded a value of 1 and the other is given a numerical value corresponding to its share of the whole. Calculating what proportion of the cases are found in the modal category serves as a simple measure of dispersion.

Randomized Experiment A type of study in which the effect of one variable can be examined in isolation through random allocation of subjects to treatment and control groups.

Random Sampling Drawing samples from the population in a manner that ensures every individual in that population has an equal chance of being selected.

Range A measure of dispersion calculated by subtracting the smallest score from the largest score.

Rank-Order Test A test of statistical significance that uses information relating to the relative order or rank of variable scores.

Ratio Scale A scale of measurement identical to an interval scale in every respect except that, in addition, a value of zero on the scale represents the absence of the phenomenon.

Regression Coefficient (b) A statistic used to assess the influence of an independent variable, X, on a dependent variable, Y. b is interpreted as the estimated change in Y that is associated with a one unit change in X.

Regression Error (e)   The difference between the predicted value of Y and the actual value of Y.

Regression Line   The line predicting values of Y. The line is plotted from knowledge of the Y-intercept and the regression coefficient.

Regression Model   The hypothesized statement by the researcher of the combined factors that define the value of the dependent variable, Y. The model is normally expressed in equation form.

Rejection Region   The area of a sampling distribution containing the test statistic values that will cause the researcher to reject the null hypothesis.

Relaxing Assumptions   When an assumption for a test may be relaxed, we need not be concerned with that assumption. The assumption that a population is normal may be relaxed if the sample size is sufficiently large to invoke the central limit theorem.

Reliability   The extent to which the measure chosen will consistently assign the same value to whatever is being measured.

Representative Sample   A sample that reflects the population from which it is drawn.

Research Hypothesis   The antithesis of the null hypothesis. The statement normally answers the initial research question by suggesting that there is a relationship or a difference.

Research Question   The question the researcher hopes to be able to answer by means of a study.

Residual Error   See Regression Error.

Sample   A set of actual observations or cases drawn from a population.

Sample Distribution   The frequency distribution of a particular variable within a sample drawn from a population.

Sample Statistic   A characteristic of a sample, for example, the mean number of previous convictions in a random sample of 1,000 prisoners drawn from the entire prison population.

Sampling Distribution   A probability distribution of all the results of a very large number of samples, each one of the same size and drawn from the same population under the same conditions.

Sampling Frame   The universe of eligible cases from which a sample is drawn.

Sampling with Replacement   A sampling method whereby individuals in a sample are returned to the sampling frame after they have been selected. This raises the possibility that certain individuals in a population may appear in a sample more than once.

Scale of Measurement   Type of categorization used to arrange or assign values to data.

Scatter Diagram   See Scatterplot.

Scatterplot   A graph whose two axes are defined by two variables, and upon which a point is plotted for each subject in a sample according to its score on the two variables.

Separate Variance   A method of obtaining the standard error of the sampling distribution for a difference of means test. The separate variance method does not require an assumption of homoscedasticity.

Significance Level   The objective risk that the researcher may make a Type I error. In a test of hypotheses, the researcher sets a significance level. This level is the risk that the researcher is prepared to take of making a Type I error.

Skewed A description of a spread of scores that is clearly weighted to one side.

Spearman's *r* (*r*_s) A measure of association between two ordinally scaled variables. Spearman's *r* measures the strength and direction of linear relationships on a standardized scale between −1 and +1. It is used mainly for rank-ordered data.

Standard Deviation A measure of dispersion calculated by taking the square root of the variance.

Standard Deviation Unit A unit of measurement used to describe the deviation of a specific score or value from the mean in a *z*-distribution.

Standard Error The standard deviation of a sampling distribution.

Standard Normal Distribution A normal frequency distribution with a mean of 0 and a standard deviation of 1. Any normal frequency distribution can be transformed into the standard normal distribution by using the *z* formula.

Statistically Significant A test statistic is deemed statistically significant if it falls within the rejection region defined by the researcher. When such a result is obtained, the researcher is prepared to reject the null hypothesis. In other words, the researcher is prepared to say that the null hypothesis is not true for the population, acknowledging a risk of error that corresponds with the level of significance chosen for the test.

Statistical Power One minus the probability of a Type II error. The greater the statistical power of a test, the less chance there is that a researcher will mistakenly fail to reject the null hypothesis.

Statistical Test of Significance A step-by-step method that enables the researcher to

come to a conclusion about the population parameter based on a sample statistic.

Sums of Squares The sum of squared deviations of scores from a mean or set of means.

Tails of the Distribution The extremes on either side of a distribution. The events represented in the tails of a sampling distribution are those deemed least likely to occur if the null hypothesis is true for the population.

Test Statistic The outcome of the study expressed in units of the sampling distribution. A test statistic that falls within the rejection region will lead the researcher to reject the null hypothesis.

Tolerance A measure of the extent of the intercorrelations of each independent variable with all other independent variables. It may be used to test for multicolinearity in a multivariate regression model.

Total Sums of Squares (TSS) A measure of the total amount of variability across all of the groups examined. The total sums of squares is calculated by summing the squared deviation of each score from the grand mean.

***t*-Test for Dependent Samples** A test of statistical significance that is used when two samples are not independent.

Two-Sample *t*-Test for Means A test of statistical significance that examines the difference observed between the means of two samples.

Two-Sample *z*-Test A test of statistical significance that may be used to test the difference between proportions when *N* is sufficiently large.

Two-Tailed Test of Significance A statistical test of significance in which the region for rejecting the null hypothesis falls on both sides of the sampling distribution. Two-tailed tests are based on nondirectional research hypotheses.

Type I Error Also known as "Alpha" error. The mistake made when a researcher rejects the null hypothesis on the basis of the sample (i.e., claiming that there is a relationship) when, in fact, the null hypothesis is true (i.e., there is actually *no* such relationship in the population).

Type II Error Also known as a "Beta" error. The mistake made when a researcher fails to reject the null hypothesis on the basis of the sample (i.e., claiming that there is no relationship) when, in fact, the null hypothesis is false (i.e., there actually *is* a relationship).

Unexplained Sums of Squares (USS) Another name for the within sums of squares. The unexplained sums of squares is the part of the total variability that cannot be explained by visible differences between the groups.

Universe The total population of cases.

Validity The extent to which the measure chosen accurately reflects the concept being measured.

Variable A trait, characteristic, or attribute of a person/object/event that can be measured at least at the nominal-scale level.

Variance A measure of dispersion calculated by adding together the squared deviations of each score from the mean and then dividing the sum by the number of cases.

Variation Ratio A measure of dispersion calculated by subtracting the proportion of cases in the modal category from 1.

Within Sums of Squares (WSS) A measure of the variability within groups. The within sums of squares is calculated by summing the squared deviation of each score from its sample mean.

Y-intercept (b_0) The expected value of Y when $X = 0$. The Y-intercept is used in predicting values of Y.

Index